Norman Lewis
is the number one teacher of vocabulary building in the United States!

WORD POWER MADE EASY presents in easily understood form the unique new methods by which he has
successfully taught hundreds of thousands of people
the secrets of building a larger vocabulary.

1. Mr. Lewis tells you how to test your present
vocabulary.

2. He tells you why people who can speak and write
effectively get to the top.

3. He proves that you can achieve word power—and
have fun doing it.

4. In three weeks, using the simple, easy, step-by-
step methods in this book, Mr. Lewis will show you
how to put new sparkle into your personality, new
confidence into your speech.

WORD POWER MADE EASY was originally published
by Doubleday & Company, Inc.

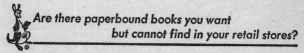

**Are there paperbound books you want
but cannot find in your retail stores?**

You can get any title in print in:
Pocket Book editions • Pocket *Cardinal* editions • Permabook editions or Washington Square Press editions. Simply send retail price, local sales tax, if any, plus 15¢ to cover mailing and handling costs for each book wanted to:

MAIL SERVICE DEPARTMENT
    POCKET BOOKS • A Division of Simon & Schuster, Inc.
    1 West 39th Street • New York, New York 10018
    Please send check or money order. We cannot be responsible for cash.
    Catalogue sent free on request.

Titles in these series are also available at discounts in quantity lots for industrial or sales-promotional use. For details write our Special Projects Agency: The Benjamin Company, Inc., 485 Madison Avenue, New York, N.Y. 10022.

WORD
POWER
MADE EASY

The Complete Three-Week
Vocabulary Builder

BY
NORMAN LEWIS

A POCKET CARDINAL EDITION
PUBLISHED BY POCKET BOOKS · NEW YORK

WORD POWER MADE EASY

Doubleday edition published November, 1949

A Pocket *Cardinal* edition

1st printing.........January, 1953
35th printing.........March, 1969

The extract from "How to Pronounce a Word," by Norman Lewis, is copyright, 1946, by Esquire, Inc. Reprinted from November 1946 *Coronet*.
The extract from "Be a Perfect Speller in 30 Minutes," by Norman Lewis, is copyright, 1946, by Esquire, Inc. Reprinted from February 1946 *Coronet*.
The extract from "How to Spell a Word," by Norman Lewis, is copyright, 1948, by Esquire, Inc. Reprinted from January 1949 *Coronet*.
The extract from "Mind Over Grammar," by Norman Lewis, is copyright, 1947, by Fawcett Publications, Inc.
The extracts from "You Can Catch a Misspelled Word," by Norman Lewis, are copyright, 1948, by Fawcett Publications, Inc.
The extracts from "Watch That Word," by Norman Lewis, are copyright, 1948, by Fawcett Publications, Inc.
The pronunciation tests in "Brief Intermission Eight" are reprinted by permission of the Curtis Publishing Company.

This Pocket *Cardinal*® edition includes every word contained in the original, higher-priced edition. It is printed from brand-new plates made from completely reset, clear, easy-to-read type.
Pocket *Cardinal* editions are published by Pocket Books, a division of Simon & Schuster, Inc., 630 Fifth Avenue, New York, N.Y. 10020.
Trademarks registered in the United States and other countries.

L

To Mary, Margie and Debbie

CONTENTS

why it is necessary to stay with your work for long periods and return to it at regular intervals.

SECOND WEEK:
GAINING INCREASED MOMENTUM

words that refer to government, feelings, names, thinness, thankfulness, and sitting.

BRIEF INTERMISSIONS

WORD POWER
MADE EASY

GETTING OFF TO A GOOD START

1

HOW TO TEST
YOUR PRESENT VOCABULARY

If you are the average adult, your vocabulary is barely one-and-one-half times as large as that of a child of ten.

And you know only one fourth as many words as the average college sophomore.

But that's the least of it—

What is infinitely more significant is that you are now increasing your vocabulary at no more than one one hundredth your rate when you were in the lower grades of elementary school!

These accusations may sound insulting—but they are not intended to be. They are only an attempt to get you to face the facts about vocabulary development that educational testing has turned up in recent years.

Let us examine some of these facts.

According to a typical investigation by Professor Robert H. Seashore, chairman of the Department of Psychology of Northwestern University, the average child of ten knows the meanings of 34,300 different terms, and since his sixth year has been learning new words at the rate of 5000 a year.

The results of a similar investigation, conducted by Columbia University Professor George W. Hartmann among the students of the Alabama Institute of Technology, show that the average college sophomore has a vocabulary of approximately two hundred thousand words.

How do these figures compare with your own? I have obtained data on adult vocabularies by testing hundreds of students in the Adult Education Program of the City College of New York. These data show:

3

1. That the average adult vocabulary is 50,000 words—one-fourth the size of the vocabulary of a college sophomore, only one-and-one-half times as large as the vocabulary of a ten-year-old.
2. That the constant rate of increase among adults is in the neighborhood of fifty words a year—one one hundredth the rate of children between six and ten.

This wide discrepancy is something to think about, isn't it? But wait—perhaps you are not the average adult. Perhaps your vocabulary is not comparatively anemic; perhaps you have come a lot further, since you were ten, than most people. Shall we put it to a test?

A TEST OF VOCABULARY RANGE

Here are sixty brief phrases, each containing one italicized word; it is up to you to check the closest definition of each such word. To keep your score valid, refrain, as far as possible, from wild guessing. The key will be found at the end of the test.

1. *disheveled* appearance: (a) untidy, (b) fierce, (c) foolish, (d) peculiar, (e) unhappy
2. a *baffling* problem: (a) difficult, (b) simple, (c) puzzling, (d) long, (e) new
3. *lenient* parent: (a) tall, (b) not strict, (c) wise, (d) foolish, (e) severe
4. *repulsive* personality: (a) disgusting, (b) attractive, (c) normal, (d) confused, (e) conceited
5. *audacious* attempt: (a) useless, (b) bold, (c) foolish, (d) crazy, (e) necessary
6. *agile* climber: (a) lively, (b) tired, (c) skillful, (d) careful, (e) stubborn
7. *prevalent* disease: (a) dangerous, (b) catching, (c) childhood, (d) fatal, (e) widespread
8. *ominous* report: (a) loud, (b) threatening, (c) untrue, (d) serious, (e) unpleasant
9. an *incredible* story: (a) true, (b) interesting, (c) well-known, (d) unbelievable, (e) unknown
10. a good *oculist:* (a) eye doctor, (b) skin doctor, (c) foot doctor, (d) heart doctor, (e) bone doctor

11. will *supersede* the old law: (a) enforce, (b) specify penalties for, (c) take the place of, (d) repeal, (e) continue

12. an *anonymous* donor: (a) generous, (b) stingy, (c) well-known, (d) one whose name is not known, (e) reluctant

13. performed an *autopsy:* (a) examination of living tissue, (b) examination of a corpse to determine the cause of death, (c) process in the manufacture of optical lenses, (d) operation to cure an organic disease, (e) series of questions to determine the causes of delinquent behavior

14. an *indefatigable* worker: (a) well-paid, (b) tired, (c) skillful, (d) tireless, (e) pleasant

15. a confirmed *atheist:* (a) bachelor, (b) disbeliever in God, (c) believer in religion, (d) believer in science, (e) priest

16. a *loquacious* woman: (a) tall, (b) beautiful, (c) homely, (d) sweet, (e) talkative

17. a *glib* talker: (a) smooth, (b) awkward, (c) loud, (d) friendly, (e) boring

18. to *philander:* (a) work hard, (b) make love triflingly, (c) save money, (d) be in doubt, (e) try unsuccessfully

19. an *ocular* difficulty: (a) unexpected, (b) insurmountable, (c) pertaining to the eye, (d) real, (e) imaginary

20. questionable *paternity:* (a) fatherhood, (b) truthfulness, (c) value, (d) knowledge, (e) wisdom

21. a *naive* attitude: (a) unwise, (b) hostile, (c) unsophisticated, (d) friendly, (e) contemptuous

22. living in *affluence:* (a) dirt, (b) countrified surroundings, (c) fear, (d) wealth, (e) poverty

23. more pleasant in *retrospect:* (a) back view, (b) freedom, (c) acceptance, (d) leisure, (e) anticipation

24. a real *gourmet:* (a) teacher, (b) greedy eater, (c) vegetarian, (d) connoisseur of good food, (e) antique

25. to *simulate* interest: (a) pretend, (b) feel, (c) lose, (d) stir up, (e) ask for

26. a *magnanimous* action: (a) puzzling, (b) generous, (c) foolish, (d) unnecessary, (e) wise

27. a *clandestine* meeting: (a) prearranged, (b) hurried, (c) important, (d) secret, (e) periodical

28. the *apathetic* populace: (a) made up of various national stocks, (b) keenly vigilant of their rights, (c) densely packed, (d) indifferent, uninterested, (e) prehistoric

29. to *placate* his wife: (a) divorce, (b) make a gift to, (c) make arrangements for, (d) help, (e) change hostility to friendliness

5

30. *vacillate* continuously: (a) avoid, (b) waver mentally, (c) inject, (d) treat, (e) scold

31. a *nostalgic* feeling: (a) nauseated, (b) homesick, (c) sharp, (d) painful, (e) delighted

32. feel *antipathy*: (a) bashfulness, (b) stage fright, (c) friendliness, (d) hostility, (e) suspense

33. be more *circumspect*: (a) restrained, (b) confident, (c) cautious, (d) honest, (e) intelligent

34. an *intrepid* campaigner: (a) fearless, (b) eloquent, (c) popular, (d) experienced, (e) famous

35. *diaphanous* material: (a) strong, (b) sheer and gauzy, (c) colorful, (d) expensive, (e) sleazy

36. a *taciturn* host: (a) stingy, (b) generous, (c) disinclined to conversation, (d) charming, (e) gloomy

37. to *malign* his friend: (a) accuse, (b) help financially, (c) disbelieve, (d) slander, (e) discard

38. a *congenital* deformity: (a) horrible, (b) crippling, (c) slight, (d) incurable, (e) occurring at or during birth

39. a definite *neurosis*: (a) plan, (b) emotional maladjustment, (c) mental derangement, (d) feeling of fear, (e) physical reaction

40. took an *unequivocal* stand: (a) indecisive, (b) well-intentioned, (c) unexpected, (d) definite, (e) dangerous

41. *vicarious* enjoyment: (a) complete, (b) unspoiled, (c) occurring from a feeling of identification with another, (d) long-continuing, (e) temporary

42. *psychogenic* ailment: (a) incurable, (b) contagious, (c) caused by the emotions, (d) intestinal, (e) imaginary

43. an *anachronous* attitude: (a) unexplainable, (b) religious, (c) belonging to a different time, (d) out-of-place, (e) unusual

44. his *iconoclastic* phase: (a) artistic, (b) sneering at tradition, (c) troubled, (d) difficult, (e) religious

45. a *tyro*: (a) dominating personality, (b) beginner, (c) accomplished musician, (d) dabbler, (e) serious student

46. a *laconic* reply: (a) immediate, (b) assured, (c) terse and meaningful, (d) unintelligible, (e) angry

47. *semantic* confusion: (a) relating to the meanings of words, (b) pertaining to money, (c) having to do with the emotions, (d) relating to mathematics, (e) scientific

48. *cavalier* treatment: (a) courteous, (b) high-handed, (c) negligent, (d) incomplete, (e) expensive

49. an *anomalous* situation: (a) dangerous, (b) intriguing, (c) unusual, (d) pleasant, (e) unhappy

50. *posthumous* child: (a) cranky, (b) brilliant beyond his years, (c) physically weak, (d) illegitimate, (e) born after the death of his father
51. feels *enervated*: (a) full of ambition, (b) full of strength, (c) completely exhausted, (d) troubled, (e) weak
52. shows true *perspicacity*: (a) sincerity, (b) mental keenness, (c) love, (d) faithfulness, (e) longing
53. a *sycophantic* attitude: (a) sneering, (b) unbelieving, (c) bootlicking, (d) surprising, (e) contemptible
54. *gregarious* person: (a) calm, (b) company-loving, (c) untrustworthy, (d) vicious, (e) self-sacrificing
55. sufficiently *phlegmatic*: (a) satisfied, (b) annoyed, (c) highstrung, (d) emotionally calm, (e) irritating
56. *consummate* scoundrel: (a) repentant, (b) punished, (c) perfect, (d) vicious, (e) unreformable
57. an *egregious* blunder: (a) outstandingly bad, (b) slight, (c) irreparable, (d) unnecessary, (e) humorous
58. *cacophony* of the city: (a) political administration, (b) crowded living conditions, (c) cultural advantages, (d) harsh sounds, (e) foul odors
59. a *prurient* adolescent: (a) tall and gangling, (b) sexually longing, (c) clumsy and awkward, (d) pimply faced, (e) soft-spoken
60. *uxorious* husband: (a) henpecked, (b) suspicious, (c) guilty of infidelity, (d) fondly and foolishly doting on his wife, (e) lovesick

---

KEY: 1—a, 2—c, 3—b, 4—a, 5—b, 6—a, 7—e, 8—b, 9—d, 10—a, 11—c, 12—d, 13—b, 14—d, 15—b, 16—e, 17—a, 18—b, 19—c, 20—a, 21—c, 22—d, 23—a, 24—d, 25—a, 26—b, 27—d, 28—d, 29—e, 30—b, 31—b, 32—d, 33—c, 34—a, 35—b, 36—c, 37—d, 38—e, 39—b, 40—d, 41—c, 42—c, 43—c, 44—b, 45—b, 46—c, 47—a, 48—b, 49—c, 50—e, 51—c, 52—b, 53—c, 54—b, 55—d, 56—c, 57—a, 58—d, 59—b, 60—d

---

Your score (allowing one point for each correct answer)

. . . . ———

THE MEANING OF YOUR SCORE

These words have been carefully chosen according to their difficulty, and the approximate evaluation of your vocabulary which you will find in the chart below is based on the results achieved by 318 students in the Adult Education Program of the City College of New York.

If you scored:

0–11 correct choices, your vocabulary is *below-average*
12–35 correct choices, your vocabulary is *average*
36–48 correct choices, your vocabulary is *above-average*
49–54 correct choices, your vocabulary is *excellent*
55–60 correct choices, your vocabulary is on a *superior* level.

VOCABULARY AND SUCCESS

Now you know where you stand. If you are in the below-average or average group, you must consider, seriously, whether an inadequate vocabulary may be holding you back socially, professionally, and intellectually. (If you are in one of the higher groups, you have doubtless already discovered the unique and far-reaching value of a rich vocabulary, and you are eager to add still further to your knowledge of words.)

Let us examine, briefly, some of the scientific evidence that points to the intimate relationship between vocabulary and personal, professional, and intellectual success.

The Human Engineering Laboratory, an institution which tests people's aptitudes, has found that the *only* common characteristic of successful people in this country is an unusual grasp of the meanings of words. The Laboratory has tested the vocabularies of thousands of people in all age groups and in all walks of life—and has discovered that the men drawing down the highest salaries have made the highest scores. I want you to consider very thoughtfully the explanation that Dr. Johnson O'Connor, director of the Laboratory, offers for the close relationship between vocabulary and success:

"Why do large vocabularies characterize executives and possibly outstanding men and women in other fields? The final answer seems to be that words are the instruments by means of which men and women grasp the thoughts of others and with which they do much of their own thinking. They are the tools of thought."

There is other evidence.

At many universities today, groups of freshmen are put into experimental classes for the sole purpose of increasing their knowledge of English words. *These groups do better in their sophomore, junior, and senior years than control groups of similarly endowed students who do not receive such freshman training.*

And still more evidence:

At the University of Illinois, entering students are given a simple twenty-nine-word vocabulary test. The results of this test can be used, according to Professor William D. Templeman, to make an accurate prediction of future academic success—or lack of success—over the entire four-year college course. "If a student has a superior vocabulary," states Professor Templeman, "it will probably follow that he will do better work academically."

And finally:

Educational research has discovered, in recent years, that a person's I.Q. is intimately related to his vocabulary. Take a standard vocabulary test and then an intelligence test—the results in both will be substantially the same.

YOU CAN INCREASE YOUR VOCABULARY

Yes, in the highly verbal, highly intellectual civilization in which we now live, the man with a better vocabulary has a better chance of success, other things being equal—a better chance of success in his personal life, his business life, his intellectual life.

And you can increase *your* vocabulary—faster and easier than you may realize.

You can, in fact, achieve a tremendous gain in just three short weeks of concentrated effort.

Furthermore—

You can start improving your vocabulary immediately—and within a few days you can be cruising along at such a rapid rate that there will be an actual change in your thinking, in your ability to express your thoughts, and in your powers of understanding.

Does this sound as if I am promising you the whole world in a neat package with a pretty pink ribbon tied around it? I am. And I am willing to make such an unqualified promise because I have seen what has happened almost overnight to those of my students who have made sincere, methodical efforts to learn more, many more, words.

2

HOW TO START
BUILDING YOUR VOCABULARY

WHEN you have finished working with this book, you will
no longer be the same person.

You can't be.

If you honestly read every page, if you do every exercise,
if you take every test, if you follow every principle, you will
go through an intellectual experience that will effect a radical
change in you.

For if you systematically increase your vocabulary, you
will also sharpen and enrich your thinking; push back your
intellectual horizons; build your self-assurance; improve your
facility in handling the English language and thereby your
ability to express your thoughts effectively; and acquire a
deeper understanding of the world in general and of yourself
in particular.

Increasing your vocabulary does not mean merely learning
the definitions of large numbers of obscure words; it does
not mean memorizing scores of unrelated terms. What it
means—what it can only mean—is becoming acquainted with
the multitudinous and fascinating phenomena of human existence for which words are, obviously, only the verbal de-
scriptions.

Increasing your vocabulary—properly, intelligently, and
systematically—means treating yourself to an all-round, liberal
education.

And surely you cannot deny that such an experience will
change you intellectually—

Will have a discernible effect on your methods of thinking
—on your store of information—on your ability to express
your ideas—on your understanding of human problems.

11

HOW CHILDREN INCREASE THEIR VOCABULARIES

In the previous chapter I mentioned Professor Robert H. Seashore's investigation of children's recognition vocabularies. Let me present some more of Seashore's findings:

> At the age of four, the average child has a vocabulary of 5,600 basic words.
> At the age of five, he knows 9,600 words.
> At the age of six, 14,700 words.
> At the age of seven, 21,200 words.
> At the age of eight, 26,300 words.
> At the age of nine, 29,300 words.

And, you will recall from Chapter 1, Professor Seashore found that at the ripe old age of ten the average child is able to recognize and understand 34,300 different words—and has been building his vocabulary at an approximate rate of 5000 words a year since his sixth birthday.

Do these figures leave you a little short of breath? They should. For you yourself were once that average child.

You yourself once increased your vocabulary at the average rate of 5000 words a year.

And how did you accomplish that Gargantuan feat?

By staying up nights poring over an unabridged dictionary?

By keeping notebooks chock-full of all the new words you ever heard or read?

By assiduously looking up the definitions of any new words your parents and friends used?

No—you had a much better, much more effective, and considerably less self-conscious method.

Your method was the essence of simplicity: day in and day out you kept learning; you kept squeezing every possible ounce of learning out of every waking moment; you were an eternal question box, for you had a constant and insatiable desire to know and understand.

Then, eventually, you lost your great drive for knowing and understanding.

When that happened, your vocabulary stopped increasing—because your intellect had slowed down its tremendous rate of growth.

HOW ADULTS STOP BUILDING THEIR VOCABULARIES

In a review of Caroline Pratt's recent book, *I Learn from Children,* Roland Gelatt states somewhat the same idea in the following words; "All normal human beings are born with a powerful urge to learn. Almost all of them lose this urge, even before they have reached maturity. It is only the few . . . who are so constituted that lack of learning becomes a nuisance. This is perhaps the most insidious of human tragedies."

Children are wonders at increasing their vocabularies because of their "powerful urge to learn." They do not learn solely by means of words, but as their knowledge increases, so does their vocabulary—for words are the symbols of ideas and understanding.

(If you are a parent, you perhaps remember that crucial and trying period in which your child constantly asked "Why?" The "Why?" is the child's method of finding out. How many adults that you know go about asking and thinking "Why?" How often do you yourself do it?)

The adults who "lose this urge," who no longer feel that "lack of learning becomes a nuisance," stop building their vocabularies. They stop learning, they stop growing intellectually, they stop developing mentally, they stop changing. When and if this period of life is finally reached, then, as Mr. Gelatt so truly says, "This is perhaps the most insidious of human tragedies."

But fortunately the process is not irreversible.

We have not yet learned to bring back life to a dead body. But we do know how to breathe life into a stalled mind, how to revive intellectual curiosity, how to restore the "powerful urge to learn." In short, we do know how to help an adult start his vocabulary growing again even if it has been quiescent for many years.

I am not talking theory. For years I have been working face to face with thousands of adults who have been taking vocabulary-improvement courses in the City College of New York.

As the result of my experience with these adults, I can state as a fact, and without qualification, that:

The person who can recapture "the powerful urge to learn" with which he was born can go on increasing his vocabulary at a prodigious rate—

No matter what his present age.

WHY AGE MAKES LITTLE DIFFERENCE IN VOCABULARY BUILDING

I repeat, *no matter what his present age.*

You may be laboring under a delusion common to many older people.

You may think that after you pass the twenties you rapidly and inevitably lose your ability to learn.

That is simply not true.

There is no doubt that the years up to eighteen or twenty are the best period for learning. Your own experience bears that out. And of course *with the average person* more learning is done up to twenty than ever after, even if he lives to be older than Methuselah. (That is why one's vocabulary increases so spectacularly for the first twenty years of one's life and comparatively little thereafter.)

But (and follow me closely)—

The fact that most learning is accomplished before the age of twenty does not mean that very little learning can be done beyond that age.

What *is* done by most people and what *can* be done under proper guidance and motivation are two very, very different things—as scientific experiments have conclusively shown.

Furthermore—

The fact that one's learning ability is best up to twenty does not mean that it is absolutely useless as soon as the twentieth birthday has passed.

Quite the contrary.

Edward Thorndike, the famous educational psychologist, found in experiments with people of all ages that although the learning curve rises spectacularly up to twenty, it *remains steady* for at least another five years. After that, ability to learn (according to Professor Thorndike) drops very, very, slowly up to the age of thirty-five, a little more rapidly but *still slowly* beyond that age.

And—

Right up to senility the *total* decrease in learning ability after age twenty is never more than 15 per cent!

That does not sound, I submit, as if no one can ever learn anything new after the age of twenty.

Believe me, the old saw that claims you cannot teach an old dog new tricks is a baseless, if popular, superstition.

So I repeat: No matter what your age, you can go on learning efficiently, or start learning once again if perhaps you have stopped.

You can be thirty, or forty, or fifty, or sixty, or seventy—or older.

No matter what your age, you can once again increase your vocabulary at a prodigious rate—providing you recapture the "powerful urge to learn" that is the key to vocabulary improvement.

Not the urge to learn "words"—words are only symbols of ideas.

But the urge to learn facts, theories, concepts, information, knowledge, understanding—call it what you will.

Words are the symbols of knowledge, the keys to accurate thinking. Is it any wonder then that the most successful and intelligent people in this country have the biggest vocabularies?

It was not their large vocabularies that made these people successful and intelligent, but their *knowledge*.

Knowledge, however, is gained largely through words.

In the process of increasing their knowledge, these successful people increased their vocabularies.

Just as the child increases *his* vocabulary at a tremendous, phenomenal rate during those years when his knowledge is increasing most rapidly.

Knowledge is chiefly in the form of words, and from now on, in this book, you will be thinking *about*, and thinking *with*, new words and new ideas.

WHAT THIS BOOK CAN DO FOR YOU

This book is designed to get you started building your vocabulary at a comparatively prodigious rate by helping you regain the intellectual atmosphere, the keen, insatiable, curiosity, the "powerful urge to learn" of your childhood.

The organization of the book is based on two simple principles: 1) words are the verbal symbols of ideas, and 2) the more ideas someone is familiar with, the more words he knows.

So, chapter by chapter, we will start with some central idea—personality types, doctors, science, unusual occupations, liars, actions, speech habits, insults, compliments, et cetera—and examine ten basic words which express various aspects of that idea. Then, using each word as a springboard, we will explore any others which are related to it in meaning or derivation, so that it is not unlikely that a single chapter may discuss, teach, and test close to 100 important words.

Always, however, the approach will be from the idea. First there will be a "teaser preview" in which the ideas are briefly hinted at; then a "headline," in which each idea is examined somewhat more closely; next a clear, detailed paragraph or more which will analyze the idea in all its ramifications; finally the word itself, which you will meet only after you are completely familiar with the idea.

In the etymology (derivation of words) section, you will learn what Greek or Latin root gives the word its unique meaning and what other words contain the same or related roots. You will thus be continuously working in related fields, and there will never be any possibility of confusion from "too muchness," despite the great number of words taken up and tested in each chapter.

Successful people have superior vocabularies. People who are intellectually, socially, and economically successful are accustomed to dealing with ideas, are constantly on the search for new ideas, build their lives and their careers on the ideas they have learned. And it is to readers whose goal is successful living that this book is addressed.

A NOTE ON TIME SCHEDULES

From my experience over many years in teaching adults, I have become a firm believer in setting a goal for all learning and a schedule for reaching that goal.

If you will work intensively several hours an evening and several evenings a week, you will have no difficulty finishing

16

each of the three main sections of this book in one week—a total of three weeks for the entire book.

If you can so organize your life that you will be able to work on your vocabulary for an hour or more *every day* (needless to say, this would be the ideal time schedule), you will be able to master the contents of this book in three weeks by completing one chapter plus its brief intermission in a sitting. (Try it—it's really easier than it may sound, even when you get to the longer chapters in the middle of the book.)

Of course you may find that you can go faster or, on the other hand, that you prefer to take longer. That is up to you —you will be your own taskmaster. But above all, decide as soon as possible at approximately what rate you can comfortably go and how long, therefore, it will take you to finish. *Then set your schedule and stick to it.* Try, also, never to interrupt your work until you have thoroughly covered that part of a chapter for which various pronunciation, comprehension, and recall tests are provided—the place to stop, if your learning is to be efficient and satisfying, is at the end of a series of tests, never anywhere else.

HOW TO TALK
ABOUT PERSONALITY TYPES

—— TEASER PREVIEW ——

How do you describe a man who:

- *is interested solely in his own welfare?*
- *constantly talks about himself?*
- *dedicates his life to helping others?*
- *turns his mind inward?*
- *turns his mind outward?*
- *hates humanity?*
- *hates women?*
- *hates marriage?*
- *leads a lonely, austere existence?*

UNLESS you are a hermit, you meet, from day to day and year to year, an amazing variety of different kinds of human beings. Psychology claims that every human being is unique —how a man (or woman) turns out is wholly dependent, in the beginning, on chance. Which one of the countless millions of the father's sperm will be the first to reach and fertilize the mother's egg? And what unpredictable forces of environment will mold and shape and develop the newborn infant into the final adult? Will he be proud or humble, friendly or moody, a genius or an imbecile, or just a so-called "average" human being?

We start our work by examining ten products of the chance interplay of the forces I have been describing.

And, of course, we begin not with the words, but with the ideas.

IDEAS

1. me first

This man's attitude to life is simple, direct, and aboveboard—every decision he makes is based on the answer to one question: "What's in it for me?" If his selfishness, greed, and ruthless desire for self-advancement hurt other people, that's too bad. "This is a tough world, pal, dog eat dog, every man for himself, and I, for one, am not going to be left behind!"

He's an *egoist*.

2. the height of conceit

"Now, let's see. Have you heard about all the money I'm making? Did I tell you about my latest amorous conquest? Let me give you *my* opinion—*I* know, because I'm an expert at practically everything!" This conceited boor is boastful to the point of being obnoxious—he has only one string to his conversational violin, namely, *himself;* and on it he plays a number of monotonous variations: what *he* thinks, what *he* has done, how good *he* is, how *he* would solve the problems of the world, et cetera ad nauseam.

He's an *egotist*.

3. let me help you

He has discovered the secret of true happiness—concerning himself with the welfare of others. Never mind his own interests, how's the next fellow getting along?

He's an *altruist*.

4. leave me alone

Like a biochemist studying a colony of bacteria under the microscope, he minutely examines his every thought, feeling, and action. Probing, futile questions like "What do other people think of me?" "How do I look?" and "Maybe I shouldn't have said that," are his constant nagging companions, for he is unable to realize that other people do not spend as much time and energy analyzing him as he thinks.

He may seem unsocial, yet his greatest desire is to be liked and accepted. He may be shy and quiet, he is often moody and unhappy, and he prefers solitude or at most the company of one person to a crowd. He has an aptitude for creative work and is uncomfortable engaging in activities that require co-operation with other people. He may even be a genius, or eventually turn into one.

He's an introvert.

5. let's do it together

He's a wonderful salesman, because he can always get interested—sincerely, vitally interested—in other people's problems. He's the life of the party, because he never worries about the effect of his actions, never inhibits himself with doubts about dignity or propriety. He is usually happy, generally full of high spirits, and he loves to be with people—lots of people. His thoughts, his interests, his whole personality are turned outward.

He's an extrovert.

6. like you and me

He has both *introverted* and *extroverted* tendencies—at different times and on different occasions. His interests are turned, in about equal proportions, both inward and outward. Indeed, he's quite normal—in the sense that his personality is like that of most of us.

He's an ambivert.

7. people are no damn good

Cynical, embittered, suspicious, he hates everyone. The perfectability of the human race? "Oh, brother, don't get me on that topic!" The stupidity, the meanness, and the crookedness of most mortals ("Most? Probably all!")—that is his favorite theme.

He's a misanthrope.

8. women are no damn good

Some time in the dim past of this unfortunate man's life he was crossed, scorned, or deeply wounded by a woman. So now he has a natural defense—he hates and fears all women. He agrees with the gloomy philosopher, Schopenhauer (or was it Nietzsche?) that "Women are the long-haired, short-brained sex"; that "Whenever you visit a woman, make sure to take a big whip with you."

He's a misogynist.

**9. "marriage is an institution—and who wants
   to live in an institution?"**

"Women are fine—they make wonderful companions, mistresses, and other men's wives." This gentleman, if we may call him a gentleman, defines a bachelor as one who is lucky in love—for he himself is definitely and irrevocably averse to wedding bells. He probably needs the help of a good psychiatrist—though who knows, maybe the single blessed state is the only one for him.

He's a *misogamist*.

10. ". . . that the flesh is heir to . . ."

Self-denial, austerity, lonely contemplation—these are the characteristics of the good life, so he claims. The simplest food and the least amount of it that will keep body and soul together, combined with a complete abstinence from indulgence in any of the earthy pleasures, will eventually lead to the spiritual and intellectual perfection which is man's ultimate goal—that is his philosophy.

He's an *ascetic*.

USING THE WORDS: 1

You have been introduced to ten valuable words—but in each case, as you have noticed, you have first considered the ideas which these words represent. Now listen to the words—each one will be respelled phonetically so that you may make sure you are pronouncing it correctly. A capitalized syllable indicates the position of the accent—other syllables are spelled exactly as they sound.

Don't be bashful; say each word aloud. This is one of the important steps to complete mastery. And as you hear the word in your own voice, think of its meaning. Are you quite clear as to the full significance of each one? If you are not, there is no law against going back and checking up on your learning.

Can you pronounce the words?

1. *egoist*   EE-go-ist
2. *egotist*   EE-go-tist
3. *altruist*   AL-troo-ist

21

4.	*introvert*	IN-tro-vurt
5.	*extrovert*	EKKS-tro-vurt
6.	*ambivert*	AM-bi-vurt
*7.	*misanthrope*	MISS-in-thrope
*8.	*misogynist*	mi-SAHDGE-in-ist
*9.	*misogamist*	mi-SOG-am-ist
10.	*ascetic*	a-SET-ik (*a* as in *hat*)

Can you work with the words?

You have taken two long steps forward toward mastery of the expressive words in this chapter—you have thought about the ideas behind them, and you have said them aloud. Now you will want to be quite sure that there is no confusion in your mind as to which words refer to which personality types. To test the success of your learning, match the words in the first column with the actions in the second column.

1. egoist	a. turns his mind inward
2. egotist	b. hates marriage
3. altruist	c. talks about his accomplishments
4. introvert	d. hates his fellow mortals
5. extrovert	e. leads an austere life
6. ambivert	f. is interested in the welfare of others
7. misanthrope	g. believes in self-advancement
8. misogynist	h. turns his mind both inward and outward
9. misogamist	i. hates women
10. ascetic	j. turns his mind outward

KEY: 1—g, 2—c, 3—f, 4—a, 5—j, 6—h, 7—d, 8—i, 9—b, 10—e

Do you understand the words?

Now that you are becoming more and more involved in these ten words, find out if they can make an immediate appeal to your understanding. Here are ten questions— Can you indicate, quickly, and without reference to any previous definitions, whether the correct answer to each of these questions is *yes* or *no?*

---

*Starred words throughout the book are demons in so far as their pronunciation is concerned—be especially careful to get them right.

1. Is an *egoist* selfish? YES NO
2. Is modesty one of the characteristics of the *egotist*? YES NO
3. Is an *altruist* selfish? YES NO
4. Does an *introvert* pay much attention to himself? YES NO
5. Does an *extrovert* prefer solitude to companionship? YES NO
6. Are most normal people *ambiverts*? YES NO
7. Does a *misanthrope* have a high respect for his fellow mortals? YES NO
8. Does a *misogynist* enjoy the company of women? YES NO
9. Does an *ascetic* lead a life of luxury? YES NO
10. Does a *misogamist* try to avoid marriage? YES NO

KEY: 1—yes, 2—no, 3—no, 4—yes, 5—no, 6—yes, 7—no, 8—no, 9—no, 10—yes

---

Can you recall the words?

These exercises are aimed toward making new words part of your everyday thinking. They not only check your learning, but also aid your memory and concentration. So don't skip a single one.

Now that you have pronounced the new words of this chapter, have matched them to their definitions, and answered questions about them, test your recall by writing next to each brief definition the specific word which applies. The answers, which immediately follow the test, will help you check your spelling as well as your understanding.

1. He lives a lonely, austere life. 1._____

2. His interests are turned outward. 2._____

3. He is supremely selfish. 3._____

4. He hates mankind. 4._____

5. His interests are turned both inward and outward. 5._____

6. He is incredibly conceited. 6._____

23

7. He is interested in the welfare of others.   7._____

8. He hates women.   8._____

9. His thinking is turned inward.   9._____

10. He hates wedlock.   10._____

KEY: 1—ascetic, 2—extrovert, 3—egoist, 4—misanthrope, 5—ambivert, 6—egotist, 7—altruist, 8—misogynist, 9—introvert, 10—misogamist

---

ORIGINS AND RELATED WORDS: I

Every word in the English language has a history—and these ten are no exception. In this section you will learn a good deal more about the words you have been working with; in addition, you will make excursions into many other words allied either in meaning, form, or history to our basic ten.

1. the ego

Egoist and *egotist* are built on the same Latin stem—the pronoun *ego*, meaning *I. I* is the greatest concern in the *egoist's* mind, the most overused word in the *egotist's* vocabulary. (Keep the words differentiated in your own mind by thinking of the *T* in *talk*, and the *T* in *egotist*.) *Ego* itself has been taken over from Latin as an important English word and is commonly used to denote one's concept of oneself, as in, "What do you think your constant criticisms do to my *ego?*" *Ego* has also a special and highly restricted meaning in psychoanalysis—but for the moment you have enough troubles without going into *that*.

The *egocentric* person considers himself the *center* of the universe—he is an extreme form of the *egoist*. And the *egomaniac* carries *egoism* to such an extreme that his needs, desires, and interests have become a morbid obsession, a *mania*. The *egoist* or *egotist* is obnoxious, the *egocentric* is intolerable, and the *egomaniac* is dangerous and slightly mad (for example, Adolf Hitler and Benito Mussolini). The adjective form for *egomaniac* is *egomaniacal*.

24

In Latin the word for *other* is *alter*, and a number of valuable English words are built on this root.

Altruism, the philosophy practiced by *altruists*, comes from one of the variant spellings of Latin *alter*, other—*altruistic* actions look toward the benefit of *others*. If you *alternate*, you skip one and take the *other*, so to speak, as when you bathe on *alternate* Saturdays. An *alternate* in a debate, contest, or conference is the *other* person who will take over if the original choice should be unable to attend. And if you have no *alternative* but to marry some girl, you have no *other* choice.

You see how easy it is to understand the meanings of these words once you realize that they all come from the same source. And keeping in mind that *alter* means *other*, you can quickly understand words like *alter ego*, *altercation*, and *alteration*.

An *alteration* is of course a change—a making into something *other*. When you *alter* your plans, you make *other* plans.

An *altercation* is a verbal dispute—when you have an *altercation* with someone you have a violent disagreement, a "fight" with words. And why? Because you have *other* ideas, plans, or opinions than those of the person on the *other* side of the argument. *Altercation*, by the way, is somewhat stronger than *quarrel* or *dispute*—the sentiment is more heated, the disagreement is likely to be angry or even hot-tempered, there may be recourse, if the disputants are human, to profanity or obscenity. You have *altercations*, in short, over pretty important issues, and the word implies that you get quite excited.

Alter ego, which combines *alter*, *other*, with our old friend *ego*, *I*, generally refers to someone with whom you are so close that you and he do the same things, think alike, react similarly, and are, in temperament, almost mirror images of each other. Any such friend is your *other I*, your *other self*, your *alter ego*.

USING THE WORDS: II

Can you pronounce the words?

Digging a little into the derivation of three of our basic words, *egoist*, *egotist*, and *altruist*, has put us in touch with two important Latin roots, *ego, I,* and *alter, other,* and has made it possible for us to explore, with little difficulty, all other words derived from these roots. Pause, now, for a moment, to digest these new acquisitions, and to make sure that you can say them correctly.

1.	*ego*	EE-go
2.	*egocentric*	ee-go-SEN-trik
3.	*egomaniac*	ee-go-MAY-nee-ak
°4.	*egomaniacal*	ee-go-ma-NYE-a-k'l
5.	*altruism*	AL-troo-izm
6.	*altruistic*	al-troo-ISS-tik
7.	to *alternate*	AWL-ter-nayt
°8.	*alternate* (adj. or noun)	AWL-ter-nit
9.	*alternative*	awl-TURN-a-tiv
10.	*alteration*	awl-ter-AY-shun
11.	to *alter*	AWL-ter
12.	*altercation*	awl-ter-KAY-shun
13.	*alter ego*	AWL-ter-EE-go

Can you work with the words? (I)

You have seen how these thirteen words stem from the two Latin roots *ego, I,* and *alter, other,* and you have pronounced them aloud and thereby begun to make them part of yourself. The question to settle at this point is whether you understand them well enough to be able to match them to their meanings. If you have studied successfully, you should make a perfect score.

1. ego	a.	one who is excessively fixated on his own desires, needs, et cetera
2. egocentric	b.	change
3. altruism	c.	argument
4. to alternate	d.	one's concept of oneself
5. to alter	e.	take one, skip one, et cetera
6. altercation	f.	philosophy of putting another's welfare above one's own

KEY: 1–d, 2–a, 3–f, 4–e, 5–b, 6–c

Can you work with the words? (II)

1. egomaniacal
2. altruistic
3. alternative
4. alteration
5. alter ego
6. alternate (adj.)

a. a change
b. other
c. interested in the welfare of others
d. one's other self
e. a choice
f. morbidly, insanely wrapped up in oneself

KEY: 1—f, 2—c, 3—e, 4—a, 5—d, 6—b

Do you understand the words?

If you have begun to understand these thirteen words, you will be able to react immediately, and correctly, to the following questions.

1. Is rejection one way for a woman to hurt a man's *ego*?   YES   NO
2. Are *egocentric* people easy to get along with?   YES   NO
3. Does an *egomaniac* have a normal personality?   YES   NO
4. Are *egomaniacal* tendencies a sign of maturity?   YES   NO
5. Is *altruism* a characteristic of selfish people?   YES   NO
6. Are *altruistic* tendencies a sign of growing up?   YES   NO
7. Is a delegate who is chosen as an *alternate* more important than the original selection?   YES   NO
8. Does an *alternative* allow you some freedom of choice?   YES   NO
9. Does *alteration* imply keeping things the same?   YES   NO
10. Do excitable people often engage in *altercations*?   YES   NO
11. Is your *alter ego* usually quite similar to yourself?   YES   NO

KEY: 1—yes, 2—no, 3—no, 4—no, 5—no, 6—yes, 7—no, 8—yes, 9—no, 10—yes, 11—yes

---

Can you recall the words?

Do you now understand each of these new words so well that you can summon it from your mind when a brief definition is offered? Review first if you feel that is necessary, then without further reference to the list in the previous tests try writing the proper word in each blank.

1. one's other self   1._____

2. to change   2._____

3. a heated dispute   3._____

4. a person insanely convinced of his own   4._____
   importance

5. unselfish (adj.)   5._____

6. one so involved with himself that he   6._____
   considers himself the center of the
   universe

7. a choice   7._____

8. one who substitutes for another   8._____

KEY: 1—alter ego, 2—alter, 3—altercation, 4—egomaniac, 5—altruistic, 6—egocentric, 7—alternative, 8—alternate

---

ORIGINS AND RELATED WORDS: II

1. depends how you turn

Introvert, extrovert, and *ambivert* are built on the Latin verb *verto, to turn.* If your thoughts are constantly turned inward *(intro),* you are an *introvert;* outward *(extro),* an *extrovert;* and in both directions *(ambi),* an *ambivert. Ambi, both,* is also found in *ambidextrous, able to use both hands with equal skill.* (The noun is *ambidexterity.) Dexterous* means *skillful, dexterity* means *skill. Dexter* is actually the Latin word for *right hand*—in the *ambidextrous* person, both hands are *right hands,* so to speak. The right hand is traditionally the more skillful one; it is only recently that we have come to accept that "lefties" or "south-paws" are just as normal as anyone else—and the term *left-handed* is still used as a synonym of *awkward.*

The Latin word for *the left hand* is *sinister.* This word, in

28

English, means *evil* or *dangerous,*° a further commentary on our traditional suspiciousness of left-handed persons. There are probably still a large number of parents who insist on forcing left-handed children to change (though left-handedness is inherited and as much an integral part of its possessor as the color of his eyes or the shape of his nose), with various unfortunate results—usually stuttering and an inability to read with normal skill.

The French word for the left hand, by the way, is *gauche,* and, as you would suspect, when we took this word over into English we invested it with an uncomplimentary meaning. Call a man *gauche* and you imply that he is awkward and clumsy, generally in a figurative rather than a physical sense. (You see we're right back to our traditional misconception that left-handed people are less skillful than right-handed ones.) A *gauche* remark is tactless; a *gauche* offer of sympathy is so bumbling as to be embarrassing; a person's *gaucherie* refers to his awkward, clumsy, tactless, embarrassing way of saying things or handling situations. The *gauche* person is totally without finesse.

Watch your pronunciation of these two words—they're French and they preserve a certain Gallic flavor. Say GO, then quickly add *sh:* GO-sh. The noun is pronounced GO-she-ree.

And the French word for the right hand is *droit,* which we have used in building our English word *adroit.* Needless to say, *adroit,* like *dexterous,* means *skillful,* but especially in the exercise of the mental faculties. Like *gauche, adroit,* or its noun *adroitness,* usually is used figuratively. The *adroit* person is quick witted, can get out of difficult spots cleverly, can handle situations ingeniously. *Adroitness* is, then, quite the opposite of *gaucherie.*

2. love, hate, and marriage

Misanthrope, misogynist, and *misogamist* are built on the Greek stem *misein, to hate.* The *misanthrope* hates mankind (Greek *anthropos, man);* the *misogynist* hates women (Greek *gyne, woman);* the *misogamist* hates marriage (Greek *gamos,*

°A book-reviewer, taking for granted that his readers were familiar with the etymology of the words, once remarked about a mystery-story writer: "Indeed, he is particularly *dexterous* when he is most *sinister.*"

marriage). *Anthropos, mankind,* is also found in *anthropology,* the study of the human race, and in *philanthropist,* one who loves mankind and shows his love by writing out big checks or by other charitable services.

Gyne, woman, is found in *gynecologist,* the doctor who treats those ailments peculiar to *women,* such as pregnancy, tumor of the uterus, tipped womb, menstrual disorders, and other feminine mysteries.

And *gamos, marriage,* occurs in *monogamy, bigamy,* and *polygamy. Monogamy* is the system of having one mate (at a time), often referred to by jokesters as *monotony; bigamy* is the legal offense of incurring a further marital obligation without having liquidated the previous one; and *polygamy* is the delightful but somewhat chaotic custom, practiced at one time by the Mormons of Utah and before them by King Solomon, of having as many wives as a man can afford financially and put up with emotionally.

Another form of *misanthrope* is *misanthropist.* The philosophy itself is called *misanthropy,* the adjective is *misanthropic.*

The philosophy of the *misogynist* is *misogyny,* the adjective is either *misogynistic* or *misogynous.* The *misogamist* practices *misogamy* and is *misogamous.*

3. living alone and liking it

Ascetic is from a Greek word *asketes, monk* or *hermit.* (The *philosophy* is *asceticism.*)

A monk lives a lonely life—not for him the pleasures of the fleshpots, the laughter and merriment of convivial gatherings, the dissipation of high living. Rather, days of contemplation, study, and rough toil, nights on a hard bed in a simple cell, and the kind of self-denial which leads to a purification of the soul.

That man is an *ascetic* who leads an existence, voluntarily of course, which compares in austerity, simplicity, and rigorous hardship with the life of a monk. The late Mahatma Gandhi is a perfect example of a believer in *asceticism.*

USING THE WORDS: III

I suppose you feel that it is time to come up for air again. Actually, this chapter is not so chock-full as it may at first seem. We have discussed only seven roots, and all the new words that we picked up along the way either directly stem from these roots or are merely other forms of the basic ten words discussed in the first part of the chapter.

Let us review the seven roots.

1. *ego*, I
   EXAMPLES: *ego*, self-concept; *egocentric*, self-centered, *egomania*, self-madness
2. *dexter*, right hand
   EXAMPLES: *ambidextrous*, both hands right hands; dexterous, skillful (right handed)
3. *anthropos*, mankind
   EXAMPLES: *anthropology*, study of mankind; *philanthropy*, love of mankind
4. *gyne*, woman
   EXAMPLE: *gynecology*, study of woman's diseases
5. *gamos*, marriage
   EXAMPLES: *monogamy*, one marriage; *bigamy*, two (or more) marriages, contrary to law; *polygamy*, many marriages, following social custom
6. *misein*, to hate
   EXAMPLES: *misanthropy*, hatred of mankind; *misogyny*, hatred of women; *misogamy*, hatred of marriage
7. *alter*, other
   EXAMPLES: *altruism*, love for others; *to alter*, change for some other; *alter ego*, other self

As you see, it's really not half so confusing as you may have thought. Review for a moment the words that come from our seven roots, refreshing your memory from the body of the text if necessary. You will then be ready for your tests.

Can you pronounce the words?

Say each word aloud, following the phonetic respelling.

1. *ambidextrous*	am-bi-DEKS-trus
2. *ambidexterity*	am-bi-deks-TER-i-tee
3. *dexterous*	DEKS-truss
4. *dexterity*	deks-TER-i-tee
5. *sinister*	SIN-is-ter
°6. *gauche*	GO-sh
°7. *gaucherie*	GO-she-ree
8. *adroit*	a-DROYT
9. *adroitness*	a-DROYT-ness

31

10. *anthropology*	an-thro-POL-o-jee
11. *philanthropist*	fil-AN-thro-pist
°12. *gynecologist*	gyne-e-KOL-o-jist
13. *monogamy*	mo-NOG-o-mee
14. *bigamy*	BIG-a-mee
15. *polygamy*	po-LIG-a-mee
°16. *misanthropist*	mis-AN-thro-pist
°17. *misanthropy*	mis-AN-thro-pee
°18. *misanthropic*	mis-an-THROP-ik
°19. *misogyny*	mi-SAHDGE-i-nee
°20. *misogynous*	mi-SAHDGE-in-us
°21. *misogynistic*	mi-SAHDGE-in-is-tik
°22. *misogamy*	mi-SOG-a-mee
°23. *misogamous*	mi-SOG-a-mus
°24. *asceticism*	a-SET-i-sizm

Can you work with the words? (I)

As before, to check on your comprehension, see how successfully you can match words and means.

1. ambidextrous	a. evil, threatening
2. dexterous	b. hating mankind
3. sinister	c. skillful
4. gauche	d. awkward
5. misanthropic	e. capable of using both hands with equal skill

KEY: 1—e, 2—c, 3—a, 4—d, 5—b

Can you work with the words? (II)

1. anthropology	a. system of only one marriage
2. gynecology	b. hatred of women
3. monogamy	c. illegal plurality of marriages
4. bigamy	d. study of human development
5. misogyny	e. study of female ailments

KEY: 1—d, 2—e, 3—a, 4—c, 5—b

Can you work with the words? (III)

| 1. polygamy | a. devotion to lonely and austere life |
| 2. misogamy | b. skill, cleverness |

32

3. asceticism   c. custom in which one man has many wives
4. philanthropy   d. love of mankind
5. adroitness   e. hatred of marriage

KEY: 1—c, 2—e, 3—a, 4—d, 5—b

Do you understand the words?

By now, if you see these words used in sentences, you should be able to respond immediately to their meanings. Answer the following questions without referring to the definitions in previous pages.

1. Can *ambidextrous* people use either the left or right hand equally well?   YES   NO
2. Should a surgeon be manually *dexterous?*   YES   NO
3. Is a *sinister*-looking person frightening?   YES   NO
4. If a man is *gauche,* is he likely to get along well with people?   YES   NO
5. Is an *adroit* speaker likely to be a successful lawyer?   YES   NO
6. Is a student of *anthropology* interested in primitive tribes?   YES   NO
7. Does a *gynecologist* have more male than female patients?   YES   NO
8. Is *monogamy* the custom in Christian countries?   YES   NO
9. Is a *misogamist* likely to show tendencies toward *polygamy?*   YES   NO
10. Is a *bigamist* breaking the law?   YES   NO
11. Is a *philanthropist* generally altruistic?   YES   NO
12. Is a *misanthropist* probably emotionally secure?   YES   NO
13. Are *misogynous* men interested in chorus girls?   YES   NO
14. Are spinsters necessarily *misogamous?*   YES   NO
15. Are bachelors necessarily *misogynous?*   YES   NO
16. Is *asceticism* a popular philosophy today?   YES   NO

KEY: 1—yes, 2—yes, 3—yes, 4—no, 5—yes, 6—yes, 7—no, 8—yes, 9—no, 10—yes, 11—yes, 12—no, 13—no, 14—no, 15—no, 16—no

Can you recall the words?

Now let us see how successfully you can react to a definition with one of the words you have just studied. Consider it a proof of your successful learning if you can fill in most of the blanks without further reference to previous lists. Let the initial letter guide your thinking.

1. Philosophy of living austerely	1. A_____
2. Hatred of women	2. M_____
3. Hatred of marriage	3. M_____
4. Hatred of mankind	4. M_____
5. Skillful	5. D_____
6. Awkward	6. G_____
7. Evil, threatening	7. S_____
8. Describing hatred of women	8. M_____
9. Skill	9. A_____
10. Pertaining to hatred of marriage (adj.)	10. M_____
11. Pertaining to hatred of mankind (adj.)	11. M_____
12. Social custom of plurality of marriages	12. P_____
13. Legal crime of having more than one spouse	13. B_____
14. Doctor specializing in female disorders	14. G_____
15. Custom of one marriage at a time	15. M_____
16. One who hates the human race	16. M_____
17. Able to use both hands with equal skill	17. A_____
18. Study of mankind	18. A_____
19. One who loves mankind	19. P_____
20. Skill in the use of both hands	20. A_____

KEY: 1—asceticism, 2—misogyny, 3—misogamy, 4—misanthropy, 5—dexterous, 6—gauche, 7—sinister, 8—misogynous or misogynistic, 9—adroitness, 10—misogamous, 11—misanthropic, 12—polygamy, 13—bigamy, 14—gynecologist, 15—monogamy, 16—misanthropist or misanthrope, 17—ambidextrous, 18—anthropology, 19—philanthropist, 20—ambidexterity

---

CHAPTER REVIEW

Do you recognize the words?

Check the word that most closely fits each definition.

1. Puts his own desires first:
   (a) egoist, (b) egotist, (c) altruist
2. Is self-analytical:
   (a) extrovert, (b) introvert, (c) ambivert
3. Hates women:
   (a) misogamist, (b) misanthrope, (c) misogynist
4. One's other self:
   (a) altercation, (b) alter ego, (c) alteration
5. Awkward, clumsy:
   (a) adroit, (b) dexterous, (c) gauche
6. Custom of having a plurality of wives:
   (a) bigamy, (b) polygamy, (c) monogamy
7. Study of human development:
   (a) asceticism, (b) philanthropy, (c) anthropology

KEY: 1—a, 2—b, 3—c, 4—b, 5—c, 6—b, 7—c

GAINING MOMENTUM

There you are—in one short evening of, I trust, not too unpleasant work, you have become acquainted with scores of new, vital, exciting words. You understand the ideas behind these words, their various forms and spellings, their pronunciation, their derivation, how they can be used, and exactly what they mean. I do not wish to press a point unduly, but it is likely that you have learned as many new words in the short time it took you to cover this chapter as the average adult learns in an entire year. This realization should make you feel both gratified and excited—sufficiently gratified and excited, I hope, to keep right on if you have the time, or come back at the very next available moment.

Funny thing about time. Aside from the fact that Arnold Bennett pointed out, namely, that we all, rich or poor, sick or well, have the same amount of time, exactly twenty-four hours every day (that is looking at time from a static point of view), it is also true that we can always find time for the things we enjoy doing, almost never for the things we find unpleasant (and that is looking at time from the dynamic point of view). I am not merely being philosophical—I am sure that you will agree with this concept if you give it a little thought. And if you have enjoyed working with this book so far, make a habit of sticking with it for as long as you can and returning to it as often as you can. Especially in the beginning—for once you gain momentum, you'll coast right along with little trouble.

BRIEF INTERMISSION ONE:
TEST YOUR GRAMMAR

How good is your English? Have you ever said *me* and then wondered if it shouldn't have been *I*—or vice versa? Do you sometimes get a little confused about *lay* and *lie* or *who* and *whom*? Perhaps you are often a little less than certain about the distinction between *effect* and *affect*, *principal* and *principle*, *childish* and *childlike*?

Here is a series of quick tests that will show you how skillful you are in using the right word in the right place, that will give you a reliable indication of how your language ability compares with the average.

TEST I—EASY

If your English is every bit as good as average, you will have no difficulty making a proper choice in at least eight of the following ten sentences.

1. There is a beautiful moon out tonight and Estelle and I are going for a stroll—would you like to come along with (she and I, her and me?)
2. Your husband doesn't believe that you are older than (I, me).
3. Maybe we're not as rich as (they, them), but I bet we're a lot happier.
4. Does your child still (lay, lie) down for a nap after lunch?
5. When we saw Mary openly flirting with Nellie's husband, we (could, couldn't) hardly believe our eyes.
6. You should (of, have) cooked the stew much longer—it's still quite tough.
7. Does your husband (leave, let) you spend your household money as freely as you'd like?
8. Harriet feels that most (mothers-in-law, mother-in-laws) are impossible to get along with.

37

9. "What (kind of, kind of a) dress are you looking for?" asked the salesgirl.
10. Mrs. White was delighted that the Fennells had invited Saul and (she, her) to their party.

Is your English up to par? HERE ARE THE CORRECT ANSWERS

1—her and me, 2—I, 3—they, 4—lie, 5—could, 6—have, 7—let, 8—mothers-in-law, 9—kind of, 10—her

TEST II—HARDER

Choose wisely in at least seven of the following problems to consider that your skill is distinctly above average—get all ten right to conclude that you rarely, if ever, make an error in grammar.

1. What (effect, affect) has the war had on juvenile delinquency?
2. Marriage, say some philosophers, is the (principle, principal) goal of most women.
3. There's no sense (in, of) carrying on that way just because your child won't eat his spinach.
4. She can't remember (who, whom) it was.
5. The child (lay, laid) quietly sucking its thumb.
6. No one but (she, her) ever objected to his attitude.
7. The judge sentenced the murderer to be (hanged, hung).
8. Neither of Bill's sisters (has, have) had much luck in snaring a husband.
9. Either the sugar or milk (go, goes) into the batter next.
10. The doctor will speak to (whoever, whomever) came in first.

Is your speech above average? HERE ARE THE CORRECT ANSWERS

1—effect, 2—principal, 3—in, 4—who, 5—lay, 6—her, 7—hanged, 8—has, 9—goes, 10—whoever

TEST III—VERY HARD

Now you can discover how close you are to being an expert in English. The next ten sentences are no cinch—you will be acquitting yourself creditably if you check the correct word in more than half of them. And you have every right to consider yourself the possessor of unusual linguistic ability if you manage to come to a proper conclusion in nine or ten of the problems.

1. Although Martin was once a confirmed bachelor, he has finally found in Alice a girl (who, whom) he thinks will make a perfect wife.
2. Ironically enough, Alice is one of those women who (believes, believe) that the success of any marriage depends entirely on the husband.
3. Martin was particularly attracted by Alice's (childish, childlike) charm and innocence.
4. Although Martin is a student of world problems, Alice is totally (uninterested, disinterested) in foreign affairs.
5. This recipe calls for two (spoonsful, spoonfuls) of vanilla.
6. Are you trying to (infer, imply) by those words that he is unworthy of her?
7. We thought the actress to be (she, her), but we weren't sure.
8. Was it (she, her) you were talking about?
9. The data on the divorce case (is, are) on the judge's desk.
10. "It is I who (is, am) the only friend you've got," she told him pointedly.

Are you an expert? HERE ARE THE CORRECT ANSWERS

1—who, 2—believe, 3—childlike, 4—uninterested, 5—spoonfuls, 6—imply, 7—her, 8—she, 9—are, 10—am

4

HOW TO TALK ABOUT
DOCTORS

———TEASER PREVIEW————————————————

What is the title of the doctor who:

- is a specialist in diagnosis?
- treats female ailments?
- delivers babies?
- specializes in the treatment of childhood
  diseases?
- treats skin disorders?
- is an eye surgeon?
- is a specialist in heart ailments?
- is a specialist in nerve disorders?
- treats sick minds?

THE FAMILY doctor is becoming practically extinct—especially in large urban areas. At one time if you felt ill you "went to the doctor." Now you go to a specialist, depending on which part of your anatomy seems to be affected.

In this chapter we discuss the functions of ten medical specialists—what they do, how they do it, what their titles are.

IDEAS

1. what's wrong with you?

His specialty is finding out what ails you—and why. To arrive at a diagnosis, he'll give you a thoroughgoing and exhaustive examination, from head to foot, inside and out. And for this purpose he will use an impressive array of tests and apparatus: X ray, fluoroscope, blood count, urinalysis, cardiogram, and so on.

This doctor is an *internist*.

2. female troubles?

This man's practice is restricted to females, and more specifically to those ailments peculiar to women which were detailed in Chapter 3.

This doctor is a *gynecologist.*

3. having a baby?

He delivers babies and takes care of the mother during and immediately after the period of her pregnancy.

This doctor is an *obstetrician.*

4. Is your baby ill?

Infancy and childhood are heir to unique diseases of their own. You know the usual childhood maladies—mumps, whooping cough, chicken pox, measles, and the rest. Here is a man who limits his practice to youngsters, taking care of babies directly after birth, watching their diets and growth, giving them the series of inoculations that has done so much to decrease infant mortality, and soothing their worried parents.

This doctor is a *pediatrician.*

5. skin clear?

You have heard the classic riddle: "What is the best use for pigskin?" Answer: "To keep the pig together." Human skin has a similar purpose: It is, if we get down to fundamentals, what keeps us all in one piece. And our outer covering, like so many of our internal organs, is subject to diseases and infections of various kinds, running the gamut from simple acne and eczemas through impetigo, to syphilis, to cancer. And there is a man whose specialty is the treatment of such ailments.

This doctor is a *dermatologist.*

6. how is your vision?

His field is the eye and all the disorders connected with it: Imperfect vision, myopia, astigmatism, cataracts, et cetera. He may prescribe glasses, administer drugs, or perform surgery.

This doctor is an *oculist.*

7. how are your bones?

His area of specialization is the skeletal structure of the body; he treats various deformities such as clubfoot, curvature of the spine, dislocation of the hip, et cetera. He is a surgeon, and may correct a condition either by operating or by the use of braces or other appliances.

This doctor is an _orthopedist_.

8. does your heart go pitter-patter?

With diseases of the heart still the number-one killer of humanity, it is not surprising that one of the medical specialists deals with the treatment of that vital organ.

This doctor is a _cardiologist_.

9. are you nervous?

He specializes in afflictions that arise from improper functioning of the nervous system—cerebral palsy, "tics," strokes, et cetera.

This doctor is a _neurologist_.

10. are you neurotic?

It is a far cry today from the attitude we took not so many generations back: "Does this man seem slightly daft, a little peculiar? The devil's got him, so lock him up in a dark dungeon and beat him until he is better."

In this modern age we have what we consider more scientific and enlightened means of treating disorders of the mind or personality—drugs, electric and insulin-shock therapy, operations on the brain to sever one or more nerves (this technique has the formidable name of _frontal lobotomy_), and the recognition, thanks to Freud, of the influence of the "unconscious mind" and of childhood experiences on future behavior.

After receiving his M.D. degree, a physician may take further training and specialize in the treatment of mental and emotional disturbances to full-blown insanity.

This doctor is a _psychiatrist_.

Anatomically speaking, let us see how our medical specialists line up.

DOCTOR	AREA OF SPECIALTY
1. *internist*	the body as a whole
2. *gynecologist*	female organs
3. *obstetrician*	delivery of babies
4. *pediatrician*	treatment of infants
5. *dermatologist*	skin
6. *oculist*	eyes
7. *orthopedist*	bones
8. *cardiologist*	heart
9. *neurologist*	nerves
10. *psychiatrist*	mind

USING THE WORDS: I

Now that you are familiar with the ideas behind our basic ten words, spend a few minutes doing the exercises that will lead to complete mastery.

Can you pronounce the words?

Words take on a new color if you hear them in your own voice; they begin to belong to you more personally, more intimately, than if you merely hear or read them. As a first step in complete mastery, say the following words aloud.

1.	*internist*	in-TURN-ist
*2.	*gynecologist*	gyne-e-KOL-o-jist
3.	*obstetrician*	obs-te-TRISH-in
4.	*pediatrician*	pee-dee-a-TRISH-in
5.	*dermatologist*	derm-a-TOL-o-jist
6.	*oculist*	OK-yoo-list
*7.	*orthopedist*	or-tho-PEE-dist
8.	*cardiologist*	car-dee-OL-o-jist
9.	*neurologist*	noo-ROL-o-jist
*10.	*psychiatrist*	sye-KYE-a-trist

Can you work with the words?

Match each doctor to his field.

FIELDS	SPECIALISTS
1. mental or emotional disturbances	a. internist
2. nerves	b. gynecologist
3. skin	c. obstetrician

4. diagnosis	d. pediatrician
5. infants	e. dermatologist
6. female complaints	f. oculist
7. eyes	g. orthopedist
8. heart	h. cardiologist
9. pregnancy	i. neurologist
10. bones	j. psychiatrist

KEY: 1—j, 2—i, 3—e, 4—a, 5—d, 6—b, 7—f, 8—h, 9—c, 10—g

Do you understand the words?

React quickly to the following questions.

1. Is an *internist* an expert in diagnosis?   YES   NO
2. Is a *gynecologist* familiar with female anatomy?   YES   NO
3. Does an *obstetrician* specialize in diseases of childhood?   YES   NO
4. Does a *pediatrician* deliver babies?   YES   NO
5. If you had a stubborn skin rash, would you visit a *dermatologist*?   YES   NO
6. If you had trouble with your vision would you visit an *orthopedist*?   YES   NO
7. Is an *oculist* a nerve-specialist?   YES   NO
8. If there were something wrong with your child's posture, would you visit a *cardiologist*?   YES   NO
9. Is a *neurologist* a nerve-specialist?   YES   NO
10. If a friend of yours seemed inexplicably depressed and unhappy, would you suggest a visit to a *psychiatrist*?   YES   NO

KEY: 1—yes, 2—yes, 3—no, 4—no, 5—yes, 6—no, 7—no, 8—no, 9—yes, 10—yes

---

Can you recall the words?

Write the name of the specialist you would visit for each of the following ailments or reasons.

1. shingles, which is a disease of nervous origin   1. _neurologist_

2. recurrent nausea, for which your family physician can find no apparent cause

2. _internist_

3. hives, a skin disease

3. _dermatologist_

4. palpitations of the heart

4. _cardiologist_

5. tensions, fears, insecurity

5. _psychiatrist_

6. pregnancy

6. _obstetrician_

7. some disorder of the female organs

7. _gynecologist_

8. a check-up for your two-month-old child

8. _pediatrician_

9. faulty vision

9. _oculist_

10. curvature of the spine

10. _orthopedist_

KEY: 1—neurologist, 2—internist, 3—dermatologist, 4—cardiologist, 5—psychiatrist, 6—obstetrician, 7—gynecologist, 8—pediatrician, 9—oculist, 10—orthopedist

---

ORIGINS AND RELATED WORDS: I

1. inside you

Internist and *internal* come of course from the same source, a Latin root meaning *inside*. The *internist* is a specialist in *internal* medicine, in the exploration of your insides. He determines the state of your various organs or discovers what's happening *within* your body to cause the troubles you're complaining of.

Do not confuse the *internist* with the *intern*, who is a young medical graduate serving his hospital apprenticeship before starting his own private practice.

2. women again

The specialist in female ills, the *gynecologist*, derives his title from the Greek *gyne, woman,* from which source comes also *misogynist*, the *woman hater*, a word we discussed in Chapter 3. This doctor's specialty is *gynecology;* the adjective

45

form is *gynecological*, as in "the *gynecological* cause of her troubles."

Though it must be a thorn in the side of every *obstetrician* who is aware of it, his medical title is derived from the Latin word *obstetrix, midwife. Obstetrix* is from a verb meaning *to stand before*—doubtless in allusion to the fact that midwives stand before the delivering woman, ready to catch the infant as it comes out. Indeed, it is still a wry (and of course highly inaccurate) medical joke that the only instrument an *obstetrician* needs is a big basket. *Obstetrics* is only recently a respectable calling—no further back than 1834, Professor William P. Dewees assumed the first chair of *obstetrics* at the University of Pennsylvania and had to brave considerable medical contempt and ridicule as a result—the delivery of children was then considered beneath the dignity of the profession. Even today it is estimated that one hundred thousand mothers yearly are delivered without *obstetrical* attention.

3. children

In *pediatrician*, the stem is *ped*—but don't let it mislead you. It's not the same *ped* you see in *pedestal, pedal,* or *pedestrian.* The root in these three words means *foot,* and comes from Latin; but the *ped* in *pediatrician* is a respelling of the Greek word *paidos, child. Pediatrics,* the specialty of the *pediatrician, is the healing of a child.*

Paidos (usually respelled *ped*), then, means *child.* And *pedagogy,* which combines *paidos* with *agogos, leading,* is, strictly, *the leading of a child.* And to what do you lead a child? You lead him to learning, to development, to growth, to maturity. From the moment of his birth, an infant is led by an adult—he is taught, first by parents and then by teachers, to be self-sufficient, to fit into the society in which he is born. Hence, *pedagogy,* which by strict derivation means *the leading of a child,* refers actually to the principles and methods of teaching. College students majoring in education take certain standard *pedagogy* courses—the history of education; education psychology; the psychology of adolescents; principles of teaching; et cetera.

One who teaches is versed in *pedagogy*—he is, in short, a *pedagogue.* But *pedagogue* has had an unhappy history.

From its original, neutral, meaning of *teacher*, it has deteriorated to the point where it refers, today, to a narrow-minded, strait-laced, old-fashioned, dogmatic teacher. It is a word of contempt and should be used with caution.

Like *pedagogue*, *demagogue* has also deteriorated in meaning. In derivation a *leader* (*agogos*) of the people (*demos*), a *demagogue* today is actually one who attempts to *mislead* the people. He is a politician who foments discontent among the voters, promises them all sorts of rewards if they will help him gain power, though he actually plans to use this political power to further his own personal fortunes. "Leaders of the people" like Hitler, Mussolini, and Huey Long come readily to mind—such figures can be accused of *demagoguery*.

4. skin-deep

The *dermatologist*, whose specialty is *dermatology*, is so named from the Greek *derma*, skin. See the syllables *derma* in any English word and you will know there is some reference to *skin*—for example, a *hypodermic* needle penetrates under (*hypo*) the *skin*; the *epidermis* is the outermost layer of *skin*; a *taxidermist* (his business is *taxidermy*) is one who prepares, stuffs, and mounts the *skins* of animals; a *pachyderm* is an animal with an unusually thick *skin*, like an elephant or a rhinoceros; and *dermatitis* is the general name for any *skin* inflammation, irritation, or infection. Every dermatologist is also a *syphilologist*, since *syphilis*, while actually an infection of the blood stream, first manifests itself in the form of a *skin* eruption.

5. the eyes have it

The *oculist* deals with eyes; his title should, logically, derive from a root meaning *eye*. You will be happy to know that it does—from the Latin *oculus*. We hear this root also in the adjective *ocular*, *pertaining to the eye*; *monocle*, *a lens for one* (*mono*) eye sported by traditional Englishmen of the so-called upper-class; *binoculars*, *field glasses* which increase the range of our two (*bi*) eyes; and, strangely enough, *inoculate*, a word commonly misspelled with two *n*'s. When you are inoculated against a disease, say diphtheria, an "eye" or

47

bud is made in your skin, through which the serum is injected by means of a *hypodermic*.

The *oculist* practices *ophthalmology*, the scientific name for the study and treatment of eye diseases. Most *oculists* prefer to be known by the title *ophthalmologist*, perhaps because this word is practically unpronounceable, and hence seems considerably more dignified, not to say more elegant, than *oculist*.

The *oculist* or *ophthalmologist* should be not be confused with two other practitioners whose business is with the eye—the *optometrist* and *optician*.

The *optometrist*, who is not a physician, is not permitted by law to perform operations or to administer drugs—his activities are largely restricted to prescribing and fitting glasses. The *optician* is even further restricted—he may only fill an *optometrist's* or *ophthalmologist's* prescription, grinding lenses according to specifications; he does not examine a patient. Many *optometrists* grind lenses, either according to their own prescription or according to the prescription brought to them from an *ophthalmologist*. Both the *optometrist* and the *oculist* are college-trained—the *optician* need not be. Only the *oculist* (or *ophthalmologist*) is a medical doctor.

USING THE WORDS: II

Our exploration of roots and related forms has turned up twenty-five new words. Let's review the major ones rapidly.

1. *intern*—a graduate of medical school serving his apprenticeship in a hospital
2. *gynecology*—the treatment of female ills
3. *obstetrics*—the delivery of babies
4. *pediatrics*—the medical specialty restricted to the care of infants and the curing of children's diseases
5. *pedagogy*—principles of teaching
6. *pedagogue*—term of contempt for a teacher
7. *demagogue*—one who stirs up discontent among the masses so he can gain political power
8. *demagoguery*—the specialty of the demagogue
9. *dermatology*—medical specialty restricted to the treatment of skin diseases
10. *hypodermic*—a needle for penetrating under the skin

11. *epidermis*—outer layer of skin
12. *taxidermy*—the stuffing and mounting of the skins of animals
13. *pachyderm*—elephant, rhinoceros, hippopotamus, et cetera
14. *dermatitis*—skin inflammation
15. *syphilologist*—medical doctor who specializes in the treatment of syphilis
16. *ocular*—pertaining to the eye
17. *monocle*—one-lens eyeglass
18. *ophthalmologist*—eye doctor
19. *optometrist*—practitioner who prescribes and fits glasses
20. *optician*—dealer in optical goods; grinder of optical lenses

These words are related either in etymology or meaning to six of our basic ten words, and can therefore be learned quickly, understood without difficulty, and remembered without undue strain. To test the success of your learning, try the following tests.

Can you pronounce the words?

1.	*intern*	IN-turn
*2.	*gynecology*	gye-ne-KOL-o-jee
3.	*obstetrics*	ob-STET-riks
4.	*obstetrical*	ob-STET-ri-k'l
*5.	*pediatrics*	pe-de-AT-riks
6.	*pedagogy*	PED-a-go-jee
*7.	*pedagogical*	ped-a-GODGE-i-k'l
8.	*pedagogue*	PED-a-gog
9.	*demagogue*	DEM-a-gog
*10.	*demagoguery*	dem-a-GOG-a-ree
*11.	*pachyderm*	PAK-i-durm
12.	*hypodermic*	hy-po-DUR-mik
13.	*epidermis*	ep-i-DUR-mis
14.	*taxidermist*	tax-i-DUR-mist
*15.	*dermatitis*	dur-ma-TYE-tis
16.	*syphilologist*	siff-i-LOLL-o-jist
17.	*taxidermy*	TAX-i-dur-mee
18.	*ocular*	OK-yoo-ler
19.	*monocle*	MON-i-k'l
20.	*binoculars*	bi-NOK-yoo-lerz
21.	*inoculate*	i-NOK-yoo-layt
*22.	*ophthalmology*	off-thal-MOL-o-jee
*23.	*ophthalmologist*	off-thal-MOL-o-jist
24.	*optometrist*	op-TOM-e-trist
25.	*optician*	op-TISH-un

49

Can you work with the words? (I)

Match words and meanings.

1. gynecology +
2. obstetrics c
3. pediatrics g

4. pedagogy a
5. demagoguery d
6. dermatology e
7. taxidermy b

a. principles of teaching
b. stuffing of skins of animals
c. specialty dealing with the delivery of newborn infants
d. stirring up discontent among the masses
e. treatment of skin diseases
f. specialty dealing with women's diseases
g. specialty dealing with the treatment of children.

KEY: 1–f, 2–c, 3–g, 4–a, 5–d, 6–e, 7–b

Can you work with the words? (II)

1. hypodermic c
2. epidermis f
3. pachyderm a
4. dermatitis g
5. ophthalmologist b
6. optometrist d
7. optician e

a. elephant
b. eye doctor
c. needle
d. one who prescribes glasses
e. lens grinder
f. skin
g. inflammation

KEY: 1–c, 2–f, 3–a, 4–g, 5–b, 6–d, 7–e

Do you understand the words?

React quickly to the following questions.

1. Does a treatise on *obstetrics* deal with childbirth?   YES   NO
2. Does *gynecology* deal with the female reproductive organs?   YES   NO
3. Is *pediatrics* concerned with the diseases of old age?   YES   NO
4. Does *pedagogy* refer to teaching?   YES   NO
5. Is a *pedagogue* an expert teacher?   YES   NO

6. Is a *demagogue* interested in the welfare of the people? YES (NO)
7. Is a lion a *pachyderm*? YES (NO)
8. Is the *epidermis* one of the layers of the skin? (YES) NO
9. Is *dermatitis* an inflammation of one of the limbs? YES (NO)
10. Is a *taxidermist* a medical practitioner? YES (NO)
11. Is an *ophthalmologist* a medical doctor? (YES) NO
12. Is an *optometrist* a medical doctor? YES (NO)
13. Does an *optician* prescribe glasses? YES (NO)

KEY: 1—yes, 2—yes, 3—no, 4—yes, 5—no, 6—no, 7—no, 8—yes, 9—no, 10—no, 11—yes, 12—no, 13—no

Can you recall the words?

Supply the proper word for each brief definition.

1. specialty of child delivery   O obstetrics
2. outer layer of skin   E pidermis
3. expert on venereal diseases   S yphibologist
4. principles of teaching   P pedagogy
5. thick-skinned animal   P achyderm
6. skin inflammation   D dermititis
7. one who foments political discontent   D demagogue
8. one who sells optical equipment   O ptician
9. medical graduate serving his apprenticeship   I ntern
10. treatment of childhood diseases   P ediatrics
11. practice of stirring up political dissatisfaction for purely personal gain   D demagoguery
12. one who stuffs the skins of animals   T axidermist
13. another title for oculist   O phthalmologist
14. study of female ailments   G ynecology

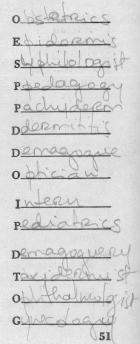

15. medical specialty relating to diseases
    of the eye

O *ophthalmology*

16. one-lens eyeglass

M *onocle*

17. pertaining to the eye

O *ocular*

18. one who measures vision

O_____

ORIGINS AND RELATED WORDS: II

1. lay them straight

The *orthopedist,* or bone surgeon, is so called from the Greek roots *ortho, change,* and *paidos, child,* the same *paidos* we met in *pediatrician.* The *orthopedist* straightens bone deformities, in children primarily, because childhood, the period when the bones are soft and pliable, is the best time for such corrections. His specialty is *orthopedics. Ortho* is also found in *orthodontia, the straightening of teeth.* The dentist who specializes in improving your "bite," retracting "buck teeth," and by means of braces and other techniques seeing to it that every molar, incisor, bicuspid, et cetera is exactly where it belongs in your mouth is an *orthodontist.*

Incidentally, words like *obstetrics, pediatrics,* and *orthopedics,* though they end in "*s,*" are used as singulars. For example, "Obstetrics *is* usually a remunerative calling," and "Pediatrics *is* a comparatively new specialty."

2. good for the heart

The *card* in *cardiologist* of course means *heart,* and is from the Greek. A sufferer from a *cardiac* condition has

52

heart trouble, and a *cardiogram* is an electrically produced record of the beats of the heart. The instrument which produces this record is called a *cardiograph*.

3. good for the nerves

In *neurologist*, the first two syllables come from the Greek root *neuron, nerve. Neuralgia* is acute pain along the nerves and their branches; *neuritis* is inflammation of the nerves, just as *dermatitis* is inflammation of the skin; *neurasthenia* is an emotional condition, rather than a physical one—the *neurasthenic* patient is worried, "nervous," depressed, emotionally exhausted; and *neurosis*, still from the same Greek word for *nerve* is best described by a *psychiatrist*, since it is an emotional disturbance. Dr. Eric Berne defines *neurosis* in his excellent book, *The Mind in Action*, as follows: "An illness characterized by excessive use of energy for unproductive purposes so that personality development is hindered or stopped. A man who spends most of his time worrying about his health, counting his money, plotting revenge, or washing his hands, can hope for little emotional growth." The victim of a neurosis is called *neurotic*.

Bear in mind that a *neurosis* is not a form of insanity or mental unbalance. A full-blown mental disorder is called a *psychosis*.

Thus *egoism*, which we discussed in Chapter 3, is simply a symptom of lack of adjustment; in a more aggravated and unpleasant form it is *egocentricity*, and is then a *neurosis*; and if it is sufficiently pronounced to be *egomania*, it is a *psychosis*. Many of us are *neurotic*, but except for the unhappiness that our *neurosis* may cause ourselves and others, we can manage to live fairly comfortable lives. When we are *psychotic*, however, we are no longer able to carry on our everyday affairs in a normal fashion—we must then be treated by a *psychiatrist* or perhaps we must even be institutionalized.

The word *psychiatrist* combines *psyche*, Greek for *mind*, with *iatreia, healing*. The *psychiatrist* is a doctor who heals sick minds. The specialty is *psychiatry*—the adjective is *psychiatric*. The clearest definition of *psychiatry* that I have ever seen appears in Dr. William C. Menninger's *Psychiatry: Its Evolution and Present Status* (1948), to wit: "Psychiatry (is) that branch of clinical medicine which concerns itself with the diagnosis, treatment, and prevention of personality disorders. . . ." Since *neuroses* and *psychoses* are both personality disorders, we might also say that the practice of psychiatry concerns itself with the diagnosis, et cetera, of *neuroses* and *psychoses*.

USING THE WORDS: III

Before you start the exercises on the new words we have uncovered, you may wish to refresh your mind on some of the roots.

1. *gyne*, woman
   EXAMPLES: *gyne*cology, misog*yn*ist
2. *paidos*, child
   EXAMPLES: *p*ediatrician, ortho*ped*ics
3. *derma*, skin
   EXAMPLES: *derma*tology, hypo*derm*ic, taxi*derm*y, *derma*titis
4. *agogos*, leader
   EXAMPLES: ped*agog*ue, dem*agog*ue
5. *oculos*, eye
   EXAMPLES: *ocul*ist, *ocul*ar, mon*ocl*e, bin*ocul*ars, in*ocul*ate
6. *ortho*, change
   EXAMPLES: *ortho*pedics, *ortho*dontia
7. *card*, heart
   EXAMPLES: *card*iologist, *card*iac, *card*iogram, *card*iograph
8. *neuron*, nerve
   EXAMPLES: *neur*algia, *neur*itis, *neur*asthenia, *neur*osis
9. *psyche*, mind
   EXAMPLES: *psych*iatry, *psych*osis

Can you pronounce the words?

1.	*orthopedics*	or-tho-PEE-diks
2.	*orthodontist*	or-tho-DON-tist
°3.	*orthodontia*	or-tho-DON-sha
4.	*cardiac*	KAR-dee-ak
5.	*cardiogram*	KAR-dee-o-gram
6.	*cardiograph*	KAR-dee-o-graff
7.	*neuralgia*	noo-RAL-ja
8.	*neuritis*	noo-RYE-tis
9.	*neurasthenia*	noo-ras-THEE-ne-a
°10.	*neurasthenic*	noo-ras-THEN-ik

11. *neurosis*	noo-RO-sis
12. *neurotic*	noo-ROT-ik
13. *psychosis*	sye-KO-sis
°14. *psychiatry*	si-KYE-a-tree
°15. *psychiatric*	sye-kee-AT-rik
16. *psychotic*	sye-KOT-ik

Do you understand the words?

Some of the words we have been working with will now be used in meaningful statements. Check your understanding of the meanings of these words by determining whether each statement is *true* or *false*.

1. A *gynecologist's* office is largely visited by men. — TRUE FALSE

2. *Ophthalmology* is the study of eye diseases. — TRUE FALSE

3. *Orthopedics* is the science of children's diseases. — TRUE FALSE

4. A *cardiac* specialist treats diseases of the liver. — TRUE FALSE

5. A person with crooked teeth may profit from *orthodontia*. — TRUE FALSE

6. *Neuralgia* is a disease of the bones. — TRUE FALSE

7. A *neurosis* is more severe than a *psychosis*. — TRUE FALSE

8. *Neuritis* is inflammation of the nerves. — TRUE FALSE

9. *Psychiatry* is a medical science which deals with mental, emotional, and personality diseases. — TRUE FALSE

10. *Neurasthenia* is more likely to afflict unstable personalities than well-adjusted people. — TRUE FALSE

11. A *cardiograph* is a device for recording heart-beats. — TRUE FALSE

12. *Psychiatric* treatment is designed to relieve tensions and dissipate conflicts. — TRUE FALSE

13. An *optometrist* may write a prescription for glasses. — TRUE FALSE

14. A *hypodermic* needle is designed to puncture the skin. — TRUE FALSE

15. A doctor who specializes in *pediatrics* restricts his practice to women. — TRUE FALSE

16. An *optician* may treat diseases of the eye. — TRUE FALSE

17. *Binoculars* increase the range of vision. ~~TRUE~~ FALSE
18. A good teacher applies the principles of *pedagogy* in his work. ~~TRUE~~ FALSE
19. *Pedagogue* is a complimentary term for a teacher. TRUE ~~FALSE~~
20. A *demagogue* thinks of the welfare of the people. ~~TRUE~~ FALSE
21. An elephant is a *pachyderm*. ~~TRUE~~ FALSE

KEY: 1–f, 2–t, 3–f, 4–f, 5–t, 6–f, 7–f, 8–t, 9–t, 10–t, 11–t, 12–t, 13–t, 14–t, 15–f, 16–f, 17–t, 18–t, 19–f, 20–f, 21–t

Can you work with the words? (I)

Match words and definitions.

1. orthopedics	a. nerve pain
2. orthodontia	b. emotional disturbance
3. neuralgia	c. straightening of teeth
4. neuritis	d. nerve inflammation
5. neurasthenia	e. treatment of skeletal deformities

KEY: 1–e, 2–c, 3–a, 4–d, 5–b

Can you work with the words? (II)

1. cardiogram	a. record of heart beats
2. cardiograph	b. mental unbalance
3. neurosis	c. emotional disturbance
4. psychosis	d. treatment of personality disorders
5. psychiatry	e. instrument for recording heart beats

KEY: 1–a, 2–e, 3–c, 4–b, 5–d

Can you recall the words?

Without further reference to the words which you have now read about and pronounced aloud, can you write the one which properly fits each of the following quick definitions?

1. Dentist who straightens teeth   1. O_____

2. A specific emotional disturbance   2. N_____

3. Top layer of skin   3. E_____

4. Baby delivery   4. O_____

5. One-lens eyeglass   5. M_____

6. Science of diseases of the eye   6. O_____

7. Science of diseases of women   7. G_____

8. Nonmedical practitioner who may prescribe glasses   8. O_____

9. Record of heartbeats   9. C_____

10. Acute nerve pain   10. N_____

11. Correction of deformities in children   11. O_____

12. Dealer in optical goods   12. O_____

13. Curing of mental illnesses   13. P_____

14. Medical apprentice   14. I_____

15. Science of children's diseases   15. P_____

16. Science of skin diseases   16. D_____

17. Inflammation of the nerves   17. N_____

18. A nonphysical disease of emotional origin   18. N_____

19. Mentally unbalanced   19. P_____

20. One who mounts and stuffs animals   20. T_____

21. Inflammation or irritation of the skin   21. D_____

22. Pertaining to the heart   22. C_____

23. Pertaining to the eye   23. O_____

24. Science of teaching   24. P_____

25. Uncomplimentary term for a teacher   25. P_____

26. A thick-skinned animal   26. P_____

27. One who foments discontent among the masses so he may gain political power   27. D_____

KEY: 1—orthodontist, 2—neurosis, 3—epidermis, 4—obstetrics, 5—monocle, 6—ophthalmology, 7—gynecology, 8—optometrist, 9—cardiogram, 10—neuralgia, 11—orthopedics, 12—optician, 13—psychiatry, 14—intern, 15—pediatrics, 16—dermatology, 17—neuritis, 18—neurasthenia, 19—psychotic, 20—taxidermist, 21—dermatitis, 22—cardiac, 23—ocular, 24—pedagogy, 25—pedagogue, 26—pachyderm, 27—demagogue

---

CHAPTER REVIEW

Can you recognize the words?

Check the word that most closely fits each definition.

1. Specialist in female ailments:
    (a) obstetrician, (b) gynecologist, (c) dermatologist
2. Specialist in children's diseases:
    (a) orthopedist, (b) pediatrician, (c) internist
3. Specialist in eye diseases:
    (a) cardiologist, (b) oculist, (c) optician
4. Specialist in mental disorders:
    (a) neurologist, (b) demagogue, (c) psychiatrist
5. Study of eye diseases:
    (a) taxidermy, (b) optometry, (c) ophthalmology
6. Straightening of teeth:
    (a) orthodontia, (b) orthopedics, (c) neurasthenia
7. Personality disorder:
    (a) neuritis, (b) neuralgia, (c) neurosis
8. Mentally unbalanced:
    (a) neurotic, (b) psychotic, (c) cardiac
9. Principles of teaching:
    (a) demagoguery, (b) pedagogy, (c) psychosis

KEY: 1—b, 2—b, 3—b, 4—c, 5—c, 6—a, 7—c, 8—b, 9—b

TWO REQUISITES OF WORD MASTERY

Not to digress too much, let me ask you to think for a moment about authors.

Everyone has a book in him—only a comparatively few people ever write that book.

Why? Lack of ability? Poor vocabulary? Not enough time? These are the obvious reasons—and every one of them is insufficient.

The only true, the only possible, reason is *lack of discipline* or *lack of patience*—or both.

Similarly, everyone can have a superior vocabulary. Our language is full of words (almost 650,000 at last count), and the words are full of ideas, and no one has a monopoly or a copyright on any of them. Yet many adults are verbal cripples, are mentally undernourished, use and know and recognize barely one- and one-half times as many words as the average ten-year-old.

Again, why? *Lack of discipline, lack of patience*—or both!

The work you will do in these pages can change your life—and I am not exaggerating for effect.

But you need *discipline* and *patience*.

To gain such discipline and patience, consider that day lost in which you do not spend at least some time using this book to improve your vocabulary—even if it is as little as one hour. Continue working as long as your time and energy permit—and never put the book down without deciding exactly when you will return to it.

There will be periods of difficulty—then is the time to exert the greatest discipline, the greatest patience. I won't pretend that any part of this book is as easy as an adventure novel—but I do insist that every page in it can help you attain a mastery over words.

And mastery over words is often the most distinguishing difference between the mediocre mind and the alert mind.

The material for such mastery is in your hands—the rest is up to you.

BRIEF INTERMISSION TWO:
WHY GRAMMAR IS CONFUSING

English grammar is confusing enough as it is—what makes it doubly confounding is that, like women's fashions, it is constantly changing.

This means that some of the strict rules which you memorized so painfully in your high-school or college English courses may no longer be completely valid. In other words, you may be knocking yourself out in an attempt to speak perfect English, and yet only achieve, at best, the doubtful distinction of sounding stuffy and pedantic.

The problem boils down to this: If grammar is becoming more liberal from one generation to another, what is the state of the language as of today? Where does educated, unaffected speech end? And where does illiterate, ungrammatical speech begin?

The following notes on current trends in modern usage are intended to help you come to a decision about certain controversial expressions. As you read each sentence, pay particular attention to the italicized word or words. Does the usage square with your own language patterns? Would you be willing to phrase your thought in just such terms? Decide whether the sentence is right or wrong, then compare your conclusion with the opinion given in the explanatory paragraphs that follow the test.

TEST YOURSELF

1. If she drinks too many dry martinis, she'll surely *get* sick.   RIGHT   WRONG
2. Have you *got* a dollar?   RIGHT   WRONG
3. No one loves you except *I*.   RIGHT   WRONG
4. Please *lay* down.   RIGHT   WRONG
5. *Who* do you love?   RIGHT   WRONG

6. Neither of these dresses *give* you that Lana Turner look.

   RIGHT WRONG

7. The murderer was *hung* at dawn.

   RIGHT WRONG

8. Mother, *can* I go out to play?

   RIGHT WRONG

9. Take two *spoonsful* of this medicine every three hours.

   RIGHT WRONG

10. Your words seem to *infer* that Marie is trying to steal your husband.

   RIGHT WRONG

11. I *will* be happy to go to the dance with you.

   RIGHT WRONG

12. It is *me*.

   RIGHT WRONG

13. Go *slow*.

   RIGHT WRONG

14. Mary and Margie are *alumni* of the College of New Rochelle.

   RIGHT WRONG

15. I *would* like to ask you a question.

   RIGHT WRONG

1. If she drinks too many dry martinis, she'll surely *get* sick.

RIGHT. This expression is established, it's correct, it's completely cultivated. The puristic objection is that *get* has only one meaning—namely, *obtain*. However, as any dictionary will attest, *get* has scores of different meanings, one of the most respectable of which is *become*. You can *get* tired, *get* dizzy, *get* drunk, or *get* sick—and your choice of words will offend no one but a pedant.

2. Have you *got* a dollar?

RIGHT. If purists get a little pale at the sound of *get* sick, they turn chalk white when they hear *have got* as a substitute for *have*. But the fact is that *have got* is an established American form of expression. Jacques Barzun of Columbia University, the noted author and literary critic, says: "*Have you got* is good idiomatic English—I use it in speech without thinking about it and would write it if colloquialism seemed appropriate to the passage."

There is no doubt that this idiom is well-established in educated speech and writing. *Harper's Magazine* used it not long ago as a title for one of its articles: "Taft—Is This The Best We've *Got*"; and Bernard De Voto writing in the same periodical, asked: "How much privilege of corrupting literature has radio *got*?" (Note: *Harper's* is one of the so-called "class" or "literary" magazines. If an expression is good enough for *Harper's*, it's good enough for the common people.)

3. No one loves you except *I*.

WRONG. For best results, use *me* after except. This problem is troublesome because, to the unsophisticated, the sentence sounds as if it can be completed to "No one loves you, except *I* do," but current educated usage adheres to the technical rule that a preposition *(except)* governs an objective pronoun *(me)*.

4. Please *lay* down.

WRONG. Liberal as grammar has become in the last thirty years, there is still no sanction for using *lay* with the meaning of *recline*. You *lie* happily in bed waiting for your husband to bring up your breakfast; and when he arrives he *lays* the tray on the night table. *Lay*, then, means to *place*; *lie* means to *rest* or *recline*.

5. *Who* do you love?

RIGHT. "The English language shows some disposition to get rid of *whom* altogether, and unquestionably it would be a better language with *whom* gone." So wrote Janet Rankin Aiken, of Columbia University, in 1936. Today, many years later, the "disposition" has become a full-fledged force. A few months ago *Life* magazine ran an advertisement in the grammatically conservative *New York Times*. The headline was bold and linguistically modern, to wit: "*Who* will you meet in this week's LIFE?" And *New York Post* editorial writer Samuel Grafton, who certainly knows as much grammar as the next fellow, shows the same partiality toward the more popular *who*. This question is from one of his recent columns: "If we don't recognize Judea, *who* are we going to recognize?"

The rules for *who* and *whom* are pretty complicated. Follow them strictly if you have the time and inclination; on the other hand, if you prefer to use the democratic *who* for informal, everyday speech, and hang the stuffy precepts of grammar, go right ahead. You'll be speaking good, idiomatic English.

6. Neither of these dresses *give* you that Lana Turner look.

WRONG. The temptation to use a plural verb in this sentence is, I admit, practically irresistible. However, "neither of" means "neither *one of*" and the singular verb *gives* is the preferable form.

7. The murderer was *hung* at dawn.

   WRONG. A distinction is made, in cultivated speech, between *hung* and *hanged*. A picture is *hung*, but a man is *hanged*—that is, if such action is intended to bring about his untimely and unhappy demise.

8. Mother, *can* I go out to play?

   RIGHT. If you insist that your child say *may*, and nothing but *may*, when asking for permission, modern parents may consider you old-fashioned and puristic. *Can* is not discourteous, incorrect, or vulgar—and the newest editions of the authoritative dictionaries fully sanction the use of *can* in requesting rights, privileges, or permission. Anyway, present-day psychological thinking warns against correcting a child's English even when he makes a real mistake—which this assuredly is not.

9. Take two *spoonsful* of this medicine every three hours.

   WRONG. There is a strange affection, on the part of people who are unduly word-conscious, for the expressions *spoonsful* and *cupsful*, even though *spoonsful* and *cupsful* do not exist as actual words. The only acceptable plurals are *spoonfuls* and *cupfuls*. I am taking for granted, of course, that you are using one spoon or cup and filling it the required number of times. If, for secret reasons of your own, you prefer to take your medicine in two separate spoons, you may then properly speak of "two *spoons full (not spoonsful)* of medicine."

10. Your words seem to *infer* that Marie is trying to steal your husband.

    WRONG. It is as incorrect to use infer with the meaning of *hint* or *suggest* as it is unethical to steal some one else's husband. The proper word for this sentence would be *imply—infer* means *to draw a conclusion*.

11. I *will* be happy to go to the dance with you.

    RIGHT. In informal speech, you need no longer worry about the delicate and unrealistic distinctions between *shall* and *will*. The theory of modern grammarians is that *shall-will* differences were simply invented out of whole cloth by the textbook writers of the 1800s. Professor Gustav Arlt, editor of the scholarly *Modern Language Forum* at the University of

California, points out: "The artificial distinction between *shall* and *will* to designate futurity is a superstition that has neither a basis in historical grammar nor the sound sanction of universal usage."

So if you are in the habit of saying *I will* because, being only human, you find the complicated *shall-will* rules too much for mortal flesh to bear, you will be relieved to learn that you may now relax. People who habitually use *will* with *I* and *we* are speaking 100 per cent correct English.

12. It is *me*.

RIGHT. This violation of grammatical law has been completely sanctioned by current usage. When Winston Churchill made a nationwide radio address from New Haven, Connecticut, a few years ago, his opening sentence was: "This is *me*, Winston Churchill." I imagine that the purists who were listening to Britain's former Prime Minister fell into a deep state of shock at these words, but of course Churchill was simply using the kind of down-to-earth, democratic English that has become standard in American speech. Novelist Louis Bromfield says, "The expression *It is me* has justification through convenience and very common usage." And Dr. A. H. Fuchs, a member of the editorial staff of the Merriam-Webster Dictionary, wrote me recently: "We assure you that *It is me* has long been established as good colloquial speech."

The question is, simply, which are you going to be—fussy or up-to-date? By all means stick to *It is I* in your own speech, if you prefer that form, but it is highly unrealistic and sometimes hazardous to look down your nose at people who use the equally correct and certainly more popular *It is me*.

13. Go *slow*.

RIGHT. "Go *slow*" is not, and never has been, incorrect English —every dictionary concedes that *slow* is an adverb as well as an adjective. Rex Stout, well-known writer of mystery novels and creator of Detective Nero Wolfe, says: "Not only do I use and approve of the idiom *Go slow*, but if I find myself with people who do not, I leave quick."

14. Mary and Margie are *alumni* of the College of New Rochelle.

WRONG. As Mary and Margie are obviously females, we call them *alumnae* (a-LUM-nee); only male graduates are *alumni* (a-LUM-nye).

15. I *would* like to ask you a question.

RIGHT. In current American usage, *would* may be used with *I*, though no die-hard purist will give an inch in this matter. Strict, old-fashioned rules demand *I should*, and perhaps if your English teacher was from the Old School, she made quite a to-do over your lapses from this now outmoded principle.

Indeed, in modern speech, *should* is almost entirely restricted to expressing duty or probability.

As in the case of the bejeweled dowager of the Depression Days, who was approached on Park Avenue by a seedy-looking character.

"Madam," he whined, "I haven't eaten in five days."

"My good man," the matron answered with great concern. "You should force yourself!"

5

HOW TO TALK
ABOUT VARIOUS PRACTITIONERS

—— **TEASER PREVIEW** ——————————

What practitioner:

- *is a student of human behavior?*
- *follows the techniques evolved by Sigmund Freud?*
- *straightens teeth?*
- *measures eyes for glasses?*
- *grinds lenses for glasses?*
- *treats minor ailments of the feet?*
- *analyzes handwriting?*
- *examines the contours of the skull?*

AN ANCIENT GREEK mused about the meaning of life, and *philosophy* was born. The first Roman decided to build a road instead of cutting a path through the jungle, and *engineering* came into existence. One day in primitive times, a human being lent to another whatever then passed for money and got back his original investment plus a little more—and *banking* had started.

Most people spend part of every workday at some gainful employment, honest or otherwise. And in so doing often contribute their little mite to the progress of the world.

We explore, in this chapter, the ideas behind people's occupations—and the words that translate these ideas into verbal symbols.

IDEAS

1. behavior

His training has made him an expert in the dark mysteries of human behavior. He knows what makes people act as they do, why they have certain feelings, how their personalities were formed—in short, what makes them tick. Therefore, he is often hired by industries, schools, and institutions to devise means for keeping workers productive and happy, students well-adjusted, and inmates contented. If he is a bona fide member of his profession, he is a college graduate who has taken advanced study in the field.

He is a *psychologist*.

2. worries

He may be a physician or psychiatrist who has been specially trained in the techniques devised by Sigmund Freud, or he may be a nonmedical person with such training. In either case, he helps you to delve into that part of your mind which he calls the "unconscious" so that, by reviewing with him the experiences and thoughts of your earlier years, you can come to a complete understanding of your present worries, fears, conflicts, repression, insecurities, and nervous tensions—thus taking the first step in eliminating them. His treatment, consisting largely in listening to, and interpreting the meaning of, your free-flowing ideas, is usually given in daily or weekly sessions that may well go on for a year or more. When (and if) you are finally discharged as cured, you are much better adjusted to the complex and frustrating world in which we all live.

He is a *psychoanalyst*.

3. teeth

He is a dentist who has taken postgraduate work in the straightening of teeth.

He is an *orthodontist*.

4. eyes

He's the man who measures your vision and prescribes the type of glasses which will give you a new and more accurate view of the world. Although not a physician, he is a trained and registered member of his profession.

He is an *optometrist*.

5. glasses

He's the man who grinds lenses according to the specifications decided upon by your optometrist or ophthalmologist. In conjunction with this activity, he may also run a store that deals in other kinds of optical goods. He does not need a college degree.

He is an *optician*.

6. bones

He is a member of the profession that originated in 1874, when Andrew T. Still devised a drugless technique of curing diseases by massaging and manipulating the bones of the body. This technique rests on the theory that illness may be caused by the undue pressure of displaced bones on nerves and blood vessels. He is a licensed practitioner and a graduate of a professional school.

He is an *osteopath*.

7. joints

The basic principle of this practitioner's work is the maintenance of the structural and functional integrity of the nervous system. He consequently treats physical ailments by manipulating most of the articulations of the body, especially those connected to the spinal column. He is licensed and legally recognized in forty-five states of the nation, and his academic studies parallel those of the major healing professions.

He is a *chiropractor*.

8. feet

He treats minor foot ailments—corns, calluses, bunions, fallen arches, et cetera. Since he is not a physician, he may not administer drugs or perform major surgery, but he is a graduate of a professional school and a licensed practitioner in most states.

He is a *chiropodist* or *podiatrist*.

9. writing

For a fee, he will analyze your handwriting, claiming to deduce therefrom what kind of person you are.

He's a *graphologist*.

10. bumps

At a price, he will examine the "bumps" in your skull and, by manual exploration, decide the state of your mental faculties. This gentleman, who at best may be charitably credited with applying pseudoscientific laws, is, in most instances, a sideshow or circus barker—he is less interested in your brain-power than in your financial resources. The theory on which his deductions are based was first advanced by a Viennese physician in the late eighteenth century, to wit: that various faculties reside in different parts of the brain and their strength or weakness can be discovered from the contours of the skull. (Needless to say, this theory has long since been discredited, but is nevertheless still a source of considerable income to unscrupulous sharpsters.)

He is a *phrenologist*.

USING THE WORDS: (I)

The four tests which cover the basic ten words of this chapter will give you a chance to *say* the words, *work* with them, *write* them, and *think* about them.

Can you pronounce the words?

1. *psychologist*	sye-KOL-o-jist
2. *psychoanalyst*	sye-ko-AN-a-list
3. *orthodontist*	or-tho-DON-tist
4. *optometrist*	op-TOM-e-trist
5. *optician*	op-TISH-un
6. *osteopath*	OSS-tee-o-path
7. *chiropractor*	KYE-ro-prak-ter
°8. *chiropodist*	ki-ROP-o-dist
° *podiatrist*	po-DYE-a-trist
9. *graphologist*	gra-FOL-o-jist
10. *phrenologist*	fre-NOL-o-jist

Can you work with the words?

Match practitioners and interests.

PRACTITIONERS		INTERESTS
1. psychologist		a. your vision
2. psychoanalyst		b. your "unconscious"
3. orthodontist		c. your bones and blood vessels
4. optometrist		d. grinding lenses
5. optician		e. your feet
6. osteopath		f. your teeth
7. chiropractor		g. your skull
8. chiropodist or podiatrist		h. the joints of your spine
9. graphologist		i. your handwriting
10. phrenologist		j. your behavior

KEY: 1–j, 2–b, 3–f, 4–a, 5–d, 6–c, 7–h, 8–e, 9–i, 10–g

Do you understand the words?

Decide whether each of the following statements is *true* or *false*.

	TRUE	FALSE
1. A *psychologist* must also be a physician.	TRUE	FALSE
2. A *psychoanalyst* follows Freudian techniques.	TRUE	FALSE
3. An *orthodontist* is a dentist who specializes in a restricted field.	TRUE	FALSE
4. An *optometrist* prescribes glasses to fit your special needs.	TRUE	FALSE
5. An *optician* may also prescribe glasses.	TRUE	FALSE
6. An *osteopath* uses drugless techniques.	TRUE	FALSE
7. A *chiropractor* has a medical degree.	TRUE	FALSE
8. A *chiropodist* is permitted by law to amputate a limb, if necessary.	TRUE	FALSE
9. A *graphologist* claims that he can read your character in your handwriting.	TRUE	FALSE
10. A *phrenologist* works with completely accredited scientific techniques and theories.	TRUE	FALSE

KEY: 1–f, 2–t, 3–t, 4–t, 5–f, 6–t, 7–f, 8–f, 9–t, 10–f

70

Can you recall the words?

Write the title of the person who fulfills each of the following functions.

1. He delves into your unconscious.

1. _psychoanalyst_

2. He is a licensed practitioner who attempts to cure illnesses by manipulating the bones.

2. _osteopath_

3. He takes care of minor ailments of the feet.

3. _podiatrist_

4. He straightens teeth.

4. _orthodontist_

5. He analyzes your handwriting.

5. _graphologist_

6. He grinds lenses and sells optical goods.

6. _optician_

7. He examines the bumps in your skull.

7. _phrenologist_

8. By manipulation and massage, this popular practitioner claims to be able to cure illnesses.

8. _chiropractor_

9. He studies and explains human behavior.

9. _psycologist_

10. He measures your visual abilities and fits you with glasses if necessary.

10. _optometrist_

KEY: 1—psychoanalyst, 2—osteopath, 3—chiropodist or podiatrist, 4—orthodontist, 5—graphologist, 6—optician, 7—phrenologist, 8—chiropractor, 9—psychologist, 10—optometrist

---

ORIGINS AND RELATED WORDS

1. the mental life

Psychologist is built upon the same Greek root as *psychiatrist—psyche, the mind.* In *psychiatrist,* the combining form is *iatreia, healing;* in *psychologist,* the combining form is the

71

Greek *logos*, which means, among other things, *the study of*—and a *psychologist* studies the human *mind*. His field is *psychology*, the adjective form of which is *psychological*.

The same Greek *psyche* is a full-fledged English word in its own right—it designates the mental life, the spiritual or nonphysical aspect of one's existence. In its adjective form, *psychic*, it refers to phenomena or qualities that cannot be explained in purely physical terms. A person, for example, is called *psychic* if he seems to possess a sixth sense, a special gift of mind reading, or any mysterious aptitudes that cannot be accounted for logically. Or we say that a person's troubles are *psychic* if they are of the mind rather than of the body.

Psyche combines with the Greek *path, suffering* or *disease*, to form *psychopathic*. We often refer to someone as "a *psychopathic* case" if we believe that he is mentally unbalanced. *Psychopathic* has essentially the same meaning as *psychotic*, a word we discussed in Chapter 4.

And *psyche* combines with Greek *soma, body*, to form *psychosomatic*, an adjective which delineates the powerful influence which the mind, especially the unconscious mind, has on bodily diseases. Thus, a person who unconsciously fears the consequence of his being present at a certain meeting will suddenly develop a bad cold, a backache, or even be injured in a traffic accident, so that his appearance at this meeting is made impossible. It's a real cold, it's far from an imaginary backache, and of course one cannot in any sense doubt the concrete reality of the automobile that ran over him. Yet, according to the *psychosomatic* theory of medicine, his unconscious mind made him susceptible to the cold germs, caused the backache, or forced him into the path of the speeding car. A *psychosomatic* disorder may actually exist in so far as symptoms are concerned—headache, excessive urination, pains, paralysis, heart palpitations—yet there is no organic cause within the body. The cause is within the *psyche*, the mind. Dr. Flanders Dunbar, in *Mind and Body*, gives a clear and exciting account of the interrelationship between emotions and diseases.

Psychoanalyst, obviously, comes from the same root as the other words we have been discussing. The technique is called *psychoanalysis*, the adjective is *psychoanalytic*. *Psychoanalysis* differs from *psychiatry* in that it relies exclusively on the deep, exhaustive, probing into the unconscious mind developed by

72

its founder, Sigmund Freud of Vienna, Austria. In oversimplified terms, the general principle of *psychoanalysis* is to guide the patient to an awareness of the deep-seated, unconscious causes of his worries, conflicts, and tensions. Once found, exposed to the light of day, and thoroughly understood, claim the *psychoanalysts*, these causes vanish like a light snow that is exposed to strong sunlight. For those who need and can afford it, *psychoanalysis* is a revelation and in most cases the means of regaining mental and emotional health; for those who cannot afford it *(psychoanalysis*, administered by a trained physician, is expensive), most welfare agencies now have *psychiatric* social workers, licensed nonmedical analysts carefully trained in the Freudian technique, whose services are considerably less costly and probably equally beneficial.

Suppose your troubles are of *psychological* origin? You have asthma, let us say, and your doctor can find no physical basis for your ailment. So he sends you to visit a *psychoanalyst*, since the asthmatic attacks are real enough, and something must cause them.

With your *psychoanalyst* you explore your past life, dig into your unconscious, and discover, let us say for the sake of argument, that your mother always used to set for you impossibly high goals. No matter what you accomplished in school, it was not good enough—in her opinion (and she always made her opinions painfully clear to you), you could do better if you were not so lazy. As a child you built up certain resentments and anxieties because you seemed unable to please your mother—and (this will sound far-fetched, but it is perfectly possible) as a result you became asthmatic. How else were you going to get the mother love, the approbation, the attention you needed and which you felt you were not receiving?

In your sessions with your analyst you learn that your asthma comes from your emotions rather than from your physical organs. It stems from the *mind*, the *psyche*. So your asthma is *psychogenic*—of psychological origin.

And your treatment? No drugs, no surgery—these help the body, not the emotions. Instead, you "work out" (this is the term *psychoanalysts* use) your troubles in talk, in remembering, in exploring, in interpreting. And if your asthma is indeed *psychogenic*, *psychoanalysis* is very likely to help you; your attacks may cease, either gradually or suddenly.

For *psychogenic* disorders, then, the most effective treatment is along psychological lines. Such treatment, whether through *psychoanalysis*, hypnosis, electric- or insulin-shock, suggestion, or any other of various techniques, is called *psychotherapy*.

2. the physical life (teeth, eyes, bones, hands, and feet)

Ortho, as we discovered in Chapter 4, is from the Greek verb *to straighten; dont* is the Greek word for *tooth*. The meaning of the title *orthodontist* is thus quite clear. The specialty, you will recall, is *orthodontia*, the adjective is *orthodontic*. The value of *orthodontia* lies not only in its beautifying effect; by keeping the "bite" regular, it also saves the teeth. Like *psychoanalysis*, it's a wonderful idea for those who need (and can afford) it.

Optometrist and *optician* are both derived from Greek *optikos, eye*. *Metr* in *optometrist* means *to measure* (again from the Greek) and is also found in such common words as *thermometer*, measurer of heat; *taximeter*, measurer of taxicab miles; *metric* system, a system of measurement; *barometer*, measurer of atmospheric pressure; and in the medical term *sphygmomanometer*, the device for measuring blood pressure. The *optometrist* is one who measures the vision of the eye; his field is *optometry*, the adjective is *optometric*. Greek *optikos, eye*, gives us the adjective *optic*, as in the *optic* nerve, or *eye nerve*, and also the adjective *optical*, as in *optical illusion, a deception of the eye*.

Osteopath is formed from two Greek words: *osteon, bone*, and *pathos, disease* or *suffering*. The *osteopath* claims that diseases arise chiefly from displacement of the bones. He practices *osteopathy*; the adjective is *osteopathic*. *Osteon* is also found in the common disease *osteomyelitis, inflammation of the bones*.

Both *chiropractor* and *chiropodist* are built on the Greek *chiros*, hand. The *chiropractor* uses his hands in the curing of ailments; the *chiropodist* treats surface ailments of the hand and foot, and received his title in an earlier time when most of us did an honest day's work with our hands so that we often developed calluses on them—life having changed the way it has, many human beings earn a livelihood today from more sedentary occupations, and so develop calluses on less respectable portions of the anatomy. The *chiropractor* engages in *chiropractic*, the *chiropodist* in *chiropody*. *Chiros* is also found in the English word *chirography*, *handwriting*.

The *pod* in *chiropodist* is from the Greek word for *foot*, and is found in the *chiropodist's* other title, *podiatrist*, which combines also the root *iatreia*, *healing*, which we last met in *psychiatry* and *pediatrics*. The *podiatrist* engages in *podiatry*; the adjective is *podiatric*. Knowing the meaning of the root *pod*, you will recognize such words as *podium*, the speaker's platform (i.e., place where he stands on his feet), and *tripod*, a three-legged stand for a camera or other device.

3. two unscientific studies

The business of the *graphologist* is *graphology*—from *graph*, writing, and *ology*, the study of. We have already met *graph* in *chirography*, *handwriting*, and *ology* in *psychology*, *the study of the mind*. *Graph* is found in many common English words, such as *telegraph*, writing from afar, *stenograph*, writing in short form, and *autograph*, writing of one's own name.

We find *ology*, *the study of*, again in *phrenology*, combined with the Greek word for *brain*, *phrenos*. The *phrenologist* claims that he can study your brain power by examining the topography of your cranium.

SUMMARY OF NEW WORDS

Let us now, as usual, take a quick review of the roots which have helped us to understand our new words.

1. *metr*, measure
    Examples: sphygmomano*meter*, opto*metrist*
2. *optikos*, eye
    Examples: *optic*, *optic*ian, *opt*ometrist
3. *osteon*, bone
    Examples: *osteo*path, *osteo*myelitis
4. *chiros*, hand
    Examples: *chiro*graphy, *chiro*practic, *chiro*pody
5. *pod*, foot
    Examples: *pod*ium, tri*pod*, *pod*iatric

Simple? If you learn new words in etymological families, it cannot be otherwise.

Now try the exercises—*say, write, work with,* and *think about* the words you have just learned.

Can you pronounce the words?

1.	*psychology*	sye-KOL-o-jee
2.	*psychological*	sye-ko-LODGE-i-k'l
*3.	*psyche*	SYE-ke
4.	*psychic*	SYE-kik
*5.	*psychopathic*	sye-ko-PATH-ik
6.	*psychosomatic*	sye-ko-so-MAT-ik
*7.	*psychogenic*	sye-ko-JEN-ik
*8.	*psychotherapy*	sye-ko-THER-a-pee
9.	*psychoanalysis*	sye-ko-a-NAL-i-sis
10.	*psychoanalytic*	sye-ko-an-a-LIT-ik
*11.	*orthodontia*	or-tho-DON-sha
12.	*orthodontic*	or-tho-DON-tik
*13.	*sphygmomanometer*	SFIG-mo-ma-NOM-e-ter
14.	*optometry*	op-TOM-e-tree
15.	*optometric*	op-to-MET-rik
16.	*optic*	OP-tik
17.	*optical*	OP-ti-k'l
*18.	*osteopathy*	oss-te-OP-a-thee
*19.	*osteopathic*	oss-te-o-PATH-ik
*20.	*osteomyelitis*	OSS-te-o-MYE-a-lye-tis
21.	*chiropractic*	ky-ro-PRAK-tik
*22.	*chiropody*	ki-ROP-o-dee
*23.	*chirography*	kye-ROG-ra-fee
*24.	*podiatry*	po-DYE-a-tree
*25.	*podiatric*	po-dee-AT-rik
26.	*podium*	PO-de-um
27.	*tripod*	TRYE-pod
28.	*graphology*	gra-FOLL-o-jee
29.	*phrenology*	fre-NOLL-o-jee

Can you work with the words? (I)

Match words and definitions.

1. psychology	a. straightening of teeth
2. psychotherapy	b. delving into the unconscious mind
3. psychoanalysis	c. treatment based on theory of pressure on blood vessels

76

4. orthodontia   d. treatment of the mind
5. optometry   e. analysis of handwriting
6. osteopathy   f. treatment of foot ailments
7. chiropractic   g. analysis of skull contours
8. chiropody   h. study of human behavior
9. graphology   i. treatment by manipulation of joints of the spinal column
10. phrenology   j. measurement and correction of vision

KEY: 1–h, 2–d, 3–b, 4–a, 5–j, 6–c, 7–i, 8–f, 9–e, 10–g

Can you work with the words? (II)

1. psyche   a. pertaining to relationships between mind and body
2. psychopathic   b. speakers' stand
3. psychosomatic   c. pertaining to the eye
4. psychogenic   d. treatment of foot ailments
5. sphygmomanometer   e. the mental life
6. optical   f. inflammation of the bones
7. osteomyelitis   g. of emotional origin
8. podiatry   h. blood-pressure apparatus
9. podium   i. mentally unbalanced

KEY: 1–e, 2–i, 3–a, 4–g, 5–h, 6–c, 7–f, 8–d, 9–b

Do you understand the words?

Show the depth of your comprehension of these new words by marking each of the following statements *true* or *false*.

1. *Psychic* phenomena can be explained on rational or physical grounds.   TRUE   FALSE
2. *Psychopathic* personalities are usually unpredictable.   TRUE   FALSE
3. A *psychosomatic* symptom is one that has no organic source.   TRUE   FALSE

77

4. Every *psychiatrist* uses *psychoanalysis*.	TRUE	FALSE
5. *Orthodontia* is a branch of dentistry.	TRUE	FALSE
6. Doctors use *sphygmomanometers* to test blood pressure.	TRUE	FALSE
7. *Osteopathy* is a registered and licensed profession.	TRUE	FALSE
8. *Chiropractic* deals with handwriting.	TRUE	FALSE
9. An *orthopedist* is especially well-trained to treat *osteomyelitis*.	TRUE	FALSE
10. *Chiropody* and *podiatry* are synonymous terms.	TRUE	FALSE
11. A *podium* is a place from which a lecture might be delivered.	TRUE	FALSE
12. *Graphology* and *phrenology* are highly scientific and accredited professions.	TRUE	FALSE
13. *Psychotherapy* is helpful in curing *psychogenic* disorders.	TRUE	FALSE

KEY: 1–f, 2–t, 3–t, 4–f, 5–t, 6–t, 7–t, 8–f, 9–t, 10–t, 11–t, 12–f, 13–t

Can you recall the words?

Write the word we have studied which satisfies each of the following definitions.

1. One's soul or mental life
   1. P s{{syche}}

2. Pertaining to teeth straightening (adj.)
   2. O {{rthodontia}}

3. Pertaining to vision (longer form)
   3. O {{ptical}}

4. The adjective which denotes the relationship, especially in illness, between mind and body
   4. P {{sychosomatic}}

5. Mentally diseased
   5. P {{sychopathic}}

6. Study of behavior
   6. P {{sychology}}

7. Pertaining to treatment of the foot (adj.)
   7. P {{odiatric}}

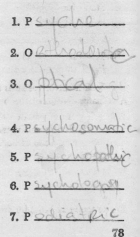

78

8. Blood-pressure apparatus

8. S _dphygmomanometer_

9. Pseudoscience which treats of the "bumps" in the skull

9. P _hrenology_

10. Three-legged stand

10. T _ripod_

11. Pertaining to the treatment of diseases by manipulation of the bones (adj.)

11. O _steopathic_

12. Extrasensory

12. P _sychic_

13. Handwriting

13. C _hirography_

14. Handwriting analysis

14. G _raphology_

15. Treatment by Freudian techniques

15. P _sychoanalysis_

16. Measurement of vision

16. O _ptometry_

17. Treatment of minor ailments of the foot

17. P _odiatry_

18. Pertaining to behavior (adj.)

18. P _sychological_

19. Pertaining to the eye (short form)

19. O _ptic_

20. Inflammation of the bones

20. O _steomyelitis_

21. Stand for a speaker

21. P _odium_

22. Pertaining to Freudian treatment (adj.)

22. P _sychoanalitic_

23. Treatment of ailments of the foot (alternate form)

23. C _hiropody_

24. Treatment of diseases by manipulation of the bones

24. O _steopathy_

25. The general practice of manipulating and massaging for the purpose of curing ailments

25. C _hiroppractic_

26. Pertaining to vision measurement (adj.)

26. O _ptometric_

27. Practice of straightening teeth

27. O _rthodontia_

28. Of psychological or
emotional origin

28. P ~~Psychogenic~~ _(handwritten)_

29. Curative techniques for
emotional or mental
disorders

29. P Psychotherapy _(handwritten)_

KEY: 1—psyche, 2—orthodontic, 3—optical, 4—psychosomatic, 5—psychopathic, 6—psychology, 7—podiatric, 8—sphygmomanometer, 9—phrenology, 10—tripod, 11—osteopathic, 12—psychic, 13—chirography, 14—graphology, 15—psychoanalysis, 16—optometry, 17—podiatry, 18—psychological, 19—optic, 20—osteomyelitis, 21—podium, 22—psychoanalytic, 23—chiropody, 24—osteopathy, 25—chiropractic, 26—optometric, 27—orthodontia, 28—psychogenic, 29—psychotherapy

---

What have you learned about roots?

From our study of words in this chapter you have become familiar with a number of important roots. Can you write the meaning of each of the following roots and supply, in addition, the required number of examples of words using each root?

1. *Psyche* means _mind_

    Examples: _psychology, psychiatrist, psychotic_

2. *ology* means _study of_

    Examples: _cardiology, psychology, graphology_

3. *path* means _suffering_

    Examples: _osteopath, psychopathic_

4. *ortho* means _straighten_

    Examples: _orthodontia, orthopedics_

5 *dont* means _tooth_

    Example: _orthodontist_

6. *metr* means _measure_

    Examples: _optometric, sphygmomanometer_

80

7. *optikos* means _eye, vision_

   Examples: _optic_, _optometry_

8. *osteon* means _bones_

   Examples: _osteopath osteomyelitis_

9. *itis* means _inflammation_

   Examples: _osteomyelitis, neuritis_

10. *chiros* means _hand_

    Examples: _chiropractic, chirography_

11. *pod* means _foot_

    Examples: _podiatry podium_

12. *iatreia* means _healing_

    Examples: _psychiatry podiatry_

13. *tri* means _three_

    Example: _tripod,_

14. *graph* means _writing_

    Example: _graphology_

15. *phrenos* means _brain_

    Example: _phrenology_

KEY: 1—mind (psychology, psychiatry, psychotic, psychopathic, psyche, psychosomatic, psychogenic, psychotherapy, et cetera); 2—study of (psychology, ophthalmology, graphology, phrenology, et cetera); 3—disease (psychopathic, osteopathic, et cetera); 4—straighten (orthodontia, orthopedics); 5—tooth (orthodontist); 6—measure (optometrist, sphygmomanometer); 7—eye (optical, optician, optometrist); 8—bone (osteopath, osteomyelitis); 9—inflammation (osteomyelitis, appendicitis, et cetera); 10—hand (chiropody, chirography); 11—foot (podium, tripod, podiatry, chiropody); 12—healing (psychiatry, podiatry); 13—three (tripod, tricycle, triangle, et cetera); 14—write (graphology, telegraphy, et cetera); 15—brain (phrenology)

CHAPTER REVIEW

Do you recognize the words?

Check the word which most closely fits each definition.

1. Practitioner trained in Freudian techniques:
    (a) psychologist, (b) psychoanalyst, (c) psychiatrist
2. Foot doctor:
    (a) podiatrist, (b) osteopath, (c) chiropractor
3. Handwriting analyst:
    (a) graphologist, (b) phrenologist, (c) optician
4. Mentally diseased:
    (a) psychological, (b) psychopathic, (c) psychic
5. Caused by the emotions:
    (a) psychic, (b) psychogenic, (c) psychoanalytic
6. Describing bodily ailments tied up with the emotions:
    (a) psychosomatic, (b) psychopathic, (c) psychic
7. Inflammation of the bones:
    (a) osteomyelitis, (b) osteopathic, (c) podiatric

KEY: 1–b, 2–a, 3–a, 4–b, 5–b, 6–a, 7–a

Becoming word conscious

Perhaps, if you have been working as assiduously with this book as I have repeatedly counseled, you have noticed an interesting phenomenon.

This phenomenon is as follows: You read a magazine article and suddenly you see one or more of the words you have recently learned. Or you open a book and there again are some of the words you have been working with in this book. In short, all your reading seems to call to your attention the very words you've been studying.

Why? Have I, with uncanny foresight, picked words which have suddenly and inexplicably become popular among writers? Obviously, that's nonsense.

The change is in you. You have now begun to be alert to words, you have developed what is known in psychology as a "mind-set" toward certain words. Therefore, whenever these words occur in your reading you take special notice of them.

The same words occurred before—and just as plentifully—but since they presented little communication to you, you reacted to them with an unseeing eye, with an ungrasping mind. You were figuratively, and almost literally, blind to them.

Do you remember when you bought, or contemplated buying, a new car? Let's say it was a Studebaker. Suddenly you began to see Studebakers all around you—you had a Studebaker "mind-set."

It is thus with anything new in your life. Development of a "mind-set" means that the new experience has become very real, very important, almost vital.

If you have become suddenly alert to the new words you have been learning, you're well along toward your goal of building a better vocabulary. You are beginning to live in a new and different intellectual atmosphere—nothing less!

On the other hand, if the phenomenon I have been describing has not yet occurred, do not despair. It will. I am alerting you to its possibilities—recognize it and welcome it when it happens.

In one's intellect, as in nature, there is rarely a vacuum. Nothing is ever static. There must be, in your mind, either growth or decay, one or the other—you cannot stand still, mentally.

Increasing your vocabulary means mental growth.

So keep right on growing—there are no limits, your horizons can always expand. Or contract!

BRIEF INTERMISSION THREE:
HOW GRAMMAR CHANGES

If you think that grammar is an exact science, get ready for a shock. Grammar is a science, all right—but it is most inexact. There are no inflexible laws, no absolutely hard and fast rules, no unchanging principles. Correctness varies with the times and depends much more on geography, on social class, and on collective human caprice than on the restrictions found in textbooks.

In mathematics, which is an exact science, five and five make ten the country over—in the North, in the South, in the West; in Los Angeles and Coral Gables and New York. There are no two opinions on the matter—we are dealing, so far as we know, with a universal and indisputable fact.

In grammar, however, since the facts are highly susceptible to change, we have to keep an eye peeled for trends. What are educated people saying these days? Which expressions are generally used and accepted on educated levels, which others are more or less restricted to the less educated levels of speech? The answers to these questions indicate the trend of usage in the United States, and if such trends come in conflict with academic rules, then the rules are no longer of any great importance.

Grammar follows the speech habits of the majority of educated people—not the other way around. That is the important point to keep in mind.

The following notes on current trends in modern usage are intended to help you come to a decision about certain controversial expressions. As you read each sentence, pay particular attention to the italicized word or words. Does the usage square with your own language patterns? Would you be willing to phrase your thoughts in just such terms? Decide whether the sentence is right or wrong, then compare your conclusion with the opinions given following the test.

84

TEST YOURSELF

1. Let's keep this between you and *I*.   RIGHT   WRONG
2. I'm your best friend, *ain't* I?   RIGHT   WRONG
3. Five and five *is* ten.   RIGHT   WRONG
4. I never saw a man get so *mad*.   RIGHT   WRONG
5. Every one of his sisters *are* unmarried.   RIGHT   WRONG
6. He visited an *optometrist* for an eye
   operation.   RIGHT   WRONG
7. Do you *prophecy* another world war?   RIGHT   WRONG
8. *Leave* us not mention it.   RIGHT   WRONG
9. If you expect to *eventually succeed*,
   you must keep trying.   RIGHT   WRONG

1. Let's keep this between you and *I*.

WRONG. Children are so frequently corrected by parents and teachers when they say *me* that they cannot be blamed if they begin to think that this simple syllable is probably a naughty word. Dialogues such as the following are certainly typical of many households—perhaps including your own.

"Mother, can me and Johnnie go out and play?"
"No, dear, not until you say it correctly. You mean 'May Johnnie and I go out to play?' "

"Who wants a jelly apple?"
"Me!"
"Then use the proper word."
(The child becomes a little confused at this point—there seem to be so many "proper" and "improper" words.)
"Me, *please?*"
"No, dear, not *me*."
"Oh. *I*, please?"
(This sounds terrible to a child's ear. It completely violates his sense of language, but he does want the jelly apple, so he grudgingly conforms.)

"Who broke my best vase?"
"It wasn't me!"
"Is that good English, Johnnie?"
"O.K., it wasn't I. But honest, Mom, it wasn't me—I didn't even touch it!"

85

And so, if the child is strong enough to survive such constant corrections, he decides that whenever there is room for doubt, it is safer to say *I*.

Some adults, conditioned in childhood by the kind of misguided censorship detailed here, are likely to believe that "between you and *I*" is the more elegant form of expression, but most educated speakers, obeying the rule that a preposition governs the objective pronoun, say "between you and *me*."

2. I'm your best friend, *ain't I?*

WRONG. As linguistic scholars have frequently pointed out, it is unfortunate that *ain't I?* is unpopular in educated speech, for the phrase fills a long-felt need. *Am I not?* is too prissy for down-to-earth people; *amn't I?* is ridiculous; and *aren't I*, though popular in England, has never really caught on in America. With a sentence like the one under discussion you are practically in a linguistic trap—there is no way out unless you are willing to choose between appearing illiterate, sounding prissy, or feeling ridiculous.

"What is the matter with *ain't I?* for am I not?" wrote Wallace Rice in *The American Mercury* some years ago. "Nothing whatever, save that a number of minor grammarians object to it. *Ain't I?* has a pleasant sound once the ears are unstopped of prejudice." Mr. Rice has a valid point there, yet educated people avoid *ain't I?* as if it were catching. In all honesty, therefore, I must say to you: Don't use *ain't I?* except humorously. What is a safe substitute? Apparently none exists, so I suggest that you manage, by some linguistic calisthenics, to avoid having to make a choice. Otherwise you may find yourself in the position of being damned if you do and damned if you don't.

3. Five and five *is* ten.

RIGHT. But don't jump to the conclusion that "five and five *are* ten" is wrong—both verbs are equally acceptable in this or any similar construction. If you prefer to think of "five-and-five" as a single mathematical concept, say *is*. If you find it more reasonable to consider "five and five" a plural idea, say *are*. The arithmetic teachers I've polled on this point are about evenly divided in preference, and so, I imagine, are the rest of us. So use whichever verb exercises the greater appeal to your sense of logic.

4. I never saw a man get so *mad*.

RIGHT. When I questioned a number of authors and editors about their opinion of the acceptability of *mad* as a synonym for *angry*, the typical reaction was: "Yes, I say *mad*, but I always feel a little guilty when I do."

Most people do say *mad* when they are sure there is no English teacher listening; it's a good sharp word, everybody understands exactly what it means, and it's a lot stronger than *angry*, though not quite as violent as *furious* or *enraged*. In short, *mad* has a special implication offered by no other word in the English language; as a consequence, educated people use it as the occasion demands and it is perfectly correct. So correct, in fact, that every authoritative dictionary lists it as a completely acceptable usage. If you feel guilty when you say *mad*, even though you don't mean *insane*, it's time you stopped plaguing your conscience with trivialities.

5. Every one of his sisters *are* unmarried.

WRONG. Are is perhaps the more logical word, since the sentence implies that he has more than one sister and they are all spinsters. In educated speech, however, the tendency is to make the verb agree with the subject, even if logic is violated in the process—and the better choice here would be *is*, agreeing with singular subject, *every one*.

6. He visited an *optometrist* for an eye operation.

WRONG. If the gentleman in question did indeed need an operation, he went to the wrong man. In most states, an optometrist is forbidden by law to perform surgery or administer drugs—he may only prescribe and fit glasses. And he is not a medical doctor. The M.D. who specializes in the treatment of eye diseases, and who may operate when necessary, is an *oculist*. (See Chapter 5.)

These two practitioners, the *optometrist* and the *oculist*, should not be confused with the *optician*, who has no degree, medical or otherwise, and is either a mechanic who grinds lenses or a businessman who sells optical goods.

Then there is also the *ophthalmologist* (off-thal-MOL-o-jist), who is identical in privileges and training with the *oculist*. *Ophthalmologist*, perhaps because it practically defies pronunciation, is the more impressive title, and most eye doctors call themselves by that term.

7. Do you *prophecy* another world war?

WRONG. Use *prophecy* only when you mean *prediction*—when you mean *predict*, as in this sentence, use *prophesy*. This distinction is simple and foolproof. Therefore we properly say: "His *prophecy* (prediction) turned out to be true," but "He really seems able to *prophesy* (predict) political trends." There is a distinction also in the pronunciation of these two words. *Prophecy* is pronounced PROFF-e-see; *prophesy* is pronounced PROFF-e-sigh.

8. *Leave* us not mention it.

WRONG. On the less sophisticated levels of American speech, *leave* is a popular substitute for *let*. On educated levels, the following distinction is carefully observed: *Let* means *allow*, *leave* means *depart*. (There are a few idiomatic exceptions to this rule, but they present no problem.) "*Let* me go" is preferable to "*Leave* me go" even on the most informal of occasions, and a sentence like "*Leave* us not mention it" would be heard only from those educated speakers whose language patterns have been irreparably corrupted by too much listening to "Duffy's Tavern."

9. If you expect to *eventually succeed*, you must keep trying.

RIGHT. We have here, in case you're puzzled, an example of that notorious bugbear of academic grammar, the "split infinitive." (An infinitive is a verb preceded by *to: to succeed, to fail, to remember.*)

Splitting an infinitive is not at all difficult—you need only insert a word between the *to* and the verb: *to eventually succeed, to completely fail, to quickly remember.*

Now that you know how to split an infinitive, the important question is, is it legal to do so? I am happy to be able to report to you that it is not only legal, it is also ethical, moral, and sometimes more effective than to not split it. Benjamin Franklin, Washington Irving, Nathaniel Hawthorne, Theodore Roosevelt, and Woodrow Wilson, among many others, were unconscionable infinitive splitters. And modern writers are equally partial to the construction.

To bring this report right up to the minute, I asked a number of editors about their attitude toward the split infinitive. Here are two typical reactions.

Ralph A. Beebe, one of the editors of Doubleday and Company: "The restriction against the split infinitive is, to my mind, the most artificial of all grammatical rules. I find that most educated people split infinitives regularly in their speech, and only eliminate them from their writing when they rewrite and polish their material."

Roger William Riis, Roving Editor of *Reader's Digest:* "I want to defend the split infinitive. The construction adds to the strength of the sentence—it's compact and clear. This is to loudly say that I split an infinitive whenever I can catch one."

And here, finally, is the opinion of humorist James Thurber, as quoted by Rudolf Flesch in *The Art of Plain Talk:* "Word has somehow got around that the split infinitive is always wrong. This is of a piece with the outworn notion that it is always wrong to strike a lady."

I think the evidence is conclusive enough—it is perfectly correct to consciously split an infinitive whenever such mayhem increases the strength or clarity of your sentence.

6

HOW TO TALK
ABOUT SCIENCE AND SCIENTISTS

—— TEASER PREVIEW ——————————

What scientist:

- *is interested in human development?*
- *is a student of the heavens?*
- *explores the physical qualities of the earth?*
- *studies living matter?*
- *is a student of plant life?*
- *is a student of the animal kingdom?*
- *is professionally interested in insects?*
- *is a student of linguistics?*
- *is a student of the psychological effects of words?*

A TRUE SCIENTIST lives up to the etymological meaning of his title—"one who knows." Anything scientific is based on facts—observable facts that can be recorded, tested, checked, and verified.

Science, then, deals with human knowledge—as far as it has gone. It has gone very far indeed since the last century or two, when we stopped basing our thinking on guesses, wishes, theories that had no foundation in reality, and concepts of how the world *ought* to be; and instead began to explore the world as it *was*, and not only the world but the whole universe. From Galileo, who looked through the first telescope atop a tower in Pisa, Italy, through Pasteur, who watched microbes through a microscope, to Einstein, who deciphered riddles of the universe by means of mathematics, man has at last begun to fill in a few of his areas of ignorance.

Who are some of the more important explorers of knowledge—and by what names are they known?

IDEAS

1. whither mankind?

His field is all mankind—how we developed in mind and body from primitive cultures and early forms.

He's an *anthropologist*.

2. what's above?

His field is the heavens, and all that's in them—planets, galaxies, stars, and other universes.

He's an *astronomer*.

3. and what's below?

His field is the comparatively little and insignificant whirling ball on which we live—the earth. He's interested in how our planet came into being, what it's made of, how its mountains, oceans, rivers, plains, and valleys were formed, and what's down deep if you start digging.

He's a *geologist*.

4. what is life?

His field is all living organisms—from the simplest one-celled amoeba to the amazingly complex and mystifying structure we call a human being. Plant or animal, flesh or vegetable, denizen of water, earth, or air—if it lives and grows, he wants to know more about it.

He's a *biologist*.

5. flora

Biology classifies life into two great divisions—plant and animal. This man's province is the former category—flowers, trees, shrubs, mosses, marine vegetation, blossoms, fruits, seeds, grasses, and all the rest that make up the plant kingdom.

He's a *botanist*.

6. and fauna

Animals of every description, kind, and condition, from birds to bees, fish to fowl, reptiles to monkey to man, are the special area of exploration of this scientist.

He's a *zoologist*.

7. and all the little bugs

There are over 650,000 different species of insects, and millions of individuals of every species—and he's interested in every one of them.

He's an *entomologist*.

8. tower of babel

This scientist explores the history, growth, change, forms, and uses of that unique tool which distinguishes human beings from all other forms of life—to wit: language. This man is, in short, a student of linguistics, ancient and modern, primitive and cultured, Chinese, Hebrew, Icelandic, Slavic, Teutonic, and every other kind spoken now or in the past by man, not excluding that delightful hodgepodge known as "pidgin English," in which a piano is described as "big box, you hit 'um in teeth, he cry," and in which Hamlet's famous quandary is translated into "Can do, no can do—how fashion?"

He's a *philologist*.

9. what do you really mean?

This man explores the subtle, intangible, elusive relationship between language and thinking, between meaning and words. His interest lies in the psychological cause and effect of the words we use and he hopes eventually to bring about in human mortals clearer, more accurate thinking by means of clearer, more accurate ways of speaking. In another sense, he demonstrates to us that because of muddled thinking and miseducation, none of us really understand what anyone else is talking about.

He's a *semanticist*.

10. who are your friends and neighbors?

He is a student of the way in which people live together, their family and community structures and customs, their housing, their social relationships, their forms of government, and their layers of caste and class.

He's a *sociologist*.

USING THE WORDS: I

Can you pronounce the words?

1.	*anthropologist*	an-thro-POL-o-jist
2.	*astronomer*	a-STRON-o-mer
3.	*geologist*	je-OL-o-jist
4.	*biologist*	bye-OL-o-jist
5.	*botanist*	BOT-an-ist
°6.	*zoologist*	zoe-OL-o-jist
7.	*entomologist*	en-to-MOL-o-jist
8.	*philologist*	fill-OL-o-jist
9.	*semanticist*	se-MAN-ti-sist
°10.	*sociologist*	so-she-OL-o-jist

Can you work with the words?

Match each scientist to his professional interest.

SCIENTIST	PROFESSIONAL FIELD
1. anthropologist	a. community and family life
2. astronomer	b. meanings and psychological effects of words
3. geologist	c. development of the human race
4. biologist	d. celestial phenomena
5. botanist	e. language
6. zoologist	f. insect forms
7. entomologist	g. the earth
8. philologist	h. all forms of living matter
9. semanticist	i. animal life
10. sociologist	j. plant life

KEY: 1—c, 2—d, 3—g, 4—h, 5—j, 6—i, 7—f, 8—e, 9—b, 10—a

Do you understand the words?

Following each scientist are two ideas, only one of which interests him professionally. Check his chief interest.

1. *anthropologist* a. bushmen of Australia
                     b. Greek grammar
2. *astronomer*   a. structure of lobsters
                     b. structure of the moon
3. *geologist*   a. volcanic craters
                     b. craters on the moon
4. *biologist*   a. housing conditions of people on relief
                     b. evolutionary processes
5. *botanist*   a. giant redwoods of California
                     b. hoof-and-mouth disease
6. *zoologist*   a. sex life of the grasshopper
                     b. sex life of fir trees
7. *entomologist*   a. social life of the ant
                     b. social life of Samoans
8. *philologist*   a. changes in social customs since the
                        industrial revolution
                     b. changes in English grammar since
                        Shakespeare
9. *semanticist*   a. pronunciation of English words
                     b. emotional implications of English words
10. *sociologist*   a. sex life of wild animals in captivity
                     b. sex life of people on relief

KEY: 1—a, 2—b, 3—a, 4—b, 5—a, 6—a, 7—a, 8—b, 9—b, 10—b

Can you recall the words?

Write the title of the scientist whose main interest is described below.

1. insects   *entomologist*
2. language   *philologist*
3. social conditions   *sociologist*
4. history of mankind   *anthropologist*
5. meanings of words   *semanticist*
6. plants   *botanist*
7. the earth   *geologist*
8. the heavenly bodies   *astronomer*

9. all living matter   *biologist*

10. animals   *zoologist*

KEY: 1—entomologist, 2—philologist, 3—sociologist, 4—anthropologist, 5—semanticist, 6—botanist, 7—geologist, 8—astronomer, 9—biologist, 10—zoologist

---

ORIGINS AND RELATED WORDS

1. man and the stars

Anthropologist contains roots we have met before: Greek *anthropos, man,* has already come up in *misanthrope, hater of mankind* (Chapter 3); *ology, study of,* has occurred in *graphology, phrenology,* and *ophthalmology.* The science is *anthropology,* the adjective is *anthropological.*

Astronomer is built on Greek *astron, star,* and *nomos, arrangement, law,* or *order.* The astronomer is interested in the arrangement of stars and other celestial bodies. His profession is *astronomy,* the adjective is *astronomical,* a word often used in a nonheavenly sense, as in "the *astronomical* size of the national debt." *Astronomy* deals in such enormous distances (the sun, for example, is 93,000,000 miles from the earth, and light from stars travels toward the earth at 186,000 miles per *second)* that the adjective *astronomical* is applied to any tremendously big figure.

The root *astron, star,* is also found, combined with our old friend *ology, study of,* in *astrology,* the pseudoscience which claims it can foretell the future by a study of the stars. The practitioner of this theory is called an *astrologer,* a man generally pictured with a pointed dunce cap adorned with stars, planets, and various portions of the moon; a flowing robe that looks like an old fashioned flannel nightgown; an unkempt gray beard; and a wise expression, as if he knows everything there is to know. All he actually knows is that he's going to separate you from some of your money if you're gullible enough to believe his baseless predictions. *Aster* is a star-shaped flower; *asterisk,* a star-shaped symbol (*), is generally used in writing or printing to tell the reader to look at the bottom of the page for a footnote; and *astrophysics is* that branch of physics which deals with the physical composition of heavenly bodies.

Disaster and *disastrous* also come from *astron, star.* In ancient times it was believed that the stars ruled human destiny; any misfortune or calamity, therefore, happened to someone because the stars were opposed to him. We realize now that a man's fate is largely fashioned by his personality, by economic forces, and by the actions of other men, but in the word *disaster* is preserved the older, more romantic, and highly inaccurate view.

Nomos, arrangement, law, or *order,* is found in two other interesting and valuable English words.

For example, if you can make your own laws for yourself, if you needn't answer to anyone else for what you do, in short, if you are independent, then you enjoy *autonomy,* a word which combines *nomos, law,* with *auto, self.* (We last met *auto, self,* in *autograph,* which etymologically is *writing by oneself.*) *Autonomy,* then, is self-law, self-government. The fifty states in our nation are fairly *autonomous,* but not completely so. On the other hand, in most colleges each separate department is pretty much *autonomous.* And of course, one of the big reasons for the revolution of 1776 was that America wanted *autonomy,* rather than direction from England.

You know the instrument which musicians use to guide their timing? A pendulum swings back and forth, making an audible click at each swing, and in that way governs or orders the measure of the player. Hence it is called a *metronome,* a word which combines *nomos* with *metron,* the root we became familiar with in our study of words like *optometrist, sphygmomanometer, taximeter,* et cetera. Etymologically, a *metronome* governs the measuring of musical time.

2. the earth and its life

The *geologist,* whose profession is *geology,* and who investigates *geological* phenomena, derives his name from a combination of Greek *geos, earth,* and *ology, study of. Geos* is also found in *geometry,* literally *measuring the earth,* or that branch of mathematics which treats of the measurement and properties of solid and plane figures, such as angles, triangles, squares, spheres, prisms, et cetera, all of which are, strictly speaking, forms found on the earth.

The *biologist* is so-called from his study of all living forms; the first two syllables of his title are from Greek *bios, life*. The field is *biology*, the adjective *biological*. *Bios, life*, is also found in *biography*, writing about someone's *life; autobiography*, the story of one's *life* written by *oneself;* and *biopsy*, a medical examination, generally through a microscope, of tissue removed from a *living* body for the purpose of determining the disease that afflicts it. A *biopsy* is normally performed in a suspected cancer. A small part of the tissue is cut from the affected area and under the microscope its cells can be investigated for evidences of cancerous growth. A *biopsy* is contrasted with an *autopsy*, which is a medical examination of a corpse in order to discover the cause of its death. The *auto* in *autopsy* means, as you know, *oneself*—in an *autopsy*, the surgeon determines for *himself*, by actual sight rather than by theorizing, what brought the corpse to its present lamentable state. *Opsis*, as in *biopsy* and *autopsy*, means *sight* or *viewing*, and is related to *optikos, eye*, a root we have already studied.

Botanist is formed on Greek *botane, plant*. The field is *botany*, the adjective *botanical*. The famed *botanical* gardens of Bronx Park, in New York, contain thousands of varieties of plants from all over the world.

The *zoologist*, who is a student of *zoology* (the adjective is *zoological*), is so-named after the Greek *zoon, animal*. The combination of the two *o*'s tempts many people to pronounce the first three letters of these words in one syllable, thus: *zoo*. However, the two *o*'s should be separated, as in *co-operate*, even though no hyphen is used in the spelling to indicate such separation. Say zoe-OL-o-jist, zoe-OL-o-jee, et cetera. *Zoo*, a park for wild animals, is a shortened form of *zoological gardens*, and is, of course pronounced in one syllable.

3. cutups

The syllable *tom* in any scientific word generally comes from the Greek *temnein*, to cut. We hear it in *appendectomy*, a cutting out of the appendix, and *tonsillectomy*, a cutting out of the tonsils. We also hear it in *entomology*, the science that deals with insects, forms of life that seem, in appearance, as if they are almost cut in two. (Take a good look at one sometime to see what I mean.) *Insect* itself is from a Latin root meaning *cut,* as in *dissection,* et cetera. The adjective form of *entomology* is, as you would guess, *entomological.*

Temnein, to cut, is usually found in English words in the spelling *tom.* Consider the following:

1. The smallest particle is of course one that cannot be cut any further. Up to recent years we felt that this unique distinction was held by the *atom,* though today almost every country in the world is going mad trying to split, or cut up, the *atom.* The first letter in *atom* is a negative Greek prefix which you will meet in many other words in later chapters of this book—whenever you do see it tacked on to the beginning of a word of Greek origin, remember that it may mean *not.*

2. In some words of Greek origin, however, the initial letter *a* may not have a negative force. In *anatomy,* it is part of a prefix meaning *on* or *up. Anatomy* was originally a *cutting* up of a living body to determine its structure; by extension, the word naturally came to mean the structure itself, since determining such structure was possible only by means of dissection, or cutting up.

3. Originally any volume which formed part of a larger work was called a *tome*—etymologically, a part *cut* from the whole. Today, a *tome* refers to any book, especially a large one physically, or a heavy one in content. The word is often applied humorously, in mock dignity, to any book.

4. *Mono,* you recall from our study of the word *monocle,* means *one.* The root for two is *di* (as in *dialogue,* speech by two people), and *dicha* means *in two.* So to describe a *cutting* into *two parts,* we use *dicha* and *tom* and get *dichotomy.* A *dichotomy* is a *splitting in two*—it is a technical word much used in astronomy, biology, botany, and the science of logic. It is also used as a nontechnical term, as when we refer to the *dichotomy* in the life of a man who is a government clerk all day and a night-school teacher after working hours, so that his life is, in a sense, split into two parts. The verb is *to dichotomize;* the adjective is *dichotomous. Dichotomous* thinking is the sort that divides everything into two parts— *good* and *bad; white* and *black; Democrats* and *Republicans;* et cetera. An unknown wit has made this classical statement about *dichotomous* thinking: "There are two kinds of people:

Those who divide everything into two parts, and those who do not."

5. Suppose you take some big thing or idea and cut out the essential part. That part then, is a condensation of the whole; and we call it an *epitome,* a word which uses *tom, to cut,* and *epi, upon* or *up.*

For example, an *epitome* may refer to a summary, condensation, or abridgment of a piece of writing or of an idea, as in "Let me have an *epitome* of the book," or "Give me the *epitome* of his speech."

More commonly, *epitome* and its verb, *to epitomize,* might be used in a phrase like "He is the *epitome* of kindness," or "That one act *epitomizes* his philosophy of life." If you cut out the essential part of something, that part in a way is representative of the whole. So a man who is the *epitome* of kindness stands for all people who are kind; and an act that *epitomizes* a philosophy of life represents, by itself, the complete philosophy. And watch your pronunciation of *epitome*—there are four syllables, not three. Say *e-PIT-o-mee.*

4. the power of words

Ology, we have long since decided, means *the study of,* but that is only one of its meanings, though admittedly its most common one. The *log* part comes from a Greek word *logos,* which means *word,* and in *philology* the last three syllables are related to *logos, word: philology,* strictly, is a *love of words,* hence, by extension, *the study of linguistics.* The first syllable *phil* is, you will recall by thinking of *philanthropist,* from *philos, love.* We meet the root in *philanderer,* one who makes love triflingly (the verb is *to philander);* in *philatelist,* one who loves and collects postage stamps (his hobby is *philately);* in *Anglophile,* a lover of British customs and forms in preference to American ones; in *bibliophile,* a lover and collector of rare books; in *Philadelphia,* the City of Brotherly Love; in *philosophy,* the love of wisdom; in *philharmonic,* the love of harmonies or music; and in *philtre,* a love potion.

Semantics, the work of the *semanticist,* is from a Greek root *semantikos, significant meaning.* It is my opinion that *semantics* is one of the most important of modern sciences, if not *the* most important; it is difficult to give a full appreciation of the meaning or use of the subject in a book such as this, since a *semanticist* needs a big book of his own to explain his science. The two best books on *semantics*, exciting, stimulating, and highly readable, are *Language in Action*, by S. I. Hayakawa (Harcourt, Brace, publishers), and *People in Quandaries*, by Dr. Wendell Johnson (Harper & Brothers, publishers).

The adjective form is *semantic*. Please note that *semantics*, like *pediatrics* and *obstetrics*, is considered a singular word despite the *s* ending. Semantics *is*, not *are*, an exciting study. However, this rule applies only when we refer to the word as a science or study. In the following sentence, *semantics* is used as a plural: "The *semantics* of your thinking *are* all wrong."

5. how people live

The *sociologist* is engaged in *sociology*—the adjective is *sociological*. The *c* in these words is preferably pronounced as it is in *social*—note the sound of *sh*: so-she-OL-o-jee, et cetera.

Sociology, a college subject of long standing, is considered one of the dullest of studies—though *sociologists* claim that economics is even duller. I have personally found both sciences practically deadly, as have many other people I know, even those who are well-educated. I suspect that the fault with both *sociology* and economics is that they are hemmed in by tradition and, paradoxically enough, unscientific thinking. To understand this attitude better, read Professor Barrows Dunham's excellent book, *Man Against Myth* (Little, Brown, publishers).

USING THE WORDS: II

In each vocabulary chapter we make fruitful excursions into words that are built upon the roots found in our basic ten. Do not feel, however, that the purpose of the section is primarily to acquaint you with the important Latin and Greek stems from which so many valuable English words are derived. That is, at best, a secondary purpose.

The primary purpose of our work with roots is to continue learning words which revolve around a central core. In the first part of each chapter our central core is an idea—learning words with common ideas is quicker, easier, and more permanent than learning isolated words. Similarly, learning words that have common roots is, again, a comparatively rapid and simple method of understanding new words in wholesale quantities. So in our occasional review of roots, pay particular attention to the examples and their relation to the common roots. For example, note how easy it is to remember the meanings of the words we have just discussed (as well as those from previous chapters) if we divide them according to their common roots.

1. *anthropos*, man
   EXAMPLES: *anthro*pology, mis*anthro*py, phil*anthro*py
2. *astron*, star
   EXAMPLES: *astron*omy, *aster*isk, *astro*logy, *astro*physics
3. *geos*, earth
   EXAMPLES: *geo*logy, *geo*graphy, *geo*metry
4. *bios*, life
   EXAMPLES: *bio*logy, *bio*graphy, auto*bio*graphy, *bio*psy
5. *temnein* (tom), cut
   EXAMPLES: en*tom*ology, epi*tom*e, frontal lobo*tom*y, dichot*om*y, tonsillec*tom*y, appendec*tom*y
6. *philos*, love
   EXAMPLES: *phil*ology, *phil*anthropy, *phil*ander, *phil*ately Anglo*phile*, biblio*phile*, *phil*osophy
7. *nomos*, order, arrangement, law
   EXAMPLES: auto*nom*y, metro*nom*e, astro*nom*y

Can you pronounce the words?

1.	*anthropology*	an-thro-POL-o-jee
2.	*anthropological*	an-thro-po-LODGE-i-k'l
3.	*astronomy*	a-STRON-o-mee
4.	*astronomical*	as-tro-NOM-i-k'l
5.	*astrology*	a-STROL-o-jee
6.	*astrologer*	a-STROL-o-jer
7.	*aster*	ASS-ter
8.	*asterisk*	ASS-ter-isk
9.	*astrophysics*	ASS-tro-FIZZ-iks
10.	*geology*	jee-OL-o-jee
11.	*geological*	jee-o-LODGE-i-k'l
12.	*geography*	jee-OG-ra-fee
13.	*geometry*	jee-OM-e-tree

14. *biological*	bye-o-LODGE-i-k'l
15. *biology*	bye-OL-o-jee
16. *biography*	bye-OG-ra-fee
17. *autobiography*	aw-to-bye-OG-ra-fee
*18. *biopsy*	BYE-op-see
*19. *autopsy*	AW-top-see
20. *botany*	BOTT-a-nee
21. *botanical*	bo-TAN-i-k'l
*22. *zoology*	zoe-OL-o-jee
*23. *zoological*	zoe-o-LODGE-i-k'l
24. *entomology*	en-to-MOL-o-jee
25. *entomological*	en-to-mo-LODGE-i-k'l
26. *philology*	fil-OL-o-jee
*27. *philological*	fill-o-LODGE-i-k'l
28. *philanderer*	fil-AND-er-er
29. *philander*	fil-AND-er
30. *philatelist*	fil-AT-el-ist
31. *philately*	fil-AT-e-lee
32. *Anglophile*	ANG-glo-fyle
*33. *bibliophile*	BIB-lee-o-fyle
34. *semantics*	se-MAN-tiks
35. *semantic*	se-MAN-tik
*36. *sociology*	soe-she-OL-o-jee
*37. *sociological*	soe-she-o-LODGE-i-k'l
38. *autonomy*	aw-TON-o-mee
*39. *antonomous*	aw-TON-o-mus
40. *metronome*	MET-ro-noam
41. *atom*	AT-'m
42. *anatomy*	a-NAT-o-mee
43. *tome*	TOAM
*44. *dichotomy*	dye-KOT-o-mee
*45. *dichotomous*	dye-KOT-a-mus
46. *dichotomize*	dye-KOT-o-myze
*47. *epitome*	e-PIT-o-mee
48. *epitomize*	e-PIT-o-myze

Can you work with the words? (I)

Match words and definitions in each group.

1. anthropology	a. pseudoscience of the stars
2. astronomy	b. story of someone's life
3. astrology	c. study of all life

4. geology	d. study of human development
5. biology	e. study of plants
6. biography	f. study of the composition of the earth
7. botany	g. study of animal life
8. zoology	h. science of the heavens

KEY: 1—d, 2—h, 3—a, 4—f, 5—c, 6—b, 7—e, 8—g

Can you work with the words? (II)

1. autopsy	a. medical examination of living tissue
2. biopsy	b. make love triflingly
3. entomology	c. study of insects
4. philology	d. stamp collecting
5. philander	e. linguistics
6. philately	f. medical examination of a corpse
7. bibliophile	g. book collector

KEY: 1—f, 2—a, 3—c, 4—e, 5—b, 6—d, 7—g

Can you work with the words? (III)

1. autonomy	a. a splitting in two
2. metronome	b. one who loves England
3. dichotomy	c. musical time measurer
4. epitome	d. structure of the body
5. Anglophile	e. self-rule
6. anatomy	f. part which represents the whole

KEY: 1—e, 2—c, 3—a, 4—f, 5—b, 6—d

Do you understand the words?

React quickly to the following questions.

1. Is *anthropology* concerned with plant life?	YES	NO
2. Does *astronomy* attempt to foretell the future?	YES	NO
3. Is *astrology* a true science?	YES	NO

103

4. Does *geology* deal with the physical properties of stars?   YES   NO

5. Is a *biopsy* performed on a dead body?   YES   NO

6. Is a *philanderer* likely to be faithful to his wife?   YES   NO

7. Does the United States have political *autonomy*?   YES   NO

8. Is a *metronome* sometimes used by music students?   YES   NO

9. Did Dr. Jekyll-Mr. Hyde lead a *dichotomous* life?   YES   NO

10. Is an egoist the *epitome* of selfishness?   YES   NO

KEY: 1—no, 2—no, 3—no, 4—no, 5—no, 6—no, 7—yes, 8—yes, 9—yes, 10—yes

---

Can you recall the words?

Write the word we have just studied which fits each of the following brief definitions.

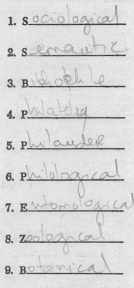

1. Pertaining to the study of social customs (adj.)

1. S _sociological_

2. Pertaining to the emotional flavor of a word (adj.)

2. S _emantic_

3. Lover and collector of books

3. B _ibliophile_

4. Stamp collecting

4. P _hilately_

5. Make love insincerely

5. P _hilander_

6. Pertaining to the science of linguistics (adj.)

6. P _hilological_

7. Pertaining to the study of insects (adj.)

7. E _ntomological_

8. Pertaining to the study of animals (adj.)

8. Z _oological_

9. Pertaining to the study of plants (adj.)

9. B _otanical_

104

10. Dissection of a corpse to determine cause of death

10. Autopsy

11. Story of one's life, self-written

11. Autobiography

12. Pertaining to the study of living matter

12. Biological

13. Measurement of figures

13. Geometry

14. Pertaining to the study of rocks, et cetera (adj.)

14. Geological

15. Branch of physics dealing with composition of celestial bodies

15. Astrophysics

16. Star-shaped flower

16. Aster

17. Very high; pertaining to science of heavens (adj.)

17. Astronomical

18. Study of heavenly bodies

18. Astronomy

19. Science of development of man

19. Anthropology

20. One who claims he can foretell the future by study of the stars

20. Astrologer

21. Star-shaped symbol

21. Asterisk

22. Story of a man's life (or a woman's)

22. Biography

23. Microscopic examination of living tissue

23. Biopsy

24. One who prefers British to American customs, et cetera

24. Anglophile

25. Science of psychological effects of words

25. Semantics

26. Self-government

26. Autonomy

27. Time measurer for music   27. M_etronome_

28. Smallest particle, so-called   28. A_tom_

29. Structure of a body   29. A_natomy_

30. A book   30. T_ome_

31. Split into two (adj.)   31. D_ichotomous_

32. To split into two   32. D_ichotomize_

33. A condensation, summary,   33. E_pitome_
    or representative of the whole

34. To stand for the whole;   34. E_pitomize_
    to summarize

How are your roots?

Now, just to check your affinity for roots, test your knowledge of seven important ones. Give a brief meaning and one
example for each.

1. *anthropos* means _mankind_

   Example: _anthropology_

2. *astron* means _star_

   Example: _astronomy_

3. *geos* means _earth_

   Example: _geology_

4. *bios* means ___life___

   Example: ___biopsy___

5. *temnein* (*tom*) means ___cut___

   Example: ___entomology___

6. *philos* means ___love___

   Example: ___philology___

7. *nomos* means ___order, arrangement, law___

   Example: ___autonomous___

KEY: 1—mankind (anthropology, misanthrope, philanthropist, et cetera); 2—star (aster, asterisk, astrology, et cetera); 3—earth (geology, geography, et cetera); 4—life (biology, biography, biopsy, et cetera); 5—cut (entomology, tonsillectomy, frontal lobotomy, et cetera); 6—love (bibliophile, philatelist, et cetera); 7—order, arrangement, law (autonomy, metronome, et cetera)

CHAPTER REVIEW

Do you recognize the words?

   Check the word that fits each definition.

1. Student of the stars:
   (a) geologist, (b) astronomer, (c) anthropologist
2. Student of plant life:
   (a) botanist, (b) zoologist, (c) biologist
3. Student of insect life:
   (a) sociologist, (b) entomologist, (c) etymologist
4. Student of word meanings:
   (a) philologist, (b) semanticist, (c) etymologist
5. Analysis of living tissue:
   (a) autopsy, (b) biopsy, (c) astrology
6. Stamp collector:
   (a) philanderer, (b) bibliophile, (c) philatelist
7. Self-governing:
   (a) autobiographical, (b) autonomous, (c) dichotomous

8. The part that represents the whole:
    (a) epitome, (b) dichotomy, (c) metronome

KEY: 1—b, 2—a, 3—b, 4—b, 5—b, 6—c, 7—b, 8—a

WHERE TO GET NEW IDEAS

The man with a superior vocabulary, I have submitted, is the man with ideas. The words he knows are verbal symbols of the ideas he's familiar with—reduce one and you must reduce the other, for ideas cannot exist without verbalization. Freud once had an idea—and had to coin a whole new vocabulary to make his idea clear to the world. Those who are familiar with Freud's theories know all the words that explain them—the *unconscious,* the *ego,* the *id,* the *superego, rationalization, Oedipus complex,* and so on. Splitting the atom is a fairly new idea—anyone familiar with it knows something about *fission, isotope, radioactive, cyclotron,* et cetera.

Remember this: Your vocabulary indicates the alertness of your mind. The words you know show the extent of your understanding of what's going on in the world. I am not exaggerating a bit when I say that the size of your vocabulary varies directly with the degree to which you are mentally alive.

We have covered, so far in this book, several hundred words. Having learned these words, you have begun to think of an equal number of new ideas. A new word is not just another pattern of syllables with which to clutter up your mind —a new word is a new idea to help you think, to help you understand the thoughts of others, to help you express your own thoughts, to help you live a richer intellectual life.

Realizing these facts, you may become impatient. You will begin to doubt that a book like this can cover all the ideas that an alert and intellectually mature adult should be acquainted with. Your doubt is well-founded.

One of the chief purposes of this book is to get you started, to give you enough of a push so that you will begin to gather momentum, to stimulate you enough so that you will want to start gathering your own ideas.

Where can you gather them? From the same inexhaustible sources from which college students gather them—from good books on new topics, from wide-ranging reading of new subjects.

Reference has repeatedly been made to psychology, psychiatry, and psychoanalysis in these pages. If your curiosity has been piqued by these references, here is a good place to start. In these fields there is a tremendous and exciting literature—and no one can stop you from reading as widely and as deeply as you wish.

What I would like to do is offer a few suggestions as to where you might profitably begin—how far you go will depend on your own interest.

I offer the following books as particularly readable, interesting, clear, and exciting.

1. *Why We Act as We Do,* by Philip Eisenberg (Knopf).
2. *You and Psychiatry,* by William Menninger and Munro Leaf (Scribner).
3. *The Human Mind,* by Karl A. Menninger (Knopf).
4. *Mind and Body,* by Flanders Dunbar (Random House).
5. *The Mind in Action,* by Eric Berne (Simon & Schuster).
6. *Self-Analysis,* by Karen Horney (Norton).
7. *Understandable Psychiatry,* by Leland E. Hinsie (Macmillan).
8. *A General Introduction to Psycho-Analysis,* by Sigmund Freud (Garden City Pub. Co.).
9. *Emotional Problems of Living,* by O. Spurgeon English and Gerald H. J. Pearson (Norton).

BRIEF INTERMISSION FOUR:
HOW TO AVOID BEING A PURIST

Life, as you have no doubt already discovered for yourself, is complicated enough these days. Yet puristic textbooks and English teachers with puristic ideas are striving like mad to make it still more complicated. Their contribution to the complexity of modern living is the repeated claim that many of the natural, carefree, and popular expressions that most of us use every day are "bad English," "incorrect grammar," "vulgar," and "illiterate." If we begin to develop a national guilt complex about our language, we'll know exactly where to place the blame.

Actually, a large number of the formal restrictions and ancient "thou shalt nots" of academic grammar are now completely outmoded—most educated speakers quite simply ignore them.

Students in my grammar classes in the Adult Education Program of the City College of New York are somewhat nonplused when they learn that correctness is not determined by textbook rules and cannot be enforced by government edict. They invariably ask: "Aren't you going to draw the line somewhere?"

It is neither necessary nor possible for any one person to "draw the line." That is done—and quite effectively—by the people themselves, by the millions of educated people throughout the nation. Of course certain expressions may be considered "incorrect" or "illiterate" or "bad grammar"—not because they violate formal rules, but only because they are rarely if ever used by educated speakers.

Correctness, in short, is determined by current educated usage, not by rules and regulations.

The following notes on current trends in modern usage are intended to help you come to a decision about certain controversial expressions. As you read each sentence, pay particular attention to the italicized word or words. Does the usage square with your own language patterns? Would you be willing to phrase your thoughts in just such terms? Decide whether the sentence is right or wrong, then compare your conclusions with the opinions given after the test.

TEST YOURSELF

1. Let's not walk any *further* right now. RIGHT WRONG
2. Some women admit that their *principle* goal in life is to marry a wealthy man. RIGHT (WRONG)
3. What a *nice* dress! RIGHT WRONG
4. He's *pretty* sick today. (RIGHT) WRONG
5. I feel *awfully* sick. RIGHT WRONG
6. Are you going to invite Alice and *I* to your party? RIGHT WRONG

1. Let's not walk any *further* right now.

RIGHT. In the nineteenth century, when professional grammarians went practically berserk in their attempt to formalize and Latinize English grammar, an artificial distinction was drawn between *farther* and *further*, to wit: *farther* refers to space, *further* means to a greater extent or additional. Today, as a result, many teachers who are still under the dour and forbidding influence of nineteenth-century restrictions insist that it is high treason to use one word for the other.

To check on current attitudes toward this distinction, I sent the test sentence above to a number of dictionary editors, authors, and professors of English, requesting their opinion of the acceptability of *further* in reference to actual distance. Sixty out of eighty-seven professors, over two thirds of those answering, accepted the usage without qualification. Of twelve lexicographers (dictionary editors), eleven accepted *further*, and in the case of the authors, thirteen out of twenty-three accepted the word as used. C. K. Thomas, Professor of English at Cornell University, remarked: "I know of no justification for any present-day distinction between *further* and *farther*," and Charles Earle Funk, consulting editor of the Funk and Wagnalls dictionary, said: "There is nothing controversial here. As applied to spatial distance, *further* and *farther* have long been interchangeable."

Perhaps the comment of Albert Edward Wiggam, the noted

author and columnist, is most to the point: "I like both *further* and *farther* as I have never been able to tell which is which or why one is any farther or further than the other."

Most up-to-date people apparently feel as Dr. Wiggam does, for the authoritative dictionaries, which keep a finger on the pulse of educated American speech, report without exception that *further* means *farther* and *farther* means *further*.

2. Some women admit that their *principle* goal in life is to marry a wealthy man.

WRONG. In speech, you can get *principal* and *principle* confused as often as you like, and no one will ever know the difference—both words are pronounced identically. In writing, however, your spelling will give you away.

There is a simple memory trick that will help you if you get into trouble with these two words. *Rule* and *principle* both end in *le*—and a princip*le* is a ru*le*. On the other hand, *principal* contains an *a*, and so does *main*—and princip*a*l means m*a*in. Get these points straight and your confusion is over.

The head of a school is called a *principal,* because he is the *main* person in that institution of learning. The money you have in the bank is your *principal,* your *main* financial assets. And the stars of a play are *principals*—the *main* actors.

Thus, "Some women admit that their *principal* (main) goal in life is to marry a wealthy man," but "Such a *principle* (rule) is not guaranteed to lead to marital happiness."

3. What a *nice* dress!

RIGHT. Purists object to the popular use of *nice* as a synonym for *pleasant, agreeable,* or *delightful.* They wish to restrict the word to its older and more erudite meaning of *exact* or *subtle.* You will be happy to hear that they aren't getting anywhere.

When I polled a group of well-known authors (including Rex Stout, Betty MacDonald, Lillian Hellman, Christopher Morley, Betty Smith, and Hervey Allen) on the acceptability in everyday speech of the popular meaning of *nice,* their opinions were unanimous; not a single dissenting voice, out of the twenty-three authors who answered, was raised against the usage. Hervey Allen remarked: "It has been right for about 150 years. . . ."

Editors of magazines and newspapers whom I questioned on

the same point were just a shade more conservative. Sixty out of sixty-nine accepted the usage. Glen Neville, executive editor of the New York *Mirror*, commented: "I think we do not have to be nice about *nice* any longer. No one can eradicate it from popular speech as a synonym for pleasant, or enjoyable, or kind, or courteous. It is a workhorse of the vocabulary, and properly so."

The only valid objection to the word is that it is *overworked* by some people, but this shows a weakness in vocabulary rather than grammar.

As in the famous story of the editor who said to his secretary: "There are two words I wish you would stop using so much. One is 'nice,' and the other is 'lousy.'"

"O. K.," said the girl, who was anxious to please, "What are they?"

4. He's *pretty* sick today.

RIGHT. The term "purist" has been used so often in these pages that it might be a good idea to explain exactly what a purist is. The dictionary describes the gentleman as one who insists on "scrupulous or excessive observance of purity in language, style, et cetera." The purist is a hidebound reactionary who wishes to keep the English language in a strait jacket despite preponderant and unmistakable evidence that English is always changing, that grammar is constantly tending to loosen up and become more liberal, and that popular deviations from old-fashioned rules freshen and invigorate American speech.

The purist listens to the language of his friends with a red pencil ever poised to make unnecessary corrections. He is a Mr. Grundy and will not tolerate split infinitives, sentences ending with prepositions or beginning with "and," or the popular and established use of *will* or *me* or *nice* or *further*. And the more evidence you present of the untenableness of his position, the more obstinate he becomes. Proof of his richly deserved unpopularity is indicated by the derogatory adjectives usually applied to him: *pedantic, prissy, nice-Nelly,* and *schoolmarmish,* among others.

One of the purist's pet targets of attack is the word *pretty* as used in the sentence under discussion. Yet all modern dictionaries accept such use of *pretty*, and a survey made by Professor Sterling Andrus Leonard of the University of Wisconsin shows that the usage is established English.

5. I feel *awfully* sick.

RIGHT. If purists have an intense dislike of the popular use of *pretty*, they are positively venomous toward *awfully*. Perhaps your own English teacher in high school or college was of a puristic inclination—if so, you probably got your knuckles rapped whenever you used *awfully* in your themes or conversation.

Yet dictionaries accept this usage in informal speech and Professor Leonard's survey shows that it is established English.

The great popularity of *awfully* in educated speech is no doubt due to the strong and unique emphasis which the word gives to a sentence—substitute *very, quite, extremely,* or *severely* and you considerably weaken the force of the idea.

On the other hand, it is somewhat less than cultivated to say "I feel *awful* sick," and the wisdom of using *awfully* to intensify a *pleasant* concept ("What an *awfully* pretty girl"; "That book is *awfully* interesting") is perhaps still debatable, though getting less and less so as the years go on.

6. Are you going to invite Alice and *I* to your party?

WRONG. Some people are almost irresistibly drawn to the pronoun *I* in constructions like this one. However, not only does such use of *I* violate a valid and useful grammatical principle, but, more important, it is rarely heard in educated speech. The meaning of the sentence is equally clear, no matter which form of the pronoun is employed, of course, but the use of *I*, the less popular choice, may stigmatize the speaker as uneducated.

Consider it this way: You would normally say, "Are you going to invite *me* to your party?" It would be wiser, therefore to say "Are you going to invite Alice and *me* to your party?"

114

7

HOW TO TALK
ABOUT LIARS AND LYING

—— TEASER PREVIEW ——

What word would describe a liar who:

- *has built up a reputation for falsehood?*
- *is particularly skillful?*
- *cannot be reformed?*
- *has become habituated to his vice?*
- *started to lie from the moment of his birth?*
- *always lies?*
- *cannot distinguish fact from fancy?*
- *suffers no pangs of conscience?*
- *is suspiciously smooth and fluent in his lying?*
- *tells outstandingly vicious falsehoods?*

IT WAS the famous Greek philosopher and cynic Diogenes who went around the streets of Athens, lantern in hand, looking for an honest man.

This was over two thousand years ago, but I presume that Diogenes would have as little success in his search today. Lying seems to be an integral weakness of mortal character—I doubt that a single human being would be so brash as to claim that he has never in his life told at least a partial untruth. Indeed, one philologist goes so far as to theorize that language must have been invented for the sole purpose of deception. Perhaps so. It is certainly true that animals seem somewhat more trustworthy than humans, maybe because they are less gifted mentally.

115

Why do people lie? To increase their sense of importance, to escape punishment, to gain an end that would otherwise be denied them, out of long-standing habit, or sometimes because they actually do not know the difference between fact and fancy. These are the common reasons for falsification. No doubt there are other, fairly unique motives that impel people to distort the truth. And come right down to it, can we always be certain what is true and what is false?

If lying is a prevalent and all-too-human phenomenon, there would naturally be a number of interesting words to describe different types of liars.

Let's look at some of these words.

IDEAS

1. he doesn't fool even some of the people

Everybody knows his propensity for avoiding facts. He has built so solid and unsavory a reputation that only a stranger is likely to be misled by him—and then, not for long.

He's a *notorious* liar.

2. to the highest summits of artistry

His ability is top-drawer—no one can lie as convincingly or as artistically as he. His skill has, in short, reached the zenith of perfection. Indeed, his mastery of the art is so great that his lying is almost always crowned with success—and he has no trouble seducing an unwary listener into believing that he is telling gospel truth.

He's a *consummate* liar.

3. beyond redemption or salvation

He is impervious to correction. Often as he may be caught in his fabrications, there is no reforming him—he goes right on lying despite the punishment, embarrassment, or unhappiness which his distortions of truth may visit upon him.

He's an *incorrigible* liar.

116

4. too old to learn new tricks

He is the victim of firmly fixed and deep-rooted habits. With him, telling untruths is as frequent and customary an activity as brushing his teeth in the morning, or ordering toast and coffee for breakfast, or lighting up a cigarette after dinner. And almost as reflective.

He's an *inveterate* liar.

5. an early start

This character has such a long history of persistent falsification that one can only suspect his vice started while he was still reposing in his mother's womb. In other words, and allowing for the normal amount of exaggeration for effect, he has been lying from the very moment of his birth.

He's a *congenital* liar.

6. no letup

He never stops lying. While normal people lie on occasion, and often for special reasons, this scoundrel lies continuously—not occasionally or even frequently, but always.

He's a *chronic* liar.

7. a little daft

He does not know the difference between truth and falsehood. Like a child of three, he cannot distinguish fact from fancy. In this one respect at least, he is not entirely sane.

He's a *psychopathic* liar.

8. no regrets

He is completely without a conscience. No matter what misery his fabrications may cause his innocent victims, he never feels the slightest twinge of guilt. Totally unscrupulous, he is a dangerous person to get mixed up with.

He's an *unconscionable* liar.

9. old smoothie

Possessed of a lively imagination and a ready tongue, he can distort facts as smoothly, as fluently, and as effortlessly as you and

I can recite the multiplication tables. But he doesn't always get away with his lies.

Ironically enough, it is his superb smoothness that makes him suspect: his answers are too quick to be true. Even if we can't immediately catch him in his lies, we have learned from unhappy past experience not to suspend our critical faculties when he is talking. We admire his nimble wit, but we listen with a skeptical ear.

He's a *glib* liar.

10. outstanding

Lies, after all, are bad—they are frequently injurious to other people, and they have a particularly dangerous effect on the liar. At best, if he is caught, the liar suffers some embarrassment—at the worst, if he succeeds in his deception, his character becomes warped and his sense of values suffers. Almost all lies are harmful; some are no less than vicious.

With one type of liar, *all* his lies are vicious—calculatedly, predeterminedly, coldly, and advisedly vicious. He is like Adolf Hitler, who almost succeeded in wrecking civilization with his lies. In short, this wretch's lies are so outstandingly terrible that normal people can only gasp in horror and amazement at hearing them.

He's an *egregious* liar.

USING THE WORDS: I

In this chapter our words revolve rather closely around their central core. Each one, however, has a distinct, a unique meaning, a special implication. Note the differences.

TYPE OF LIAR	SPECIAL IMPLICATION
1. *notorious*	he is *famous*—or infamous—for his lying; his propensities *are known far and wide*
2. *consummate*	great *skill*
3. *incorrigible*	too far gone to be *reformed—impervious to rehabilitation*
4. *inveterate*	lying has become a *deep-rooted habit*
5. *congenital*	his lying had *very early beginnings*—as if he was *born with the vice*
6. *chronic*	*continuity*

7. *psychopathic*	has an irresistible *compulsion* to lie—often for no rational or sane reason
8. *unconscionable*	*lack of regret* or remorse
9. *glib*	great *smoothness*
10. *egregious*	*viciousness* of his lies

These ten expressive adjectives, needless to say, are not restricted to lying or liars. Note their general meanings:

1. *notorious*	well-known for some bad quality—a *notorious* philanderer
2. *consummate*	perfect, highly skilled—his *consummate* artistry at the piano keyboard
3. *incorrigible*	beyond reform—an *incorrigible* optimist
4. *inveterate*	long-accustomed, deeply habituated—an *inveterate* narcotic addict (this adjective, like *notorious*, is restricted to unfavorable conditions)
5. *congenital*	happening at or during birth—a *congenital* deformity
6. *chronic*	going on for a long time—*chronic* appendicitis
7. *psychopathic*	mentally or emotionally diseased—a *psychopathic* fear of dogs
8. *unconscionable*	without pangs of conscience—his *unconscionable* and cavalier treatment of his wife
9. *glib*	smooth, suspiciously fluent—a *glib* talker
10. *egregious*	outstandingly bad or vicious—an *egregious* error

With the exception of *consummate* and *congenital*, all ten adjectives have strongly derogatory implications and are generally used to describe people, characteristics, or conditions of which we disapprove.

Can you pronounce the words?

1. *notorious*	no-TORE-e-us
*2. *consummate*	kon-SUMM-it
*3. *incorrigible*	in-KORR-i-ji-b'l
4. *inveterate*	in-VET-er-it
5. *congenital*	kon-JEN-i-t'l
6. *chronic*	KRON-ik

7. *psychopathic*   sye-ko-PATH-ik
°8. *unconscionable*   un-KON-shon-a-b'l
9. *glib*   GLIB
°10. *egregious*   e-GREE-jus

Can you work with the words?

Match words and definitions.

WORD	DEFINITION
1. notorious	a. beyond reform
2. consummate	b. continuing over a long period of time
3. incorrigible	c. insane; mentally unbalanced
4. inveterate	d. from long-standing habit
5. congenital	e. suspiciously smooth
6. chronic	f. without conscience or scruples
7. psychopathic	g. outstandingly bad
8. unconscionable	h. unfavorably known
9. glib	i. from birth
10. egregious	j. finished, perfect, artistic

KEY: 1—h, 2—j, 3—a, 4—d, 5—i, 6—b, 7—c, 8—f, 9—e, 10—g

Do you understand the words?

React quickly to the following questions.

1. Do people become *notorious* for good acts?   YES   (NO)
2. Is Yehudi Menuhin considered a *consummate* musical genius?   YES   NO
3. If a criminal is truly *incorrigible*, is there any point to attempting to rehabilitate him?   YES   (NO)
4. Does an *inveterate* smoker smoke only occasionally?   YES   (NO)
5. Is a *congenital* deformity one that occurs late in life?   YES   (NO)
6. Is a *chronic* invalid ill most of the time?   (YES)   NO
7. Has a *psychopathic* personality lost touch with reality?   (YES)   NO

8. Does an *unconscionable* act of cruelty cause its perpetrator remorse or compunction? YES (NO)

9. Is a *glib* talker awkward and hesitant in his speech? YES (NO)

10. Is an *egregious* error very bad? (YES) NO

KEY: 1—no, 2—yes, 3—no, 4—no, 5—no, 6—yes, 7—yes, 8—no, 9—no, 10—yes

---

Can you recall the words?

Now that you have begun to get used to the words both as to meaning and sound, try, without further reference to any previous list, to supply the proper word for each definition.

1. Outstandingly vicious; so bad as to be in a class by itself	1. _egregious_
2. Starting at birth	2. _congenital_
3. Happening over and over again; continuing for a long time	3. _chronic_
4. Well-known for some bad habit or moral weakness	4. ~~inveterate~~ _notorious_
5. Beyond correction	5. _incorrigible_
6. Smooth and persuasive; unusually, almost suspiciously fluent	6. _glib_
7. Long addicted to a habit	7. _inveterate_
8. Perfect in the practice of an art; extremely skillful	8. _consummate_
9. Unscrupulous; entirely without conscience	9. _unconscionable_
10. Not sane or normal	10. _psychopathic_

KEY: 1—egregious, 2—congenital, 3—chronic, 4—notorious, 5—incorrigible, 6—glib, 7—inveterate, 8—consummate, 9—unconscionable, 10—psychopathic

---

Can you use the words?

As a result of the tests you are taking, you are becoming more and more familiar with these ten valuable and expressive words. Now, to show the depth of your understanding, decide which one of the ten words we have discussed thus far in this chapter fits each of the following situations.

1. He has gambled, day in and day out, for as long as anyone can remember—gambling has become, for him, a deep-rooted habit.

    1. An *inveterate* gambler

2. He was born with a clubfoot.

    2. A *congenital* deformity

3. Al Capone was known the world over for his criminal acts.

    3. A *notorious* racketeer

4. Storm troopers killed, maimed, and tortured without mercy, compunction, or regret.

    4. *Unconscionable* acts of cruelty

5. He answered the detective's questions easily, fluently, almost too smoothly.

    5. *glib* responses

6. Charlie Chaplin reached the acme of perfection in the art of pantomime.

    6. A *consummate* actor

7. No one can change his absurdly romantic attitude toward life; nothing anyone can do or say will alter his outlook.

    7. An *incorrigible* romantic

8. He has made a mistake that is so bad that it defies description.

    8. An *egregious* blunder

9. He is drunk almost all the time—periods of sobriety are few and very, very far between.

    9. A *chronic* alcoholic

10. His behavior cannot be explained in normal terms. He has passed the dividing line between sane and insane.

   10. A _psychopathic_ case

KEY: 1—an _inveterate_ gambler; 2—a _congenital_ deformity; 3—a _notorious_ racketeer; 4—_unconscionable_ acts of cruelty; 5—_glib_ responses; 6—a _consummate_ actor; 7—an _incorrigible_ romantic; 8—an _egregious_ blunder; 9—a _chronic_ alcoholic; 10—a _psychopathic_ case

---

ORIGINS AND RELATED WORDS

1. well-known

"Widely but unfavorably known" is the common definition for _notorious_. Just as a _notorious_ liar is well-known for his unreliable habits, so a _notorious_ gambler, a _notorious_ thief, or a _notorious_ scoundrel has achieved a wide, and probably deserved, reputation for some form of antisocial behavior. The noun is _notoriety_. The words are derived from the Latin adjective _notus, known_, from which we also get _noted_. It is an interesting philological characteristic that the addition or change of syllables can alter the emotional atmosphere of a word. Thus, an admirer of a businessman will speak of him as a "_noted_ industrialist"; this same man's enemy will call him a "_notorious_ exploiter." Similarly, if we admire a woman's unworldliness, we refer to it by the complimentary term "_childlike_ innocence"; but if we are annoyed by the trait, we describe it, derogatively, as "_childish_ naïveté." Change "-like" to "-ish" and our emotional tone has undergone a complete reversal.

2. plenty of room at the top

The top of a mountain, the very highest point, is called, as you know, the _summit_, a word derived from Latin _summa, total, highest amount_, which also gives us, of course, our mathematical term _sum_, as in addition. A _consummate_ artist has reached the very highest point of perfection; and to *consummate* a marriage, a business deal, or a contract is to put the finishing touches to it that bring it to perfect completion. The noun form is *consummation*.

3. no help

Call a man *incorrigible* if he does anything to excess and all efforts to change or reform him have been to no avail. Thus, one can be an *incorrigible* idealist, an *incorrigible* criminal, or an *incorrigible* flirt. The noun is *incorrigibility*. Make sure to stress the second syllable (*corr*) of both noun and adjective —in-KORR-i-ji-bi-li-tee and in-KORR-i-ji-b'l.

4. veterans

Inveterate is from a Latin root *vetus, old* (from which we also derive *veteran*), and typically applies to something which is bad or harmful. An *inveterate* gambler is a gambler from way back; an *inveterate* drinker has been imbibing for so long that he has, figuratively speaking, grown old with the vice; and, of course, an *inveterate* liar has been lying for so long, and his habits are by now so deep-rooted, that one can scarcely remember (the word implies) when he ever told a truth. Don't use *inveterate* in reference to a person or quality you admire, for the word is intended to have a derogatory implication.

5. birth

There are a host of valuable, expressive words, words teeming with ideas, which are built on the classical root *gen,* to *give birth to* or *to be born. Genetics* is the science which treats of the transmission of hereditary characteristics from parents to offspring; the scientist specializing in the field is a *geneticist,* and the actual part of the germ cell containing these hereditary characteristics is known as a *gene.*

Continuing our exploration, we find *genealogy* (often misspelled *geneology*), the study of a person's ancestors or family tree; *eugenics,* the science which studies means of improving the human race by mating of people whose *genes* will produce the best possible offspring (*eu* is a Greek prefix meaning *good*—so the name *Eugene* or *Eugenia* literally

124

means *well-born*); the *genital*, or sexual, organs, which operate for the purpose of giving birth; *genesis*, the beginning, birth, or origin of anything (that portion of the Bible, for example, which is called *Genesis* is concerned with the birth of the world); and *psychogenic*, born of the mind or emotions.

Congenital, then, means acquired at birth; it should not be confused with *hereditary*, which describes a condition acquired at the conception of the individual, when the male sperm meets the female egg, or *ovum*. Thus, eye color, nose shape, hair texture, and other such qualities are *hereditary;* they are determined by the *genes* in the germ cells of the mother and father. But if the mother has syphilis at the time of the actual delivery of the infant, the child may be born with *congenital* blindness—during the passage from the mother's *uterus*, or womb, he will become infected. Any *congenital* condition is acquired during the nine-month residence within the mother's womb; any *hereditary* condition is acquired at the split second of conception. To go deeper into this subject (and it is, believe me, a most fascinating subject), read Amram Scheinfeld's lively and informative book, *You and Heredity* (J. B. Lippincott Company, publishers).

Congenital is used both literally and figuratively. Literally, it generally refers to some medical deformity acquired at birth: *congenital* syphilis, *congenital* clubfoot, et cetera. Figuratively, it exaggerates, for effect, the implication of strength and very early existence of some quality: *congenital* liar, a *congenital* aversion to blondes, *congenital* fear of the dark, et cetera. And don't confuse *congenital* with *congenial,* which comes from a different root. Two people are *congenial* if they have the same tastes and interests, if they get along agreeably; a *congenial* atmosphere is conducive to one's *physical* comfort, suitable to one's temperament.

6. of time and place

A *chronic* liar lies constantly, continuously, without a break in time; a *chronic* invalid is always, or almost always, sick; a *chronic* smoker does not light up a cigarette occasionally, but is a steady devotee of nicotine. You can thus see the strong implication of the idea of *time* in *chronic*—which is only natural, since the word is derived from Greek *chronos, time*.

This root is also found in *anachronism*, something out of time, out of date, or belonging to a different era, either earlier or later. For example, a mother scolds her sixteen-year-old daughter for using lipstick and going to dances. Daughter responds: "Oh mother! Your attitude is so *anachronous!*" The girl, who not only has more common sense, but also, perhaps, a better vocabulary, than her parents, means that her mother's ideas belong to an earlier century, when, indeed, girls of sixteen did not wear lipstick (at least not the respectable ones) or go to dances unchaperoned. Today social conditions are very different. Or wander along Fifty-ninth Street and Central Park in New York some Sunday. You will see horse-drawn carriages with top-hatted coachmen—a vestige of the 1800s. Surrounded by twentieth century motorcars and modern skyscraper buildings, these romantic vehicles of a bygone era are *anachronous*. We are dealing with an *anachronism*—something which does not belong to the present time.

An *anachronism*, anything you call *anachronous*, or *anachronistic* (both adjective forms are equally popular) must be out of *time* with its surroundings; if something is out of *place*, call it *incongruous*. Thus, it is *incongruous* to wear a sweater and slacks to a full-dress wedding; it is *anachronous* to wear the wasp waist, conspicuous bustle, and powdered wig of the eighteenth century. The noun form of *incongruous* is *incongruity*.

Continuing with *chronos, time,* we also have *chronological, in correct time order* (to tell a story *chronologically,* that is, in the order of its occurrence); *chronometer,* a time-measuring device, such as a watch or clock; and *chronicle,* a history or record of events that happened at one time.

Not to omit *synchronize,* a verb which combines the Greek root *syn, same,* with *chronos, time.* If you and your friends *synchronize* your watches, you set them *at the same time.* If you *synchronize* the activity of your arms and legs, as in swimming, you move them *at the same time.* The adjective is *synchronous.*

7. suffering and feeling

We are already familiar with the parts of *psychopathic*—the first half is from Greek *psyche,* mind, the second from Greek *patheia, disease, suffering, feeling.* A *psychopathic* liar has a mental illness which makes it impossible for him to distinguish fact from fantasy—his lying is, therefore, without discernible or rational purpose, and, odd as it may sound, he has no consciousness that he is telling an untruth.

Patheia, disease, suffering, or feeling is found in a number of other English words.

1. If you have the *same feeling* as someone else, if you *suffer* in the *same* way, you are *sympathetic.* (*Sym, same,* is another spelling of the root *syn* which we discovered in *synchronize.*)

2. On the other hand, if your feeling is *against* someone, you are unfriendly or hostile—then we speak of your *antipathy,* a word which is somewhat stronger than *dislike* or *aversion.* The adjective is *antipathetic.* (*Anti* is a root meaning *against* or *opposite.*)

3. To take a third possibility, you may have no feeling at all—then you are *apathetic.* Here again we find the initial *a* giving a negative force to a word of Greek derivation, as it did earlier to *atom* and *anachronous. Apathy* is a lack of feeling or interest where one would normally expect some feeling to be shown.

4. In medical school, students study anatomy, physiology, materia medica, surgery, et cetera. They also study the origin, nature, cause, and cure of diseases. We already know that the root for *study of* is *ology*—combining it with *path,* we get *pathology,* the study of disease. The adjective *pathological* means *diseased*—a *pathological* condition in a person is an unhealthy, diseased condition.

5. If something can evoke in you a reaction to someone's *suffering,* it is *pathetic. Pathos* is the quality in speech, music, literature, or drama which can make you sad or sympathetic —in other words, make you suffer or understand the suffering of someone else.

6. A good deal of research is being done today by Dr. J. B. Rhine and his associates at Duke University on extrasensory perception; you will find an interesting account of Rhine's work in his book *The Reach of the Mind.* What makes it possible for two people separated by miles of space to communicate with each other without recourse to messenger, telephone, telegraph, or the postal service? It can be done, say the believers in *telepathy,* though they do not yet admit to knowing how. How can one person read the mind of another?

Simple—he's *telepathic;* but no one can explain the chemistry or biology of it. *Telepathy* is built by combining *patheia, feel,* with *tele, from afar. Telepathic* communication occurs when people can *feel* each other's thoughts *from afar. Tele, from afar,* is found also in *telephone, sound from afar,* and *telegraph, writing from afar.*

Two other interesting words containing our root *patheia, homeopathy* and *allopathy,* will be discussed in a later chapter.

8. no conscience

Unconscionable is, of course, related to the word *conscience.* An *unconscionable* act or crime is one that shows the perpetrator to be wholly without *conscience.* The *conscience* of the *unconscionable* liar gives him no uncomfortable moments, despite the agony or misery he may cause others.

9. fool some of the people . . .

Glib is from an old English root which means *slippery.* A *glib* liar or a *glib* talker is smooth and *slippery;* he has a ready answer, a fluent tongue, a persuasive air—but, such is the implication of the word, he fools only the most ignorant, for his smoothness lacks sincerity and conviction.

10. herds and flocks

In *egregious* we find the useful Latin root *greg,* which means *herd.* Any *egregious* lie, act, crime, mistake, et cetera is so vicious that it actually stands out from the *herd,* the way a black sheep is conspicuous among white ones. The same root *(greg)* is also found in *gregarious,* an adjective applied to a person who enjoys companionship, who, literally, likes to be "with the herd." *Extroverts* are *gregarious*—they prefer mixing with people to being alone. All normal human beings are *gregarious* at least to a degree—they get a feeling of warmth and kinship from engaging in group activities such as going to the theater, taking part in or watching athletic events, or attending parties. A *congregation* is a religious "herd"; and to *segregate* someone or something is to remove him or it from the herd.

USING THE WORDS: II

Can you pronounce the words?

1. *notoriety*	no-to-RYE-e-tee
2. *to consummate*	KON-su-mayt (but the adjective is pronounced kon-SUM-it)
3. *consummation*	KON-su-may-shun
4. *incorrigibility*	in-KORR-i-ji-bi-li-tee
5. *genetics*	je-NET-iks
6. *geneticist*	je-NET-i-sist
7. *gene*	JEAN
8. *eugenics*	yoo-JEN-iks
9. *genital*	GEN-i-t'l
10. *ovum*	O-vum
11. *uterus*	YOO-ter-us
12. *heredity*	he-RED-i-tee
13. *hereditary*	he-RED-i-ter-ee
14. *anachronism*	a-NAK-ro-nizm
15. *anachronous*	a-NAK-ro-nuss
16. *anachronistic*	a-NAK-ro-niss-tik
17. *incongruous*	in-KONG-groo-us
18. *incongruity*	in-kong-GROO-i-tee
19. *chronological*	kron-o-LODGE-i-k'l
20. *chronometer*	kro-NOM-e-ter
21. *chronicle*	KRON-i-k'l
22. *synchronize*	SIN-kro-nyze
23. *synchronous*	SIN-kro-nus
24. *pathetic*	pa-THET-ik
25. *pathos*	PAY-thoss
26. *pathology*	pa-THOL-o-jee
27. *pathological*	path-o-LODGE-i-k'l
28. *apathetic*	ap-a-THET-ik
29. *antipathy*	an-TIP-a-thee
30. *apathy*	AP-a-thee
31. *gregarious*	gre-GAIR-ee-us
32. *antipathetic*	an-tee-pa-THET-ik
33. *segregate*	SEG-re-gayt
34. *telepathy*	te-LEP-a-thee
35. *telepathic*	tel-a-PATH-ik

Can you work with the words? (I)

Match words and definitions.

1. notoriety
2. consummation
3. incorrigibility
4. genetics
5. gene
6. eugenics
7. ovum

a. impossibility of reforming or correcting
b. that part of the cell which transmits characteristics
c. completion
d. science of favorable births
e. public knowledge of one's misdeeds
f. human egg
g. science dealing with the transmission of characteristics from parents to offspring

1-e, 2-c, 3-a, 4-g, 5-b, 6-d, 7-f

KEY: 1—e, 2—c, 3—a, 4—g, 5—b, 6—d, 7—f

Can you work with the words? (II)

1. incongruity
2. chronicle
3. pathos
4. apathy
5. pathology
6. synchronization
7. chronometer
8. antipathy
9. uterus
10. telepathy

a. record of events
b. power of evoking sadness
c. setting to the same time
d. study of disease
e. aversion, dislike
f. timepiece
g. something out of place
h. lack of feeling or interest
i. womb
j. mind reading; extrasensory communication

1-g, 2-a, 3-b, 4-h, 5-d, 6-c, 7-f, 8-e, 9-i, 10-j

KEY: 1—g, 2—a, 3—b, 4—h, 5—d, 6—c, 7—f, 8—e, 9—i, 10—j

Can you work with the words? (III)

1. segregated
2. gregarious
3. apathetic
4. pathological

a. out of time
b. unfeeling
c. in order of time
d. at the same time

130

5. pathetic	e. diseased
6. synchronous	f. received from parents
7. anachronous	g. separated
8. chronological	h. causing a feeling of sadness
9. hereditary	i. reproductive
10. genital	j. company-loving

KEY: 1—g, 2—j, 3—b, 4—e, 5—h, 6—d, 7—a, 8—c, 9—f, 10—i

Can you work with the words? (IV)

1. notorious	a. beyond correction
2. consummate (adj.)	b. from birth
3. incorrigible	c. mentally deranged
4. inveterate	d. highly skilled; artistic
5. congenital	e. suspiciously smooth
6. chronic	f. without conscience
7. psychopathic	g. remaining for a long time
8. unconscionable	h. unfavorably known
9. glib	i. viciously bad
10. egregious	j. long-habituated

KEY: 1—h, 2—d, 3—a, 4—j, 5—b, 6—g, 7—c, 8—f, 9—e, 10—i

Do you understand the words?

Check the correct response.

1. Does *notoriety* usually come to perpetrators of grisly murders?   YES   NO
2. Is the product of a *consummately* skillful counterfeiter likely to be taken as genuine?   YES   NO
3. Is an *incorrigible* child usually obedient and well-mannered?   YES   NO
4. Is a *geneticist* interested in your parents' characteristics?   YES   NO
5. Is the *uterus* part of the male anatomy?   YES   NO
6. Does a fertilized *ovum* turn into a human being?   YES   NO
7. Are *eugenists* attempting to improve the human race?   YES   NO
8. Is religion *anachronous*?   YES   NO

131

9. Is obscenity *incongruous* in young children? YES NO
10. Are these dates in *chronological* order? 1942, 1941, 1586 YES NO
11. Is *pathology* the study of healthy tissue? YES NO
12. Are ascetics *gregarious*? YES NO
13. Are *apathetic* citizens interested in their political representatives? YES NO
14. Is *telepathic* communication carried on by telephone? YES NO
15. Does one have an *antipathy* for something one loves? YES NO

KEY: 1—yes, 2—yes, 3—no, 4—yes, 5—no, 6—yes, 7—yes, 8—no, 9—yes, 10—no, 11—no, 12—no, 13—no, 14—no, 15—no

---

Can you recall the words?

Now that you have read about, mentally digested, said aloud, and worked with the new words we have been discussing, you are sufficiently alert to them to be able to write each one next to its short definition—and if you wish to make this an acid test of your affinity for words, attempt to fill in as many blanks as you can without referring to any foregoing list.

1. sexual; reproductive   1. G_enital_

2. to complete   2. C_onsummate_

3. out of place   3. I_ncongruous_

4. the womb   4. U_terus_

5. the science of better births 5. E_ugenics_

6. a history   6. C_hronicle_

7. the egg which, when fertilized, grows into a baby   7. O_vum_

8. in order of time   8. C_hronological_

9. liking to be with other people 9. G_regarious_

10. a feeling against   10. A_ntipathy_

11. reputation for doing something bad

11. N<u>otoriety</u>

12. something out of time with its surroundings

12. A<u>nachronism</u>

13. that part of the human germ cell which transmits a characteristic from parent to offspring

13. G<u>ene</u>

14. completion

14. C<u>onsummation</u>

15. inability to be reformed

15. I<u>ncorrigibility</u>

16. the science which deals with the transmission of characteristics

16. G<u>enetics</u>

17. referring to a quality or characteristic which is inherited (adj.)

17. H<u>ereditary</u>

18.-19. out of time (two forms)

18. A<u>nachronous</u>

19. A<u>nachronistic</u>

20. something which is out of place (noun)

20. I<u>ncongruity</u>

21. lack of feeling

21. A<u>pathy</u>

22. a measurer of time

22. C<u>hronometer</u>

23. the scientist who studies heredity

23. G<u>eneticist</u>

24. make happen at the same time

24. S<u>ynchronize</u>

25. happening at the same time (adj.)

25. S<u>ynchronous</u>

26. evoking sadness (adj.)

26. P<u>athetic</u>

27. power to evoke sadness (noun)

27. P<u>athos</u>

28. study of disease

28. P<u>athology</u>

29. diseased (adj.)

29. P<u>athological</u>

133

30. to separate from others   30. S~~egregate~~

31. skilled in thought transference   31. T~~elepathic~~

KEY: 1—genital, 2—consummate, 3—incongruous, 4—uterus, 5—
eugenics, 6—chronicle, 7—ovum, 8—chronological, 9—gregarious,
10—antipathy, 11—notoriety, 12—anachronism, 13—gene, 14—
consummation, 15—incorrigibility, 16—genetics, 17—hereditary,
18–19—anachronous or anachronistic, 20—incongruity, 21—
apathy, 22—chronometer, 23—geneticist, 24—synchronize, 25—
synchronous, 26—pathetic, 27—pathos, 28—pathology, 29—pathological, 30—segregate, 31—telepathic

---

CHAPTER REVIEW

Can you recognize the words?

Check the word that most closely fits each definition.

1. Highly skilled:
     (a) consummate, (b) inveterate, (c) notorious
2. Beyond reform:
     (a) inveterate, (b) incorrigible, (c) glib
3. Dating from birth:
     (a) inveterate, (b) congenital, (c) psychopathic
4. Outstandingly bad:
     (a) egregious, (b) unconscionable, (c) chronic
5. Science of heredity:
     (a) pathology, (b) genetics, (c) orthopedics
6. Womb:
     (a) ovum, (b) gene, (c) uterus
7. Science of good births:
     (a) eugenics, (b) heredity, (c) genealogy
8. Out of time:
     (a) incongruous, (b) anachronous, (c) synchronous
9. Study of diseases:
     (a) pathology, (b) telepathy, (c) antipathy
10. Fond of company, friends, group activities, et cetera:
     (a) apathetic, (b) gregarious, (c) chronological
11. Indifferent:
     (a) antipathetic, (b) pathetic, (c) apathetic

KEY: 1—a, 2—b, 3—b, 4—a, 5—b, 6—c, 7—a, 8—b, 9—a, 10—b, 11—c

FOUR LASTING BENEFITS

This brings us close to the end of your first week's work. You know by now that it is easy to build your vocabulary if you work diligently and intelligently. Diligence is important —to come to the book occasionally is to learn new words and ideas in an aimless fashion, rather than in the continuous way that characterizes the natural, uninterrupted, intellectual growth of a child. (You will recall that children are top experts in increasing their vocabularies.) And an intelligent approach is crucial—new words can be completely understood and permanently remembered only as symbols of vital ideas, never if memorized in long lists of isolated forms.

If you have worked diligently and intelligently, you have done much more than merely learned a few hundred new words. Actually, I needn't tell you what else you've accomplished, since, if you really have accomplished it, you can feel it for yourself; but it may be useful if I verbalize the feelings you may have.

In addition to learning the meanings, pronunciation, background, and use of some 250 valuable words, you have:

1. *Begun to sense a change in your intellectual atmosphere.* (You have begun to do your thinking with many of the words, with many of the ideas behind the words. You have begun to use the words in your speech and writing, and have become alert to their appearance in your reading.)

2. *Begun to develop a new interest in words as expressions of ideas.*

3. *Begun to be conscious of the words you hear about you and that you yourself use.*

4. *Begun to gain a new feeling for the relationship between words.* (For you realize that many words are built on roots from other languages and are related to other words which stem from the same roots.)

These accomplishments may not sound like much—they only mean that you have given yourself a chance to continue your intellectual growth. It's a little hard to think, however, what more anyone can ask of life!

But, in fine, vocabulary building is just that—a method of continuing one's intellectual growth.

Now, before we go on, suppose we pause to see how successful your learning has been.

Directly after the next "Brief Intermission," I will offer you a comprehensive test of the first week of your work. Take it only when you feel that you have absorbed all that has gone before. You may first wish to skim through the previous chapters, nailing down once again all the words, ideas, forms, pronunciations, and spellings. Or, on the other hand, you may have been working so carefully that you now feel competent to answer any question I may put to you—if so, go right ahead with the test.

BRIEF INTERMISSION FIVE:
HOW TO SPEAK NATURALLY

Consider this statement by Louis Bromfield, noted author of *Malabar Farm:* "If I, as a novelist, wrote dialogue for my characters which was meticulously grammatical, the result would be the creation of a speech which rendered the characters pompous and unreal."

And this one by Jacques Barzun, former literary critic for *Harper's:* "Speech, after all, is in some measure an expression of character, and flexibility in its use is a good way to tell your friends from the robots."

Consider also this puckish remark by the late Clarence Darrow: "Even if you do learn to speak correct English, who are you going to speak it to?"

These are typical reactions of professional people to the old restrictions of formal English grammar. Do the actual teachers of English feel the same way? Again, some typical statements:

"Experts and authorities do not make decisions and rules, by logic or otherwise, about correctness," says E. A. Cross, Professor of English at the Greeley, Colorado, College of Education. "All they can do is observe the customs of cultivated and educated people and report their findings."

"Grammar is only an analysis after the facts, a post-mortem on usage," says Stephen Leacock in *How To Write,* "Usage comes first and usage must rule."

One way to discover current trends in usage is to poll a cross section of people who use the language professionally, inquiring as to their opinion of the acceptability, in everyday speech, of certain specific and controversial expressions. A questionnaire I prepared recently was answered by eighty-two such people—thirty-one authors, seven book reviewers, thirty-three editors, and eleven professors of English. The results, some of which will be detailed below, may possibly prove startling to you if you have been conditioned to believe, as most of us have, that correct English is rigid, unchangeable, and exclusively dependent on grammatical rules.

TEST YOURSELF

1. Californians boast of the *healthy* climate of their state. RIGHT WRONG
2. Her new novel is not *as* good as her first one. RIGHT WRONG
3. We *can't* hardly believe it. RIGHT WRONG
4. This is *her*. RIGHT WRONG
5. *Who* are you waiting for? RIGHT WRONG
6. Please take care of *whomever* is waiting. RIGHT WRONG
7. *Whom* would you like to be if you weren't yourself? RIGHT WRONG
8. My wife has been *robbed*. RIGHT WRONG
9. Is this *desert* fattening? RIGHT WRONG

1. Californians boast of the *healthy* climate of their state.

RIGHT. There is a distinction, says formal grammar, between *healthy* and *healthful*. A person can be *healthy*—I am still quoting the rule—if he possesses good health. But climate must be *healthful*, since it is *conducive* to health. This distinction is sometimes observed in writing but rarely in everyday speech, as you have probably noticed. Even the dictionaries have stopped splitting hairs—they permit you to say *healthy* no matter which of the two meanings you intend.

"*Healthy* climate" was accepted as current educated usage by twenty-six of the thirty-three editors who answered the questionnaire, six of the seven book reviewers, nine of the eleven professors of English, and twenty of the thirty-one authors. The earlier distinction, in short, is rapidly becoming obsolete.

2. Her new novel is not *as* good as her first one.

RIGHT. If you have studied formal grammar, you will recall that after a negative verb the "proper" word is *so*, not *as*. Is this rule observed by educated speakers? Hardly ever, I should say, unless they are of pedantic inclination, or believe that a grammar censor, armed with a sharp red pencil, is listening.

In reference to the sentence under discussion, Thomas W. Duncan, author of *Gus the Great*, remarked: "I always say—

138

and write—*as*, much to the distress of my publisher's copy-reader. But the fellow is a wretched purist."

The tally on this use of *as* showed seventy-four for, only eight against.

3. We *can't* hardly believe it.

WRONG. Of the eighty-two professional people who answered my questionnaire, seventy-six rejected this sentence; it is evident that *can't hardly* is far from acceptable in educated speech. Preferred usage: We *can* hardly believe it.

4. This is *her.*

WRONG. This substitution of *her* where the rule requires *she* was rejected by fifty-seven of my eighty-two respondents. Paradoxically enough, although "It's *me*" and "This is *me*" are fully established in educated speech, "This is *her*" still seems to be condemned by the majority of cultivated speakers. Nevertheless, the average person, I imagine, may feel a bit uncomfortable saying "This is *she*"—it sounds almost too sophisticated.

This is more than an academic problem. If the voice at the other end of a telephone conversation makes the opening move with "I'd like to speak to Jane Doe" (your name, for argument's sake), you are, unfortunately, on the horns of a very real dilemma. "This is *she*" may sound prissy—"This is *her*" may give the impression that you're uneducated. Other choices are equally doubtful. "Talking!" is suspiciously businesslike if the call comes to your home, and "I am Jane Doe!" may make you feel like the opening line of a high-school tableau. The need for a decision arises several times in a busy day—and, I am sorry to report, the English language is just deficient enough not to be of much help. I wonder how it would be if you just grunted affably?

5. *Who* are you waiting for?

RIGHT. *Formal* grammar not only requires *whom* but demands that the word order be changed to: "For whom are you waiting?" (Just try talking with such formality on everyday occasions and see how long you'll keep your friends.)

Who is the normal, popular form as the first word of a sentence, no matter what the grammatical construction; and an opinion by Kyle Crichton, formerly an editor of *Collier's* magazine, is typical of the way many educated people feel. Mr. Crichton said: "The most loathsome word (to me at least) in the English language is *whom*. You can always tell a half-educated buffoon by the care he takes in working the word in. When he starts it, I know I am faced with a pompous illiterate who is not going to have me long as company."

The score for acceptance of the sentence as it stands (with *who*) was sixty-six out of eighty-two. If, like most unpedantic speakers, you prefer *who* to *whom* for informal occasions, or if you feel as strongly about *whom* as Mr. Crichton did, you will be happy to hear that modern trends in English are all on your side.

6. Please take care of *whomever* is waiting.

WRONG. Whomever is awkward and a little silly in this sentence and brings to mind Franklin P. Adams's famous remark on grammar: " 'Whom are you?' asked Cyril, for he had been to night school." It is also contrary to grammatical rule. People who are willing to be sufficiently insufferable to use *whomever* in this construction have been tempted into error by the adjacent word *of*. They believe that since they are following a preposition with an objective pronoun they are speaking impeccable grammar. In actuality, however, *whomever* is not the object of the preposition *of* but the subject of the verb *is waiting*. Preferable form: Please take care of *whoever* is waiting.

7. *Whom* would you like to be if you weren't yourself?

WRONG. Here is another and typical example of the damage which an excessive reverence for *whom* can do to an innocent person's speech. Judged by grammatical rule, *whom* is incorrect in this sentence (the verb *to be* requires *who*); judged by normal speech patterns, it is absurd. This use of *whom* probably comes from an abortive attempt to sound elegant.

8. My wife has been *robbed!*

RIGHT—if something your wife owns was taken by means of thievery. However, if your wife herself was kidnaped, or in some way talked into leaving you, she was *stolen*, not *robbed*. To *rob* is to abscond with the contents of something—to *steal* is to walk off with the thing itself. Needless to say, both forms of activity are highly antisocial and equally illegal.

9. Is this *desert* fattening?

WRONG. The dessert that is fattening is spelled with two *s*'s. With one *s*, it's a desert, like the Sahara. Remember the two *s*'s in dessert by thinking how much you'd like two portions, if only your waistline permitted them.

8

HOW TO CHECK YOUR FIRST
WEEK'S PROGRESS

THE first section of the book should not have taken you more than a week to go through. In that time, if you have worked diligently, you have accomplished the following feats:

1. Become acquainted, or perhaps reacquainted, with approximately 250 expressive words—
2. Learned over forty important Latin and Greek roots—
3. Set up valuable habits of self-discipline and self-directed learning—
4. Explored your attitudes toward grammar and current usage, meanwhile erasing any confusion you may once have felt about specific problems of correctness in your use of words—
5. And, finally, taken good, long steps toward your ultimate goal —namely, the development of a better, richer, more expressive vocabulary.

Now let us pause for breath, let us take a quick review of all you have learned. For this purpose, I shall select, at random, a number of words and roots from each chapter, and ask you to test your memory of their meanings and uses.

Methods of scoring your achievement on this test, and the significance of your results, will be explained shortly.

I—roots

Directions: In the table below you will find a number of roots we have discussed, with an example of their use. It is your job to fill in the meaning of each one.

ROOT	MEANING	EXAMPLE
1. *ego*	_oneself_	egoism
2. *misein*	_hate_	misanthrope
3. *gamos*	_marriage_	bigamy

4. *gyne*	<u>women</u>	gynecology
5. *derma*	<u>skin</u>	dermatology
6. *ortho*	<u>streighten</u>	orthodontia
7. *psyche*	<u>mind</u>	psychotic
8. *neuron*	<u>nerves</u>	neurology
9. *ology*	<u>study of</u>	astrology
10. *bios*	<u>life</u>	biopsy

II—more roots

Directions: Here are ten words we have studied, each with its roots italicized. In the appropriate blank, write the meaning of that root.

1. ent*omo*logy   1. <u>cut</u>
2. *phil*atelist   2. <u>love</u>
3. opto*metr*ist   3. <u>measure</u>
4. ortho*ped*ics   4. <u>child</u> — ✓
5. *cardi*ac   5. <u>heart</u>
6. *pod*iatry   6. <u>foot</u>
7. psycho*path*ic   7. <u>deisese</u> — ✓
8. *greg*arious   8. <u>herd</u>
9. ana*chron*ism   9. <u>time</u>
10. con*gen*ital   10. <u>birth</u>

III—same or opposite?

Directions: If each pair of words is similar in meaning, check S; if more nearly opposite, check O.

1. egoistic—altruistic   S   O
2. misanthropic—philanthropic   S   O
3. misogamous—polygamous   S   O
4. dexterous—skillful   (S)   O

5. sinister—threatening   (S)   O

6. ocular—visual   (S)   O

7. notorious—infamous   (S)   O

8. consummate (adj.)—unskilled   S   (O)

9. chronic—acute   (S)   O

10. glib—halting   (S)   O

IV—true or false?

Directions: If the statement is factually accurate, check *T*; if factually inaccurate, check *F*.

1. An *introvert* is generally *gregarious.*   T   (F)
2. An *ascetic* is generally *gregarious.*   T   (F)
3. An *astronomical* number is very large.   (T)   F
4. An *Anglophile* dislikes Great Britain.   T   (F)
5. A *neurotic* person must be institutionalized.   T   (F)
6. The *epidermis* is the outermost layer of skin.   (T)   F
7. An *optician* is licensed to examine eyes and prescribe glasses.   T   (F)
8. An *inveterate* gambler rarely indulges his vice.   T   (F)
9. A *congenital* condition occurs at or during birth.   (T)   F
10. An *anachronous* attitude is modern, up-to-date.   T   (F)

V—matching

Directions: Choose the word from second column which belongs to each function in first column.

1. dislikes women	a. entomologist
2. is pathologically self-interested	b. taxidermist
3. studies the development of the human race	c. egomaniac
4. is an expert on insects	d. bibliophile
5. collects books	e. ophthalmologist
6. mounts and stuffs animals	f. psychopath
7. is an eye doctor	g. philologist
8. is a student of linguistics	h. anthropologist
9. is anxious and unadjusted	i. neurotic
10. is insane	j. misogynist

144

VI—more matching

Directions: As on Test V.

I	II
1. delivers babies	a. pediatrician
2. treats female ailments	b. cardiologist
3. treats infants	c. psychiatrist
4. treats skin diseases	d. chiropodist
5. treats deformities	e. dermatologist
6. heart specialist	f. psychoanalyst
7. treats mental abnormalities	g. obstetrician
8. treats nervous disorders	h. neurologist
9. treats minor ailments of the feet	i. orthopedist
10. applies Freudian techniques	j. gynecologist

1g, 2j, 3a, 4e, 5d, 6b, 7c, 8h, 9i, 10f

VII—recall a word

Directions: Write the word we have studied that best fits each definition. The initial letter is offered to guide your thinking.

1. ruthless   1. U*nconscionable*

2. fluent   2. G*lib*

3. outstandingly bad   3. E*gregious*

4. out of place   4. I*ncongrous*

5. study of family tree   5. G*enealogy*

6. study of heredity   6. G*enetics*

7. in order of time   7. C*hronological*

8. skin eruptions   8. D*ermatitis*

9. record of heartbeats   9. C*ardiogram*

10. agreeable, pleasant   10. C*ongenial*

145

VIII—choose a word

Directions: Check the one word, of the three offered, which best fits each definition.

1. science of the heavens: a. astrology, b. astronomy, c. phrenology.
2. science of the composition of the earth: a. geography, b. astrophysics, c. geology.
3. dissection of a corpse: a. biopsy, b. autopsy, c. zoology.
4. eye doctor: a. oculist, b. optometrist, c. optician.
5. foot doctor: a. pediatrician, b. podiatrist, c. taxidermist.
6. student of word meanings: a. semanticist, b. geneticist, c. graphologist.
7. diagnostician: a. cardiologist, b. intern, c. internist.
8. conceited: a. egoist, b. egotist, c. misanthropist.
9. equally skilled in both hands: a. ambivert, b. ambidextrous, c. bigamist.
10. to complete: a. to consummate, b. to segregate, c. to psychoanalyze.

IX—pronounce a word

Directions: Check the correct pronunciation.

1. *psychiatrist:* a. sye-kee-AT-rist, b. sye-KYE-a-trist.
2. *misanthropy:* a. miss-in-THROE-pee, b. miss-AN-thro-pee.
3. *ascetic:* a. a-SEE-tic, b. a-SET-ic.
4. *egomaniacal:* a. ee-go-MAY-nee-ak'l, b. ee-go-ma-NYE-a-k'l
5. *anachronism:* a. AN-a-kro-nizm, b. a-NACK-ro-nizm.
6. *misogynous:* a. miss-o-JYE-nus, b. mi-SODGE-in-us.
7. *podiatric:* a. poe-DYE-a-trik, b. poe-dee-AT-rik.
8. *consummate:* (adj.): a. KON-su-mit, b. kon-SUM-it.
9. *incorrigible:* a. in-ko-RIDGE-a-b'l, b. in-KORR-i-ji-b'l.
10. *egregious:* a. e-GREG-ee-us, b. e-GREE-jus.

X—choose the correct word

Directions: Check the preferable grammatical form.

1. I (can, can't) hardly hear you.
2. Send in (whoever, whomever) is waiting.
3. (Who, whom) do you think you are, anyway?

4. My watch has been (robbed, (stolen)).
5. What kind of ((dessert,) desert) would you like?
6. What is your ((principle,) principal) occupation?
7. Are you going to ask my wife and ((I,) me) to your party?
8. It's strictly between you and ((I,) me).
9. Every one of his friends (hate, (hates)) him.
10. No one passed the test except (I, (me)).
11. Do you want to ((lay,) lie) down for a while?
12. They (hung, (hanged)) the horse thief.
13. How many ((spoonfuls,) spoonsful) of baking soda does the recipe call for?
14. Are you ((implying,) inferring) that I'm a liar?
15. The general and colonel are ((alumni,) alumnae) of West Point.

XI—change a word

Directions: Write the required part of speech.

1. Change *pediatrician* to the noun denoting the specialty

   pediatrics is an interesting profession.

2. Change *orthodontist* similarly:

   His specialty is _orthodontia_

3. Change *anachronism* to an adjective:

   It was an _anachronistic_ sight.

4. Change *neurasthenia* to the word that applies to a person.

   He's a _neurasthenic_

5. Change *ambidextrous* to a noun.

   His total _ambidexterity_ is amazing.

SCORING

Each correct answer counts one point. Score your points next to each part of the test, then add for a total. Significance of your credits will be explained directly after the answers.

I. 1—I, 2—hate, 3—marriage, 4—woman, 5—skin, 6—change, 7—mind, soul, spirit, 8—nerve, 9—study of, 10—life
II. 1—cut, 2—love, 3—measure, 4—child, 5—heart, 6—foot, 7—disease, feeling, suffering, 8—herd, 9—time, 10—birth

III. 1–O, 2–O, 3–O, 4–S, 5–S, 6–S, 7–S, 8–O, 9–O, 10–O

IV. 1–f, 2–f, 3–t, 4–f, 5–f, 6–t, 7–f, 8–f, 9–t, 10–f

V. 1–j, 2–c, 3–h, 4–a, 5–d, 6–b, 7–e, 8–g, 9–i, 10–f

VI. 1–g, 2–j, 3–a, 4–e, 5–i, 6–b, 7–c, 8–h, 9–d, 10–f

VII. 1–unconscionable, 2–glib, 3–egregious, 4–incongruous, 5–genealogy, 6–genetics, 7–chronological, 8–dermatitis, 9–cardiogram, 10–congenial

VIII. 1–b, 2–c, 3–b, 4–a, 5–b, 6–a, 7–c, 8–b, 9–b, 10–a

IX. All b pronunciations are correct.

X. 1–can, 2–whoever, 3–who, 4–stolen, 5–dessert, 6–principal, 7–me, 8–me, 9–hates, 10–me, 11–lie, 12–hanged, 13–spoonfuls, 14–implying, 15–alumni

XI. 1–pediatrics, 2–orthodontia, 3–anachronous or anachronistic, 4–neurasthenic, 5–ambidexterity

SIGNIFICANCE OF YOUR SCORE

The 110 responses you were asked to make were no child's play, and I shall not pretend for a moment that they were. Your score indicates, then, how successfully you have mastered the preceding chapters of this book. Add up your individual points and locate your total in the following table:

100–110   Masterly work; you are ready to shoot right ahead.

85–99   Good work; however, be more careful in the next sections of the book.

75–84   Average work; you're getting a good deal out of your study, but not enough. Perhaps you should review more carefully after you do each day's stint.

60–74   Barely acceptable; work harder.

40–59   Poor; further review is suggested before you go on.

0–39   You can do much better if you really try; start again with firmer resolve and more interest.

All right. That seals off, temporarily, this first section. Go right ahead now to further adventures and explorations as you bring closer and closer your goal of acquiring a bigger and better vocabulary.

[SCORE]

First week's Achievement Test: _____ out of *110*

148

BRIEF INTERMISSION SIX:
DO YOU ALWAYS
USE THE PROPER WORD?

The fact is that grammar is getting more liberal every day. Common usage has put a stamp of approval on many expressions which your grandmother would not have dared utter in her most intimate conversation—not if she believed she was in the habit of using good English. *It is me; have you got a cold?; it's a nice day; can I have another piece of cake?; she is a most aggravating child; will everybody please remove their hats*—all these today represent perfectly correct grammar for everyday conversation. Modern grammar research reports that these expressions have become universal in educated speech.

However, such a liberal policy does not mean that all bars are down. Only a person whose speech borders on the illiterate would make such statements as: *Can you learn me to swim?; he don't live here no more; we ain't working so good; me and my husband are glad to see you.* There are still certain minimum essentials of good English which the cultivated speaker carefully observes.

Is your grammar as good as the next person's? Here's a quick test by which you can measure your ability.

Check the preferable choice in each sentence. then compare your results with the key at the end. Allowing 4 per cent for each correct answer, consider 92–100 excellent, 76–88 good, 68–72 average, and any lower score an indication that your English leaves something to be desired.

1. What (a—effect, b—affect) does Frank Sinatra have on you?
2. What's the sense (a—in, b—of) looking for a husband after you're thirty?
3. She won't (a—leave, b—let) us see her new boy friend.
4. What (a—kind of, b—kind of a) dress do you want?

149

5. Her (a—principle, b—principal) objection to neurotics is that they are difficult to live with.

6. The murderer was (a—hanged, b—hung) two hours before the governor's pardon arrived.

7. The trouble with most men's family lives is their (a—mother-in-laws, b—mothers-in-law).

8. For a light cake, use two (a—spoonfuls, b—spoonsful) of baking powder.

9. Everyone likes you but (a—she, b—her).

10. Sally sent a gift for (a—him and me, b—he and I).

11. The data which you've sent me (a—is, b—are) inconclusive.

12. The cost of new houses (a—is, b—are) finally dropping.

13. Irene as well as her husband (a—has, b—have) come to see you.

14. (a—Is, b—Are) either of your sisters working?

15. If Robert Taylor or Franchot Tone (a—is, b—are) your ideal, you are no bobby soxer.

16. One or two of her features (a—is, b—are) very attractive.

17. Can you visit Mary and (a—I, b—me) tonight?

18. He is totally (a—uninterested, b—disinterested) in your personal affairs.

19. She (a—laid, b—lay) on the beach while her son splashed at the water's edge.

20. (a—Who, b—Whom) would you rather be if you weren't yourself?

21. You should not (a—have, b—of) spoken so harshly.

22. She is one of those women who (a—is, b—are) always making up in public.

23. It is I who (a—is, b—am) your best friend.

24. What we need in this country (a—is, b—are) more blondes.

25. I'm smarter than Gladys, but she's prettier than (a—I, b—me).

ANSWERS: 1—a, 2—a, 3—b, 4—a, 5—b, 6—a, 7—b, 8—a, 9—b, 10—a, 11—b, 12—a, 13—a, 14—a, 15—a, 16—b, 17—b, 18—a, 19—b, 20—a, 21—a 22—b, 23—b, 24—a, 25—a

GAINING INCREASED MOMENTUM

HOW TO TALK
ABOUT ACTIONS

—— TEASER PREVIEW ——

What verb means to:

- *belittle?*
- *be purposely confusing?*
- *tickle someone's fancy?*
- *flatter fulsomely?*
- *prohibit some food or activity?*
- *make unnecessary?*
- *work against?*
- *spread slander?*
- *give implicit forgiveness for a misdeed?*
- *change hostility to friendliness?*

THERE are words, as you doubtless recall from your high-school study of grammar, which describe action.

These words are called *verbs*.

Every sentence which you think, say, read, or write contains an implied or expressed verb, for it is the verb which carries the action, the message, the thought of the sentence.

Young children learning to talk use verbs fairly early.

Their very first words, of course, are likely to be *nouns*, as they name the things or people around them.

Mama, dada, doll, baby, bottle, et cetera will probably be the first standard syllables (intelligible naturally only to its fond parents) that an infant will utter, for naming concrete things or real persons is the first step in the development of language ability.

153

Soon there will come the ability to express *intangible* ideas, and then the growing child begins to use simple verbs—*go, stop, stay, want, eat, sleep*, et cetera.

As maturity is reached, the verbs express ideas of greater and greater complexity; and the intelligent, mature adult can describe the most involved actions in a few simple syllables—if he has a good store of useful verbs at his command.

The richer and more extensive a person's vocabulary of verbs, the more accurately and expressively he can describe the subtlest actions, reactions, attitudes, and emotions.

With the proper verb you can pin-point an action down to the last detail.

Let's be specific.

IDEAS

1. playing it down

Harry Truman couldn't win the 1948 election. The pollsters said so, the Republicans heartily agreed, even the Democrats, some in high places, believed it. Mr. Truman himself was perhaps the only voter in the country who was not entirely convinced.

Came the first Tuesday after the first Monday in November—well, if you were one of those who stayed up most of the night listening to the returns, and then kept your ear to the radio most of the next day, you recall how you reacted to the unique Truman triumph.

It was no mean accomplishment, thought many people. Pure accident, said others. If one out of twelve voters in a few key states had changed his ballot, Harry could have gone back to selling ties, one Republican apologist pointed out. It wasn't anything Truman did, said another; it was what Dewey didn't do. No credit to Truman, said a third; it was the farmers—or labor—or the Republicans who hadn't bothered to vote—or the ingenious miscounting of ballots. No credit to Truman, insisted a fourth; it was Wallace's candidacy—it was the Democrats—it was Republican overconfidence—it was sunspots—it was the Communists—it was the civil service workers who didn't want to lose their cushy jobs—it was really Roosevelt who won the election.

Anyway Harry didn't accomplish a thing—he was just a victim of good fortune.

What were the apologists for Dewey's failure doing?

They were *disparaging* Truman's achievement.

2. playing it safe

Of course, Dewey did campaign, in his own way, for the presidency. As the Republican aspirant, he had to take a stand on the controversial Taft-Hartley act.

Was he for it? He was for that part of it which was *good*. Naturally, he was against any of the provisions which were *bad*. Was he for it? The answer was *yes*—and also *no*. Take whichever answer you wanted most to hear.

What was Dewey doing?

He was *equivocating*.

3. enjoying the little things

Have you ever gone through a book that was so good you kept hugging yourself mentally as you read? Have you ever seen a play or motion picture that was so charming that you felt sheer delight as you watched? Or perhaps you have had a portion of pumpkin-chiffon pie, light and airy and mildly flavored, and with a flaky, delicious crust, that was the last word in gustatory enjoyment?

Now notice the examples I have used. I have not spoken of books that grip you emotionally, of plays and movies that keep you on the edge of your seat in suspense, or of food that satisfies a ravenous hunger. These would offer quite a different, perhaps more lasting and memorable, type of enjoyment. I have detailed, rather, mental or physical stimuli that excite enjoyably but not too sharply—a delightful novel, a charming play, a delicious dessert.

How do such things affect you?

They *titillate* you.

4. playing it way up

You know how the "bobby soxers" once adored, idolized, and overwhelmed Frank Sinatra—or how mature women had had similar reactions to Charles Boyer and, earlier, to Rudolph Valentino.

And of course you know how certain unpleasant types of people fall all over a visiting celebrity—a best-selling author, a much publicized general, or a famous entertainer. They show him (such is life that it is more likely to be "him" than "her") fierce and servile attention, they worship and flatter him fulsomely, excessively, almost sickeningly—and 100 per cent insincerely.

How do we say it in a single word?

They *adulate* him.

5. accentuating the negative

What does the doctor say to the *diabetic?* No sugar, no pastries, no ice cream, no white bread, et cetera, the patient's morale dropping lower and lower as each food is placed on the *verboten* list.

And what does the sufferer from a heart ailment hear? No stairs, no more than a few hours of work each day, no excitement, very little sex, stay off the tennis courts . . .

And if it's a question of ulcers? No pickled herring, no salami or frankfurters, no martinis, manhattans, or tom collinses . . .

What's the doctor doing?

He's *proscribing* foods, pleasures, activities.

6. accentuating the explosive

Consider a young woman aged twenty-four. She has the svelte slimness that plumper women would gladly die for, and a rich, proud, bosom that would stop a healthy man at fifty yards. Her face would put Helen of Troy to shame, and her profile (which she is never reluctant to show) is devastating.

That's on the physical side of the ledger. Emotionally, she's warm, sympathetic, gay, alternately serious and saucy, passionately interested in life and people, free of complexes, conflicts, or inhibitions. In addition, she's a fascinating talker but an even better listener.

Now don't get excited—I know that this is an idealized, and perhaps impossible, picture. But if such a woman did exist, would she need to have any worries about attracting male companionship?

Such physical, emotional, and mental characteristics would entirely *obviate* such worries.

7. playing it wrong

Theodor Reik, in his penetrating book on psychoanalysis, *Listening With the Third Ear,* talks about neurotic people who unconsciously wish to fail. In business interviews they say exactly the wrong words, they do exactly the wrong things, they seem intent (as, *unconsciously,* they actually are) on insuring failure in every possible way, though consciously they are doing their best to court success.

What effect does such a neurotic tendency have?

It *militates* against success.

156

8. thinking the worst

Agnes is always in character. She will meet you on the street, her face wreathed in smiles. "Have you heard about Mrs. Gray?" she gurgles. "Her husband is getting a divorce—he caught her with the milkman!" (Meanwhile, Mr. and Mrs. Gray are probably having a happy lunch in town, just as much in love as ever.)

Or Agnes has come to your home for the evening. "Oh isn't it terrible about Dick Black?" You know, of course, that even if it is terrible, Agnes feels wonderful about it. "The bank discharged him—his accounts were short; I think he spent it on slow horses and fast women!" (Dick likely doesn't know the front end of a horse from the rear—and if he's not quite so ignorant about women, it's only because he has six daughters. The truth is, no doubt, that another bank offered him a better job. But Agnes always figures it out her own way.)

How does Agnes speak about her neighbors? (*Why* is perhaps a more important question, but one that only a psychoanalyst could eventually answer.)

She (*maligns*) them.

9. giving the benefit of any doubt

Do you think it's all right to cheat on your income taxes? At least just a little? It's wrong, of course, but doesn't everybody do it?

How do you feel about marital infidelity? Are you inclined to overlook the occasional transgressions of the male partner, since, after all, men are essentially polygamous by nature?

If your answer to these questions is in the affirmative, how are you reacting to such transgressions of legal or moral principles?

You *condone* them.

10. changing hostility

Unwittingly you have done something which has aroused anger and resentment in your best friend. You had no desire to hurt him, yet he makes it obvious that he feels pretty bitter about the whole situation. (Perhaps you failed to invite him to a gathering to which he wanted to come; or you neglected to ask his advice on a matter which he felt was important to him.) His friendship is valuable to you and you wish to restore yourself in his good graces. What would you do?

You would (*placate*) your friend.

157

Can you pronounce the words?

The basic ten words which open this section offer no important pronunciation difficulties, and you may therefore be tempted to neglect or ignore this exercise. Don't. The purpose of the pronunciation tests is not only to give you confidence that you are saying new words correctly—their secondary but very valuable purpose is to get you used to the words by letting you hear them from your own mouth. In psychoanalysis a patient truly believes something only if he says it himself—in vocabulary building a student truly acquires a word only after he has heard it issuing through his own vocal cords.

So say these verbs aloud, as often as you may consider necessary, thinking of their meanings as you go along.

1.	*disparage*	diss-PAR-idge (AR as in *carriage*)
2.	*equivocate*	ee-KWIV-o-kayt
3.	*titillate*	TITT-i-layt
4.	*adulate*	AJ-yoo-layt
5.	*proscribe*	pro-SCRIBE
6.	*obviate*	OB-vee-ayt
7.	*militate*	MILL-i-tayt
8.	*malign*	ma-LYNE
9.	*condone*	kon-DOAN
10.	*placate*	PLAY-kayt

Can you work with the words?

Match words and definitions.

1.	disparage	a. flatter lavishly
2.	equivocate	b. work against
3.	titillate	c. prohibit
4.	adulate	d. forgive
5.	proscribe	e. change hostility to friendliness
6.	obviate	f. purposely talk in such a way as to be vague and misleading
7.	militate	g. slander
8.	malign	h. play down

158

9. condone	i. make unnecessary
10. placate	j. tickle

Do you understand the words?

React quickly to the following questions.

1. Do you normally *disparage* something you admire?   YES   (NO)
2. Do you *equivocate* if you think it unwise to take a definite stand?   (YES)   NO
3. Do pleasant things *titillate* you?   (YES)   NO
4. Do emotionally mature people enjoy *adulation*?   YES   (NO)
5. Is sugar *proscribed* for diabetics?   (YES)   NO
6. Does a substantial fortune *obviate* financial fears?   (YES)   NO
7. Does a woman's coldness often *militate* against her chances of marriage?   (YES)   NO
8. Do people enjoy being *maligned*?   YES   (NO)
9. Do we generally *condone* the faults of those we love?   (YES)   NO
10. Can you sometimes *placate* a hostile child with a lollipop or cookie?   YES   NO

Can you use the words?

In this exercise you can test your ability to put a word to proper use, and in addition gain the value of actually writing a new word as a meaningful solution to a significant problem. To think about a word, to say it, to write it, to use it—that is the road to word mastery. So, without reference to previous tests, write one of our ten verbs that best fits each of the following situations.

1. You've been asked to take a stand on a certain issue, but you don't have the courage to be either definitely for or against.

    You _equivocate_

2. You spread around an unpleasant story that you know will besmirch someone's reputation.

    You _malign_ him.

3. Your wife has stopped talking to you since you paid so much attention to that gorgeous blonde at the Schapper's party. So you bring home a big bouquet of roses.

    You are trying to _placate_ her.

4. Your boss is a god—at least so you pretend. And you flatter and kowtow to him to a degree that even he finds annoying.

    You _adulate_ him.

5. You are crowding 260 on the scales—and without a stitch of clothing. So your doctor warns against rich desserts, second helpings, and other such gustatory pleasures.

    He _proscribe_s these foods.

6. Your child Johnnie has smacked the neighbor's kid—entirely unprovoked, you are forced to admit. But after all, you think, tomorrow the other kid will smack Johnnie. That's what childhood is like.

    You _condone_ Johnny's behavior.

7. When your wife, understandably looking for praise, shows you the wonderful bargain she has just bought, you say, "Oh, well! If that's all you do with your time—just go looking for silly bargains!"

    You _disparage_ her accomplishment.

8. You were planning to go to the bank to draw some money for a new suit, but an unexpected and big check has come in the morning's mail.

    Receipt of the money _obviate_ed a trip to the bank.

9. You are the soul of honesty, but unfortunately, you have a sneaky, thievish, sinister look—and no one ever trusts you.

    Your appearance _militates_ against you.

160

10. A beautiful, curly-haired, blonde little girl of four captures your fancy. You could spend all day delightedly staring at her.

   She _titillates_ you.

Can you recall the words?

Write the proper verb next to each definition.

1. Change hostility into friendliness   1. _placate_
2. Make unnecessary   2. _obviate_
3. Belittle   3. _disparage_
4. Overlook or forgive a transgression   4. _condone_
5. Tickle; delight   5. _titillate_
6. Spread malicious rumors about   6. _malign_
7. To purposely use language susceptible of opposite interpretations   7. _equivocate_
8. Act to the disadvantage of   8. _militate_
9. Forbid   9. _proscribe_
10. Worship; flatter servilely   10. _adulate_

ORIGINS AND RELATED WORDS

1. equality

If you play golf, you know that each course or hole has a certain *par,* the number of strokes allowed according to the results achieved by expert players. Your own accomplishment on the course will be at *par,* above *par;* or, if you slept badly

161

or your mother-in-law dropped in for a visit, below *par*. *Par*, as you might expect, comes from a Latin word meaning *equal;* it's up to you, when you play, to *equal* the standard, expert score. When we speak of *parity* payments to farmers, we refer to payments that show an equality to those for some agreed-upon year. So, when you *disparage*, you lower someone's *par*, or feeling of *equality*.

Be careful to use the word properly. You do not *disparage* a person, but only his achievements, accomplishments, attempts, et cetera. Thus: "She *disparaged* his love-making, claiming she had seen better." However, you may *speak disparagingly of* a person, or *in disparagement of* a person or his work. Thus: "She spoke *disparagingly* of his love-making, saying she had expected better," or "She spoke *in disparagement of* his efforts to make love to her, pointing out that she had turned down better offers."

Parity as a noun means *equality*, and its opposite, *disparity*, means a lack of *equality*, or a *difference*. We may speak for example, of the *disparity* between someone's promise and his performance; or of the *disparity* between the rate of vocabulary growth of a child and an adult. The common word *compare* and all its forms (*comparable, comparative*, et cetera) also derive from *par, equal*. Two things are *compared* when they have certain *equal* or similar qualities.

2. how to say yes and no

Speaking of *equality*, that is one of the Latin roots in *equivocate;* that plus *voc, voice* or *call*. When you *equivocate*, you seem to be saying both *yes* and *no* with *equal voice*. An *equivocal* answer, therefore, is designedly vague, indefinite, and susceptible of contradictory interpretations, quite the opposite of an *unequivocal* answer, which says *Yes!* or *No!*, and no kidding. Professional politicians are masters of *equivocation*—they are, on most vital issues, mugwumps; they sit on a fence with their *mugs* on one side and their *wumps* on the other. When Truman *unequivocally* extended recognition to the new state of Israel, he did not hedge, qualify, or leave any doubt as to his meaning. You will often hear a candidate for office say, publicly, that he *unequivocally* promises, if elected, to . . . ; and then he starts *equivocating* for all he is worth. Like the salesman who says, "Let me be perfectly *frank* with you"—and then promptly and glibly lies through his teeth.

You will encounter the root *equi, equal,* in scores of English words; *equality, equidistant, equinox, equation, equanimity, equilibrium,* et cetera. Knowing the meaning of the first two syllables of these words will help you puzzle out any that are unfamiliar to you.

And you will encounter *voc, voice,* or *call* (also spelled *vox* and *vok*) in other scores of English words: *magnavox* (radio), *large voice; vocal, using the voice; vocation, calling; avocation, hobby* or something not one's actual *calling; vociferous, in a loud voice; revoke, call back* or cancel; *convoke, call together;* et cetera.

3. statements of various kinds

Do not confuse *equivocal* with *ambiguous.* An *equivocal* statement is purposely, designedly (and with malice aforethought) couched in language that will be deceptive; an *ambiguous* statement is *accidentally* couched in such language. *Equivocal* is, in short, *purposely ambiguous.* You recall that *ambi,* which we last met in *ambivert* and *ambidextrous,* is a root which means *both;* anything *ambiguous* may have *both* one meaning and an opposite meaning. If you say, "That sentence is the height of *ambiguity,*" you mean that you find it vague because it admits of both affirmative and negative interpretations, or it may mean two different things.

Certain other types of statements contain possibilities of two interpretations—one of which is suggestive or sexy. Such statements are neither *ambiguities* nor *equivocations,* but bear the special French (as you would expect) name of *double entendres,* which literally translates into "double meanings." I will refrain, despite great temptation, from offering an example of the *double entendre*—this out of deference to the postal authorities, but if you are over sixteen years old, I'm sure you understand what I mean, and I am being neither *ambiguous* nor *equivocal*—just *cautious.*

4. how to tickle

Titillate comes from a Latin verb meaning *tickle,* and may be used both literally and figuratively. That is (literally), you can *titillate* someone by stroking him gently in strategic places; you are then causing an actual (and always very pleasant) physical sensation; or you can (figuratively) *titillate him,* or *his mind,* or *his fancy,* or *his palate* (and this is the more common use of the word), by your *charm, brilliance, cuteness, attractive appearance,* or by any other device your imagination can conceive. And I hope you have a good imagination. The noun is *titillation.*

5. how to flatter

A *compliment* is a pleasant and courteous expression of praise; *flattery* is stronger than a compliment and always insincere. *Adulation* is flattery carried to a ridiculous, a fantastic degree. There are certain public figures who want, indeed seem to need, the *adulation* of the mob, probably because they must have constant bolstering of their egos. An *adulatory* attitude is, remember, basically unwholesome; it springs not out of true and deep admiration, but more often out of a self-seeking wish to identify with someone important or famous.

6. write it down, O'Toole!

Fundamentally, *proscribe* means to *forbid,* to *prohibit,* but the word is commonly restricted today to the medical sense of forbidding the use of any food or drug, of prohibiting any activity that might prove harmful to the patient. You recognize in *proscribe* the Latin root *scrib, to write.* In ancient Roman times, a man's name was written on a public bulletin board if he had committed some crime for which his property or life were to be forfeited; Roman citizens in good standing would thereby know to avoid him. In a similar sense, the doctor writes down those foods or activities which are likely to commit crimes against the patient's health—in that way the patient knows he must avoid them. The word is occasionally used also in a religious sense. The church *proscribes,* or announces a *proscription* against, such activities as may harm its parishioners. Generally, one might concede, *proscribed* activities are the most pleasant ones—as Alexander Woollcott once remarked, if something is pleasurable, it's sure to be either immoral, illegal, or fattening.

The Latin root *scrib* is found in a host of English words:

164

prescribe, exactly opposite in meaning to *proscribe; scribe; scribble; inscribe;* and, in the spelling *scrip, scriptures; script; conscription*, et cetera.

7. it's obvious

You are familiar with the word *via, by way of*, which is from the Latin word for *road*. (The Via Appia is one of the famous highways of ancient Roman times.) Thus, if you wish to go to New York from Boston by car, you may travel *via* Providence or *via* Newport and the Jamestown Ferry. When something is *obvious*, it is right there in the middle of the road where no one can fail to see it—hence, *easily seen, not hidden, conspicuous*. And if you meet an obstacle in the road and dispose of it forthwith, you are performing the action of *obviate*. Thus, if you review your work daily in some high-school or college subject, frenzied "cramming" at the end of the semester will be *obviated*. A good, healthy bank balance *obviates* fears of financial insecurity; leaving for work in plenty of time to catch the train will *obviate* worry about being late. In short, then, *to obviate* means *to make unnecessary;* but notice that the subject of the verb is rarely a person. Thus, you cannot say, "John makes a lot of money; he *obviates* his wife's looking for a job"; instead, "John's high salary *obviates* the need for Sally's going to work."

8. war

When you see *militate*, you naturally think of *military*—and the connection is valid not only in form but also in meaning. Latin *militaris* means *pertaining to a soldier or fighting man*, and if something *militates* against you, it fights against your advantage. Thus, your timidity may *militate against* your making new friends; or your aggressiveness may *militate against* your keeping your friends. (*Militate* is always followed by the preposition *against* and, like *obviate*, never takes a personal subject—*you* don't *militate* against anyone, but some habit, action, tendency, et cetera *militates* against someone or something.)

The adjective *militant* comes from the same root, *militaris*. A *militant* reformer is one who *fights* for his reforms; a *mili-*

165

tant campaign is one waged aggressively and with determination.

9. bad and good

Working from the root of *malign*, we can track down valuable words in wholesale quantities; and we can double our yield, as they say in farming, by considering *bene* (pronounced BAY-nay), a root which has the opposite meaning to the root in *malign*.

Let's see how it works.

Malign, to spread slander about, is built on Latin *male* (pronounced MAH-lay), *badly*—*malign* means *to speak badly about. Malign* is also used as an adjective meaning *harmful, hateful,* in short *bad,* as in "the *malign* influence of his unconscious will to fail." Another adjective form is *malignant,* as in "a *malignant* glance," i.e., one showing deep hatred, or "a *malignant* growth," i.e., one that is cancerous (*bad*) and will likely spread to other parts of the body.

Now, working with the opposite root, *bene, well,* we have *benign* and *benignant,* both of which mean *kindly,* as in "a *benign* tumor," one that is not cancerous and will not spread.

That's simple enough, I submit. Let's chart some words so that we can see the contrast more sharply.

MALE: *bad, badly*	BENE: *well, good*
malign, malignant—bad, harmful, hateful	*benign, benignant*—kindly, good
malediction—a curse, etymologically a "bad saying"	*benediction*—a blessing, etymologically a "good saying"
maleficent—causing harm, etymologically "doing badly"	*beneficent*—causing good, etymologically "doing well"
malevolent—ill-disposed, etymologically "wishing badly"	*benevolent*—well-disposed, etymologically "wishing well"
malefactor—a criminal, etymologically "a bad doer"	*benefactor*—one who confers a favor, one who is helpful, etymologically "a good doer"
maladroit—awkward, clumsy, etymologically "having a bad right hand"	
malaise—indefinite feeling of bodily discomfort, illness, etymologically "bad ease"	

166

When we examine these words etymologically, we find that a *malediction* is *a bad saying*, a *benediction* is *a good saying*, from the root *dict, to say*. *Maleficent* is *bad doing*, *beneficent good doing*, from the root *fac, to do*.

Malevolent is *bad wishing*, *benevolent* is *good wishing*, from the root *volent, to wish*; *malefactor* is *a bad doer*, *benefactor* is *a good doer*, from the root *fac, to do*; *malaise* is *a bad feeling*, and *maladroit* combines *male, bad*, with *adroit*, the French form we have previously studied which means *the right hand*. An *adroit* debater, figuratively one with a good right hand, is a *skillful* debater. Hence a *maladroit* person is *badly skillful*, or *awkward, unskilled*.

10. say, do, and wish

It's really not too confusing if you take it slowly and have the patience to go through it. The *dict* in *benediction* and *malediction* means *to say*; we hear it in *dictaphone, predict, dictation*, et cetera. The *fic* in *maleficent* and *beneficent* and the *fac* in *malefactor* and *benefactor* are variant spellings of the Latin root which means *to do*; we hear it in *factory, a place where things are done*, and in *fact, something which was done*, hence *something true*. The *volent* in *benevolent* and *malevolent* means *to wish*; we hear it in *voluntary, involuntary, volunteer*, and *volition*. I take it for granted that you are familiar with these common words and will not stop at this point to define them, but I think you can see an extension of the idea of *wishing* or *willing* in each one.

11. if you please!

The root in *placate* is also a rich source of new words. The first four letters come from a Latin verb *to please*; when you *placate* someone, you please him, especially at a time when he is most displeased. Hence, you change his *malevolence*, in a manner of speaking, to *benevolence*. Or you make a *placatory* gesture, offering, or suggestion, that is, one intended to *please* or to remove hostility. If someone is *implacable*, he

167

cannot be pleased; he's got a mad on and nothing can be done to soften his resentment or weaken his hostility. Or maybe he's *placid*—he is calm, easy-going, undisturbed, everything *pleases* him.

Finally, if someone is *complacent*, he is well-pleased, generally with himself; in other words, smug, self-satisfied, content—perhaps foolishly content—with his merits, advantages, accomplishments, et cetera. *Complacency*, however, is not a word used as a complimentary or even neutral term. It contains a mild insult—when you accuse someone of being *complacent* you imply that he has very little to feel so smug about; soon will come the awakening, the hour of disillusionment. Americans were often accused by government leaders, during World War II, of *complacency*—we were too assured (baselessly, was the implication) that we would win, and as a result we did not try hard enough.

12. how to give——and forgive

To *condone* is to *forgive;* a *donation* is a *gift*—you can see the connection. *Condone* comes from the Latin verb *donare,* *to give* (as does *donation*); when you *condone* an act, you *give* freedom from punishment, almost mild approval, to the perpetrator of that antisocial act. Of course you only *condone* such actions as other people are likely to disapprove of.

USING THE WORDS: II

We have worked, in the previous section of this chapter, with twelve important and productive roots, all of them from Latin. Suppose we chart them for a quick once-over and fresh view.

ROOT	MEANING	EXAMPLE
1. *par*	equality	*disparagement*
2. *equi*	equal	*equivocal*
3. *voc*	voice, call	*vocal*
4. *ambi*	both	*ambiguity*
5. *scrib, scrip*	write	*proscription*
6. *via*	road	*obviate*
7. *male*	badly	*malignant*

8. *bene*	good, well	*benignant*
9. *fac, fic*	do	*malefactor*
10. *dic*	say	*benediction*
11. *volent*	wish, will	*malevolence*
12. *plac*	please	*implacable*

As you see, a knowledge of roots and an application of that knowledge make it simple to learn new words almost by the carload—we have taken, in a few pages, thirty-four such derivatives. Now see how you make out with our usual exercises.

Can you pronounce the words?

1. *parity*	PAR-I-tee†
2. *disparagingly*	dis-PAR-a-jing-lee†
3. *disparagement*	dis-PAR-idge-ment†
4. *disparity*	dis-PAR-*i*-tee†
5. *equivocal*	ee-KWIV-o-k'l
°6. *unequivocal*	un-ee-KWIV-o-k'l
7. *equivocation*	ee-kwiv-o-KAY-shun
8. *ambiguous*	am-BIG-yoo-us
°9. *ambiguity*	am-bi-GYOO-i-tee
10. *double entendre*	DOO-b'l ahn-TAHN-dre
11. *titillation*	tit-i-LAY-shun
12. *adulation*	aj-oo-LAY-shun
°13. *adulatory*	AJ-oo-la-toar-ee
14. *proscription*	pro-SKRIP-shun
°15. *via*	VYE-a
16. *obvious*	OB-vee-us
17. *militant*	MILL-i-tant (a as in husband)
18. *malignant*	ma-LIG-nant (a as in husband)
19. *malediction*	mal-e-DIK-shun
°20. *malaise*	ma-LAYZ
°21. *maleficent*	ma-LEFF-i-sent
°22. *malevolent*	ma-LEV-o-lent
23. *malefactor*	MAL-e-fak-ter
24. *benign*	be-NYNE
25. *benignant*	bi-NIG-nant (a as in husband)
26. *benediction*	ben-e-DIK-shun
°27. *beneficent*	be-NEFF-i-sent
°28. *benevolent*	be-NEV-o-lent

---

†PAR rhymes with CAR in *carriage*.

29. *benefactor*	BEN-e-fak-ter
°30. *placatory*	PLAY-ka-toar-ee
°31. *implacable*	im-PLAY-ka-b'l
32. *placid*	PLASS-id
33. *complacent*	kom-PLAY-sent
34. *complacency*	kom-PLAY-sen-see

Can you work with the words? (I)

Match words and definitions.

1. parity	a. indefinite and confusing expression of thought
2. disparagement	b. fulsome flattery
3. equivocation	c. prohibition
4. *double entendre*	d. tickling, mild excitement
5. titillation	e. equality
6. adulation	f. belittlement
7. proscription	g. an expression that has two meanings, one of them sexy

1e, 2f, 3a, 4g, 5d, 6b, 7c

KEY: 1—e, 2—f, 3—a, 4—g, 5—d, 6—b, 7—c

Can you work with the words? (II)

1. malediction	a. feeling of general discomfort
2. benediction	b. good wishes
3. malaise	c. curse
4. malevolence	d. criminal
5. benevolence	e. ill will
6. malefactor	f. blessing
7. benefactor	g. one who does a good deed
8. disparity	h. lack of equality

1e, 2f, 3a, 4e, 5b, 6d, 7g, 8h

KEY: 1—c, 2—f, 3—a, 4—e, 5—b, 6—d, 7—g, 8—h

Can you work with the words? (III)

1. benign	a. impervious to pacifying
2. malign	b. harmful, hateful
3. placatory	c. smug

4. implacable	d. confusing because of possibility of mis-understanding
5. placid	e. tending to soothe
6. complacent	f. calm
7. ambiguous	g. kindly

1g, 2b, 3e, 4a, 5f, 6c, 7d

KEY: 1—g, 2—b, 3—e, 4—a, 5—f, 6—c, 7—d

Can you work with the words? (IV)

1. unequivocal	a. ill-disposed
2. adulatory	b. aggressive
3. militant	c. kindly disposed
4. maleficent	d. clear, not confusing
5. beneficent	e. servilely attentive and flattering

1d, 2e, 3b, 4a, 5c

KEY: 1—d, 2—e, 3—b, 4—a, 5—c

Do you understand the words? (I)

React quickly to the following questions.

1. Has Spain lost its one-time *parity* with other great nations?	**YES**	NO
2. Do Republican congressmen often speak *disparagingly* of Kennedy's legislative program?	**YES**	NO
3. Is there a *disparity* in age between a child and his grandfather?	**YES**	NO
4. Is an *equivocal* statement clear and direct?	YES	**NO**
5. Is an *unequivocal* answer difficult to understand?	YES	**NO**
6. Are politicians often masters of *equivocation*?	**YES**	NO
7. Are *ambiguous* sentences often found in the works of good writers?	YES	**NO**
8. Is *ambiguity* to be desired in writing?	YES	**NO**
9. Can a young child usually understand a *double entendre*?	YES	**NO**
10. Is *titillation* a pleasant sensation?	**YES**	NO

KEY: 1—yes, 2—yes, 3—yes, 4—no, 5—no, 6—yes, 7—no, 8—no, 9—no, 10—yes

Do you understand the words? (II)

1. Are movie stars often victims of *adulation*?   YES   NO
2. Is an *adulatory* remark insulting?   YES   NO
3. Do some religions issue a *proscription* against eating meat on Fridays?   YES   NO
4. Did Truman wage a *militant* campaign in 1948?   YES   NO
5. Does one normally enjoy receiving *malignant* glances?   YES   NO
6. Does one utter *maledictions* against those one loves?   YES   NO
7. Is there often a feeling of *malaise* before an illness?   YES   NO
8. Was Hitler *maleficent*?   YES   NO
9. Does a *malevolent* act show nobleness of character?   YES   NO
10. Is a *malefactor* usually respected?   YES   NO

KEY: 1—yes, 2—no, 3—yes, 4—yes, 5—no, 6—no, 7—yes, 8—yes, 9—no, 10—no

---

Do you understand the words? (III)

1. Is a *benign* old man usually popular?   YES   NO
2. Are *benedictions* given in houses of worship?   YES   NO
3. Is it pleasant to be the recipient of a *beneficent* act?   YES   NO
4. Are kind people *benevolent*?   YES   NO
5. Do *placatory* gestures often heal wounds and soothe disgruntled friends?   YES   NO
6. Do corrupt politicians often claim to be *implacable* foes of corruption?   YES   NO
7. Does a child grow best if the atmosphere of the household is *placid*?   YES   NO
8. Are some unambitious people *complacent*?   YES   NO
9. Is *complacency* a pleasant quality?   YES   NO

KEY: 1—yes, 2—yes, 3—yes, 4—yes, 5—yes, 6—yes, 7—yes, 8—yes, 9—no

Do you understand the words? (IV)

Is each pair of words the same or opposite in meaning?

1. disparaging—laudatory	SAME	OPPOSITE
2. equivocal—ambiguous	SAME	OPPOSITE
3. adulate—disparage	SAME	OPPOSITE
4. proscribe—prescribe	SAME	OPPOSITE
5. obvious—confusing	SAME	OPPOSITE
6. militant—timid	SAME	OPPOSITE
7. malaise—discomfort	SAME	OPPOSITE
8. maleficent—unkind	SAME	OPPOSITE
9. malefactor—criminal	SAME	OPPOSITE
10. malevolent—hostile	SAME	OPPOSITE
11. benign—unkind	SAME	OPPOSITE
12. benediction—curse	SAME	OPPOSITE
13. placatory—irritating	SAME	OPPOSITE
14. placid—calm	SAME	OPPOSITE
15. complacent—discontent	SAME	OPPOSITE
16. disparity—similarity	SAME	OPPOSITE

KEY: 1—o, 2—s, 3—o, 4—o, 5—o, 6—o, 7—s, 8—s, 9—s, 10—s, 11—o, 12—o, 13—o, 14—s, 15—o, 16—o

Can you recall the words?

And now, finally, here is the acid test of your learning. Can you supply most or all of the thirty-four words we have just been discussing if a brief definition and the initial letter are supplied?

1. accidentally vague   1. A_mbiguous_

2. purposely vague   2. E_quivocal_

3. prohibition   3. P_roscription_

4. kindly (short form)   4. B_enign_

5. kindly (longer form)   5. B_enignant_

6. blessing   6. B_enediction_

7. unyieldingly hostile   7. I_mplacable_

8. by way of   8. V_ia_

9. pleasant excitation   9. T_itillation_

10. equality   10. P_arity_

11. favorably disposed;
    well-wishing   11. B_enevolent_

12. belittlingly   12. D_isparaging_

13. a word or expression with two
    possible meanings, one sexy 13. D_ouble entendre_

14. excessive flattery   14. A_dulation_

15. one who does a kind deed 15. B_enefactor_

16. calm   16. P_lacid_

17. hateful; doing bad   17. M_alefiaent_

18. inequality   18. D_isparity_

19. a criminal   19. M_alefactor_

20. a curse   20. M_alediction_

21. helpful; doing good   21. B_enefiaent_

22. aiming to please   22. P_lacatory_

23. smugness   23. C_omplacency_

24. self-satisfied   24. C_omplacent_

25. hateful   25. M_alignant_

26. feeling of general discomfort 26. M_alaise_

27. fighting; aggressive   27. M_ilitant_

28. ill-disposed; wishing harm 28. M_alevolent_

29. derogatoriness   29. D_isparagement_

30. clear, definite   30. U_nequivocal_

31. purposeful vagueness   31. E_quivocation_

32. accidental vagueness   32. A_mbiguity_

33. worshipful; excessively flattering	33.	_Adulatory_
34. easily seen	34.	O_bvious_

KEY: 1—ambiguous, 2—equivocal, 3—proscription, 4—benign, 5—benignant, 6—benediction, 7—implacable, 8—via, 9—titillation, 10—parity, 11—benevolent, 12—disparagingly, 13—_double entendre_, 14—adulation, 15—benefactor, 16—placid, 17—maleficent, 18—disparity, 19—malefactor, 20—malediction, 21—beneficent, 22—placatory, 23—complacency, 24—complacent, 25—malignant, 26—malaise, 27—militant, 28—malevolent, 29—disparagement, 30—unequivocal, 31—equivocation, 32—ambiguity, 33—adulatory, 34—obvious

CHAPTER REVIEW

Do you recognize the words?

Check the word which most closely fits each definition.

1. To belittle:
    (a) titillate, (b) disparage, (c) adulate
2. To be purposely confusing:
    (a) equivocate, (b) obviate, (c) proscribe
3. To work to the disadvantage of:
    (a) malign, (b) militate, (c) placate
4. To slander:
    (a) malign, (b) condone, (c) placate
5. Lack of equality:
    (a) parity, (b) disparity, (c) ambiguity
6. Phrase which may have two interpretations, one of them being indelicate or off-color:
    (a) equivocation, (b) ambiguity, (c) _double entendre_
7. Hateful:
    (a) malignant, (b) benignant, (c) malaise
8. Ill will:
    (a) malefactor, (b) malevolence, (c) maleficence
9. Kindly:
    (a) benevolent, (b) placid, (c) complacent
10. Inflexibly hostile:
    (a) implacable, (b) placatory, (c) militant

KEY: 1—b, 2—a, 3—b, 4—a, 5—b, 6—c, 7—a, 8—b, 9—a, 10—a

GETTING THE TOTAL VIEW

Well! You have not, I hope, spent more than one sitting with this chapter. It really does not matter a bit how long a sitting any one chapter requires; what does matter is that you get a total view of the material by sticking with a chapter until you have satisfactorily, successfully mastered its contents.

So I'll assume you are developing the proper intensity and tenaciousness, and have conquered these pages without interruption.

If you have, pause to consider what that means.

You have learned, or become reacquainted with, forty-four exciting words and twelve valuable Latin roots, all in one evening!

Is that good? Brother (or sister, if such is the case), stand up and pat yourself on the back. *The average adult, remember, learns only fifty new words in an entire year!*

Don't you begin to feel, now that you have been working intensively with these forty-four words all evening, as if you have known them all your life? If you have worked properly, you should have such a feeling. And as time goes on and you begin to catch these words in your reading, begin to notice them when other people use them, begin to find yourself thinking with them and using them yourself—then you will be *certain* that you have known them all your life!

No, I am not being evangelical—I simply expect that you will go through the same exhilarating intellectual experiences, as a result of learning new words and exploring new ideas, that my students have constantly reported to me.

BRIEF INTERMISSION SEVEN:
HOW TO PRONOUNCE A WORD

"Art thou an Ephraimite?"
"Nay."
"Say now the word for 'an ear of corn'."
"Sibboleth."

This is undoubtedly the earliest recorded instance of a pronunciation quiz. It was administered in Biblical times (you will find an account of it in the Book of Judges) by a Gileadite who caught a suspected Ephraimite trying to cross the River Jordan. The prisoner would vow that he *was* a Gileadite, but pronunciation gave him away; Gileadites called an ear of corn *shibboleth,* not *sibboleth.* The error generally cost the Ephraimite his life; which, you are probably reflecting, is rather a harsh penalty for a single mispronunciation.

Times have not changed quite as much as you may think. During the World War II fighting in the Pacific Islands, a suspected Japanese who claimed to be a Chinese or Filipino was given a quick pronunciation test by his American captors —he was asked to say *lalapalooza.* To the Japanese ear, *L* is an alien sound—so, if the prisoner was not what he pretended to be, the best he could manage was *raraparooza.* He had flunked the test—his pronunciation had given him away.

Your pronunciation gives you away. Only under the most highly exceptional circumstances could an error cost you your life (as in the case of the Ephraimites), or your freedom (as in the case of the Japanese), or even your job or your friends, as some speech missionaries solemnly and absurdly proclaim. But under ordinary circumstances an expert can draw from your pronunciation a number of interesting conclusions about your geographical background, your education, your cultural environment, and your personality.

For instance, if you say something approaching *ahl* for all or *pak* for park, you are advertising that you have grown up in or around Boston. If you call the city *Shi-kaw-go*

(Chicago), you are probably a Westerner or Midwesterner (especially if you also pronounce log *lawg* and hog *hawg*), while if you say *Shi-kah-go, lahg* and *hahg* you more likely come from the East. *Greezy* for greasy shows that you have Southern or Western speech habits; a sharp *R* in *park* will similarly identify you with the western part of the country, and the complete omission of the *R* in the same word will indicate your background as the Eastern Seaboard. Explode your *Ts* (*wettt, hurtt, et cetera*) or click your *NGs* (*singg ga songg, Longg glsland*) and you almost reveal the street you live on in the Bronx; or pronounce the three words *Mary, marry, merry,* and you name the section of the country in which you formed your linguistic habits: the West if you say these words almost identically, the East if the three words are distinctly different in sound. If you're from the East, especially one of the larger cities, you call it a *creek* and a *vayz* (vase); but if you hail from the North or West you refer to it as a *crick* and a *vayss.*

And of course if you're from certain parts of England you call a ski a *shee* and a schedule a *shedule;* you speak of medicine as *med-sin* and insist that a laboratory is a *la-BORE-a-tree.*

Your pronunciation of certain other words, for example *either, aunt, athletic, film, grimace, comparable,* and *verbatim,* will give away, to an experienced ear, more secrets about you than you may realize. If you are willing to take a few simple tests, we can arrive at a fairly accurate analysis of the impression your speech habits give the world.

FIRST ANALYSIS

Do you avoid illiterate forms?

Check in each case the form of the word which you *habitually* and naturally use. As this is not a test of your knowledge, but of your speech patterns, you should be guided solely by what you believe you say, not by what you may think is right.

1. *aviator*	a. AVV-ee-ay-ter	b. AY-vee-ay-ter
2. *bronchial*	a. BRON-ikle	b. BRONK-ee-al
3. *radiator*	a. RADD-ee-ay-ter	b. RAY-dee-ay-ter

4. *vanilla*	a. vi-NELL-a	b. va-NILL-a
5. *modern*	a. MOD-ren or MAR-den	b. MOD-urn
6. *February*	a. FEB-yoo-ar-y	b. FEB-roo-ar-y
7. *mischievous*	a. mis-CHEE-vee-us	b. MISS-chi-vus
8. *attacked*	a. at-TACK-ted	b. at-TACKT
9. *athletic*	a. ath-a-LET-ic	b. ath-LET-ic
10. *elm, film*	a. ellum, fillum	b. elm, film

In the test you have just taken, the first of the two choices was in each case the illiterate form, the second was the accepted or educated pronunciation. If you checked form b right down the line, or did not wander from this straight path more than once, you may feel assured that your speech bears no stigma of illiteracy. If, however, you made an unfortunate choice in several items, consider your action a danger signal. As a further check on your habits, ask yourself whether you are ever guilty of saying *axed* for asked, *myoo-ni-SIP-'l* for municipal, *tra-JET-ic* for tragic, *lyeberry* for library, *fasset* for faucet, *rassle* for wrestle, *drownedded* for drowned, or *lenth* and *strenth* for length and strength.

SECOND ANALYSIS

Does your pronunciation have a college education?

People of more than average education pronounce each of the following words in a certain way. How do you say them? Make an honest choice in accordance with your actual speech habits: do not be influenced by what you may believe is correct.

1. *genuine*	a. JEN-yoo-wyne	b. JEN-yoo-win
2. *orgy*	a. OR-jee	b. OR-gee
		(*g* as in *girl*)
3. *status*	a. STAY-tus	b. STAT-us
4. *zoology*	a. zoo-OL-o-gy	b. zoe-OL-o-gy
5. *coupon*	a. KOO-pon	b. KYOO-pon
6. *comparable*	a. com-PAR-able	b. COM-par-able
7. *bouquet*	a. boe-KAY	b. boo-KAY
		b. BOE-kay
8. *human*	a. YOO-man	b. HYOO-man
9. *robust*	a. ROE-bust	b. ro-BUST
10. *grimace*	a. gri-MAYCE	b. GRIM-iss
11. *garage*	a. ga-RAHDJ	b. ga-RAHZH
		(*ZH* like the *S* in pleasure)

179

12. *impious*	a. IM-pee-us	b. im-PYE-us
13. *impotent*	a. IM-po-tent	b. im-PO-tent
14. *infamous*	a. IN-fa-mous	b. in-FAY-mous
15. *clandestine*	a. CLAN-de-styne	b. clan-DESS-tin
16. *verbatim*	a. ver-BAY-tim	b. ver-BAT-im
17. *preferable*	a. pre-FER-able	b. PREF-er-able
18. *chiropodist*	a. ki-ROP-o-dist	b. tchi-ROP-o-dist
19. *plebeian*	a. PLEE-bee-an	b. ple-BEE-an
20. *culinary*	a. KYOO-li-nary	b. KULL-i-nary

Compare your results with this key: 1—b, 2—a, 3—a, 4—b, 5—a, 6—b, 7—b, 8—b, 9—b, 10—a, 11—b, 12—a, 13—a, 14—a, 15—b, 16—a, 17—b, 18—a, 19—b, 20—a.

If you made one or two slips only, your speech is up to the standard of our better educated citizenry. Three to five errors would mean that your pronunciation habits are in general good, though not perfect. Six to nine errors would place you with the merely average speakers, and ten or more unfortunate choices would again be a warning signal that perhaps your speech does not give the world a picture of you as a person of any degree of linguistic maturity.

THIRD ANALYSIS

Do you avoid affected speech?

Check, as before, the forms you habitually use.

1. *again*	a. a-GAYNE	b. a-GEN
2. *either*	a. EYE-ther	b. EE-ther
3. *vase*	a. vahz	b. vayze or vayse
4. *tomato*	a. to-MAH-to	b. to-MAY-to
5. *chauffeur*	a. sho-FURR	b. SHO-fer
6. *aunt*	a. ahnt	b. ant (rhyme with *slant*)
7. *secretary*	a. SEC-re-tree	b. SEC-re-terry
8. *rather*	a. rah-ther	b. ra-ther (rhyme with *gather*)
9. *program*	a. pro-grum	b. pro-gramm
10. *ask*	a. ahsk	b. ask

Except for certain sections of New England and parts of the South, the second alternative offered above is in every case the popular, current, and standard form. The greater number of *b* pronunciations that you checked, the more natural and unaffected will your listeners consider your speech. If you generally mix in social, business, or geographical groups in which *ahnt, tomahto,* and *eyether* are accepted pronunciations you are, of course, relatively safe in using some or all of the *a* forms in the test; nevertheless, you should bear in mind that these are not the pronunciations common to the majority of Americans and that you may occasionally run the risk of being thought "snooty" or supercilious by your less dramatic and more down-to-earth listeners.

And now, the fourth and last analysis is just for fun, and will serve to prove that we cannot become too fussy about "correct" pronunciation. The words in this test are "catch" words; that is, you are expected, if you are normal, to get most of them wrong. They are, with one exception, bookish words that are rarely used in everyday speech—there is thus no reason why you should be expected to be familiar with their dictionary pronunciations. You may flop ignominiously on this test, and while you will suffer a temporary deflation of your ego as a result, you will have as compensation proof positive that you are normal.

FOURTH ANALYSIS

Are you normal?

Most people taking this test will make seven or more errors. If you get more than three right, you may credit yourself with unusual language sophistication. If you come anywhere near a perfect score, you are absolutely phenomenal. In doing this test, check the form you believe is correct.

1. *finis* (the end) a. FIN-iss, b. fee-NEE, c. FYE-niss
2. *eighth* (the number) a. ayt-th, b. ayth
3. *secretive* (concealing) a. SEEK-re-tive, b. se-KREE-tive
4. *cerebrum* (portion of the brain) a. SER-ebrum, b. se-REE-brum
5. *dour* (stern, forbidding) a. to rhyme with *poor*, b. to rhyme with *sour*

6. *congeries* (a heap) a. CON-je-reez, b. con-JEE-ree-eez
7. *ignominy* (disgrace) a. IG-no-mi-ny, b. ig-NOM-i-ny
8. *gramercy!* (a Shakespearian exclamation) a. GRAM-er-see, b. gra-MUR-see
9. *vagary* (a whim) a. VAG-a-ree, b. VAY-ga-ree, c. va-GARE-ee
10. *quay* (a wharf) a. kway, b. kay, c. key

KEY: 1–c, 2–a, 3–b, 4–a, 5–a, 6–b, 7–a, 8–b, 9–c, 10–c

(These are the pronunciations required by the Merriam-Webster Collegiate Dictionary, 5th edition.)

In your own pronunciation, you are following the wisest course if you avoid illiterate and uneducated forms, pronounce your words without being guilty of affectation or pedantry, and simply conform to the natural dictates of that part of the country in which you developed your speech habits. Actions may speak louder than words, but the world bases its first impression of you on what you say and how you say it.

10

HOW TO TALK
ABOUT VARIOUS SPEECH HABITS

―――― TEASER PREVIEW ――――――――――――――

What adjective describes a person who:

- *is disinclined to conversation?*
- *is brief and pithy in his speech?*
- *is confused and incoherent in his speech?*
- *shows by his speech that he is trite and unimaginative?*
- *uses more words than necessary?*
- *is forcefully compelling and logical in his speech?*
- *talks rapidly and fluently?*
- *is noisy and clamorous?*
- *is talkative?*

PERHAPS some of your richest and most satisfying experiences have been with people to whom you can just talk, talk, talk. As you speak, previously untapped springs of ideas and emotions begin to flow; you hear yourself saying things you never thought you knew.

Happiness, in the final analysis, comes from other people, from a feeling of kinship with the world. An evening of good conversation with congenial friends is about the cheapest form of happiness you can buy—and about the most exhilarating.

Of course there are all kinds of talkers, and all kinds of talk.

Let's look at some of them.

IDEAS

1. saying little

"S. Jay Kaufman, a colyuming pioneer along Broadway two decades ago, recalls when he met Herbert Hoover, just defeated for re-election. The ex-President told about Cal Coolidge, who inaugurated the idea of seeing anyone who wished to see him—one hour a week.

"Mr. Hoover tried the plan but not happily. When he next saw Coolidge he asked 'Silent Cal' how he could see so many persons in an hour, while he (Hoover) could see so few.

"'Because,' dead-panned Cal, 'You answer back!'"

—Walter Winchell

What adjective best describes Coolidge?

He's *taciturn*.

2. saying little—meaning much

There is another well-known anecdote about "Silent Cal":
A young newspaperwoman was sitting next to him at a banquet, so the story goes, and turned to him mischievously.

"Mr. Coolidge," she said, "I have a bet with my editor that I can get you to say more than two words to me this evening."

"*You lose,*" Coolidge rejoined simply.

Now, how would you describe Coolidge?

He's *laconic*.

3. much emotion, little talk

"One day, late for his train, a Chinese traveling in this country rushed over to the baggage room in Grand Central Station, threw his check on the counter, and demanded his bag. The attendant couldn't find it. As precious minutes went by, the Chinese began jumping up and down with rage. Finally he couldn't stand it any longer. His train was going—his bag was nowhere to be found—and he pounded the counter with his fist and yelled:

"'Pretty damn seldom where my bag go. She no fly. You no more fit run station than godsake. That's all I hope!'"

—J. P. McEvoy, in *Reader's Digest*, January, 1947

How would you characterize the Chinese traveler?

He was *inarticulate*.

184

4. much talk, little sense

Miss Bates, a character in *Emma,* a novel by Jane Austen:

"So obliging of you! No, we should not have heard, if it had not been for this particular circumstance, of her being able to come here so soon. My mother is so delighted! For she is to be three months with us at least. Three months, she says so, positively, as I am going to have the pleasure of reading to you. The case is, you see, that the Campbells are going to Ireland. Mrs. Dixon has persuaded her father and mother to come over and see her directly. I was going to say, but, however, different countries, and so she wrote a very urgent letter to her mother, or her father, I declare I do not know which it was, but we shall see presently in Jane's letter . . ."

How would you characterize Miss Bates?

She is *garrulous.*

5. dull and flat

Some people are completely lacking in originality and imagination—and their speech shows it. Everything they say is trite, hackneyed, commonplace—their words and speech patterns are an indication of dull, unquestioning minds.

How would you characterize such people's speech?

It is *banal.*

6. words, words, words!

He talks and talks and talks—it's not so much the quantity you object to as the repetitiousness. He phrases, rephrases, and re-rephrases his thoughts—using far more words than necessary, overwhelming you with words, drowning you with them, until your only thought is how to escape, or maybe how to die.

He's *verbose.*

7. words in quick succession

He's a rapid, fluent talker, the words seeming to roll off his tongue with such ease and lack of effort, and sometimes with such copiousness, that you listen with amazement, if not always with delight.

He's *voluble.*

185

8. words that convince

He expresses his ideas forcefully, almost brilliantly, and in a way that calls for whole-hearted assent and agreement from an intelligent listener.

He's *cogent.*

9. the sound and the fury

His talk is loud, noisy, clamorous, vehement. What may be lacking in content is compensated for in force and strength.

He's *vociferous.*

10. quantity, if not quality

He (or should one preferably say *she?*) talks a lot—a very lot. He (or she) may be voluble, vociferous, garrulous, verbose, but never inarticulate, taciturn, or laconic. No matter. It's the quantity and continuity that are most conspicuous. "Were you vaccinated with a phonograph needle?" is the question you are tempted to ask as you listen.

He's *loquacious.*

Our words, in this chapter, revolve closely around the idea of varying quantities and kinds of talking. Many of the adjectives are synonymous, but each contains its unique difference. You can be quite clear on these differences by examining the chart.

To emphasize		
	quietness	*taciturn*
	economy	*laconic*
	awkwardness	*inarticulate*
	meaninglessness	*garrulous*
	hackneyed phraseology	*banal*
	wordiness and repetition	*verbose*
	rapidity and fluency	*voluble*
	mental keenness	*cogent*
	noisiness	*vociferous*
	quantity	*loquacious*

USING THE WORDS

Can you pronounce the words?

*1. *taciturn*   TASS-i-turn
 2. *laconic*   la-KON-ic
 3. *inarticulate*   in-ar-TIK-yoo-lit
*4. *garrulous*   GAR-oo-lus (AR as in *carriage*)
*5. *banal*   BAY-n'l
 6. *verbose*   ver-BOSE
*7. *voluble*   VOL-yoo-b'l
*8. *cogent*   KOE-jent
 9. *vociferous*   vo-SIFF-er-us
10. *loquacious*   lo-KWAY-shus

Can you change adjectives to nouns?

In preceding chapters you may have observed some general laws for making an adjective into a noun or vice versa. For example, *ambiguous—ambiguity; complacent—complacency,* et cetera. Now draw on your native ingenuity and your verbal sophistication to change each adjective into a noun that will fit the phrase that accompanies it.

1. *taciturn*—his depressing _taciturnity_
2. *laconic*—speech full of _laconisms_
3. *inarticulate*—no doubt about his _inarticulateness_
4. *garrulous*—an amazing _garrulosity_
5. *banal*—replete with _banalities_
6. *verbose*—agonizing _verbosity_
7. *voluble*—astonishing _volubility_
8. *cogent*—inimitable _cogency_
9. *vociferous*—annoying _vociferousness_
10. *loquacious*—uncontrollable _loquacity_

KEY: 1—taciturnity, 2—laconisms, 3—inarticulateness, 4—garrulity or garrulousness, 5—banalities, 6—verbosity, 7—volubility, 8—cogency, 9—vociferousness, 10—loquacity or loquaciousness

Can you work with the words?

Match words and definitions.

1. taciturn		a.	chattering meaninglessly
2. laconic		b.	wordy
3. inarticulate		c.	trite, hackneyed, unoriginal
4. garrulous		d.	fluent and rapid
5. banal		e.	noisy, loud
6. verbose		f.	speaking unintelligibly
7. voluble		g.	talkative
8. cogent		h.	brilliantly compelling, persuasive
9. vociferous		i.	unwilling to engage in conversation
10. loquacious		j.	using few words packed with meaning

1 i, 2 j, 3 f, 4 a, 5 c, 6 b, 7 d, 8 h, 9 e, 10 g

KEY: 1–i, 2–j, 3–f, 4–a, 5–c, 6–b, 7–d, 8–h, 9–e, 10–g

Do you understand the words?

React quickly to these questions.

1. Do *taciturn* people usually make others feel comfortable and welcome? YES NO
2. Does a *laconic* speaker use more words than necessary? YES NO
3. Does rage make some people *inarticulate*? YES NO
4. Is it interesting to listen to *garrulous* old men? YES NO
5. Do *banal* speakers show a great deal of originality? YES NO
6. Is *verbosity* an admirable quality? YES NO
7. Is it easy to be *voluble* when you don't know the subject you are talking about? YES NO
8. Do unintelligent people usually make *cogent* statements? YES NO
9. Is a *vociferous* demand ordinarily made by a shy, quiet person? YES NO
10. Do women have a greater reputation for *loquacity* than men? YES NO

KEY: 1—no, 2—no, 3—yes, 4—no, 5—no, 6—no, 7—no, 8—no, 9—no, 10—yes

---

Can you recall the words?

Do you know that new nerve patterns are formed by repeated actions? As a child, you laced your shoes with great concentration—the activity was directed, controlled, purposive, and, at the beginning, quite exciting. As you grew older and more skillful, you laced your shoes with scarcely a thought of what you were doing. Your fingers flew about their task almost automatically—for the habit had formed a nerve pattern and the action needed little if any conscious attention.

That's simple enough to understand. If you do not remember your own experiences with shoe lacing, you can observe the phenomenon of struggling with a skill, mastering it, and finally making it a self-starting habit, by watching any child, preferably your own, between the ages of two and five. Or you can simply take my word for it.

You need not take my word for the way a mastery of new words is acquired. You can see in yourself, as you work with this book, how adding words to your vocabulary is exactly analogous to a child's mastery of shoe lacing. First you struggle with the concepts; then you eventually master them; finally, by frequent work with the new words (now you see the reason for the great number of exercises, the repetitious writing, saying, thinking) you build up new nerve patterns and you begin to use the new words with scarcely any consciousness of what you are doing.

Watch this common but important phenomenon closely as you do the next exercise. I contend that your total absorption of the material in this chapter has given you complete mastery of our ten basic words. Prove that you are beginning to form new nerve patterns in relation to these words by writing the one which fits each brief definition. The quicker you think of the word that applies and the higher your score, the surer you can be that using these words will soon be as automatic and unselfconscious as putting on your shoes in the morning.

1. talkative   1. _loquacious_

2. noisily talkative   2. _vociferous_

3. forming words and sentences
   incoherently   3. _inarticulate_

4. gabbing ceaselessly and with little meaning   4. _garrulous_

5. disinclined to talk   5. _taciturn_

6. talking in hackneyed phraseology   6. _banal_

7. showing a fine economy in the use of words   7. _laconic_

8. forceful and convincing   8. ~~_voluble_~~ _cogent_

9. talking rapidly and fluently   9. _voluble_

10. using more words than necessary   10. _verbose_

KEY: 1—loquacious, 2—vociferous, 3—inarticulate, 4—garrulous, 5—taciturn, 6—banal, 7—laconic, 8—cogent, 9—voluble, 10—verbose

---

ORIGINS AND RELATED WORDS

1. about keeping one's mouth shut

If you let your mind play over some of the *taciturn* people you know, you will realize that their abnormal disinclination to conversation makes them seem morose, sullen, and unfriendly. Cal Coolidge's *taciturnity* was world famous, and no one, I am sure, ever conceived of him as cheerful, over-friendly, or particularly sociable. There are doubtless many possible causes of such verbal rejection of the world: perhaps lack of self-assurance, feelings of inadequacy or hostility, excessive seriousness or introspection, or just plain having nothing to say. Maybe, in Coolidge's case, he was saving up his words—after he did not "choose to run" in 1928, he wrote a daily column for the *New York Herald Tribune* at a rumored price of two dollars a word—and, according to most critics (probably all Democrats), he had seemed wiser when he had kept silent. Coolidge hailed from New England, and *taciturnity* in that part of the country is considered a virtue. Who knows, the cause may be geographical and climatic, rather than psychological.

Taciturn is from a Latin verb *taceo, to be silent,* and is one of those words whose full meaning cannot be expressed by any other combination of syllables. It has many synonyms, among them *silent, uncommunicative, reticent, reserved, secretive, close-lipped,* and *close-mouthed;* but no other word indicates the *permanent, habitual,* and *temperamental* disinclination to talk implied by *taciturn.* In short, we have here a valuable and unique word which no literate citizen can get along without.

2. better left unsaid

Equally valuable and equally unique is another word derived from *taceo, be silent,* namely *tacit.*

Here is a man dying of cancer. He suspects what his disease is, and everyone else, of course, knows. Yet he never mentions the dread word, and no one who visits him ever breathes a syllable of it in his hearing. It is *tacitly* understood by all concerned that the word will remain forever unspoken.

Consider another situation:

An executive is engaging in extracurricular activities with his young and pretty secretary. Yet during office time they are as formal and distant as any two human beings can well be. Neither of them ever said to the other, "Now, look here, we may be lovers after five o'clock, but between nine and five we must preserve the utmost decorum. O.K.?" Such speech, such a verbal arrangement, is considered unnecessary—so we may say that the boss and his mistress have a *tacit* agreement (i.e., nothing was ever actually *said)* to maintain a complete employer-employee relationship during office hours.

Anything *tacit,* then, is *unspoken, unsaid, not verbalized.* We speak of a *tacit agreement, arrangement, acceptance, rejection, assent, refusal,* et cetera. A *person* may never be called *tacit.*

3. talk, talk, talk!

Garrulous, verbose, voluble and *loquacious* people are all talkative; but each type, you will recall, has a special quality. Working backward *loquacity* is the most neutral of the conditions: when you speak of "female *loquacity*" you imply that women wag their tongues more than men do. *Volubility* includes fluency and *rapidity* of speech, as well as great quantity; *verbosity* implies such an overabundance of words as to cause confusion and dullness. (A *loquacious* person may talk a lot because he has a lot to say—a *verbose* person smothers his ideas with words.) And *garrulity* implies constant talking, usually aimless and meaningless, about trifles. Often you hear the expression "A *garrulous* old man" or "A *garrulous* old woman," since in advanced age the mind may wander and lose the ability to discriminate between the important and the unimportant, between the interesting and the dull.

Garrulous is from a Latin verb *to chatter;* a *garrulous* person reminds you of a chattering monkey. *Verbose* is from the Latin *verbum, word,* from which useful root we also derive *verbal, using words; verbatim, quoted word-by-word;* the grammatical term *verb;* and *verborrhea,* a word formed on analogy to *diarrhea,* and obviously meaning an incessant, overwhelming cascade of words. *Voluble* is from Latin *volvere, to roll;* in *volubility* the words just roll out, apparently without effort. *Revolve,* to roll *around,* comes from the same root.

And *loquacious* comes from Latin *loquor, to speak.* Eloquent, *speaking expressively,* is the most common word containing this root, but mention should also be made at this point of two less common derivatives, *grandiloquent* and *magniloquent,* which are virtually identical in meaning. The *grandiloquent* or *magniloquent* person uses lofty, pompous, overelegant phraseology; his *home* is his *residence,* his *wife* is his *helpmate,* his *children* are *offspring,* in short his speech is always togged out in a full-dress suit or evening gown, and as a result he usually sounds absurd.

Loquor, to speak, has also given us the words *soliloquy, ventriloquist, colloquial,* and *circumlocution.*

1. A *soliloquy* is a speech made to oneself. We often talk to ourselves, but usually silently, the words going through our minds but not actually passing our lips. A *soliloquy* is the utterance of this speech, not to some listener, but to ourselves. The letters *soli* in *soliloquy* come from the Latin word for *alone;* the same root is found in *solitude, solitary, solo,* et cetera.

2. A *ventriloquist* is one who can throw his voice, so that a listener thinks it is coming from some source other than the *ventriloquist's* lips. (The *ventri* is from the Latin word for

192

stomach, and is found also in *ventral,* an adjective referring to the front or stomach side of an animal or person. *Ventral* is contrasted to *dorsal,* which refers to the back of an animal or person). A *ventriloquist* acts as if he is speaking from his stomach, rather than from his mouth. The art is *ventriloquism.*

3. *Colloquial* combines *loquor, to speak,* with *con, together.* When people speak together they are engaging in conversation—and their language is usually more informal and less rigidly grammatical than what you might expect in writing or in public addresses. *Colloquial* patterns are perfectly correct—they are simply informal, and suitable to everyday conversation. A *colloquialism,* therefore, is a *conversational-style* expression, like "He hasn't got any" or "Who are you going with?" as contrasted to the formal or literary style, namely, "He has none" or "With whom are you going?" *Colloquial* English is the English you and I talk on everyday occasions—it is not slangy, vulgar, or illiterate.

4. A *circumlocution* is, etymologically, a *talking-around.* Any way of expressing an idea that is roundabout or indirect is *circumlocution.*

To keep our roots straight, let us look at them once again.

Garrulous is the Latin for *chattering—a garrulous* person chatters meaninglessly.

Verbum is the Latin for *word—a verbose* person uses more words than necessary.

Volvo is the Latin for *roll—a voluble* person is one out of whose mouth speech seems to roll off effortlessly, rapidly, fluently.

Loquor is the Latin for *talk—a loquacious* person is full of talk.

That's all there is to it.

4. a Spartan virtue

In ancient Sparta, which was originally known as *Laconia,* the citizens were long-suffering, hard-bitten, stoical, and military minded, and were even more noted for their economy of speech than Vermonters, if that is possible. Legend has it that when Philip of Macedonia was storming the gates of Sparta (or Laconia), he sent a message to the besieged king saying, "If we capture your city we will burn it to the ground." A one-word answer came back: "If." It was now probably Philip's turn to be speechless, though history does not record his reaction.

It is from the name *Laconia* that we derive our word *laconic*—and bear in mind that it is a highly complimentary term, showing our admiration for anyone who can deliver so much punch in so few words.

Like the man who was waiting at a lunch counter for a ham sandwich. When it was ready the clerk inquired politely, "Will you have it here, or take it with you?"

"Both," was the *laconic* reply.

Or like the man who was watching the lush imbibing dry martinis at a Third Avenue bar. The drunk downed the contents of his cocktail glass at one gulp, then daintily nibbled and swallowed the bowl, finally turned the glass over and ate the base. The stem he threw into a corner. This amazing gustatory feat went on for half an hour, until a dozen stems were lying shattered in the corner, and the drunk had chewed and swallowed enough bowls and bases to start a glass factory. Then he turned to our friend and asked belligerently, "I suppose you think I'm cuckoo, don't you?" "Sure—the stem is the best part," was the *laconic* answer.

I think you see the full implication of the word, and realize that no other word in the whole language would serve quite as well.

5. hardly short of brilliant

Cogent, like *laconic*, is a term of admiration. A *cogent* argument is well-put, convincing, hardly short of brilliant. *Cogency* shows a keen mind, an ability to think clearly and logically. *Cogent* derives from a Latin verb *cogere, to drive together, compel, force.* A *cogent* remark compels acceptance because of its sense and logic.

6. the noise and the fury

Like all the other words in this chapter, *vociferous* also derives from the Latin; it uses a stem *voc, voice,* which you have met before (in *equivocal*) plus a root *fer, to bear.* A *vociferous* rejoinder bears a lot of voice—i.e., it is vehement, loud, noisy, clamorous, shouting. The noun is *vociferousness.*

7. to sleep or not to sleep

The root *fer, to bear,* is found also in *somniferous, bearing sleep.* (*soporific,* from another Latin root for *sleep,* has the same meaning.) So a *somniferous* or *soporific* lecture is so dull and boring that it is sleep-inducing If we work from the other root in *somniferous, somnus, sleep,* we will turn up three interesting new words, to wit:

insomnia—inability to fall asleep
somnolent—sleepy, drowsy
somnambulism—sleepwalking

8. a walkaway

In *insomnia* we find the negative prefix *in;* in *somnambulism* we find the root *ambul, to walk.* An *ambulatory* hospital case is one that can walk around; to *amble* is *to walk aimlessly;* an *ambulance* is so called because originally it was composed of two stretcher bearers who *walked* off the battle field with a wounded soldier; and a *perambulator* is a carriage in which Daddy takes the baby for a *walk.*

So many of our English words come from Latin that it is particularly fruitful, as you can see, to start anywhere and work with a root to learn new words in wholesale quantities. *Vociferous* takes us to *somniferous;* the latter in turn leads us to other words referring to sleep, finally pointing to *somnambulism;* which in turn opens up for us all words containing *ambul, to walk.*

It is perfectly possible, by this means, to keep going almost endlessly, wandering along any etymological road which may beckon, and never quite knowing where we'll arrive. This much, however, we do know: each such road will carry us along to a bigger and bigger vocabulary.

USING THE WORDS: II

Working from our basic words we have discovered twenty-nine others, all of them related in meaning or derivation. Note that our etymological explorations have acquainted us with the following roots:

1. *taceo, be silent*
    taciturnity—disinclination to engage in conversation
    tacit—unspoken
2. *volvo—to roll*
    volubility—rapidity and fluency of speech, words rolling off one's tongue.
3. *loquor, to talk*
    loquacious—full of talk
    soliloquize—talk alone, to oneself
    ventriloquist—one who talks as if from his stomach
    grandiloquent or *magniloquent*—talking in high-sounding words
4. *verbum, word*
    verbosity—wordiness
    verbatim—quoted word for word
5. *fer, to bear*
    vociferousness—a bearing of loud voice
    somniferous—bearing sleep
    (*soporific* has the same meaning)
6. *somnus, sleep*
    somnolent—sleepy
    insomnia—inability to fall asleep
    insomniac—one who is habitually unable to fall asleep
    somnambulism—sleepwalking
7. *ambulo, walk*
    ambulatory—walking
    perambulator—baby carriage

I submit that a realization of the meaning of the etymological parts of a word makes that word easy to understand, simple to remember. To prove to yourself that learning words through their etymology is as quick and easy as I say, try the next few tests.

Can you pronounce the words?

1.	*taciturnity*	tass-i-TURN-i-tee
2.	*tacit*	TASS-it
3.	*loquacity*	lo-KWASS-i-tee
°4.	*garrulity*	ga-ROOL-i-tee
°5.	*volubility*	vol-yoo-BILL-i-tee
°6.	*verbosity*	ver-BOSS-i-tee

*7. *verbatim*	ver-BAY-tim
8. *verborrhea*	ver-bo-REE-a
*9. *grandiloquent*	gran-DILL-o-kwent
*10. *magniloquent*	mag-NILL-o-kwent
*11. *soliloquy*	so-LILL-o-kwee
12. *soliloquize*	so-LILL-o-kwyze
13. *ventriloquist*	ven-TRILL-o-kwist
14. *ventriloquism*	ven-TRILL-o-kwizm
15. *ventral*	VEN-tr'l
16. *dorsal*	DOR-s'l
*17. *colloquial*	ko-LO-kwee-il
*18. *colloquialism*	ko-LO-kwee-a-lizm
19. *circumlocution*	sur-kum-lo-KYOO-shun
*20. *cogency*	KO-jen-see
21. *vociferousness*	vo-SIFF-er-us-ness
*22. *somniferous*	som-NIFF-er-us
*23. *soporific*	sop-er-IFF-ik
24. *insomnia*	in-SOM-nee-a
25. *insomniac*	in-SOM-nee-ak
*26. *somnolent*	SOM-no-lent
27. *somnambulism*	som-NAM-byoo-lizm
28. *ambulatory*	AM-byoo-la-tore-ee
29. *perambulator*	per-AM-byoo-lay-ter

Do you understand the words?

1. *Taciturnity* is a mark of cheerfulness. — TRUE — **FALSE**
2. A *tacit* agreement is put into words. — TRUE — **FALSE**
3. *Loquacity* is a characteristic of the *laconic* person. — TRUE — **FALSE**
4. *Garrulity* makes a man interesting. — TRUE — **FALSE**
5. *Volubility* usually accompanies inarticulateness. — TRUE — **FALSE**
6. *Verbosity* shows an accurate vocabulary. — TRUE — **FALSE**
7. A *verbatim* report makes a general summary. — TRUE — **FALSE**
8. Quiet people usually suffer from *verborrhea*. — TRUE — **FALSE**
9. A *grandiloquent* (or *magniloquent*) style prefers short, simple words. — TRUE — **FALSE**
10. *Cogency* is the mark of a confused speaker. — TRUE — **FALSE**
11. *Vociferousness* marks the shy person. — TRUE — **FALSE**

197

12. Coffee is generally *somniferous*.	TRUE	FALSE
13. *Insomnia* is a pleasant condition.	TRUE	FALSE
14. When you feel *somnolent* you are wide awake.	TRUE	FALSE
15. An *ambulatory* patient is bed-ridden.	TRUE	FALSE
16. A *soliloquy* is a speech to oneself.	TRUE	FALSE
17. A fish's *dorsal* fin is located on the back, a *ventral* fin on the front.	TRUE	FALSE
18. *Colloquial* English is correct for everyday usage.	TRUE	FALSE
19. *Circumlocution* is an indirect way of expressing an idea.	TRUE	FALSE

KEY: 1–15 are false; 16–19 are true

Can you work with the words? (I)

Match words and meanings.

1. taciturnity	a. talkativeness
2. tacit	b. quoted word for word
3. loquacity	c. clamorous talk
4. verbosity	d. high-flown, pompous speech
5. verbatim	e. inability to sleep
6. grandiloquence	f. drowsiness
7. cogency	g. disinclination to talking
8. vociferousness	h. sleep-inducing
9. somniferous	i. wordiness
10. insomnia	j. sleepwalking
11. somnolence	k. forceful talk
12. somnambulism	l. unspoken

KEY: 1–g, 2–l, 3–a, 4–i, 5–b, 6–d, 7–k, 8–c, 9–h, 10–e, 11–.
12–j

Can you work with the words (II)

1. volubility	a. speech to oneself
2. verborrhea	b. expression suitable to conversation
3. magniloquence	c. excessive flow of words

4. soliloquy	d. pertaining to the front or stomach
5. ventriloquism	e. unimaginative way of talking
6. colloquialism	f. roundabout way of talking
7. circumlocution	g. great amount of meaningless talk
8. ventral	h. elegance in talk
9. dorsal	i. pertaining to the back
10. garrulity	j. incoherence
11. banality	k. throwing of one's voice
12. inarticulateness	l. fluency
13. soporific	m. sleep-inducing

KEY: 1—l, 2—c, 3—h, 4—a, 5—k, 6—b, 7—f, 8—d, 9—i, 10—g, 11—e, 12—j, 13—m

Can you recall the words?

1. disinclination to conversation	1. T_aciturnity_
2. unspoken	2. T_acit_
3. talkativeness	3. L_oquacity_
4. incessant chattering	4. G_arrulity_
5. fluency	5. V_olubility_
6. wordiness	6. V_erbosity_
7. word for word	7. V_erbatim_
8. excessive word flow	8. V_erborrhea_
9. describing elegant speech (two words)	9. G_randiloquence_ M_agniloquence_
10. to speak to oneself	10. S_oliloquize_
11. one who can throw his voice	11. V_entriloquist_
12. pertaining to the back	12. D_orsal_
13. pertaining to the stomach	13. V_entral_
14. suitable for everyday conversation	14. C_olloquial_

199

15. a roundabout way of talking

16. forcefulness of logic in speech

17. noisily talkative

18. sleep-inducing (two words)

19. inability to fall asleep

20. sleepy

21. sleepwalking

22. able to walk

23. baby carriage

24. incoherence

25. hackneyed phraseology

15. C*ircumlocution*

16. C*ogency*

17. V*ociferous*

18. S*oporific*
    s*omniferous*

19. I*nsomnia*

20. S*omnolent*

21. S*omnambulism*

22. A*mbulatory*

23. P*erambulator*

24. I*narticulateness*

25. B*anality*

KEY: 1—taciturnity, 2—tacit, 3—loquacity, 4—garrulity, 5—volubility, 6—verbosity, 7—verbatim, 8—verborrhea, 9—grandiloquence, magniloquence, 10—soliloquize, 11—ventriloquist, 12—dorsal, 13—ventral, 14—colloquial, 15—circumlocution, 16—cogency, 17—vociferous, 18—somniferous, soporific, 19—insomnia, 20—somnolent, 21—somnambulism, 22—ambulatory, 23—perambulator, 24—inarticulateness, 25—banality

---

CHAPTER REVIEW

Do you recognize the words?

Check the word which most closely fits each definition.

1. Disinclined to conversation:
    (a) loquacious, (b) laconic, (c) taciturn
2. Trite:
    (a) inarticulate, (b) banal, (c) verbose
3. Rapid and fluent:
    (a) voluble, (b) verbose, (c) garrulous
4. Forceful and compelling:
    (a) vociferous, (b) cogent, (c) laconic

5. Unspoken:
     (a) verbatim, (b) eloquent, (c) tacit
6. Using elegant and impressive words:
     (a) verbose, (b) grandiloquent, (c) colloquial
7. Back:
     (a) dorsal, (b) ventral, (c) somniferous
8. Sleep-inducing:
     (a) soporific, (b) somnolent, (c) ventral
9. Inability to fall asleep:
     (a) somnambulism, (b) ambulatory, (c) insomnia

KEY: 1—c, 2—b, 3—a, 4—b, 5—c, 6—b, 7—a, 8—a, 9—c

BECOMING ALERT TO NEW IDEAS

Some chapters back I suggested that since words are symbols of ideas, one of the most effective means of building your vocabulary is to read books that deal with new ideas. Along that line, I further suggested that the fields of psychology, psychiatry, and psychoanalysis would be good starting points, and I mentioned nine exciting books to work with.

Needless to say, you will not wish to neglect other fields, and so I want to recommend, at this point, highly readable books in other subjects. All these books will increase your familiarity with the world of ideas—all of them, therefore, will help you build a superior vocabulary.

I. *Semantics*
  1. *Language in Action,* by S. I. Hayakawa (Harcourt, Brace).
  2. *People in Quandaries,* by Wendell Johnson (Harper & Brothers).
  3. *The Tyranny of Words,* by Stuart Chase (Harcourt, Brace).
  4. *Folklore of Capitalism,* by Thurman Arnold (Yale University).

II. *Conservation*
  1. *Our Plundered Planet,* by Fairfield Osborn (Little, Brown).

2. *Road to Survival,* by William Vogt (William Sloane Associates).

III. *History*

1. *Only Yesterday,* by Frederick Lewis Allen (Harper & Brothers).

2. *Fantastic Interim,* by Henry Morton Robinson (Harcourt, Brace).

3. *Since Yesterday,* by Frederick Lewis Allen (Harper & Brothers).

4. *They Also Ran,* by Irving Stone (Doubleday).

IV. *Science*

1. *Treasury of Science,* edited by Harlow Shapley (Harper & Brothers).

2. *Mankind So Far,* by William W. Howells (Doubleday).

3. *You and Heredity,* by Amram Scheinfeld (Lippincott).

4. *Women and Men,* by Amram Scheinfeld (Harcourt, Brace).

5. *The Human Body,* by Logan Clendening (Knopf).

V. *Art*

The Arts, by H. W. Van Loon (Simon and Schuster).

These sixteen books, together with the nine previously recommended, will give you practically a liberal education. They will introduce you to ideas that no alert adult can well afford to be ignorant of. And, of course, they will add immeasurably to your vocabulary and verbal power.

BRIEF INTERMISSION EIGHT:
HOW GOOD
IS YOUR PRONUNCIATION?

Do you go around correcting other people's pronunciation? And are you always sure you know what you're talking about when you brashly tell someone: "That's not the way to say it!"?

Here's a chance to find out—in ten minutes or less—whether you knowledge of *OR-tho-e-py* (the art of pronouncing words correctly) is as good as you think it is.

TEST I

Your speech meets an accepted standard of literacy if you can check the correct form of at least *nine* of the following words:

1. (a) RAD-ee-ay-ter or (b) RAY-dee-ay-ter? (*radiator*)
2. (a) MOD-ren or (b) MOD-urn? (*modern*)
3. (a) LYE-brerry or (b) LYE-berry? (*library*)
4. (a) MISS-chi-vuss or (b) miss-CHEE-vee-us? (*mischievous*)
5. (a) ath-LET-ic or (b) ath-a-LET-ic? (*athletic*)
6. (a) FILL-um or (b) FILM? (*film*)
7. (a) JEN-yoo-wyne or (b) JEN-yoo-win? (*genuine*)
8. (a) pre-FER-able or (b) PREFF-er-able? (*preferable*)
9. (a) LENTH or (b) LENGGTH? (*length*)
10. (a) IN-trik-a-see or (b) in-TRIK-a-see? (*intricacy*)

TEST II

Your speech is on the college-graduate level if you can check the correct pronunciation of at least *seven* of the following words:

1. (a) gri-MAYCE or (b) GRIMM-iss? (*grimace*)
2. (a) IM-pee-us or (b) im-PYE-us? (*impious*)

3. (a) SEEK-re-tive or (b) se-KREE-tiv? (*secretive*)
4. (a) nah-eev-TAY or (b) NAY-ve-tee? (*naïveté*)
5. (a) YOO-min- or (b) HYOO-min? (*human*)
6. (a) RO-bust or (b) ro-BUST? (*robust*)
7. (a) HOSS-pit-ab'l or (b) hos-SPIT-ab'l? (*hospitable*)
8. (a) press-TEEDGE or (b) press-TEEZH? (*prestige*) (ZH like the S in *pleasure*)
9. (a) ver-BAY-tim or (b) ver-BAT-im? (*verbatim*)
10. (a) OR-gee (*g* as in *girl*) or (b) OR-jee? (*orgy*)

TEST III

You are a veritable expert in orthoepy if you can check the correct pronunciation of at least *five* of the following words—and you are perfectly normal if you flunk every one of them, for these are "catch" words that are frequently mispronounced.

1. (a) AIR, (b) ERR, or (c) URR (*err*)
2. (a) diff-THEER-ee-a or (b) dipp-THEER-ee-a? (*diphtheria*)
3. (a) FYE-niss, or (b) FINN-iss, or (c) fee-NEE? (*finis*)
4. (a) DIRR-i-jib'l, or (b) DERR-i-jib'l, or (c) di-RIDGE-ib'l? (*dirigible*)
5. (a) vi-RAH-go, (b) vi-RAY-go, or (c) VIRR-a-go? (*virago*)
6. (a) repp-er-tee or (b) ray-par-TAY? (*repartee*)
7. (a) ig-NOM-in-ee or (b) IG-no-min-ee? (*ignominy*)
8. (a) SER-e-bral or (b) se-REE-bral? (*cerebral*)
9. (a) gon-DOAL-a or (b) GON-do-la? (*gondola*)
10. (a) diss-a-BEEL or (b) DISH-a-bill? (*dishabille*)

KEY:
  Test I: 1—b, 2—b, 3—a, 4—a, 5—a, 6—b, 7—b, 8—b, 9—b, 10—a
  Test II: 1—a, 2—a, 3—b, 4—a, 5—b, 6—b, 7—a, 8—b, 9—a, 10—b
  Test III: 1—c, 2—a, 3—a, 4—a, 5—b, 6—a, 7—b, 8—a, 9—b, 10—a

---

(Syllabication is not exact, and is intended only to indicate approximate sounds.)

11

HOW TO INSULT
YOUR ENEMIES

—— TEASER PREVIEW ——————

What do you call a person who:

- *insists on complete and blind obedience?*
- *bootlicks the rich and influential?*
- *dabbles at the fine arts?*
- *is a loud-mouthed, quarrelsome woman?*
- *has a one-track mind?*
- *sneers at other people's cherished traditions?*
- *does not believe in God?*
- *commits acts of gross lewdness?*
- *has imaginary ailments?*

THE PHENOMENAL sales of Dale Carnegie's *How to Win Friends and Influence People* attest to the human enough desire, the almost universal need, to keep on friendly terms with the world. A serious book which presented the other side of the coin, and which might be titled *How to Lose Friends and Insult Your Enemies* would, to begin with, stand little chance of achieving the dignity of print, and, if published, would likely sell only to the author's most devoted (and most prosperous) friends.

Psychoanalysis bolsters Carnegie's conviction that we all want to make friends, but it also points out in no equivocal terms the necessity for expressing, rather than repressing, our hostilities—that is, if we wish to preserve our mental health and not eventually have to seek psychotherapy.

You can express your hostility in many ways, but the most satisfying and least harmful is to do so in words And in this chapter we shall consider some of the epithets you can hurl at your enemies.

IDEAS

1. slave driver

He makes you toe the mark—right down to the last centimeter. He exacts blind, unquestioning, obedience; demands the strictest conformity to rules, however arbitrary or tyrannical; and will not tolerate the slightest deviation from his orders. He is, in short, the epitome of the army top sergeant.

He is a *martinet.*

2. bootlicker

He toadies to rich or influential people, catering to their vanity, flattering their ego. He's the personification of the traditional ward heeler, he out-yesses the Hollywood yes-men. And on top of all these unpleasant characteristics, he's a complete hypocrite. All his servile attentions and unceasing adulation spring from his own selfish desires to get ahead, not out of any sincere admiration. He cultivates people of power or property so that he can curry favor at the opportune moment.

He's a *sycophant.*

3. dabbler

Often, though not necessarily, a person of independent income, he engages superficially in the pursuit of one of the fine arts—painting, writing, sculpturing, composing, et cetera. He does this largely for his own amusement and not to achieve any professional competence; nor is he at all interested in monetary rewards. For him, it is simply a means of passing time pleasantly.

He's a *dilettante.*

4. battle-ax

She's a loud-mouthed, shrewish, turbulent woman; she's quarrelsome and aggressive, possessing none of those gentle and delicate virtues we like to associate with femininity. Watch out when she's around, brother—she's strong-minded, unyielding, sharp-tongued, and dangerous. She'll curse like a stevedore and yell like a fishwife—and if you're the butt of her anger, nothing on earth can help you.

She's a *virago*.

5. superpatriot

Anything he owns or belongs to is better—simply because he owns it or belongs to it, although he will be quick to find more justifiable explanations. His religion, whatever it may be, is far superior to any other; his political party is the only honest one; his neighborhood puts all others in the city in the shade; his wife is the best cook in Christendom; the kind of car he runs is faster, smoother, more economical, and more beautiful than any other, no matter in what price range; and of course his country and its customs leave nothing to be desired, and inhabitants of other nations are in comparison barely civilized. In short, he is exaggeratedly, aggressively, absurdly, and excessively devoted to his own affiliations—and makes no bones about advertising such devotion.

He's a *chauvinist*.

6. fanatic

He has a one-track mind—and when he's riding a particular hobby, he rides it hard. He has such an exaggerated, all-inclusive zeal for one thing (and it may be his business, his profession, his wife, his children, his stomach, money, photography, or whatever) that it amounts almost to insanity. He talks, eats, sleeps, that one thing—to the point where he bores everyone to distraction.

He's a *monomaniac*.

7. attacker

He's violently against established beliefs, revered traditions, cherished customs—such, says he, stand in the way of reform and progress and are always based on superstition and irrationality. Religion, family, marriage, ethics—he wasn't there when these were started and by God he's not going to conform simply because most unthinking people do.

He's an *iconoclast*.

8. skeptic

There is no God—that's his position and you're not going to budge him from it.

> He's an *atheist*.

9. self-indulger

He's lascivious, libidinous, lustful, lewd, wanton, immoral—but more important, he habitually indulges his sexual lust and no woman is safe within his arm's reach.

> He's a *lecher*.

10. worrier

He is always sick, though no doctor can find an organic cause for his ailments. He knows he has ulcers, though medical tests show a healthy stomach. He has heart palpitations, but a cardiogram fails to show any abnormality. His headaches are caused (he's sure of it) by a rapidly growing brain tumor—yet X rays show nothing wrong. Do not think that these maladies are imaginary, however; to him they are most real, nonexistent as they may be in fact And as he travels from doctor to doctor futilely seeking confirmation of his imminent death, he becomes more and more convinced that he's too weak to go on much longer.

Physically, of course, there's nothing the matter with him. But psychically he is indeed a very sick man. His mental tenseness, insecurities, and frustrations are simply taking the form of simulated bodily ills.

> He's a *hypochondriac*.

USING THE WORDS: I

Can you pronounce the words?

In this chapter we have got into real pronunciation demons —so watch your step every inch of the way. These are top-drawer words, all of them; you will shortly be thinking with them and using them in conversation and writing—so make sure you can say them correctly.

1. *martinet*   mahr-ti-NETT
*2. *sycophant*   SICK-o-fint
*3. *dilettante*   dill-e-TAN-tee
*4. *virago*   vi-RAY-go
*5. *chauvinist*   SHO-vi-nist
6. *monomaniac*   mon-o-MAY-nee-ak
7. *iconoclast*   eye-KON-o-klast
8. *atheist*   AY-thee-ist
*9. *lecher*   LETCH-er
*10. *hypochondriac*   hye-po-KON-dree-ak

Can you work with the words?

Now for a quick once-over before we dig deeper into the meanings and origins of the new words in this chapter. Can you, with little or no hesitation, match the words in the first column to the key ideas in the second column? With the ever-growing background you now have you should, if your learning has been successful, complete this exercise in no more than ninety seconds, and with a perfect score. Can you do it?

WORDS	KEY IDEAS
1. martinet	a. superficiality
2. sycophant	b. patriotism
3. dilettante	c. godlessness
4. virago	d. single-mindedness
5. chauvinist	e. antitradition
6. monomaniac	f. sex
7. iconoclast	g. illness
8. atheist	h. discipline
9. lecher	i. turbulence
10. hypochondriac	j. flattery

1-h, 2-j, 3-a, 4-i, 5-b, 6-d, 7-e, 8-c, 9-f, 10-g

KEY: 1—h, 2—j, 3—a, 4—i, 5—b, 6—d, 7—e, 8—c, 9—f, 10—g

Do you understand the words?

React quickly to each question.

1. Does a *martinet* condone carelessness and neglect of duty?   YES   NO

2. Is a *sycophant* a sincere person?   YES   (NO)
3. Is a *dilettante* a hard worker?   YES   (NO)
4. Is a *virago* sweet and gentle?   YES   (NO)
5. Is a *chauvinist* modest and self-effacing?   YES   (NO)
6. Does a *monomaniac* have a one-track mind?   (YES)   NO
7. Does an *iconoclast* scoff at tradition?   (YES)   NO
8. Does an *atheist* believe in God?   YES   (NO)
9. Is a *lecher* misogynous?   YES   (NO)
10. Does a *hypochondriac* have a lively imagination?   (YES)   NO

KEY: 1—no, 2—no, 3—no, 4—no, 5—no, 6—yes, 7—yes, 8—no, 9—no, 10—yes

---

Can you recall the words?

Write the word that fits each brief definition.

1. A person whose emotional disorder is reflected in nonorganic or imaginary bodily ailments.   1. H*ypochondriac*

2. A strict disciplinarian   2. M*artinet*

3. A lewd and sexually aggressive person   3. L*echer*

4. A toady to people of wealth or power   4. S*ycophant*

5. A disbeliever in God   5. A*theist*

6. A dabbler in the arts   6. D*ilettante*

7. A shrewish, loud-mouthed female   7. V*irago*

8. A scoffer at tradition   8. I*conoclast*

9. Person with a one-track mind   9. M*onomaniac*

10. A blatant superpatriot   10. C*hauvinist*

KEY: 1—hypochondriac, 2—martinet, 3—lecher, 4—sycophant, 5—atheist, 6—dilettante, 7—virago, 8—iconoclast, 9—monomaniac, 10—chauvinist

Can you use the words?

If one of your friends (or enemies) reacted in each of the following ways, what would you call him?

1. He scoffs at beliefs you have always held dear.

1. _iconoclast_

2. You know he's hale and hearty—but he constantly complains of his illness.

2. _hypochondriac_

3. He insists his political affiliations are superior to yours.

3. _chauvinist_

4. He insists on his subordinates toeing the mark.

4. _martinet_

5. He makes sexual advances to everyone else's wife—and is too often successful.

5. _lecher_

6. He cultivates friends that can do him good—financially.

6. _sycophant_

7. He dabbles with water colors.

7. _dilettante_

8. He insists there is no Deity.

8. _atheist_

9. She's a shrew, a harridan, a scold, and a nag.

9. _virago_

10. His only interest in life is his fish-collection—and he is fanatically, almost psychotically, devoted to it.

10. _monomaniac_

KEY: 1—iconoclast, 2—hypochondriac, 3—chauvinist, 4—martinet, 5—lecher, 6—sycophant, 7—dilettante, 8—atheist, 9—virago, 10—monomaniac

---

ORIGINS AND RELATED WORDS: I

1. the French drillmaster

Jean Martinet was the Inspector-General of Infantry during the reign of King Louis XIV—and a stricter, more fanatic

211

drillmaster France had never seen. It was from this time that the French Army's reputation for discipline dates (a reputation somewhat tarnished since 1940, alas), and it is from the name of this Frenchman that we derive our English word *martinet*. The word is always used in a derogatory sense and generally shows resentment and anger on the part of the user. The secretary who calls her boss a *martinet*, the wife who applies the epithet to her husband, the worker who thus refers to his foreman—these speakers all show their contempt for the excessive, inhuman discipline to which they are asked to submit.

Since *martinet* comes from a man's name (in the Brief Intermission which follows we shall discover that a number of picturesque English words are similarly derived), there are no related forms built on the same root. There is an adjective *martinetish* and another noun form, *martinetism*, but these are used only rarely.

2. a Greek "fig-shower"

Sycophant comes to us from the Greeks. According to Shipley's Dictionary of Word Origins:

> "When a fellow wants to get a good mark, he may polish up an apple and place it on teacher's desk; his classmates call such a lad an apple-shiner. Less complimentary localities use the term bootlicker. The Greeks had a name for it: *fig-shower*. Sycophant is from Gr. *sykon, fig, phanein, to show*. This was the fellow that informed the officers in charge when (1) the figs in the sacred groves were being taken, or (2) when the Smyrna fig-dealers were dodging the tariff."

Thus, a *sycophant* may appear to be a sort of "stool pigeon," since the latter curries the favor of police officials by "peaching" on his fellow criminals. The *sycophant* may use this means of ingratiating himself with influential citizens of the community; or he may use flattery, servile attentions, or any other form of insinuating himself in someone's good graces. A *sycophant* practices *sycophancy*, and has a *sycophantic* attitude. All three forms of the word are highly uncomplimentary—use them with care.

Material may be so delicate or fine in texture that anything behind it will show through. The Greek prefix *dia* means *through;* and *phanein,* as we now know, means *to show*—hence such material is called *diaphanous.* Do not use the adjective in reference to all material that is transparent (for example, you would not call glass *diaphanous,* even though you can see right through it), but only material which is silky, gauzy, filmy, and, in addition, transparent or practically transparent. The word is often applied to female garments—nightgowns, negligees, et cetera.

3. just for his own amusement

Dilettante is from the Italian verb *dilettare,* to *delight.* The *dilettante* paints, writes, composes, plays a musical instrument, or engages in scientific experiments purely for his own delight or amusement—never to develop his ability, make money, become famous, or to satisfy a deep creative urge (the latter, I presume, being the more normal justifications for the time that professional artists, writers, composers, musicians, poets, and scientists spend at their chosen work). A *dilettantish* attitude is superficial, unprofessional; *dilettantism* is superficial part-time dabbling in the type of activity which usually engages the full time and energy of the true artist or scientist.

Do not confuse the *dilettante,* who has a certain amount of native talent or ability, with the *tyro,* who is the inexperienced beginner in some art, but who may be full of ambition, drive, and energy. To call a man a *tyro* is to imply that he is just starting in some artistic or scientific field—he's not much good yet because he has not had time to develop his skill, if any. The *dilettante* usually has some skill but isn't doing much with it. On the other hand, anyone who has developed consummate skill in an artistic field, generally allied to music, is called a *virtuoso*—like Heifetz or Menuhin on the violin, Horowitz on the piano, Adler on the harmonica. Pluralize *virtuoso* in the normal way—*virtuosos;* or if you wish to sound more elegant, give it the continental form—*virtuosi.* The *i* ending for a plural is the Italian form and is common in musical circles. For example, *libretto,* the story (or book) of an opera, may be pluralized to *libretti; concerto,* a form of musical composition, is pluralized *concerti.* However, the Anglicized *librettos* and *concertos* are perfectly correct also.

213

Libretto is pronounced *li-BRETT-o; libretti* is *li-BRETT-ee; concerto* is *kon-CHUR-to;* and *concerti* is *kon-CHUR-tee.* Suit your plural form, I would suggest, to the sophistication of your audience.

4. violent women

Virago, the term that most men secretly apply to their mothers-in-law (few husbands have the temerity to use the word openly believing no doubt that discretion is better than valor), comes oddly enough, from the Latin word for *man, vir.* Perhaps the derivation is not so odd after all; a *virago,* far from being traditionally feminine (i.e., timid, delicate, low-spoken, et cetera), is most masculine—coarse, troublesome, loud-mouthed. *Termagant* and *harridan* are words with essentially the same uncomplimentary meaning as *virago*—to call a brawling woman a *virago,* a *termagant,* and a *harridan* is admittedly repetitious, but is successful in relieving your feelings. And if you need still more relief, you may add *battle-ax, war-horse, shrew,* and *harpy*—or do you get along so well with women that you do not need these expressive terms in your vocabulary?

5. the old man

Nicholas Chauvin, soldier of the French Empire, so vociferously and unceasingly aired his veneration of Napoleon Bonaparte that his name became the laughingstock of all Europe. Thereafter, an exaggerated and blatant patriot was known as a *chauvinist*—and still is today. In addition, as you have learned earlier in this chapter, *chauvinism,* by natural extension, applies to blatant veneration of any other affiliation besides one's country.

To be *patriotic* is to be normally proud of and devoted to one's country—to be *chauvinistic* is to carry such pride and devotion to an obnoxious and pathological point.

We might digress here to investigate an etymological sideroad down which the word *patriotic* beckons. *Patriotic* is built on the Latin word *pater, father*—one's country is, in a sense, one's *fatherland.*

Let us see what other interesting words are built on this same root.

1. *patrimony*—an inheritance from one's father. The *-mony* comes from the same root which gives us *money*, namely *Juno Moneta*, the Roman goddess who guarded the temples of finance.

2. *patronymic*—a name formed on the father's name, like *Johnson* (son of John), *Martinson, Aaronson*, et cetera. The *nym* is from a Greek root meaning *name*, and is also found in *synonyms*, words of the same name (or meaning), *antonyms*, words of opposite names (or meanings), and *homonyms*, words of similar sounding names but different spellings and meanings, like *bear—bare, way—weigh*, et cetera.

3. *paternity*—fatherhood.

4. *patriarch*—a venerable, fatherlike, old man; an old man in a ruling, fatherlike position.

5. *patricide*—killing of one's father.

This list does not necessarily exhaust the number of words built on *pater, father*, but is sufficient to give you an idea of how closely related many English words are. In your reading you will come across other words containing the letters *pater* or *patr*—you will be able to figure them out once you realize that the base is the word *father*. You might, if you feel ambitious, puzzle out the relationship to the "father idea" in the following words, checking with a dictionary to see how good your linguistic intuition is:

1. paternal
2. patrician
3. patron
4. patronize
5. paterfamilias
6. padre
7. patriarchy
8. paternalism

6. the old lady

As we come to the end of the *pater* or "father" road, it is only natural to swing off to a side lane labeled *mater* or "mother road."

Here we will find valuable words like the following:

1. *matriarch*—the mother-ruler; the "mother person" who controls a large household, tribe, or country. This word, like *patriarch,* is built on the root *arch, to rule.* During the reign of Queen Elizabeth or Queen Victoria, England was a *matriarchy*—and a few primitive tribes, ruled by women, were *matriarchies.*

2. *maternity*—motherhood

3. *maternal*—motherly

4. *matron*—an older woman, one sufficiently mature to be a mother

5. *alma mater*—strictly, soul mother. Actually, the school or college from which one has graduated, and which in a sense is one's intellectual mother.

6. *matrimony*—marriage. Though this word is similar to *patrimony* in spelling, it does not refer to *money,* as *patrimony* does; unless, that is, you are cynical enough to believe that women marry for money. As the language was growing, *marriage* and *children* went hand in hand—it is therefore not surprising that the word for *marriage* should be built on the Latin stem for *mother.* Of course, times have changed, but we won't go into that.

7. *matricide*—killing of one's mother, fortunately not a very common occurrence in civilized life.

7. murder of all sorts

We've explored the "father road" and the "mother road" and before we return to our starting place, there is an inviting road indicated by the words *patricide* and *matricide.* This "cide road" (no pun intended) comes from a Latin verb *caedo, to cut down, or kill.* Murder being an integral part of human life, there is a word for almost every kind of killing you can think of. Let's look at some of them.

1. *suicide*—killing oneself

2. *fratricide*—killing one's brother

3. *sororicide*—killing one's sister

4. *homicide*—killing a human being. In law, *homicide* is the general term for slaying. If intent and premeditation can be proved, the act is murder and punishable as such. If no such intent is present, the act is called *man-*

216

slaughter and receives a lighter punishment. Thus, if your mother-in-law makes your life unbearable and you decide to slip some arsenic into her coffee one bright morning, you are committing murder—that is, if the old lady succumbs. On the other hand, if you run her down —quite accidentally—with your car, bicycle, or wheelchair, with no intent to kill her, you will be accused of *manslaughter*—that is, if she dies and you can prove you didn't really mean it. It's all rather delicate, however, and you might do best to put thoughts of justifiable violence out of your mind.

5. *regicide*—killing of one's king, president, or other governing official

6. *uxoricide*—killing of one's wife

7. *infanticide*—killing of a newborn child

8. *genocide*—killing of a whole race or nation. This is a fairly new word, coined in 1944 by a UN official named Raphael Lemkin, to refer to the mass murder indulged in by Hitler and his henchmen.

These words are built by combining *cide, to kill,* with the Latin root that applies. It will be profitable to consider these roots for a moment, without going into too much detail or getting bogged down.

Just glance through this chart quickly, not so much to learn any new words, but more to see the relationship of the preceding -*cide* words to others that you probably know.

MURDER	ROOT	RELATED ENGLISH WORDS
1. *suicide*	*sui—self*	no common ones
2. *fratricide*	*frater—brother*	fraternize fraternal fraternity
3. *sororicide*	*soror—sister*	sorority
4. *homicide*	*homo—mankind*	homo sapiens
5. *regicide*	*reg—king, rule*	regal regent regulate
6. *uxoricide*	*uxor—wife*	*uxorious* (excessively devoted to and doting on one's wife)

217

7. *infanticide*	*infans—baby*	infantile
		infantilism
		infantry (originally made up of young boys who accompanied, on foot, the mounted knights of ancient times—hence, *foot soldiery*)
8. *genocide*	*genos—race*	*eugenics*, improvement of the race. (We have previously defined this word as the science of good births, which is essentially the same meaning. *Race* and *birth* are connected in meaning; and the roots for both words come from a common source.)

USING THE WORDS: II

We have only half finished exploring the etymological by-paths suggested by the basic words of this chapter, but we might pause for a moment to digest the new words and roots which we have already turned up. First, let us see whether you can recall the meaning of the following important roots.

Can you recognize roots?

Fill in the meaning of each root.

ROOT	MEANING	RELATED WORD
1. *pater, patr*	father	paternal
2. *arch*	ruler	patriarch
3. *mater, matr*	mother	maternity
4. *frater, fratr*	brother	fraternity
5. *soror*	sister	sorority

6. *uxor*	_____wife_____	uxoricide
7. *cide (caedo)*	__cut down, kill__	homicide
8. *infans*	_____baby_____	infantile
9. *genos*	_____Race._____	genocide

KEY: 1—father, 2—rule, 3—mother, 4—brother, 5—sister, 6—wife,
7—kill, 8—not speaking (baby), 9—race

Before we go on to the second half of our explorations with
the basic chapter words, suppose you tighten up your comprehension of the thirty-two new words we've learned thus
far.

Can you pronounce the words?

*1.	sycophancy	SICK-o-fin-see
*2.	sycophantic	sick-o-FAN-tik
3.	diaphanous	dye-AFF-in-us
*4.	dilettante	dil-e-TAN-tee
5.	dilettantism	dil-e-TAN-tizm
6.	tyro	TYE-ro
*7.	virtuoso	vur-choo-O-so
*8.	virtuosi	vur-choo-O-see
*9.	termagant	TUR-ma-guint
10.	harridan	HAR-i-din (HAR as in Harry)
*11.	chauvinism	SHO-vi-nizm
12.	chauvinistic	sho-vi-NISS-tik
13.	patrimony	PAT-ri-moe-nee
14.	patronymic	pat-ro-NIM-ik
15.	paternity	pa-TUR-ni-tee
16.	patriarch	PAY-tree-ark
17.	patricide	PAT-ri-syde
18.	matriarch	MAY-tree-ark
19.	maternity	ma-TUR-ni-tee
20.	matron	MAY-trun
*21.	alma mater	AL-ma MAY-ter
22.	maternal	ma-TUR-nil
23.	matricide	MAT-ri-syde
24.	fratricide	FRAT-ri-syde
*25.	sororicide	so-RAHR-i-syde
26.	homicide	HOM-i-syde

°27.	regicide	REDGE-i-syde
°28.	uxoricide	uk-SORE-i-syde
29.	infanticide	in-FAN-ti-syde
30.	genocide	ʃEN-o-syde
°31.	uxorious	uk-SORE-ee-us
32.	matrimony	MAT-ri-moe-nee

Can you work with the words? (I)

Match words and definitions.

1.	sycophancy	a.	murder of one's father
2.	dilettantism	b.	excessive patriotism
3.	chauvinism	c.	murder of one's ruler
4.	patrimony	d.	inheritance from father
5.	patricide	e.	murder of one's sister
6.	matricide	f.	murder of one's brother
7.	fratricide	g.	murder of a person
8.	sororicide	h.	toadying
9.	homicide	i.	murder of one's mother
10.	regicide	j.	dabbling

1h, 2f, 3b, 4d, 5a, 6i, 7f, 8e, 9g, 10c

KEY: 1—h, 2—j, 3—b, 4—d, 5—a, 6—i, 7—f, 8—e, 9—g, 10—c

Can you work with the words? (II)

1.	uxoricide	a.	marriage
2.	infanticide	b.	killing of one's child
3.	genocide	c.	fatherhood
4.	matrimony	d.	mother-ruler
5.	matriarch	e.	killing of one's wife
6.	maternity	f.	older woman
7.	matron	g.	one's school or college
8.	alma mater	h.	motherhood
9.	paternity	i.	old man in governing position
10.	patriarch	j.	killing of whole groups of people

1e, 2b, 3j, 4a, 5d, 6h, 7f, 8g, 9c, 10i

KEY: 1—e, 2—b, 3—j, 4—a, 5—d, 6—h, 7—f, 8—g, 9—c, 10—i

Can you work with the words? (III)

1. uxorious	a. catering to people of power or position
2. patronymic	b. name from father
3. chauvinistic	c. dabblers
4. sycophantic	d. an accomplished musician
5. diaphanous	e. filmy, gauzy
6. dilettanti	f. blatantly overpatriotic
7. tyro	g. loud-mouthed woman
8. virtuoso	h. a beginner
9. termagant, harridan	i. excessively doting on one's wife

1 i, 2 b, 3 f, 4 a, 5 e, 6 c, 7 h, 8 d, 9 g

KEY: 1–i, 2–b, 3–f, 4–a, 5–e, 6–c, 7–h, 8–d, 9–g

Do you understand the words?

Answer each question.

1. Does a *sycophantic* attitude show sincere admiration? — YES **NO**

2. Is a *diaphanous* gown revealing? — **YES** NO

3. Does *dilettantism* show firmness and tenacity? — YES **NO**

4. Is a *tyro* particularly skillful? — YES **NO**

5. Is a violin *virtuoso* an accomplished musician? — **YES** NO

6. Is a *termagant* a pleasant person? — YES **NO**

7. Does *chauvinism* show modesty? — YES **NO**

8. Does a substantial *patrimony* obviate financial insecurity? — **YES** NO

9. If you know a person's *patronymic* can you deduce his father's name? — **YES** NO

10. Is a *patriarch* a male? — **YES** NO

11. Does a *matriarch* have a good deal of power? — **YES** NO

12. Does *fratricide* mean murder of one's sister? — YES **NO**

13. Did the assassin of Abraham Lincoln commit *regicide*? — **YES** NO

14. Was Hitler guilty of *genocide*? (YES) NO
15. Does an *uxorious* man cater to his wife? (YES) NO

KEY: 1—no, 2—yes, 3—no, 4—no, 5—yes, 6—no, 7—no, 8—yes, 9—yes, 10—yes, 11—yes, 12—no, 13—yes, 14—yes, 15—yes

---

Can you recall the words?

With the thirty-two words well fixed in your mind, your task now is to recall the one which fits each definition. Refer to the list of words only when absolutely necessary. Greatest benefit will come from saying the complete list in the pronunciation test several times, thinking of the meaning in each case, then keeping your eyes off the list as you aim for a perfect score in this test.

1. father-killing — 1. P*atricide*
2. wife-killing — 2. U*xoricide*
3. mature woman — 3. M*atron*
4. toadying to people of influence (adj.) — 4. S*ycophantic*
5. skilled musician — 5. V*irtuoso*
6. exaggerated patriotism — 6. C*hauvinism*
7. turbulent female (three words) — 7. T*ermagant*
7. H*arridan*
7. V*irago*
8. name derived from father's name — 8. P*atronymic*
9. venerable and powerful old man — 9. P*atriarch*
10. the same applying to an old woman — 10. M*atriarch*
11. motherly — 11. M*aternal*
12. motherhood — 12. M*aternity*
13. marriage — 13. M*atrimony*
14. one's school or college — 14. A*lma Mater*

222

15. attitude of catering to wealth or prestige (noun)

15. S*ycophancy*

16. killing of a race or nation

16. G*enocide*

17. dabbling in the fine arts (noun)

17. D*ilettantism*

18. a beginner in a field

18. T*yro*

19. plural of *virtuoso* (Italian form)

19. V*irtuosi*

20. having an attitude of excessive patriotism (adj.)

20. C*hauvinistic*

21. inheritance from father

21. P*atrimony*

22. sheer, transparent

22. D*iaphanous*

23. mother-killing

23. M*atricide*

24. brother-killing

24. F*ratricide*

25. sister-killing

25. S*ororicide*

26. killing of a human being

26. H*omicide*

27. killing of one's ruler

27. R*egicide*

28. killing of a baby

28. I*nfanticide*

29. excessively fond of one's wife

29. U*xorious*

KEY: 1—patricide, 2—uxoricide, 3—matron, 4—sycophantic, 5—virtuoso, 6—chauvinism, 7—termagant, harridan, virago, 8—patronymic, 9—patriarch, 10—matriarch, 11—maternal, 12—maternity, 13—matrimony, 14—alma mater, 15—sycophancy, 16—genocide, 17—dilettantism, 18—tyro, 19—virtuosi, 20—chauvinistic, 21—patrimony, 22—diaphanous, 23—matricide, 24—fratricide, 25—sororicide, 26—homicide, 27—regicide, 28—infanticide, 29—uxorious

---

ORIGINS AND RELATED WORDS: II

1. madness of all sorts

This is a long chapter and I have cut it up into several parts to give a boost to your learning. By now you can see how easy it is to learn great numbers of new words easily, quickly, and successfully if these words have some central core of similarity. In the second part of our study of derivations we shall discover scores of new words by continuing to wander down any etymological bypath that looks inviting.

Let's start with *monomaniac*, the man (or woman, of course) who develops an abnormal obsession in respect to one particular thing, but is otherwise normal. The abnormal, almost psychotic part of his nature is indicated by the last half of the word—*maniac*; the lone, single, separate, and isolated quality of the obsession is indicated by the Greek root *mono*, which means *one*.

We'll further explore *mono*, *one*, and *mania*, *madness*, in just a moment—right now let's be quite sure we understand the full implications of *monomaniac*.

When you call a man a *monomaniac* you imply that he carries his interest in some one thing to such a point that it scarcely makes sense. It may not be the same thing all his life or for any great length of time—but whatever it is, and for however long it engages his attention, nothing else in the world matters, and everything else in the world is subordinated to it.

Psychiatry recognizes other abnormal states, all more dangerous than *monomania*, all psychotic, all defined by words built on the Greek stem *mania*, madness.

1. *dipsomania*—morbid compulsion to keep on absorbing alcoholic beverages. The *dipsomaniac* has been defined as the person for whom one drink is too many, a thousand not enough. Recent investigations suggest that *dipsomania* may not necessarily be caused by anxieties or frustrations, but possibly by metabolic or physiological weaknesses.

Adjective: *dipsomaniacal* (dip-so-ma-NYE-a-k'l)

2. *Kleptomania*—morbid compulsion to steal, not from any economic motive, but simply because the urge to take another's possessions is irresistible.

Adjective: *kleptomaniacal* (klep-to-ma-NYE-a-k'l)

3. *Pyromania*—morbid compulsion to set fires. *Pyromania* should not be confused with *incendiarism*, which is malicious burning of another's property and is not morbidly or psychotically impelled. The *pyromaniac* is mentally unbalanced; the *incendiary* is simply antisocial. In law, setting fire to another's

or to one's own property for the purpose of economic gain (such as the collection of an insurance policy) is called _arson_ and is a felony. The perpetrator of such a crime is an _arsonist_ In short, the _pyromaniac_ sets first for the thrill; the _incendiary_ for revenge; the _arsonist_ for money.

Adjective: _pyromaniacal_ (pye-ro-ma-NYE-a-k'l)

4. _Megalomania_—morbid delusions of one's grandeur, importance, godliness, et cetera. Jokes accusing the heads of governments of _megalomania_ are common, the most recent being:

Churchill, Roosevelt, and Stalin were talking about their dreams.

Churchill: I dreamed last night that God had made me _prime minister_ of the whole world.

Roosevelt: I dreamed that God had made me _president_ of the whole world.

Stalin: How could you gentlemen have such dreams. I didn't dream of offering you those positions!

Perhaps the purest cases of _megalomania_ in history were Napoleon and Hitler; both gentlemen were obviously psychotic and had delusions of their invincibility.

Do not confuse the _megalomaniac_ with the _egomaniac_ (see Chapter 3); the latter is morbidly, psychotically wrapped up in himself.

Adjective: _megalomaniacal_ (meg-a-lo-ma-NYE-k'l)

5. _Nymphomania_—morbid, incessant, and intense desire, on the part of a _female_, for sexual intercourse. A woman with such desires is considered insane and is called a _nymphomaniac;_ a _man_, on the other hand, is considered dangerous, and is called a _lecher_.

Adjective: _nymphomaniacal_ (nim-fo-ma-NYE-a-k'l)

So much for _manias_. There is another side to the coin. Just as personality disorders can cause morbid _attraction_ toward certain things or acts (stealing, fire, power, sex, et cetera), so also other emotional ills can cause violent or morbid _repulsions_ to certain conditions, things, or situations. There are people who have irrational and deep-seated dread of cats, dogs, fire, the number thirteen, snakes, thunder or lightning, various colors, and so on literally without end. Such morbid dread or fear is called, in the language of psychiatry, a *phobia*, and we might pause to investigate the three most common ones. These are:

1. *Claustrophobia*—a dread of being physically hemmed in, of enclosed spaces, of crowds, et cetera.

2. *Agoraphobia*—a dread of space, the reverse of *claustrophobia*. People suffering from *agoraphobia* prefer to stay shut in their homes as much as possible, and become panic-stricken in such places as open fields, large public buildings like railroad terminals, et cetera.

3. *Acrophobia*—fear of high places. The victims of this malady cannot climb ladders or trees, or stand on tops of furniture. They refuse to go onto the roof of a building or look out the window of one of the higher floors.

A true *claustrophobe*, *agoraphobe*, or *acrophobe* is not an emotionally balanced personality.

As for *mono*, *one*, it will suffice to recognize that a number of common words are built on this Greek stem. *Monocle, monk, monastery, monotonous, monarchy, monogamy, monoplane, monopoly, monosyllable* all have relationships to the idea of "oneness" which you can readily see.

2. an adolescent characteristic

The *iconoclast*, who sneers at convention and tradition, is more likely than not to be an adolescent either chronologically or emotionally. Adolescence is the confused and rebellious time of life in which *iconoclasm* is quite normal—indeed, the adolescent who is not *iconoclastic* to some degree should be considered either immature or maladjusted. The word is from *icon, a religious image*, plus *clast, to break*. Iconoclasm does not of course have to be restricted to religion.

3. is there a God?

Atheist combines the Greek negative prefix *a, not, without*, and *theos, God*. *Do not confuse atheism* with *agnosticism*, the philosophy which claims that God is unknowable, and may or may not exist, but man can never come to a final conclusion about Him. The *agnostic* does not deny the existence of a deity, as does the *atheist;* he simply holds that no proof can be adduced one way or the other.

4. how to know

In *agnostic* we find the root *gnos*, from the Greek verb *to know*, and the familiar negative particle *a* which we met in *atheism* and *anachronism* and will meet later on in *atrophy*. Thus, an *agnostic*, etymologically speaking, *does not know.*

Note how handy it is to be acquainted with the root *gnos* when we examine the words *diagnosis* and *prognosis*. A *diagnosis* is an examination, medically or scientifically, to determine the cause and nature of ills—so that these may be *known* and therefore properly treated.

A *prognosis* on the other hand is, strictly, a *knowing beforehand.*

Thus, you may say to a doctor: "What's the *diagnosis*, Doc?"

"Diabetes."

Then you say, "And what's the *prognosis?*"

"If the patient takes insulin and watches his diet, he'll soon be as good as new."

The doctor's *prognosis*, then, is a forecast of the development or trend of a disease. He knows, beforehand, from previous similar cases, what to expect.

The verb from *diagnosis* is *diagnose;* the verb from *prognosis* is *prognosticate*. To use the verb *prognosticate* correctly, be sure that your meaning involves the forecasting of developments from a consideration of symptoms—whether the disease be physical, mental, political, economic, or what have you.

In school, you doubtless recall taking *diagnostic* tests; these measured not what you were supposed to have learned during the semester, but your general knowledge in a field so that your teachers would know what remedial steps to take, just as a doctor relies on his *diagnosis* (praying it is correct) to decide what drugs or treatments to prescribe.

In a Reading Clinic, for example, various *diagnostic* machines and tests are used—these tell the clinician what is wrong with a student's reading and what measures will probably increase such a student's reading efficiency.

5. getting back to God

Theos, God, is also found in:

1. *Monotheism:* belief in *one* God
2. *Polytheism:* belief in *many* gods, as in ancient Greece or Rome
3. *Pantheism:* belief that God is not in man's image, but is a combination of *all* the forces of the universe
4. *Theology:* the *study* of God and religion
5. *Theocracy:* *rule* by the church

The roots which combined with *theos* to produce *monotheism, polytheism, pantheism, theology,* and *theocracy* are worth considering. *Mono* (one) and *ology* (the study of) we have already worked with, and *poly* (many) we have met before.

ROOT	MEANING	RELATED WORDS
1. *mono*	one	*monomania* *monopoly*
2. *poly*	many	*polygon*, a geometric figure of many sides *polyglot*, speaking many languages *polygamy*, many marriages
3. *pan*	all	*pandemonium*, John Milton's coinage for such noise as could be made only by *all* the devils and demons of hell *panorama*, a view *all around* Pan-American
4. *ology*	study of	*biology* *gynecology*
5. *crac*	rule	*democracy*, rule of the people *autocracy*, rule by one person (auto—self) *bureaucracy*, rule by bureaus

6. eight way of saying the same thing

A *lecher* is a devotee of *lechery* and is so called from an old French verb *lechier, to lick.* The adjective *lecherous* has

228

many synonyms, most of them also, and significantly, starting with the letter *l*, a sound formed with the tongue, supposedly the seat of sensation. These all mean about the same as *lecherous*, but are not quite so strong or quite so significant of successful action. Among them are:

1. *libidinous*—from *libido, pleasure*
2. *lascivious*—from *lascivia, wantonness*
3. *lubricious*—from *lubricus, slippery*
4. *licentious*—from *licere, to be permitted*, the root from which we get *license*
5. *lewd*—the previous four words derive from Latin, but this one is from simple Anglo-Saxon *lewed, vile*.
6. *lustful*—also from an Anglo-Saxon word, meaning *pleasure, desire*.

Libidinous, lascivious, lubricious, licentious, lewd, lecherous, lustful are seven ways of saying the same thing—*sexy*. The implication of all seven words is *derogatory*. Perhaps it is a commentary on our puritanical civilization that there are few, if any, words that mean *sexy* with a complimentary or admiring connotation.

Another valuable synonym, which does not begin with *l*, is *prurient*, which comes from the Latin verb *to itch*. *Prurience* is excessive sexual inquisitiveness, desire, longing, et cetera.

7. more—and less

Hypochondria is built on two Greek roots: *hypo—under* and *chondria—the cartilage of the breastbone.* This may sound farfetched until you realize that under the breastbone is the abdomen; the ancient Greeks believed that morbid anxiety about one's health arose in the abdomen—and no one is more morbidly, unceasingly, and unhappily anxious about his health than the *hypochondriac.*

Hypo, under or *less*, is a useful root to know. The *hypodermic*, which we have already discussed in a previous chapter, penetrates *under* the skin; a *hypothyroid* person has an *underworking* thyroid gland.

On the other hand, *hyper* is the Greek root meaning *over*

229

or *above* and is just the opposite in meaning to *hypo*. The *hypercritical* person is excessively fault-finding; *hyperthyroidism* is an *overworking* of the thyroid gland; *hypertension* is the medical term for excessively high blood pressure; and you can easily figure out the meanings of *hyperacidity*, *hyperactive*, *hypersensitive*, *hyperconscious*, et cetera.

8. too much growth—and not enough

Hypertrophy combines *hyper, too much,* with *trephein, to nourish; hypertrophy* of any bodily organ or limb is excessive and abnormal growth. Contrariwise, *atrophy* (*a, not,* plus *trephein, nourish*) of a limb is a wasting away, an underdevelopment.

USING THE WORDS: III

We have discussed sixty-three or more related and derived forms—all springing from our last five basic words, *monomaniac, iconoclast, atheist, lecher,* and *hypochondriac*. If you have worked carefully, conscientiously, and with good comprehension, you are ready for your tests, the first of which, as usual, will be the important one that guides you in the correct pronunciation of these important words.

Can you pronounce the words?

You can tell, by the rate of your learning, by the speed with which you can absorb—and remember—new words in carload lots, that you are well into the book by now; and, more important, well into the natural, simple, and practically foolproof technique of building a bigger vocabulary by concentrating on ideas and on relationships, etymological and otherwise.

The sixty-three new words we discussed in the last section are for the most part sophisticated, advanced words. To make sure you will say them properly, I am going to divide this test into several parts, giving you a short section at a time.

I—difficult words

WATCH THE "NYE" SYLLABLE

* °1. monomaniacal — mon-o-ma-NYE-a-k'l
* °2. kleptomaniacal — klep-to-ma-NYE-a-k'l
* °3. pyromaniacal — pye-ro-ma-NYE-a-k'l
* 4. megalomaniacal — meg-a-lo-ma-NYE-a-k'l
* °5. nymphomaniacal — nim-fo-ma-NYE-a-k'l
* °6. dipsomaniacal — dip-so-ma-NYE-a-k'l
* °7. egomaniacal — ee-go-ma-NYE-a-k'l
* °8. maniacal — ma-NYE-a-k'l

II—manias and maniacs

  9. monomania — MON-o-may-nee-a
 10. kleptomania — KLEP-to-may-nee-a
 11. pyromania — PYE-ro-may-nee-a
 12. megalomania — MEG-a-lo-may-nee-a
 13. nymphomania — NIM-fo-may-nee-a
 14. dipsomania — DIP-so-may-nee-a
 15. egomania — EE-go-may-nee-a
 16. mania — MAY-nee-a
 17. monomaniac — MON-o-may-nee-ak
 18. kleptomaniac — KLEP-to-may-nee-ak
 19. pyromaniac — PYE-ro-may-nee-ak
 20. megalomaniac — MEG-a-lo-may-nee-ak
 21. nymphomaniac — NIM-fo-may-nee-ak
 22. dipsomaniac — DIP-so-may-nee-ak

III—sex

 23. lechery — LETCH-er-ee
 24. libidinous — li-BID-in-us
 25. lascivious — la-SIV-ee-us
°26. lubricious — loo-BRISH-us
 27. licentious — lye-SEN-shus
 28. lewd — LOOD (rhyme with FOOD)
 29. lustful — LUST-ful
°30. lubricity — loo-BRISS-i-tee
 31. prurient — PROO-ree-ent
 32. prurience — PROO-ree-ence

IV—God

33. atheism	AY-the-izm
34. agnosticism	ag-NOSS-ti-sizm
35. agnostic	ag-NOSS-tik
36. monotheism	MON-o-thee-izm
37. polytheism	POLL-ee-thee-izm
38. pantheism	PAN-thee-izm
39. theology	thee-OL-o-jee
40. theocracy	thee-OK-ra-see

V—hypo and hyper

41. hypochondria	hye-po-KON-dree-a
42. hypothyroid	hye-po-THYE-royd
43. hyperthyroidism	hye-pur-THYE-roy-dizm
44. hypertension	hye-pur-TEN-shun
°45. hyperthrophy	hye-PUR-tro-fee

VI—other words

°46. incendiarism	in-SEN-dee-er-izm
47. incendiary	in-SEN-dee-er-ee
48. arson	AR-s'n
49. arsonist	AR-s'n-ist
°50. iconoclasm	eye-KON-o-klazm
51. iconoclastic	eye-kon-o-KLASS-tik
52. atrophy	AT-ro-fee
53. diagnosis	dye-ag-NO-sis
54. diagnose	DYE-ag-noce
55. prognosis	prog-NO-sis
56. diagnostic	dye-ag-NOSS-tik
57. prognosticate	prog-NOSS-ti-kayt

VII—phobias

58. claustrophobia	klaw-stro-FOE-be-a
°59. agoraphobia	AG-or-a-FOE-be-a
°60. acrophobia	AK-ro-FOE-be-a
°61. claustrophobe	CLAW-stro-fobe
°62. agoraphobe	AG-or-a-fobe
°63. acrophobe	AK-ro-fobe

232

Can you work with the words? (I)

This has been a long chapter, and we have discussed, more or less in detail, close to 100 words or forms. Just to keep everything straight in your mind now, see how successfully you can work out the following matching exercises, which will concern any of the words we have discussed in this chapter.

WORDS	DEFINITIONS
1. martinet	a. lack of seriousness
2. sycophancy	b. harridan, shrew
3. dilettantism	c. excessive patriotism
4. tyro	d. name from father
5. virtuoso	e. venerable and influential old man
6. termagant	f. beginner
7. chauvinism	g. brilliant performer
8. patrimony	h. bootlicking
9. patronymic	i. inheritance from father
10. patriarch	j. strict disciplinarian

KEY 1—j, 2—h, 3—a, 4—f, 5—g, 6—b, 7—c, 8—i, 9—d, 10—e

Can you work with the words? (II)

WORDS	DEFINITIONS
1. patricide	a. mother-killing
2. alma mater	b. tending to fixate on one thing
3. matricide	c. wife-killing
4. fratricide	d. father-killing
5. uxoricide	e. tending to set fires
6. uxorious	f. alcoholic
7. monomaniacal	g. wife-doting
8. pyromaniacal	h. school or college
9. megalomaniacal	i. tending to delusions of grandeur
10. dipsomaniacal	j. brother-killing

KEY: 1—d, 2—h, 3—a, 4—j, 5—c, 6—g, 7—b, 8—e, 9—i, 10—f

Can you work with the words? (III)

WORDS	DEFINITIONS
1. kleptomania	a. disbelief in God
2. libidinousness	b. belief in many gods
3. atheism	c. lewdness
4. agnosticism	d. belief that God is nature
5. polytheism	e. morbid anxiety about health
6. monotheism	f. belief in one god
7. theology	g. study of religion
8. pantheism	h. psychotic thievery
9. theocracy	i. rule by church
10. hypochondria	j. skepticism about God

KEY: 1–h, 2–c, 3–a, 4–j, 5–b, 6–f, 7–g, 8–d, 9–i, 10–e

Can you work with the words? (IV)

WORDS	DEFINITIONS
1. hypothyroidism	a. too much thyroid
2. lasciviousness	b. malicious fire setting
3. hyperthyroidism	c. not enough thyroid
4. hypertrophy	d. fire setting for gain
5. incendiarism	e. deficient development
6. arson	f. determining causes
7. iconoclasm	g. excessive development
8. atrophy	h. prurience
9. diagnosis	i. foretelling probable development
10. prognosis	j. scoffing at tradition

KEY: 1–c, 2–h, 3–a, 4–g, 5–b, 6–d, 7–j, 8–e, 9–f, 10–i

Can you work with the words? (V)

WORDS	DEFINITIONS
1. prurience	a. morbid self-interest
2. egomania	b. fear of enclosed places
3. agoraphobia	c. high blood pressure
4. claustrophobia	d. sexual longing
5. acrophobia	e. fear of heights
6. hypertension	f. fear of open spaces

KEY: 1–d, 2–a, 3–f, 4–b, 5–e, 6–c

Can you recall the words?

I—manias

Now refresh your memory by reviewing in your mind the meanings of words 1 through 22, as numbered in the pronunciation test (page 231). Then making no further references to the list, write the word that correctly fits each of the following definitions.

1. single fixed obsession — 1. *monomania*

2. irresistible compulsion to set fires — 2. *pyromania*

3. unceasing desire, on the part of a woman, for sexual intercourse — 3. *nymphomania*

4. morbid desire to steal — 4. *kleptomania*

5. delusions of grandeur — 5. *megalomania*

6. alcoholism — 6. *dipsomania*

7. morbid obsession with oneself — 7. *egomania*

II—sex

Now review words 23 through 32 and, when ready, write five adjectives beginning with *l* which are synonymous with *sexy*.

8. *libidinous*

9. *lubricious*

10. *lewd*

11. *lustful*

12. *lascivious*

Write one beginning with *p*.

13. *prurient*

235

III—God

Review words 33 through 40, then write the word that fits each definition.

14. study of religion

14. _theology_

15. rule by priests

15. _theocracy_

16. God is the sum total of natural laws

16. _pantheism_

17. there is no God

17. _atheism_

18. no one knows about God

18. _agnosticism_

19. belief in one God

19. _monotheism_

20. belief in many gods

20. _polytheism_

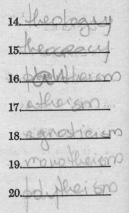

IV—hypo and hyper

Review words 41 through 45.

21. morbid anxiety about one's health

21. _hypochondria_

22. excessive development of an organ or limb

22. _hypertrophy_

23. deficient working of the thyroid gland

23. _hypothyroidism_

24. excessive working of same

24. _hyperthyroidism_

25. high blood pressure

25. _hypertension_

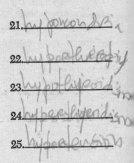

V—other words

Review words 46 through 66.

26. wasting-away or deficient development of an organ or limb

26. _atrophy_

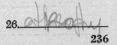

27. malicious fire setting   27. _incendiarism_

28. the felony of setting fire for eco-
    nomic gain   28. _arson_

29. sneering contempt of convention
    or tradition   29. _iconoclasm_

30. a forecast of development   30. _prognosis_

31. designed to discover causes   31. _diagnostic_

32. dread of enclosed places   32. _claustrophobia_

33. fear of heights   33. _acrophobia_

34. one who has a morbid dread of
    open spaces   34. _agoraphobia_

KEY: 1—monomania, 2—pyromania, 3—nymphomania, 4—kleptomania, 5—megalomania, 6—dipsomania, 7—egomania, 8–12 (in
any order, five of the following) libidinous, lecherous, licentious,
lascivious, lewd, lustful, lubricious, 13—prurient, 14—theology,
15—theocracy, 16—pantheism, 17—atheism, 18—agnosticism, 19—
monotheism, 20—polytheism, 21—hypochondria, 22—hypertrophy,
23—hypothyroidism, 24—hyperthyroidism, 25—hypertension, 26—
atrophy, 27—incendiarism, 28—arson, 29—iconoclasm, 30—prognosis, 31—diagnostic, 32—claustrophobia, 33—acrophobia, 34—
agoraphobe

Can you remember roots?

Now, as a final clincher, can you write the root with each
of the following meanings, and also give one example of the
use of such root?

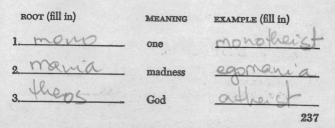

ROOT (fill in)	MEANING	EXAMPLE (fill in)
1. _mono_	one	_monotheist_
2. _mania_	madness	_egomania_
3. _theos_	God	_atheist_

237

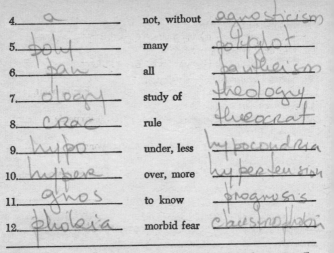

4.	_a_	not, without	agnosticism
5.	_poly_	many	polyglot
6.	_pan_	all	pantheism
7.	_ology_	study of	theology
8.	_crac_	rule	theocrat
9.	_hypo_	under, less	hypocondria
10.	_hyper_	over, more	hypertension
11.	_gnos_	to know	prognosis
12.	_phobia_	morbid fear	claustrophobia

KEY: 1—mono, 2—mania, 3—theos (the), 4—a, 5—poly, 6—pan, 7—ology, 8—crac, 9—hypo, 10—hyper, 11—gnos, 12—phobia (for examples, refer to the body of the chapter)

CHAPTER REVIEW

Do you recognize the words?

Check the word which most closely fits each definition.

1. Disciplinarian:
   (a) martinet, (b) virago, (c) dilettante
2. Bootlicker:
   (a) chauvinist, (b) sycophant, (c) lecher
3. Scoffer at tradition:
   (a) monomaniac, (b) hypochondriac, (c) iconoclast
4. Disbeliever in God:
   (a) agnostic, (b) atheist, (c) chauvinist
5. Accomplished musician:
   (a) tyro, (b) dilettante, (c) virtuoso
6. Sheer, flimsy:
   (a) diaphanous, (b) uxorious, (c) paternal
7. Abusive woman:
   (a) termagant, (b) virtuoso, (c) matriarch

8. Murder of one's wife:
   (a) genocide, (b) uxoricide, (c) sororicide
9. Old man in ruling position:
   (a) matriarch, (b) patricide, (c) patriarch
10. Morbid compulsion to steal:
    (a) dipsomania, (b) nymphomania, (c) kleptomania
11. Delusions of grandeur:
    (a) megalomania, (b) egomania, (c) pyromania
12. Lewd, lustful:
    (a) prurient, (b) agnostic, (c) hypochondriac
13. Belief in many Gods:
    (a) polytheism, (b) monotheism, (c) agnosticism
14. Setting fire for economic gain:
    (a) pyromania, (b) incendiarism, (c) arson
15. Overgrowth:
    (a) atrophy, (b) hypertrophy, (c) hypertension
16. Morbid fear of heights:
    (a) agoraphobia, (b) acrophobia, (c) claustrophobia

KEY: 1–a, 2–b, 3–c, 4–b, 5–c, 6–a, 7–a, 8–b, 9–c, 10–c, 11–a, 12–a, 13–a, 14–c, 15–b, 16–b

---

MAGAZINES THAT WILL HELP YOU

When a pregnant woman takes calcium pills, she must make sure also that her diet is rich in vitamin B, since this vitamin makes the absorption of the calcium possible. In building your vocabulary by learning great quantities of new words, you too must take a certain vitamin, metaphorically speaking, to help you absorb, understand, and remember these words. This vitamin is reading—for it is in books and magazines that you will find the words used that we have been discussing in these pages. To learn new words without seeing them applied in the context of your reading is to do only half the job and to run the risk of gradually forgetting the new additions to your vocabulary, once you have completed the final chapter. To combine your vocabulary building with increased reading is to make assurance doubly sure.

You are now so alert to the words and roots we have discussed that you will find that most of your reading will be full of the new words you have learned—and every time you do see one of the words used in context in a book or magazine, you will understand it more fully and will be taking long steps toward using it yourself.

Among magazines, I would like particularly to recommend the following, which will act both to keep you mentally alert and to set the new words you are learning:

1. *Harper's Magazine*
2. *Atlantic Monthly*
3. *The New Yorker*
4. *American Mercury*
5. *The Nation*
6. *The New Republic*
7. *Saturday Review of Literature*

These periodicals are aimed at the alert, verbally sophisticated, educated reader; you will see in them, without fail, most of the words we have been studying together—not to mention hosts of other valuable words you will want to add to your vocabulary.

BRIEF INTERMISSION NINE:
SOME INTERESTING DERIVATIONS

PEOPLE WHO MADE OUR LANGUAGE

Bloomers: Mrs. Elizabeth Smith Miller invented them in 1849, and showed a working model to a famous woman's rights advocate, *Amelia J. Bloomer*. Amelia was fascinated by the idea of garments that were both modest (they then reached right down to the ankles) and convenient—and promptly sponsored them. . . .

Boycott: *Charles C. Boycott* was an English land agent whose difficult duty it was to collect high rents from Irish farmers. In protest, the farmers ostracized him, not even allowing him to make purchases in town nor hire workers to harvest his crops.

Marcel: *Marcel* was an ingenious Parisian hairdresser who felt he could improve on the button curls popular in 1875. He did, and made a fortune.

Silhouette: Finance Minister of France just before the Revolution, *Etienne De Silhouette* advocated the *simple* life, so that excess money could go into the treasury instead of into luxurious living. And the profile is the *simplest* form of portraiture, if you get the connection.

Derrick: A seventeenth-century English hangman, *Derrick* by name, hoisted to their death some of the most notorious criminals of the day.

Sadist: Because *Count de Sade*, an eighteenth-century Frenchman, found his greatest delight torturing friends and mistresses, the term *sadist* was derived from his name. His memoirs shocked his nation and the world by the alarming frankness with which he described his morbid and bloodthirsty cruelty.

Galvanism: *Luigi Galvani*, the Italian physiologist, found by accident that an electrically charged scalpel could send a frog's corpse into muscular convulsions. Experimenting further, he eventually discovered the principles of chemically

241

produced electricity. His name is responsible not only for the technical expressions *galvanism, galvanized iron,* and *galvanometer,* but also for that highly graphic phrase, "*galvanized* into action.*"

Guppies: In 1868, *R. J. Lechmere Guppy,* president of the Scientific Association of Trinidad, sent some specimens of a tiny tropical fish to the British Museum. Ever since, fish of this species have been called *guppies.*

Nicotine: Almost four hundred years ago, *Jean Nicot,* a French ambassador, bought some tobacco seeds from a Flemish trader. Nicot's successful efforts to popularize the plant in Europe brought him linguistic immortality.

PLACES WHICH MADE OUR LANGUAGE

Bayonne, France: Where was first manufactured the daggerlike weapon which fits over the muzzle of a rifle—the *bayonet.*

Cantalupo, Italy: The first place in Europe to grow those luscious melons we now call *cantaloupes.*

Calicut, India: The city from which we first imported a kind of cotton cloth now known as *calico.*

Tuxedo Park, New York: In the country club of this exclusive and wealthy community, the short evening coat for men, or *tuxedo,* was popularized.

Egypt: It was once supposed that the colorful, fortune-telling wanderers, or *gypsies,* hailed from this ancient land.

Damascus, Syria: Where an elaborately patterned silk, *damask,* was first made.

Tzu-t'ing, China: Once a great seaport in Fukien Province. Marco Polo called it *Zaitun,* and in time a silk fabric made there was called *satin.*

Frankfurt, Germany: Where the burghers once greatly enjoyed their smoked beef and pork sausages, which we now ask for in delicatessen stores by the name of *frankfurters.*

12

HOW TO FLATTER
YOUR FRIENDS

—— TEASER PREVIEW ——————————

What adjective aptly describes a person who is:

- *friendly and easy to get along with?*
- *tireless?*
- *simple, frank, aboveboard?*
- *keen-minded?*
- *generous, noble, and forgiving?*
- *able to do many things skillfully?*
- *unflinching in the face of pain or disaster?*
- *brave, fearless?*
- *charming and witty?*
- *smooth, polished, cultured?*

WORDS are the symbols of emotions, as well as of ideas. You can show your feeling by the tone you use ("You're silly" can be an insult, an accusation, or an endearment, depending on how you say it) or by the words you choose (you can label a quality either "childish" or "childlike," depending on whether you admire it or condemn it—it's the same quality, no matter what you call it).

In Chapter 11 we discussed ten basic words that you might use to show your disapproval. In this chapter we discuss ten words which indicate wholehearted approval.

IDEAS

1. put the kettle on, Polly

He's a friendly chap, happy, extroverted, and gregarious. He's the sort of person who will invite you out for a drink, who likes to transact business around the lunch table, who puts the coffee to perking as soon as company drops in. He's sociable, genial, cordial, affable—and he likes parties and all the eating and drinking that goes with them.

He's *convivial*.

2. you can't tire him

Arnold Bennett once pointed out that we all have the same amount of time—twenty-four hours a day. Strictly speaking, that's as inconclusive an observation as Bennett ever made. It's not time that counts, but energy—and of that wonderful quality we all have very different amounts, from the person who wakes up tired, no matter how much sleep he's had, to that lucky, well-adjusted mortal who hardly ever needs to sleep.

Energy comes from a healthy body, of course; it also comes from a psychological balance, a lack of conflicts and insecurities.

And this man apparently has boundless, illimitable energy—he's on the go from morning to night, and often far into the night, working hard, playing hard, never tiring, never "pooped" or "bushed"—and getting twice as much done as any three other people.

He's *indefatigable*.

3. no tricks, no secrets

He is pleasingly frank, utterly lacking in pretense or artificiality, in fact quite unable to hide his feelings or thoughts—and so honest and aboveboard that he can scarcely conceive of trickery, chicanery, or dissimulation in anyone. There is, then, about him, the simple naturalness and unsophistication of a child.

He's *ingenuous*.

244

4. sharp as a razor

He has a mind like a steel trap; his insight into problems that would confuse or mystify people of less keenness or discernment is just short of amazing.

> He's *perspicacious*.

5. no placating necessary

He is most generous about forgiving a slight, an insult, an injury. Never does he harbor resentment, store up petty grudges, or waste energy or thought on means of revenge or retaliation. How could he? He's much too big a person.

> He's *magnanimous*.

6. one-man orchestra

The range of his aptitudes is truly formidable. If he's a writer, he has professional facility in poetry, fiction, biography, criticism, essays—you just mention it and he'll do it, and very competently. If he's a musician, he can play the oboe, the bassoon, the French horn, the bass viol, the piano, the celesta, the xylophone, even the clavichord if you can dig one up for him. If he's an artist, he'll use oils, water colors, *gouache*, charcoal, pen and ink—he can do anything! Or maybe the range of his abilities cuts across all fields, as in the case of Michelangelo, who was an expert sculptor, painter, poet, architect, and inventor. In case you're thinking "Jack of all trades . . . ," you're wrong—he's *master* of all trades.

> He's *versatile*.

7. no grumbling

He bears his troubles bravely, never begs for sympathy, never yields to sorrow, never winces at pain. It sounds almost superhuman, but it's true.

> He's *stoical*.

8. no fear

There is not, as the hackneyed phrase has it, a cowardly bone in his body. He is a stranger to fear, he's audacious, dauntless, contemptuous of danger and hardship.

> He's *intrepid*.

245

9. no dullness

He's witty, clever, delightful, a brilliant and entertaining conversationalist.

He's scintillating.

10. city slicker

He's cultivated, poised, tactful, socially so experienced, sophisticated, and courteous that he is at home in any group, at ease under all circumstances of social intercourse. You cannot help admiring (perhaps envying) his smoothness and self-assurance, his blandness, tact, and congeniality.

He's urbane.

USING THE WORDS: I

Can you pronounce the words?

1.	convivial	kon-VIV-ee-il
*2.	indefatigable	in-de-FAT-i-ga-b'l
*3.	ingenuous	in-JEN-yoo-us
4.	perspicacious	pur-spi-KAY-shus
5.	magnanimous	mag-NAN-i-mus
*6.	versatile	VUR-sa-till
7.	stoical	STO-i-k'l
*8.	intrepid	in-TREP-id
9.	scintillating	SIN-ti-lay-ting
10.	urbane	ur-BAYN

Can you work with the words?

Match words and definitions.

1.	convivial	a.	frank
2.	indefatigable	b.	unflinching
3.	ingenuous	c.	noble
4.	perspicacious	d.	capable in many directions
5.	magnanimous	e.	tireless
6.	versatile	f.	fearless
7.	stoical	g.	keen-minded
8.	intrepid	h.	witty

246

9. scintillating   i. friendly
10. urbane   j. polished, bland

KEY: 1–i, 2–e, 3–a, 4–g, 5–c, 6–d, 7–b. 8–f, 9–h, 10–j

Do you understand the words? (I)

Mark each statement *true* or *false*.

1. *Convivial* people are unfriendly.	TRUE	FALSE
2. Anyone who is *indefatigable* tires easily.	TRUE	FALSE
3. An *ingenuous* person is artful and untrustworthy.	TRUE	FALSE
4. A *perspicacious* person is hard to fool.	TRUE	FALSE
5. A *magnanimous* old man is easily insulted.	TRUE	FALSE
6. A *versatile* person does many things well.	TRUE	FALSE
7. A *stoical* person always complains of his hard lot.	TRUE	FALSE
8. An *intrepid* explorer is not easily frightened.	TRUE	FALSE
9. A *scintillating* speaker is interesting to listen to.	TRUE	FALSE
10. Someone who is *urbane* is always making enemies.	TRUE	FALSE

KEY: 1–3–false, 4–true, 5–false, 6–true, 7–false, 8–9–true, 10–false

---

Do you understand the words? (II)

Decide whether each pair of words is the *same* or *opposite* in meaning.

1. convivial—hostile	SAME	OPPOSITE
2. indefatigable—enervated	SAME	OPPOSITE
3. ingenuous—worldly	SAME	OPPOSITE
4. perspicacious—obtuse	SAME	OPPOSITE
5. magnanimous—petty	SAME	OPPOSITE
6. versatile—well-rounded	SAME	OPPOSITE
7. stoical—unflinching	SAME	OPPOSITE
8. intrepid—timid	SAME	OPPOSITE

9. scintillating—banal	SAME	OPPOSITE
10. urbane—awkward	SAME	OPPOSITE

KEY: 1—opposite, 2—opposite, 3—opposite, 4—opposite, 5—opposite, 6—same, 7—same, 8—opposite, 9—opposite, 10—opposite

Can you recall the words?

Write the word suggested by each brief description.

1. witty   1._____

2. noble, forgiving   2._____

3. capable in many fields   3._____

4. keen-minded   4._____

5. uncomplaining   5._____

6. friendly   6._____

7. poised   7._____

8. courageous   8._____

9. tireless   9._____

10. simple and honest   10._____

KEY: 1—scintillating, 2—magnanimous, 3—versatile, 4—perspicacious, 5—stoical, 6—convivial, 7—urbane, 8—intrepid, 9—indefatigable, 10—ingenuous

By now, having finished these five intensive tests on our ten basic words, you are practically an expert on every one of them. Naturally, there's a lot more to these expressive adjectives than has been intimated in the few brief paragraphs that have thus far been presented. For a completer and richer understanding, see the next section which will enrich your comprehension by offering side lights, examples, derivations, and related forms and words.

ORIGINS AND RELATED WORDS: I

1. eat, drink, and be merry

The Latin verb *vivere, to live,* and the corresponding noun *vita, life,* have given us a goodly number of important English words.

Convivere is the Latin compound verb *to live together;* from this, in Latin, was formed the noun *convivium* (don't get impatient; we'll be back to English directly), which meant a *feast or banquet;* and from *convivium* we get our English word *convivial,* an adjective which describes the kind of person who likes to attend feasts and banquets because he enjoys (and supplies) the jovial good-fellowship usually characteristic of such gatherings.

Politicians, salesmen, presidents of colleges, and other such folk are noted for their *conviviality;* they are, says psychiatrist Eric Berne in his excellent introduction to psychoanalysis, *The Mind in Action,* "stomach-minded" or "visceratonic"—sociable, tending to roundness if not stoutness, gay, extroverted, pleasant company. Dr. Berne roughly (he admits that there is a good deal of overlapping) divides humanity into three types: *visceratonic*—stomach-minded people; *cerebratonic*—brain-minded people; and *somatotonic*—body-minded people. *Visceratonic* individuals are interested in food and companionship, *cerebratonic* individuals are interested in intellectual pursuits, and *somatotonic* individuals are interested in movement and action: walking, athletics, bodily discharge of energy. Each group, says Berne, attacks its troubles in a characteristic way:

The *visceratonic* goes out to supper, inviting some friends along so he can talk his problems over with them while eating.

The *cerebratonic* reads a book, sits alone and ruminates, or in some way *thinks* his way to a solution.

The *somatotonic* scrubs the floor, polishes his car, puts up a shelf, *does* something that requires physical energy.

2. life

The stem *vivere* (Latin, to *live*) is found in such common words as:

1. *vivacious*—full of the joy of living; animated; peppy—*a vivacious girl*
2. *vivid*—possessing the freshness of life; strong; sharp; *a vivid imagination; a vivid color*
3. *revive*—bring back to life—*spirits of ammonia will revive an unconscious person*
4. *vivisection*—operating on a live animal. *Sect* is the Latin root *to cut*. *Vivisection* is the process of experimenting with live animals, by scientists, to discover causes and cures of disease. *Antivivisectionists* are those misguided souls who, out of foolish sentimentality, object to the procedure, though many of our most important medical discoveries were made through *vivisection*.

Viviparous, also from *vivere*, means *producing young (babies) from the living body*—the means by which all human beings and most other animals are born. *Viviparous* is contrasted to *oviparous, producing young from eggs*, the process by which most fish, all fowl, and other lower forms of life are born. Your mental pronunciation of *viviparous* and *oviparous* is likely to be incorrect—put your accent on the second (*vip*), not the third syllable of each word.

Ov comes of course from the Latin *ovum, egg*. We hear it in *oval, egg-shaped;* and also in *ovulation*, the process of forming an egg, which human females in the child-bearing age do once a month.

3. more about life

The Latin noun *vita, life*, is found in:

1. *vital*—essential to life; of crucial importance—*a vital matter*
2. *vitality*—life and strength
3. *vitamin*—one of the many elements on which life is dependent. Good eyesight requires vitamin A (found, for example, in carrots); strong bones need vitamin D (found in sunlight and cod-liver oils); et cetera

4. *vitalize*—to impart vigor or life to
5. *devitalize*—to rob of vigor or life

Both *vitalize* and *devitalize* are used figuratively—for example, a program or plan is *vitalized* or *devitalized*, according to how it's handled.

4. French life

Sometimes, instead of getting our English words directly from Latin, we work through one of the Latin-derived or Romance languages. (The Romance languages—French, Spanish, Italian, Portuguese, and Roumanian—are so called because they were originally dialects of the old Roman tongue imposed on Western Europe by Roman conquerors.) English, by the way, is not a Romance language, but a Teutonic one. Our tongue is a development of a German dialect imposed on the natives of Britain by the Angles, Saxons, and Jutes of early English history. Though we have taken over into English more than 50 per cent of Latin words and almost 30 per cent of Greek words, our basic language is nevertheless German.

The French, using the same Latin root *vivere*, to *live*, formed two expressive phrases much used in English. French pronunciation is, of course, tricky, and if you are not at least superficially acquainted with that language, I cannot in all honesty recommend that you use these phrases in speech, as your pronunciation of them may sound a little awkward to the sophisticated ear—but you should know what they mean. These phrases are:

1. *joie de vivre*—pronounced something like ZHWAHD VEEV (ZH is identical with the S of PLEASURE)

Literally *joy of living*, this phrase describes an immense delight in being alive, an effervescent keenness for all the daily activities that human beings indulge in. A person who possesses *joie de vivre* is never moody, depressed, bored, or apathetic—on the contrary, he is full of sparkle, eager to engage in all group activities, and, most important, always seems to be having a good time, no matter what he is doing. *Joie de vivre* is precisely the opposite of *ennui* (this is also a word of French origin, but is easy to pronounce: ON-wee), which is a feeling of boredom, discontent, or weariness resulting sometimes from having a jaded, over-sophisticated appetite, sometimes from just finding all of life tedious and unappetizing, and sometimes implying in addition physical lassitude and general inactivity. Young children and simple people rarely experience *ennui*—to them life is always exciting, always new.

2. *bon vivant,* pronounced something like BOE(ng) vee-VAH(ng)—(ng) being a special muted nasal sound that only someone who speaks French knows how to make. If you have not studied French, it's futile even to try it.

A *bon vivant* is a person who lives luxuriously, especially in respect to rich food, good liquor, expensive theater parties, operas, and other accouterments of upper-class shenanigans. *Bon vivant* means, literally, *a good liver;* actually, *a high liver.* When you think of a *bon vivant,* you get the picture of someone attired in top hat, "soup and fish" or tuxedo, raising his cane to call a taxi while a beautiful evening-gowned and sophisticated-looking woman, sparkling in diamonds and furs, waits at his side. They're going to a champagne and partridge supper at the Stork Club, et cetera, et cetera—fill in your own details of the high life.

The *bon vivant* is of course a *convivial* person—and also likely to be a *gourmand* as well as very much *visceratonic* rather than *cerebratonic* or *somatotonic.*

5. food and how to enjoy it

The *gourmand* enjoys food with an almost sensual pleasure —to him the high spots of the day are the times for breakfast, lunch, dinner, and midnight supper. In short, he likes to eat, but the eating must be good. The verb form, *gormandize,* however, has suffered a degeneration in meaning—it signifies to stuff oneself like a pig.

A *gourmand* is significantly different from a *gourmet,* who has also a keen interest in food and liquor, but is much more fastidious, is more of a connoisseur, has a most discerning palate for delicate tastes, flavors, and differences; goes in for rare delicacies (like hummingbirds' tongues and other such absurdities); and really approaches the whole business from a scientific, rather than sensual, viewpoint. *Gourmet* is always a complimentary term, *gourmand* somewhat less so.

The man who eats voraciously, with no discernment whatever, but merely for the purpose of stuffing himself ("I know I haven't had enough to eat till I feel sick"), is called a *glutton*—obviously a highly derogatory term. The verb *gluttonize* is stronger than *gormandize;* the adjective *gluttonous* is about the strongest epithet you can apply to someone whose voracious eating habits you find repulsive. *Gluttonous* is sometimes also applied to a voracious insatiable appetite for money, sex, punishment, et cetera.

USING THE WORDS: II

Working from the single word *convivial,* we have turned up twenty-six related words, and before we go on let's check on your ability to pronounce, recall, understand, and use these words.

Can you pronounce the words?

1.	*conviviality*	kon-VIV-ee-AL-i-tee
2.	*visceratonic*	VISS-er-a-ton-ik
°3.	*cerebratonic*	SER-a-bra-ton-ik
4.	*somatotonic*	so-MAT-o-ton-ik
°5.	*vivacious*	vye-VAY-shus
6.	*vivid*	VIV-id
7.	*revive*	re-VYVE
8.	*vivisection*	viv-i-SECK-shun
9.	*antivivisectionist*	AN-tee-viv-i-SECK-shun-ist
°10.	*viviparous*	vi-VIPP-er-us
°11.	*oviparous*	o-VIPP-er-us
12.	*ovulation*	ov-you-LAY-shun
13.	*vital*	VYE-t'l
14.	*vitality*	vye-TAL-i-tee
15.	*vitamin*	VYE-ta-min
16.	*vitalize*	VYE-ta-lyze
17.	*devitalize*	de-VYE-ta-lyze
°18.	*joie de vivre*	ZHWAHD VEEV
°19.	*ennui*	ON-wee
°20.	*bon vivant*	BOE(ng) vee-VAH(ng)
°21.	*gourmand*	GOOR-m'nd
°22.	*gourmet*	goor-MAY
23.	*gormandize*	GORE-min-dyze

253

24. *glutton*	GLUT-in
25. *gluttonous*	GLUT-in-us
26. *gluttonize*	GLUT-in-yze

Can you work with the words? (I)

Match words and meanings.

1. visceratonic	a. peppy
2. cerebratonic	b. bearing live young
3. somatotonic	c. strong, sharp
4. vivacious	d. "body-minded"
5. vivid	e. "stomach-minded"
6. viviparous	f. greedy
7. oviparous	g. bearing young in eggs
8. gluttonous	h. "brain-minded"

KEY: 1—e, 2—h, 3—d, 4—a, 5—c, 6—b, 7—g, 8—f

Can you work with the words? (II)

1. conviviality	a. ripening of the egg
2. vivisection	b. a "high liver"
3. antivivisectionist	c. experimentation on live animals
4. ovulation	d. one who is a connoisseur of good food
5. vitality	e. effervescence
6. joie de vivre	f. one who enjoys food
7. ennui	g. one who eats greedily
8. bon vivant	h. boredom
9. gourmand	i. congeniality
10. gourmet	j. strength, vigor
11. glutton	k. one who is against experimentation on live animals

KEY: 1—i, 2—c, 3—k, 4—a, 5—j, 6—e, 7—h, 8—b, 9—f, 10—d, 11—g

Can you work with the words? (III)

1. revive	a. rob of life or strength
2. vital	b. element necessary for life
3. vitalize	c. important, crucial
4. devitalize	d. stuff oneself like a pig
5. gluttonize	e. breathe life into
6. vitamin	f. bring back to life

KEY: 1–f, 2–c, 3–e, 4–a, 5–d, 6–b

Do you understand the words? (I)

Decide whether each pair of words is the same or opposite in meaning.

1. conviviality—asceticism	SAME	OPPOSITE
2. vivacious—apathetic	SAME	OPPOSITE
3. vivid—dull	SAME	OPPOSITE
4. revive—kill	SAME	OPPOSITE
5. vitalize—rejuvenate	SAME	OPPOSITE
6. ennui—boredom	SAME	OPPOSITE
7. bon vivant—"man about town"	SAME	OPPOSITE
8. gormandize—starve	SAME	OPPOSITE
9. glutton—ascetic	SAME	OPPOSITE
10. joie de vivre—boredom	SAME	OPPOSITE

KEY: 1–o, 2–o, 3–o, 4–o, 5–s, 6–s, 7–s, 8–o, 9–o, 10–o

Do you understand the words? (II)

Are the following statements true or false?

1. The *visceratonic* individual is gregarious.	TRUE	FALSE
2. The *cerebratonic* individual likes to spend time in contemplation.	TRUE	FALSE
3. The *somatotonic* person enjoys taking part in athletics or exercise.	TRUE	FALSE

255

4. *Vivisection* is scientifically unreliable.	TRUE	FALSE
5. Humans are *viviparous*.	TRUE	FALSE
6. Cows are *oviparous*.	TRUE	FALSE
7. *Ovulation* takes place in females only when they are married.	TRUE	FALSE
8. An *antivivisectionist* believes in experimenting on live animals.	TRUE	FALSE
9. *Vitamins* are essential to good health.	TRUE	FALSE
10. A *bon vivant* lives like a hermit.	TRUE	FALSE
11. A *gourmet* stuffs himself with food.	TRUE	FALSE
12. It is normal for young children to be overwhelmed with *ennui*.	TRUE	FALSE
13. People who are keenly alive possess *joie de vivre*.	TRUE	FALSE

KEY: 1–t, 2–t, 3–t, 4–f, 5–t, 6–f, 7–f, 8–f, 9–t, 10–f, 11–f, 12–f, 13–t

---

Can you recall the words?

Now let's choose some of the more difficult words from the list and ask you to write them next to their proper definitions.

1. bearing young by eggs   1. O_____

2. bearing live young   2. V_____

3. "stomach-minded"   3. V_____

4. "brain-minded"   4. C_____

5. "body-minded"   5. S_____

6. good-fellowship   6. C_____

7. operating on living animals   7. V_____

8. one who is opposed to such an activity   8. A_____

9. the process, on the part of a female, of producing an egg   9. O_____

10. remove life or vigor   10. D_____

11. joy of living   11. J_____

256

12. one who eats like a pig   12. G_____

13. a "high liver"   13. B_____

14. one who is a connoisseur of good
    food; choice and dainty in his
    food habits   14. G_____

15. one who likes to eat good food in
    large quantities   15. G_____

16. to stuff oneself (weaker form)   16. G_____

17. to stuff oneself (stronger form) 17. G_____

18. boredom; discontent; tedium   18. E_____

19. lively, peppy   19. V_____

KEY: 1—oviparous, 2—viviparous, 3—visceratonic, 4—cerebratonic,
5—somatotonic, 6—conviviality, 7—vivisection, 8—antivivisection-
ist, 9—ovulation, 10—devitalize, 11—*joie de vivre*, 12—glutton,
13—*bon vivant*, 14—gourmet, 15—gourmand, 16—gormandize,
17—gluttonize, 18—ennui, 19—vivacious

ORIGINS AND RELATED WORDS: II

1. able demons

Indefatigable comes of course from the simple word *fatigue*
—the *in* is a negative particle, the suffix *able* means *able to be*
—hence, literally, *indefatigable* means *unable to be fatigued*.
The noun is *indefatigability*.

Indefatigable presents a pronunciation hazard of the first
magnitude—the temptation to accent the fourth syllable must
be stoutly, manfully, and successfully resisted. Place all your
emphasis on syllable three—FAT.

Thus: in-de-FAT-i-ga-b'l and in-de-FAT-i-ga-bil-i-tee.

There are a number of other words ending in *-able* which
offer the same pronunciation hazards. These are:

1. lamentable	LAM-en-ta-b'l
2. comparable	KOM-per-a-b'l
3. hospitable	HOSS-pi-ta-b'l
4. preferable	PREF-er-a-b'l
5. amicable	AM-i-ka-b'l
6. formidable	FOR-mi-da-b'l
7. despicable	DESS-pi-ka-b'l
8. revocable	REV-o-ka-b'l
9. reparable	REP-er-a-b'l
10. admirable	AD-mir-a-b'l

These first-syllable-accent pronunciations are admittedly difficult if you're not accustomed to them—but they're worth practicing and cultivating, since they are used by sophisticated speakers.

2. how simple can one be?

Ingenuous is a complimentary term, though its synonyms *naïve, gullible,* and *credulous* are faintly derogatory.

To call a person *ingenuous* implies that he is frank, open, artless—in other words, he is not likely to try to put anything over on you nor is he apt to hide feelings or thoughts that a more sophisticated person would consider it wise, tactful, or expedient to hide.

Ingenuous should not be confused with *ingenious* (note the slight difference in spelling), which on the contrary means shrewd, clever, inventive. *Ingenious* as a noun becomes *ingenuity; ingenuous* becomes *ingenuousness.*

To call a person *naïve* is to imply that he has not learned the ways of the world, and is therefore idealistic and trusting beyond the point of safety; such idealism and trust having come from ignorance and inexperience. The noun is *naïveté.* (Let me indicate the correct pronunciations at this point before you begin to form any bad habits—nah-EEV and nah-eev-TAY.)

Credulous implies a willingness to believe almost anything, no matter how fantastic. Such an attitude, like *naïveté,* usually results, again, from ignorance and inexperience.

Gullible means easily tricked, easily fooled, easily imposed on. It is stronger than *credulous* and is a more derogatory term. *Gullibility* results more from stupidity than from ignorance or inexperience.

These four synonyms, *ingenuous, naïve, credulous,* and *gullible* are fairly close, but they contain areas of distinction worth remembering. Let's review them.

1. *ingenuous*—frank, not given to concealment
2. *naïve*—inexperienced, unsophisticated, trusting
3. *credulous*—willing to believe; not suspicious or skeptical
4. *gullible*—easily tricked

3. belief and disbelief

Credulous comes from the Latin *credo, believe,* the same root found in *credit* (if someone *believes* in your honesty, he will extend *credit* to you; he will *credit* what you say; et cetera). *Ous* is a suffix which usually signifies *full of.* So, strictly, *credulous* means *full of believingness.*

Do not confuse *credulous* with *credible.* In the latter word we see combined the root *cred, believe,* with *ible,* a suffix which means *able to be.* Something *credible can be believed.*

Let's chart some differences;

a *credulous* listener—one who fully believes what he hears
a *credible* story—one that invites belief
an *incredulous* attitude—an attitude of skepticism
an *incredible* story—one that cannot be believed
an *incredible* character—a person who is so unique that you can scarcely believe that he exists

Nouns are formed as follows:

credulous—credulity
incredulous—incredulity
credible—credibility
incredible—incredibility

To check your understanding of these distinctions, try the next test.

Can you use these words correctly?

Use *credulous, credible,* or corresponding negative or noun forms in the following sentences:

1. She listened _____ly to her husband's confession of his continuous infidelity, for she had always considered him a paragon of virtue.

2. He told his audience an _____ and fantastic story of his narrow escapes.

3. He'll believe you—he's very _____.

4. Make your characters more _____ if you want your reader to believe in them.

5. We listened dumb-struck, full of _____, to the shocking details of corruption and vice.

6. He has the most _____ good luck.

7. The _____ of it! How can such things happen?

8. In November of 1948, the Republicans listened to the national election returns, their _____ strained to the utmost.

9. "Do you believe me?" "Sure—your story is _____ enough."

10. I'm not objecting to the total _____ of your story, but only to your thinking that I'm _____ enough to take it all in!

KEY: 1—incredulously, 1—incredible, 3—credulous, 4—credible, 5—incredulity, 6—incredible, 7—incredibility, 8—credulity, 9—credible, 10—incredibility, credulous

---

4. what people believe in

Cred, the Latin root which means believe, is the origin of four other useful English words.

1. Credo—a personal belief, a code of ethics, the principles by which someone guides his actions.
2. Creed—a close synonym of credo; in addition, a religious belief, such as Catholicism, Judaism, Protestantism, et cetera.

3. *Credence*—belief, as in "I place no *credence* in his stories," or "Why should I give any *credence* to what you say?"
4. *Credentials*—a document or documents proving a person's right to a title or privilege (i.e., a right to be believed) as in: "The new ambassador presented his *credentials* to the State Department."

5. heads and tails

We can hardly close our book on the words suggested by *ingenuous* without looking at the other side of the coin. If *ingenuous* means *frank*, its opposite, *disingenuous* would mean *not frank*. But a *disingenuous* person is far more than simply a person who is not *ingenuous*. He is crafty, cunning, dishonest, artful, insincere, untrustworthy—and he is all of these while making a pretense of being simple, frank, and aboveboard. You are thinking of a wolf in sheep's clothing? It's a good analogy.

Similarly, a remark may be *disingenuous*, as may also a statement, an attitude, a confession, et cetera.

USING THE WORDS: III

Let's pause for a moment now to work with the twenty-one new words we've turned up.

Can you pronounce the words?

1.	indefatigability	in-de-FAT-i-ga-bil-i-tee
*2.	ingenuousness	in-JEN-yoo-us-ness
3.	ingenious	in-JEEN-yus
*4.	ingenuity	in-je-NOO-i-tee
*5.	naïve	nah-EEV
*6.	naïveté	nah-eev-TAY
7.	credulous	KREJ-yoo-lus
8.	gullible	GULL-i-b'l
9.	gullibility	gull-i-BILL-i-tee
10.	incredulous	in-KREJ-yoo-lus
11.	credible	KRED-i-b'l
12.	incredible	in-KRED-i-b'l
13.	credo	KREE-do
14.	creed	KREED

°15. credence   KREE-dence
 16. credentials   kre-DEN-shulz
 17. disingenuous   diss-in-JEN-yoo-us
°18. credulity   kre-JOO-li-tee
°19. incredulity   in-kre-JOO-li-tee
 20. credibility   kred-i-BILL-i-tee
 21. incredibility   in-kred-i-BILL-i-tee

Can you work with the words? (I)

Match the definitions to the words.

WORDS	DEFINITIONS
1. indefatigability	a. cunning
2. ingenuousness	b. skepticism
3. disingenuousness	c. personal code of ethics
4. naïveté	d. frankness
5. credibility	e. belief, trust
6. incredulity	f. tirelessness
7. credence	g. believability
8. credo	h. inexperience

KEY: 1—f, 2—d, 3—a, 4—h, 5—g, 6—b, 7—e, 8—c

Can you work with the words? (II)

WORDS	DEFINITIONS
1. ingenious	a. easily tricked
2. credulous	b. religious belief
3. gullible	c. inexperienced, unworldly
4. incredible	d. document proving privileges, et cetera
5. creed	e. unbelievable
6. credentials	f. shrewdness
7. ingenuity	g. clever, inventive
8. naïve	h. willing to believe

KEY: 1—g, 2—h, 3—a, 4—e, 5—b, 6—d, 7—f, 8—c

Do you understand the words?

React quickly to each question.

1. Is *indefatigability* a sign of physical and emotional health?	YES	NO
2. Is *ingenuousness* a normal quality of young childhood?	YES	NO
3. Is *ingenuity* a characteristic of inventors?	YES	NO
4. Are most adolescents *naïve?*	YES	NO
5. Are unintelligent people often *gullible?*	YES	NO
6. Is *incredulity* the mark of the agnostic?	YES	NO
7. Does an *incredible* story invite belief?	YES	NO
8. Do men generally live by a *credo?*	YES	NO
9. Does our constitution guarantee certain rights and privileges to American citizens irrespective of their *creed?*	YES	NO
10. Are *ingenious* people often *disingenuous?*	YES	NO
11. Do we generally give *credence* to *incredible* statements?	YES	NO

KEY: 1—yes, 2—yes, 3—yes, 4—no, 5—yes, 6—yes, 7—no, 8—yes, 9—yes, 10—yes, 11—no

Can you recall the words?

Now, without further reference to the twenty-one words of this section, it's your job to write the proper one next to its definition. Be guided by the initial letter.

1. inexperience, unsophistication   1. N_____

2. believing   2. C_____

3. religious belief   3. C_____

4. believable   4. C_____

5. great reservoir of energy   5. I_____

6. frankness   6. I_____

7. crafty, dishonest   7. D_____

8. inventive, clever   8. I_____

9. easily tricked   9. G_____

10. skeptical   10. I_____

11. unbelievable   11. I_____

12. personal code   12. C_____

KEY: 1—naïveté, 2—credulous, 3—creed, 4—credible, 5—indefatigability, 6—ingenuousness, 7—disingenuous, 8—ingenious, 9—
gullible, 10—incredulous, 11—incredible, 12—credo

ORIGINS AND RELATED WORDS: III

1. how to look

The Latin verbs *specto* and *specere*, to *look*, have fathered
a host of common English words; *spectacle, spectator, inspect,
retrospect* (looking back), *prospect* (a looking ahead), et
cetera. In a variant spelling *spic,* the root is found in *conspicuous* (easily seen or looked at), *perspicacious* and *perspicuous.*

A *perspicacious* person is keen-minded, mentally sharp,
astute. A man of *perspicacity* is a man of keen intelligence,
a person of *acumen.*

Perspicacious should not be confused with the similar word
perspicuous. Here is the important distinction:

Perspicacious means *smart, able to look at and understand
quickly.* This adjective applies to persons.

Perspicuous is the obverse side of the coin—it means *easily
understood from one look,* and applies to writing, style, books,
and like things that have to be understood. Hence it is a
synonym of *clear, simple, lucid.* If a man writes with *perspicuous* style, he is easy to understand. If a man is *perspicacious,* he understands.

The noun form of *perspicuous* is *perspicuity.*

So the idea of *looking* may be represented by either *spec* or *spic:*

A *spectacle* is something to *look at; spectacles* (eyeglasses) are the means by which you get a comfortable and accurate *look* at the world.

A *spectator* is one who *looks at* what's happening.

To *inspect* is to *look into* something.

Retrospect is a backward *look*—generally the word is preceded by the preposition *in*, for instance "His life *in retrospect* seemed dreary and dull," or "Most experiences seem more enjoyable *in retrospect* than in actuality."

Prospect is a forward look; *prospective* is the adjectival form. What's the *prospect* for prosperity, for world peace, for better living conditions? Your *prospective* mother-in-law is the one you can look forward to having if you marry a certain person; similarly, your *prospective* bride, groom, child, job, vacation, et cetera.

Conspicuous means easily *looked at*, catching the eye.

A *perspicacious* person can *look through* something—he's clever, ingenious, intelligent, sharp, et cetera. The noun is *perspicacity*.

Anything *perspicuous* can be *looked through*—hence it is clear, easily understood. The noun is *perspicuity*.

That reviews the words we've discussed. Now consider some others derived from the root *spec, to look:*

1. If you enjoy *looking at* yourself, figuratively speaking, then you like to examine your mental processes and emotional reactions, in the same intense way characteristic of the *introvert* (see Chapter 3). Your mind's eye turns inward, and you spend a good deal of time analyzing yourself, your character, your personality, your actions. Hence, since you *look inward*, you are *introspective*. If you are told to *introspect*, you start to *look inward* and to examine your inner reactions. Too much *introspection* generally leads to unhappiness and sometimes to thoughts of suicide—few people have the courage or stamina to analyze themselves minutely. Adolescence is that confused period of a person's life when he spends a good deal of time and energy in *introspection*.

During psychoanalysis, of course, you are constantly *introspecting*—but with the wise guidance and gentle interpretation of the analyst, your *introspection* helps you to a better understanding of your emotions.

2. There are times when you have to *look around* most carefully; you must then be *circumspect—watchful, cautious, alert.* (*Circum,* around, is the root we met in *circumlocution.*) The noun is *circumspection.*

3. If something *looks* good or sensible, but actually is not, we call it *specious.* A *specious* argument sounds plausible, but in reality is based on an error, a fallacy, or an untruth. The noun is *speciousness.*

2. minds and souls

Anima, in Latin, is the word for *soul, spirit, breath of life.* We find the root in *animal, animate* and *inanimate, animated,* and *animation;* knowing the meaning of the root, you have a better understanding of any word that contains it.

Magnanimous contains, in addition to *anima,* the root *magna, large, great,* which you will recall from *magniloquent.* A *magnanimous* person has such a great, noble, soul that he is beyond seeking petty revenge. The noun form is *magnanimity.*

On the other hand, someone who has a tiny, tiny, soul is *pusillanimous—*this word uses the Latin *pusil,* very small. Hence, he would be contemptibly petty and mean. The noun is *pusillanimity.*

Anima, by extension, means *mind* as well as *soul.* It is from this extended meaning of the root that we get the following interesting words:

1. *unanimous—*of one *mind.* If the Supreme Court hands down a *unanimous* opinion, all the judges were of one *mind. Un* is a shortened form of the Latin word *unus, one.* The noun form is *unanimity.*

2. *equanimity—*composure; literally, equal or balanced *mind;* evenness or calmness of mind. If you preserve your *equanimity* under trying circumstances, you keep your temper, you do not get confused, you remain calm.

3. *animus—*hostility, ill will, malevolence. Strictly, *animus* is simply *mind,* but has degenerated, as words often do, to mean *unfriendly mind.* The word is most often used in a pattern like this: "I bear you no *animus,* even though you have wronged me."

4. *animosity—*ill will, hostility. An exact synonym of *animus,* and a more common word, it is used in patterns like: "You

266

feel a good deal of *animosity,* don't you?," "There is real *animosity* between Bill and Ernie," "If you bear me no *animosity,* why do you treat me so badly?"

3. ile demons

Versatile comes from a Latin verb *to turn*—a *versatile* person can turn his hand to many things successfully. The noun is of course *versatility.* The preferred pronunciation of *versatile* is VUR-*sa-till,* not VUR-*sa-tyle.* Most words of more than one syllable ending in *-ile* are preferably pronounced with a short *i* (*ill*), for example:

hostile	HOSS-till
juvenile	JOO-ve-nill
textile	TEX-till
fertile	FUR-till
sterile	STER-ill
docile	DOSS-ill

There are, however, a number of important exceptions. The following are preferably pronounced *yle* (long *i,* as in *tie*).

exile	EX-yle
senile	SEE-nyle
profile	PRO-fyle
infantile	IN-fin-tyle
reconcile	RECK-in-syle
bibliophile	BIB-lee-o-fyle

4. Zeno and the front porch

Almost 2300 years ago, in ancient Greece, the philosopher Zeno lectured on a topic which still piques the human mind, to wit: "How to Live a Happy Life." Zeno would stand on a porch (the Greek word for which is *stoa*) and hold forth somewhat as follows: Men should free themselves from intense emotion, be unmoved by both joy and sorrow, and submit without complaint to unavoidable necessity. Today, Freudians preach almost the exact opposite—let your emotions flow freely, express your love or animosity, don't bottle up your feelings. But in the fourth century B.C., when Zeno was expounding his credo, his philosophy of control of the passions fell on receptive ears. His followers were called *Stoics*, after the *stoa,* or porch, from which the master lectured.

If we call someone a *stoic,* we mean that he bears his pain or sorrow without complaint, he meets adversity with unflinching fortitude. This sounds very noble, you will admit—actually, according to modern psychological belief, it is healthier not to be so *stoical. Stoicism* may be an admirable virtue (mainly because we do not then have to share the *stoic's* troubles), but it can be overdone.

5. fear and trembling

Intrepid (the accent belongs on the second syllable—in-TREP-id) comes from the Latin *trepido, to be alarmed.* The *intrepid* person exhibits courage and fearlessness when confronted by dangers from which you and I would run like hell. The noun is *intrepidity* (here the accent shifts to the third syllable: in-tre-PID-i-tee).

Trepido is found also in *trepidation*—great fear, trembling, alarm.

6. quick flash

Scintilla, in Latin, is a quick, bright, spark; in English the word may also mean a spark, but more commonly refers to a very small particle (which, in a sense, a spark is), as in the phrase, "there was not a *scintilla* of evidence against him."

In the verb *scintillate,* the idea of the spark is kept; someone who *scintillates* sparkles with charm and wit, flashes brightly with humor. The noun is *scintillation.*

7. city and country

People who live in the city go to theaters, attend the opera, listen to concerts, take part in adult-education programs, visit museums and picture galleries, browse in book stores, shop at Macy's, Marshall Field's, or other big department stores, see radio and television broadcasts in the flesh, and can ride the trolley, bus, or subway to college. And they take a taxi from here to there when they are too lazy or too rich to walk. Evenings they spend in night clubs, listening to stale jokes and drinking fresh whiskey.

These activities fill them with culture and sophistication.

Also, they crowd into jammed subway trains and busses, squeeze into packed elevators, cross the street in competition with high-powered motor cars, patiently stand in line outside of movie houses, and then wait for hours in the lobby for the seats to be vacated. They have telephones, inside toilets, electric refrigerators, automatic washing machines, milk delivered to their door, and the relaxation of spending two hours a day going to and coming from work.

Such privileges and possessions fill them with polish, refinement, and courtesy.

On the other hand, what do people in the country have? Nothing but trees, flowers, good food, clean air, honest friendships, and long walks down wooded lanes. Hence they are narrowminded, practically illiterate, completely unsophisticated, politically backward, and lamentably unenlightened— so it is claimed.

Now you understand why the drift of population has consistently been from the farms to the towns, from the towns to the big cities.

And you will also understand why the Latin words for *city* and *country* are used to describe entirely different species of mortals.

Urbs, for example, is the Latin word for *city.* An *urbane* person is, literally, a city dweller—hence, polished, refined, courteous, gracious, affable, cultivated, suave, sophisticated, tactful—add your own adjectives to describe any other qualities you deem admirable.

Rus and *ruris* are two forms of the Latin word for *country.* A *rustic* person is therefore awkward, boorish, lacking in refinement and polish.

Urbane and *rustic,* when applied to people, are emotionally charged words. *Urbane* is highly complimentary, *rustic* highly derogatory. The noun form of *urbane* is *urbanity.*

But each of these words has a neutral form. *Urban* means, simply, *pertaining to the city; rural, pertaining to the country.* And no moral judgment implied in either word. We speak, for instance, of the tensions of *urban* life as contrasted to the peacefulness of *rural* life; of *urban* communities and *rural* communities. (*Suburban*, of course, signifies near a *city*.)

The verb to *rusticate* has, also, a slightly derogatory implication—it means, strictly, to spend some time in the country, but since, as I have very patiently pointed out, there's really nothing to do in the country, *rusticate* implies a departure from the excitement and nervous tensions of city life, hence, by extension, getting out of circulation, so to speak.

USING THE WORDS: IV

We have discussed thirty-four new words in the preceding section, every one of them useful, expressive, and well worth knowing. Remember that you can best master new words by using all possible means of experience with them—your mind, your eyes, your voice, your ears, your fingers. In the first test you let your voice (as you say the words aloud) and your ears (as you listen to yourself saying them) help you along the road to mastery.

Can you pronounce the words?

1.	*retrospect*	RET-ro-spect
°2.	*astute*	ass-TOOT
°3.	*perspicacity*	pur-spi-KASS-i-tee
°4.	*acumen*	a-KYOO-men
°5.	*perspicuous*	pur-SPICK-yoo-us
°6.	*perspicuity*	pur-spi-KYOO-i-tee
°7.	*magnanimity*	mag-na-NIM-i-tee
°8.	*pusillanimous*	pyoo-si-LAN-i-mus
°9.	*pusillanimity*	pyoo-si-la-NIM-i-tee
10.	*unanimous*	yoo-NAN-i-mus
°11.	*unanimity*	yoo-na-NIM-i-tee
12.	*equanimity*	ee-kwa-NIM-i-tee
13.	*animus*	AN-i-mus
14.	*animosity*	an-i-MOSS-i-tee
15.	*versatility*	vur-sa-TILL-i-tee
16.	*stoic*	STO-ic
°17	*stoicism*	STO-i-sizm
°18.	*intrepidity*	in-tre-PID-i-tee
19.	*trepidation*	trep-i-DAY-shun
°20	*scintilla*	sin-TILL-a

21. *scintillate*	SIN-ti-layt
22. *scintillation*	sin-ti-LAY-shun
°23. *urbanity*	ur-BAN-i-tee
24. *rustic*	RUSS-tick
25. *rural*	ROOR-il
26. *urban*	UR-ban†
27. *rusticate*	RUSS-ti-kayt
28. *introspective*	in-tro-SPEK-tiv
29. *introspect*	IN-tro-spekt
30. *introspection*	in-tro-SPEK-shun
31. *circumspect*	SUR-kum-spekt
32. *circumspection*	sur-kum-SPEK-shun
°33. *specious*	SPEE-shus
°34. *speciousness*	SPEE-shus-ness

Can you work with the words? (I)

Match words and definitions.

1. retrospect	a. complete agreement
2. acumen	b. pettiness
3. magnanimity	c. malevolence
4. pusillanimity	d. backward look
5. unanimity	e. calmness
6. equanimity	f. ability in many fields
7. animosity	g. mental keenness
8. versatility	h. generosity

KEY: 1—d, 2—g, 3—h, 4—b, 5—a, 6—e, 7—c, 8—f

Can you work with the words? (II)

1. stoicism	a. fearlessness
2. intrepidity	b. sparkle
3. trepidation	c. inward look
4. scintillation	d. uncomplaining attitude to pain or trouble
5. urbanity	e. falsity
6. introspection	f. polish, cultivation

† *a* as in the last syllable of *husband*.

7. circumspection	g. care, cautiousness
8. speciousness	h. fear

Can you work with the words? (III)

1. astute	a. of one mind
2. pusillanimous	b. ill will
3. unanimous	c. pertaining to the city
4. animus	d. petty
5. rustic	e. self-analytical
6. urban	f. sharp
7. introspective	g. cautious
8. circumspect	h. false
9. specious	i. countrified

Can you work with the words? (IV)

1. perspicacity	a. clearness
2. perspicuity	b. to be witty
3. stoic	c. spend time in the country
4. scintilla	d. one who controls his emotions
5. scintillate	e. look inward
6. rural	f. a very small amount
7 rusticate	g. keen intelligence
8 introspect	h. clear, understandable
9. perspicuous	i. keen-minded
10. perspicacious	j. pertaining to the country

Do you understand the words? (I)

React to each question.

1. Does life often seem pleasanter in *retrospect*?	YES	NO
2. Are *astute* people gullible?	YES	NO
3. Is *perspicacity* a common characteristic?	YES	NO
4. Is a man of *acumen* likely to be naïve?	YES	NO
5. Is a *perspicuous* style of writing easy to read?	YES	NO
6. Should all writers aim at *perspicuity*?	YES	NO
7. Is *magnanimity* a characteristic of small-minded people?	YES	NO
8. Does a person of *pusillanimous* mind often think of petty revenge?	YES	NO
9. Is a *unanimous* opinion one in which all concur?	YES	NO
10. Do dictators demand *unanimity* of thought?	YES	NO

KEY: 1—yes, 2—no, 3—no, 4—no, 5—yes, 6—yes, 7—no, 8—yes, 9—yes, 10—yes

---

Do you understand the words? (II)

1. Is it easy to preserve one's *equanimity* under trying circumstances?	YES	NO
2. Do we bear *animus* to our enemies?	YES	NO
3. Do we usually feel great *animosity* toward our friends?	YES	NO
4. Do we admire *versatility*?	YES	NO
5. Does a *stoic* usually complain?	YES	NO
6. Is *stoicism* a mark of an uninhibited personality?	YES	NO
7. Do cowards show *intrepidity* in the face of danger?	YES	NO
8. Do cowards often feel a certain amount of *trepidation*?	YES	NO
9. Is a *scintilla* of evidence a great amount?	YES	NO
10. Do dull people *scintillate*?	YES	NO

11. Is *urbanity* a characteristic of brusque people? YES NO

12. Is a *rustic* quality one that shows poise and sophistication? YES NO

KEY: 1—no, 2—yes, 3—no, 4—yes, 5—no, 6—no, 7—no, 8—yes, 9—no, 10—no, 11—no, 12—no

---

Do you understand the words? (III)

1. Is New York a *rural* community? YES NO
2. Is a village an *urban* community? YES NO
3. Do you *rusticate* in the city? YES NO
4. Are extroverts very *introspective?* YES NO
5. Does an introvert spend a good deal of time in *introspection?* YES NO
6. In dangerous circumstances, is it wise to be *circumspect?* YES NO
7. Do *specious* arguments often sound convincing? YES NO

KEY: 1—no, 2—no, 3—no, 4—no, 5—yes, 6—yes, 7—yes

Do you understand the words? (IV)

Decide whether each pair is the same or opposite in meaning.

1. retrospect—prospect SAME OPPOSITE
2. astute—perspicacious SAME OPPOSITE
3. acumen—stupidity SAME OPPOSITE
4. perspicuous—confused SAME OPPOSITE
5. magnanimous—noble SAME OPPOSITE
6. pusillanimous—petty SAME OPPOSITE
7. unanimous—divided SAME OPPOSITE
8. equanimity—nervousness SAME OPPOSITE
9. animosity—hostility SAME OPPOSITE
10. animus—friendliness SAME OPPOSITE
11. versatility—monomania SAME OPPOSITE
12. stoicism—cowardice SAME OPPOSITE

13. intrepidity—fear	SAME	OPPOSITE
14. trepidation—courage	SAME	OPPOSITE
15. scintilla—slight amount	SAME	OPPOSITE
16. urbanity—refinement	SAME	OPPOSITE
17. rustic—crude	SAME	OPPOSITE
18. rural—urban	SAME	OPPOSITE
19. introspective—self-analytic	SAME	OPPOSITE
20. circumspect—careless	SAME	OPPOSITE
21. specious—true	SAME	OPPOSITE

KEY: 1—o, 2—s, 3—o, 4—o, 5—s, 6—s, 7—o, 8—o, 9—s, 10—o, 11—o, 12—o, 13—o, 14—o, 15—s, 16—s, 17—s, 18—o, 19—s, 20—o, 21—o

Can you recall the words? (I)

You used your mind when you read about these thirty-four words; your voice and ears and mind in the preceding tests; now you will again use your mind in remembering, and your fingers in writing, the words. Let the initial letters guide you in recalling each word for which a definition is given.

1. ability in many fields   1. V_____

2. pertaining to the city   2. U_____

3. spend time in the country   3. R_____

4. merest spark; small amount   4. S_____

5. courage   5. I_____

KEY: 1—versatility, 2—urban, 3—rusticate, 4—scintilla, 5—intrepidity

Can you recall the words? (II)

1. unflinching fortitude   1. S_____

2. countrified; unpolished   2. R_____

275

3. pertaining to the country   3. R_____

4. process of looking back to the past   4. R_____

5. nobleness of mind or spirit   5. M_____

KEY: 1—stoicism, 2—rustic, 3—rural, 4—retrospect, 5—magnanimity

Can you recall the words? (III)

1. keen-minded   1. A_____

2. clear, lucid   2. P_____

3. petty, mean   3. P_____

4. all of one mind or opinion   4. U_____

5–6. ill will (two forms)   5. A_____

     6. A_____

KEY: 1—astute, 2—perspicuous, 3—pusillanimous, 4—unanimous, 5—animus, 6—animosity

Can you recall the words? (IV)

1–2. keenness of mind (two forms)   1. P_____

     2. A_____

3. clearness   3. P_____

4. one who keeps his emotions, during times of trouble, hidden   4. S_____

5. sophistication, courtesy, refinement   5. U_____

KEY: 1—perspicacity, 2—acumen, 3—perspicuity, 4—stoic, 5—urbanity

Can you recall the words? (V)

1. pettiness of character	1. P_____
2. noun form of *unanimous*	2. U_____
3. mental calmness, balance	3. E_____
4. fear and trembling	4. T_____
5. sparkle with wit and humor	5. S_____

KEY: 1—pusillanimity, 2—unanimity, 3—equanimity, 4—trepidation, 5—scintillate

Can you recall the words? (VI)

1. looking inward; examining one's mental processes or emotional reactions	1. I_____
2. cautious	2. C_____
3. seemingly true, actually false	3. S_____
4. to think of one's mental processes	4. I_____
5. care, watchfulness	5. C_____

KEY: 1—introspective, 2—circumspect, 3—specious, 4—introspect, 5—circumspection

FIVE REVIEW TESTS

This has been a long, but I hope not a tedious, chapter. From a consideration of ten complimentary adjectives we have wandered far afield, discovering twelve important roots and many related and derived forms. To tie the whole business up neatly in a single package, try the following four tests of your success with this chapter. Review first, if you wish; or, if you feel particularly intrepid today, go right into the tests.

I. matching

WORD	MEANING
1. convivial	a. frank
2. indefatigable	b. noble, forgiving
3. ingenuous	c. unflinching
4. perspicacious	d. courteous
5. magnanimous	e. companionable, gregarious
6. versatile	f. witty
7. stoical	g. capable in many directions
8. intrepid	h. brave
9. scintillating	i. keen-minded
10. urbane	j. tireless

KEY: 1—e, 2—j, 3—a, 4—i, 5—b, 6—g, 7—c, 8—h, 9—f, 10—d

II. same or opposite?

1. vivacious—sluggish	SAME	OPPOSITE
2. vital—crucial	SAME	OPPOSITE
3. ennui—boredom	SAME	OPPOSITE
4. *bon vivant*—gourmand	SAME	OPPOSITE
5. gourmet—ascetic	SAME	OPPOSITE
6. ingenuous-crafty	SAME	OPPOSITE
7. naïve—sophisticated	SAME	OPPOSITE
8. credulous—skeptical	SAME	OPPOSITE
9. disingenuous—insincere	SAME	OPPOSITE
10. credo-belief	SAME	OPPOSITE

KEY: 1—opposite, 2—same, 3—same, 4—same, 5—opposite, 6—opposite, 7—opposite, 8—opposite, 9—same, 10—same

III. changing parts of speech

Change these adjectives to nouns.

1. indefatigable   1. _____

2. perspicacious   2. _____

3. stoical   3. _____

278

4. urbane	4. _____	
5. naïve	5. _____	
6. incredulous	6. _____	
7. incredible	7. _____	
8. perspicuous	8. _____	
9. magnanimous	9. _____	
10. pusillanimous	10. _____	

KEY: 1—indefatigability, 2—perspicacity, 3—stoicism, 4—urbanity, 5—naïveté, 6—incredulity, 7—incredibility, 8—perspicuity, 9—magnanimity, 10—pusillanimity

IV. roots

Fill in the meanings of the roots.

ROOT	MEANING	EXAMPLE
1. SPECT	_____	retrospect
2. URB	_____	urban
3. CRED	_____	credo
4. ANIM	_____	animate
5. MAGN	_____	magnanimous
6. TREP	_____	trepidation
7. VIV	_____	viviparous
8. VIT	_____	vital
9. RUS, RUR	_____	rural
10. IN	_____	incredible
11. OUS	_____	vivacious
12. IBLE, ABLE	_____	credible

KEY: 1—look, 2—city, 3—believe, 4—spirit, soul, mind, 5—large, 6—alarm, 7—live, 8—life, 9—country, 10—not, 11—full of, 12—able to be

Check the word which most closely fits each definition.

1. Tireless:
    (a) convivial, (b) indefatigable, (c) versatile
2. Frank, unsophisticated:
    (a) ingenuous, (b) ingenious, (c) intrepid
3. Unflinching, uncomplaining:
    (a) perspicacious, (b) urbane, (c) stoical
4. Noble, forgiving, generous:
    (a) pusillanimous, (b) unanimous, (c) magnanimous
5. Brain-minded:
    (a) cerebratonic, (b) somatotonic, (c) visceratonic
6. Giving birth to live young:
    (a) oviparous, (b) ovulation, (c) viviparous
7. Tedium, boredom:
    (a) ennui, (b) *joie de vivre,* (c) vitality
8. Connoisseur of choice food:
    (a) gourmet, (b) gourmand, (c) glutton
9. Inexperienced in the ways of the world:
    (a) credulous, (b) naïve, (c) credible
10. Easily tricked:
    (a) gullible, (b) incredulous, (c) ingenious
11. Backward look:
    (a) prospect, (b) retrospect, (c) introspection
12. Clearness:
    (a) perspicacity, (b) perspicuity, (c) intrepidity
13. Resentment:
    (a) animosity, (b) stoicism, (c) urbanity
14. Countrified:
    (a) rustic, (b) specious, (c) circumspect

KEY: 1—b, 2—a, 3—c, 4—c, 5—a, 6—c, 7—a, 8—a, 9—b, 10—a, 11—b,
    12—b, 13—a, 14—a

WORDS INFLUENCE YOUR THINKING

In the second week of our work together we have thoroughly explored over 270 valuable words and more than 40 important Greek and Latin roots.

As we went along we stopped at frequent intervals to check on the success of your learning and to give you opportunities to say aloud, think about, work with, and recall the words you were learning.

By now, therefore, the words in Week II are probably old friends of yours; they have started to influence your thinking, have perhaps begun to appear in your conversation, and have certainly become conspicuous in your reading. In short, they have been effective in making further changes in your intellectual climate.

Let us pause now for our periodic checkup of the success of your study. Directly after the next Brief Intermission you will find another Achievement Test. Take the test cold if you feel that all the material is at your fingertips; or spend a little time reviewing the chapters in Week II if you believe such review is necessary.

BRIEF INTERMISSION TEN:
TRY THIS PRONUNCIATION TEST

Is your speech an asset or a liability? Does your pronunciation meet the standards set by educated people? In a phrase, *do you pronounce your words correctly?*

These are not easy questions to answer, but if you will give just ten minutes of your time to three short tests, you can determine whether you speak as effectively as you should.

TEST I—EASY

Your speech is free of illiterate patterns if you can check the correct form of at least seven of the following words.

1. *aviator:* AVV-ee-ay-ter or AY-vee-ay-ter?
2. *athletic:* ath-a-LET-ic or ath-LET-ic?
3. *elm:* ELL-um or ELM?
4. *preferable:* pre-FER-ab'l or PREFF-er-ab'l?
5. *genuine:* JEN-yoo-wyne or JEN-yoo-win?
6. *grievous:* GREE-vee-us or GREE-vus?
7. *percolator:* PER-kyo-lay-ter or PER-ko-lay-ter?
8. *accessory:* a-SESS-o-ry or ack-SESS-o-ry?

TEST II—HARD

Your speech is on the college-graduate level if you can check the correct form of at least seven of the following words.

1. *grimace:* gri-MAYCE or GRIM-iss?
2. *impotent:* IM-po-tent or im-PO-tent?
3. *human:* HYOO-man or YOO-man?
4. *comparable:* COM-per-ab'l or com-PAR-ab'l?
5. *verbatim:* ver-BAY-tim or ver-BAT-im?
6. *orgy:* OR-jee or OR-guee?
7. *chiropodist:* ki-ROP-o-dist or tchi-ROP-o-dist?
8. *acumen:* a-KYOO-men or ACK-yoo-men?

TEST III—VERY HARD

You rarely, if ever, make an error in pronunciation if you can check the correct form of seven or more of the following words.

1. *ignominy:* ig-NOM-i-ny or IG-no-mi-ny?
2. *dishabille:* DISH-a-bill or diss-a-BEEL?
3. *piquant:* pe-KAHNT or PEE-kint?
4. *plethora:* ple-THORE-a or PLETH-o-ra?
5. *anathema:* a-na-THEE-ma or a-NATH-e-ma?
6. *vagary:* VAY-ga-ry or va-GAIR-y?
7. *combatant:* com-BAT-ant or COM-ba-tant?
8. *machinations:* match-i-NAY-shunz or mack-i-NAY-shunz?

KEY: In Test I, all *second* choices are correct; in Test II, all *first* choices are correct; and in Test III, all *second* choices are correct.

13

HOW TO CHECK YOUR
SECOND WEEK'S PROGRESS

I—roots

Directions: In the table below you will find a number of roots we have discussed, with examples of their use. It is your job to fill in the meaning of each root.

ROOT	MEANING	EXAMPLE
1. *voc*	_____	equivocal
2. *male*	_____	malignant
3. *bene*	_____	benign
4. *fac*	_____	factory
5. *plac*	_____	placatory
6. *tac*	_____	tacit
7. *verbum*	_____	verbose
8. *loquor*	_____	soliloquy
9. *somn*	_____	insomnia
10. *ambul*	_____	ambulatory

II—more roots

Directions: Here are twenty words we have studied, each with its root italicized. In the appropriate blank write the meaning of that root.

1. dia*phan*ous 　　 1. _____

2. *a*theist 　　 2. _____

3. *hypo*chondria   3. _____

4. *hyper*trophy   4. _____

5. *matro*n   5. _____

6. patri*cide*   6. _____

7. patro*nym*ic   7. _____

8. dipso*mania*   8. _____

9. pan*the*ism   9. _____

10. prog*nos*is   10. _____

11. con*viv*ial   11. _____

12. *cred*ible   12. _____

13. retro*spect*   13. _____

14. un*anim*ity   14. _____

15. *circum*spect   15. _____

16. *magn*animous   16. _____

17. indefatig*able*   17. _____

18. *patri*arch   18. _____

19. vivaci*ous*   19. _____

20. sub*urb*an   20. _____

III—same or opposite?

Directions: If each pair of words is similar in meaning, check
S; if more nearly opposite, check *O.*

1. disparage—praise   S   O
2. proscribe—prohibit   S   O
3. placate—irritate   S   O
4. taciturn—talkative   S   O
5. cogent—brilliant   S   O
6. atheistic—religious   S   O
7. convivial—unfriendly   S   O
8. ingenuous—naïve   S   O
9. perspicacious—astute   S   O
10. intrepid—fearful   S   O

IV—true or false?

Directions: If the statement is factually accurate, check *T*; if factually inaccurate, check *F*.

1. An *ambiguous* statement is easy to understand. T F
2. *Malaise* is a feeling of comfort. T F
3. An *implacable* person is easily pleased. T F
4. A *vociferous* person is quiet. T F
5. The *dorsal* part of an animal is its front. T F
6. A *soporific* personality is generally boring. T F
7. If you feel *somnolent* you are wide-awake. T F
8. A *martinet* insists on strict obedience. T F
9. A *virago* is sweet-tempered. T F
10. An *uxorious* husband is most devoted to his wife. T F

V—matching

Directions: Choose the word from the second column which belongs to each function in the first column.

1. is lewd and lustful	a. chauvinist
2. caters to the rich	b. sycophant
3. is an accomplished musician	c. dilettante
4. sneers at traditions	d. iconoclast
5. is the mother-ruler of a family, tribe, or nation	e. lecher
6. has an irresistible urge to steal	f. tyro
7. is excessively patriotic	g. virtuoso
8. is a loud-mouthed woman	h. termagant
9. is a beginner	i. matriarch
10. is a dabbler	j. kleptomaniac

VI—more matching

Directions: As on Test V.

1. does not know whether or not God exists	a. dipsomaniac
2. is a criminal	b. pyromaniac
3. is a connoisseur of good food	c. agnostic
4. sets fires for revenge	d. hypochondriac

5. meets adversity or pain without
   flinching   e. gourmet
6. walks in his sleep   f. stoic
7. is morbidly addicted to drink   g. malefactor
8. has imaginary ailments   h. somnambulist
9. cannot help setting fires   i. nymphomaniac
10. is a woman who is sexually
    insatiable   j. incendiary

VII—recall a word

Directions: Write the word we have studied that best fits
each definition. The initial letter is offered to guide your thinking.

1. to make unnecessary   1. O_____

2. to flatter fulsomely   2. A_____

3. to spread slander   3. M_____

4. economical in speech   4. L_____

5. trite and hackneyed   5. B_____

6. word for word   6. V_____

7. killing of masses of people   7. G_____

8. inheritance from one's father   8. P_____

9. belief in many gods   9. P_____

10. excessive growth of a part
    of the body   10. H_____

VIII—choose a word

Directions: Check the one word, of the three offered, which
best fits each definition.

1. To predict, from the symptoms, the probable course of a
   disease: a. devitalize, b. diagnose, c. prognosticate.
2. tireless: a. indefatigable, b. versatile, c. scintillating.
3. polished, refined, suave: a. rustic, b. urbane, c. magnanimous.

4. "stomach-minded": a. cerebratonic, b. somatotonic, c. viscera-tonic.
5. giving birth to live young: a. viviparous, b. oviparous, c. ovulation.
6. boredom, lassitude: a. ennui, b. *joie de vivre*. c. vitality.
7. one who enjoys lots of good food a. glutton, b. gourmand, c. *bon vivant*.
8. easily tricked. a. credulous, b. gullible, c. disingenuous.
9. keen-minded: a. perspicuous, b perspicacious, c. pusillanimous.
10. fear and trembling: a. intrepidity, b. stoicism, c. trepidation.

IX—pronounce a word

Directions: Check the correct pronunciation.

1. *implacable*
   a. im-PLAK-a-b'l
   b. im-PLAY-ka-b'l

2. *taciturn*
   a. TASS-i-turn
   b. TACK-i-turn

3. *colloquial*
   a. ko-LOE-kwee-il
   b. ko-LOE-kee-il

4. *somnolent*
   a. sum-NOE-lent
   b. SOM-no-lent

5. *sycophant*
   a. SYE-ko-fant
   b. SICK-o-fint

6. *virago*
   a. vi-RAY-go
   b. VEER-a-go

7. *dilettante*
   a. DILL-e-tant
   b. dill-e-TAN-tee

8. *uxoricide*
   a. uk-SOR-i-syde
   b. yook-SOR-i-syde

9. *megalomaniacal*
   a. MEG-a-lo-MAY-nee-a-k'l
   b. meg-a-lo-ma-NYE-a-k'l

10. *oviparous*
   a. o-VIP-er-us
   b. o-vi-PAR-ous

X—change a word

Directions: Write the required part of speech.

1. Change *equivocal* to a verb.   1.＿＿＿＿＿＿＿

2. Change *garrulous* to a noun.   2.＿＿＿＿＿＿＿

3. Change *soliloquy* to a verb. 3._____

4. Change *sycophantic* to a noun denoting the action (not the person). 4._____

5. Change *iconoclast* to the noun denoting the philosophy. 5._____

6. Change *monomania* to an adjective. 6._____

7. Change *prognosticate* to a noun. 7._____

8. Change *magnanimous* to a noun. 8._____

9. Change *stoical* to a noun denoting the attitude, not the person. 9._____

10. Change *introspective* to a noun. 10._____

KEY

I: 1—voice, 2—badly, 3—well, 4—make, do, 5—please, 6—be silent, 7—word, 8—speak, 9—sleep, 10—walk

II: 1—show, 2—not, without, 3—under, less, 4—over, more, excessive, 5—mother, 6—kill, 7—name, 8—madness, 9—God, 10—know, 11—live, 12—believe, 13—look, 14—mind, soul, spirit, 15—around, 16—large, 17—able to be, 18—father, 19—full of, 20—city

III: 1—O, 2—S, 3—O, 4—O, 5—S, 6—O, 7—O, 8—S, 9—S, 10—O

IV: 1—F, 2—F, 3—F, 4—F, 5—F, 6—T, 7—F, 8—T, 9—F, 10—T

V: 1—e, 2—b, 3—g, 4—d, 5—i, 6—j, 7—a, 8—h, 9—f, 10—c

VI: 1—c, 2—g, 3—e, 4—j, 5—f, 6—h, 7—a, 8—d, 9—b, 10—i

VII: 1—obviate, 2—adulate, 3—malign, 4—laconic, 5—banal, 6—verbatim, 7—genocide, 8—patrimony, 9—polytheism, 10—hypertrophy

VIII: 1—c, 2—a, 3—b, 4—c, 5—a, 6—a, 7—b, 8—b, 9—b, 10—c

IX: 1—b, 2—a, 3—a, 4—b, 5—b, 6—a, 7—b, 8—a, 9—b, 10—a

X: 1—equivocate, 2—garrulity, 3—soliloquize, 4—sycophancy, 5—iconoclasm, 6—monomaniacal, 7—prognosis, 8—magnanimity, 9—stoicism, 10—introspection

SCORING

A perfect score is 110—one point for each correct response. Allowing some margin for error, and conceding that after all no one is perfect, I would call any score of 90 or better an indication of successful learning.

You might turn back for a moment to page 148, on which you recorded your score on the first week's Achievement Test. Did you do better this time? Let's make a record of both scores at this point for the sake of comparison and to give you a mark to shoot at in the Achievement Test which you will take at the end of the third week of your work.

[SCORES]

First week's Achievement Test

—————— out of *110*

Second week's Achievement Test

—————— out of *110*

FINISHING WITH A FEELING
OF COMPLETE SUCCESS

14

HOW TO TALK ABOUT
COMMON PHENOMENA AND
OCCURRENCES

—— TEASER PREVIEW ———————————

What word aptly describes:

- *dire poverty?*
- *emotion experienced without direct participation?*
- *something which lasts a very short time?*
- *an inoffensive word for an unpleasant idea?*
- *light and easy banter?*
- *someone who is cowlike in his stolidity?*
- *homesickness?*
- *harsh sound?*
- *a meat-eating animal?*
- *something kept secret?*

THIS WORLD, Robert Louis Stevenson once claimed—with, I think, questionable logic—is so full of a number of things that we should all be as happy as kings.

I doubt very strongly that happiness comes from the outside, or that kings are necessarily happy. But I will go this far (and no farther) with Stevenson. The world is certainly full of a number of things. For instance, poverty and misery, hospitals and insane asylums, slums and racial restrictions, cut-down forests and once fertile lands becoming progressively more arid, war and death and taxes and bumbling diplomats. I know that Stevenson had a different sort of thing in mind, for romantic poets tend to view the world through rose-tinted spectacles, but it is often necessary to counter one extreme with another—and I simply wish to set the record straight.

In this chapter we are going to discuss a number of things to be found in the world and in the minds of its inhabitants—poverty and wealth; secondhand emotions; the relativity of time; praise of various sorts; small talk and how to indulge in it; animals; longings for the past; sounds; eating habits; and many kinds and conditions of secrecy.

As you see, when you start exploring ideas, as we constantly do in these chapters, you never know what you'll turn up.

IDEAS

1. for want of the green stuff

There are those people who are forced (often through no fault of their own) to pursue an existence not only devoid of such luxuries (radios, television sets, sunken bathtubs, electric orange-juice squeezers, automobiles, et cetera) as many of us take for granted, but lacking also in many of the pure necessities of living —sufficient protein in their diets (Southern sharecroppers who die of pellagra); sufficient food (inhabitants of India, who die of simple starvation); heated homes, hot water, clean surroundings, clothing (people on relief); et cetera.

Such people live in *penury*.

2. at least watch it

Every normal woman, no matter how unattractive, wants and needs love and romance—so say the psychologists. If no one will love her, and if she can find no one on whom to lavish her own love, she may often satisfy her emotional longings and needs by getting her feelings secondhand—through reading love stories and *True Romances*, listening to radio serials, attending motion pictures, et cetera.

Thus feelings that are denied to her through actual participations can be experienced secondhand.

These are *vicarious* feelings.

3. time is fleeting

During the late winter and early spring of 1948–49, great numbers of unstable people went practically berserk joining and forming "Pyramid Clubs." If you have not heard of this amazing phenomenon, I won't attempt to describe it in any of its multifarious ramifications, but the main point was that you paid two dollars, treated some people to coffee and doughnuts, and shortly thereafter (if you were gullible enough to fall for this get-rich-quick scheme) received a return of some fantastic amount like $2,064 for your investment.

For a short time, pyramid clubs were a rage—soon they had vanished from the American scene.

> Anything which lasts for but a short time and leaves no trace is *ephemeral*.

4. how not to call a spade . . .

Words are only *symbols* of things—they are not the things themselves. (This, by the way, is one of the basic tenets of semantics.) But many people identify the word and the thing so closely that they fear to use certain words that symbolize unpleasant (to them) things, lest they invite the full force of the things that the words symbolize.

I know that this is confusing, so let me illustrate.

Words having to do with death, sex, certain portions of the anatomy, venereal disease, cancer, et cetera, are avoided by certain types of people.

These people prefer circumlocutions—words that mean or imply the same idea but don't come right out and say so.

For example:

WORD	CIRCUMLOCUTION
die	breathe his last
	depart this life
	go to one's maker
sexual intercourse	intimate relations
prostitute	lady of the evening
	fille de joie
syphilis, gonorrhea	social disease
rape	statutory crime
	moral offense

WORD	CIRCUMLOCUTION
buttocks	derrière
	rear end
breasts	bosom
	bust
	curves
menstruation	unwell
	period
toilet	powder room
cancer	wasting disease
brassière, panties, et cetera	unmentionables
	intimate apparel
leg	limb
insane	odd
	queer
feeble-minded	not bright

The left-hand column is the direct, non-pussyfooting, method of expressing an idea. The right-hand column is made up of *euphemisms*.

5. small talk

"Whenever I'm in the dumps, I get me a new hat."
"Oh, so that's where you get them!"

. . . . .

"Lend me a dime—I want to phone one of my friends."
"Here're two dimes—call them all."

. . . . .

These are examples of *badinage*.

6. everything but give milk

You've seen a cow contentedly munching its cud. Nothing seems capable of disturbing this animal—and the animal seems to want nothing more out of life than to lead a simple, vegetable existence.

Some people are like a cow—calm, patient, placid, phlegmatic, vegetablelike.

They are *bovine*.

7. good old days

Do you sometimes experience a keen, almost physical, longing for associations or places of the past?

When you pass the neighborhood in which you were born and

where you spent your early years, do you have a sharp, funny reaction, almost akin to mild nausea?

When you are away from home and friends and family, do pleasant remembrances crowd in on your mind to the point where your present loneliness becomes almost unbearable, and you actually feel a little sick?

This common feeling is called *nostalgia*.

8. modern music

Some sounds are so harsh, grating, and discordant that they offend the ear. They lack all sweetness, harmony, pleasantness. Traffic noises of a big city, modern jazz rhythms, some of the works of Shostakovitch or Stravinsky, the thunder of New York's old Third Avenue "El" . . . such are the blaring, ear-splitting, sounds to which I refer.

These are *cacophonous*.

9. eating habits

Lions, tigers, wolves, and other animals subsist entirely on flesh. No spinach, salad greens, whole-wheat cereals, sugar, or spices— just good, red meat.

They are *carnivorous*.

10. private and public

There are certain things you just naturally do in private, like taking a bath, for instance. Some people (not the visceratonic types, of course) like to engage in other activities in complete privacy—eating, reading, sleeping, for example.

The point is that, while these activities may be conducted in privacy, there is never any reason for keeping them secret.

But there are other activities which are kept not only private, but well-shrouded in secrecy and concealed from public gaze and information with the greatest of care. These are activities which are considered sinful, shameful, illegal, or unsafe—like having an affair with a married woman, betraying military secrets to the enemy, trading in narcotics, patronizing the black market, et cetera.

Arrangements, activities, or meetings that fall under this category are called *clandestine*.

USING THE WORDS: I

Can you pronounce the words?

1.	penury	PEN-yoor-ee
2.	vicarious	vye-KAIR-ee-us
°3.	ephemeral	e-FEM-er-il
°4.	euphemism	YOO-fe-mizm
°5.	badinage	BAD-i-nidge
°6.	bovine	BO-vyne
7.	nostalgia	noss-TAL-ja
°8.	cacophony	ka-KOFF-i-nee
°9.	carnivorous	kar-NIV-er-us
°10.	clandestine	klan-DESS-tin

Can you work with the words?

Match words and definitions.

WORD	DEFINITION
1. penury	a. impermanent
2. vicarious	b. banter
3. ephemeral	c. homesickness
4. euphemism	d. meat-eating
5. badinage	e. circumlocution
6. bovine	f. harsh noise
7. nostalgia	g. poverty
8. cacophony	h. secret
9. carnivorous	i. placid, stolid
10. clandestine	j. secondhand

KEY: 1–g, 2–j, 3–a, 4–e, 5–b, 6–i, 7–c, 8–f, 9–d, 10–h

Do you understand the words? (I)

React quickly to the following questions.

1. Do wealthy people normally live in *penury?*   YES   NO

2. Is a *vicarious* thrill one that comes from direct participation?   YES   NO
3. Do *ephemeral* things last a very short time?   YES   NO
4. Is a *euphemism* the substitution of an inoffensive term for another of the same import, but which may sound vulgar or insulting?   YES   NO
5. Does *badinage* show light-hearted frivolity?   YES   NO
6. Are *bovine* people high-strung and nervous?   YES   NO
7. Does one get a feeling of *nostalgia* for past occurrences and relationships?   YES   NO
8. Is *cacophony* pleasant and musical?   YES   NO
9. Do *carnivorous* animals eat meat?   YES   NO
10. Is a *clandestine* meeting conducted in secrecy?   YES   NO

KEY: 1—no, 2—no, 3—yes, 4—yes, 5—yes, 6—no, 7—yes, 8—no, 9—yes, 10—yes

Do you understand the words? (II)

Is each pair of words *similar* or *opposed* in meaning?

1. penury—affluence   SIMILAR   OPPOSED
2. vicarious—actual   SIMILAR   OPPOSED
3. ephemeral—eternal   SIMILAR   OPPOSED
4. euphemism—less offensive word   SIMILAR   OPPOSED
5. badinage—light, teasing talk   SIMILAR   OPPOSED
6. bovine—high-strung   SIMILAR   OPPOSED
7. nostalgia—longing for the past   SIMILAR   OPPOSED
8. cacophony—euphony   SIMILAR   OPPOSED
9. carnivorous—herbivorous   SIMILAR   OPPOSED
10. clandestine—hidden   SIMILAR   OPPOSED

KEY: 1—opposed, 2—opposed, 3—opposed, 4—similar, 5—similar, 6—opposed, 7—similar, 8—opposed, 9—opposed, 10—similar

(The new words used in this test will be discussed in later sections of this chapter.)

Can you recall the words?

Fill in the proper word for each definition.

1. harsh sound	1. _____
2. having a short life	2. _____
3. dire poverty	3. _____
4. substitution of an indirect or pleasant word for a possibly offensive one of the same meaning	4. _____
5. Experienced as a spectator, rather than as a participant	5. _____
6. acute feeling of homesickness	6. _____
7. light, half-teasing banter	7. _____
8. subsisting solely on meat	8. _____
9. cowlike, stolid	9. _____
10. secret, concealed	10. _____

KEY: 1—cacophony, 2—ephemeral, 3—penury, 4—euphemism, 5—vicarious, 6—nostalgia, 7—badinage, 8—carnivorous, 9—bovine, 10—clandestine

ORIGINS AND RELATED WORDS: I

1. money, and what it will buy

The modern world operates largely by means of a price structure—wealth and poverty are therefore words that indicate the possession, on one hand, or the lack, on the other, of money. *Penury*, from Latin *penuria, want*, is dire, abject poverty, complete lack of financial resources. It is one of the two strongest English words there are to denote absence of money. The adjective form, *penurious*, strangely enough, means not so much poverty-stricken as stingy, close-fisted, niggardly; so sparing in the use of money as to *give the appearance of* penury. *Penurious* is a synonym of *parsimonious*, but is much stronger in implication. A *parsimonious* person is stingy; a *penurious* person is twice as stingy. *Penury*, then, is *poverty; penuriousness* is *stinginess*, excessive frugality. The noun form of *parsimonious* is *parsimony*, which means *niggardliness*.

A somewhat milder word than *penury* for poverty (if you can imagine a mild degree of poverty) is *indigence*. The *indigent* person is not absolutely penniless—he is simply living in reduced circumstances, foregoing many creature comforts, forced to undergo the type of humiliating hardships that accompany a lack of sufficient funds.

On the other hand, a close synonym of *penury*, and one of equal strength, is *destitution*. The *destitute* person does not even have the means for mere subsistence—as such, he is perhaps on the verge of starvation; *penury* and *destitution* are not merely straitened circumstances—they are downright desperate circumstances.

To turn now to the brighter side of the picture, the possession of money, especially in increasing quantities, is expressed by *affluence*. An *affluent* person, a man of *affluence*, or one living in *affluent* circumstances is more than comfortable; in addition, there is the implication that his wealth is increasing, rather than decreasing (you know the old adage, the rich get richer, and the poor get children). A man who lives in *affluence* probably owns his own home, runs a big, new car, has a servant or two, belongs to an expensive golf club, and wears Hickey-Freeman suits.

A much stronger term is *opulence*, which not only implies much greater wealth than *affluence* but in addition suggests lavish expenditures and ostentatiously luxurious surroundings. A man of *opulence* owns not a house but an estate; drives only Cadillacs and Mercedes (owning at least one of each); has a corps of servants, including a major-domo; belongs to golf and yacht and country clubs; wears no suit that costs less than $250; and in general is only a few rungs under an Indian Maharajah. *Opulent* may describe people, surroundings, appointments, or the like.

2. doing and feeling

If you watch a furious athletic event, and *you* get tired, though the athletes expend all the energy—that's *vicarious* fatigue.

If your friend goes on a bender, and as you watch him absorb one drink after another, *you* begin to feel giddy and stimulated, that's *vicarious* intoxication.

If you watch a mother in a motion picture or dramatic play

suffer horribly at the death of her child, and *you* go through the same agony, that's *vicarious* torment.

You can experience an emotion, then, in two ways: first-hand, through actual participation; or *vicariously*, by becoming sympathetically involved in another person's feelings.

Many people, for example, lead essentially dull and colorless lives. Through their children, through reading or attending the theater, however, they can experience all the emotions felt by others whose lives move along at a swift, exciting pace. These people live at secondhand; they live *vicariously*.

There are many words in the English language whose full meanings cannot be expressed by any other combination of syllables. *Vicarious* is one of these words. Not to know the word, not to use it, is to be unable to express the ideas for which it stands.

3. time is relative

Elephants and turtles live almost forever; human beings have a life expectancy in general of fifty odd years (though the gradual conquest of disease is constantly lengthening our span); dogs live from seven to ten years; and some insects exist for only a day.

One such short-lived creature is the dayfly, which in Greek was called *ephemera*. Hence anything so short-lived, so unenduring that it scarcely seems to outlast the day, may be called *ephemeral*.

A synomym of *ephemeral* is *evanescent*, which means *fleeting, staying for a remarkably short time, vanishing*. Something delicate, intangible, like a feeling, may be called *evanescent;* it's here, and before you can quite comprehend it, it's gone—vanished.

The noun is *evanescence*, the verb is *to evanesce*.

The root *esce* often means *beginning to*. Thus:

> *adolescent*—beginning to grow up
> *evanesce*—begin to vanish
> *convalesce*—begin to get well
> *putrescent*—beginning to rot, becoming putrid

4. an exploration of various good things

A *euphemism* is a word or expression that has been substituted for another that is likely to offend—it comes from *eu*, Greek for *good* (which you recall from *eugenics*, discussed in an earlier chapter) and *phem*, Greek *to say*. Hence, it is good, or inoffensive, saying. The adjective is *euphemistic*.

Eu, good, is found in a number of interesting words:

1. *euphony*—good sound, pleasant lilt or rhythm.
   ADJECTIVE: *euphonic* or *euphonious*
2. *eulogy*—good speech; a formal speech of praise, usually delivered as a funeral oration
   ADJECTIVE: *eulogistic*
   VERB: *to eulogize*
3. *euphoria*—good feeling, a sense of mental buoyancy and physical well-being
   ADJECTIVE: *euphoric*
4. *euthanasia*—good death; method of painless death inflicted on people suffering from incurable diseases—not legal in this country, but advocated by many doctors

5. exploration of modes of expression

Badinage is a half-teasing, nonmalicious, frivolous banter, intended to amuse rather than wound. *Badinage* has as a close synonym *persiflage*, which is a little more derisive, a trifle more indicative of contempt or mockery—but still totally unmalicious.

In line with *badinage* and *persiflage* (the former has been Anglicized in pronunciation, the latter still retains its Gallic flavor—PUR-si-flahzh, *zh* being the sound of the *s* in measure), there are four other forms of expression you should be familiar with: *cliché*, *bromide*, *platitude*, and *anodyne*.

A *cliché* is a pattern of words which was once new and fresh, but which now is so old, worn, and threadbare that only banal, unimaginative speakers and writers ever use it. Examples are: *fast and furious, unsung heroes, by leaps and bounds; conspicuous by its absence, green with envy*, et cetera. The most devastating criticism you can make of a piece of writing is to say, "It is full of clichés"; the most pointed insult of a man's way of talking is, "He speaks in clichés."

A *bromide* is any trite, dull, and probably fallacious remark which shows little evidence of original thinking, and which therefore convinces a listener of the total absence of perspicacity on the part of the speaker.

For instance, some cautious, dull-minded individual might warn you not to take a chance in these words: "Remember it's better to be safe than sorry!"

Your sneering response might be: "Oh, that old *bromide!*"

A *platitude* is similar to a cliché or bromide, in that it is a dull, trite, hackneyed, unimaginative pattern of words—but, to add insult to injury (cliché), the speaker uses it with an air of novelty—as if he just made it up, and isn't he the brilliant fellow! Such speakers are called *platitudinous*, and are the most boring, insufferable, and obnoxious people on earth—as you know if you've ever been stuck with one at a party.

An *anodyne* in the medical, literal sense, is a drug which allays pain without curing an illness, like aspirin or morphine. Figuratively, an *anodyne* is a statement made to allay someone's fears or anxieties, not believed by the speaker, but intended to be believed by the listener. "Prosperity is just around the corner" was a popular *anodyne* of the 1930s.

USING THE WORDS: II

Can you pronounce the words?

°1.	*penurious*	pe-NYOOR-ee-us
°2.	*penuriousness*	pe-NYOOR-ee-us-ness
3.	*parsimonious*	par-si-MO-nee-us
°4.	*parsimony*	PAR-si-mo-nee
5.	*indigence*	IN-di-jence
6.	*indigent*	IN-di-jent
7.	*destitution*	dess-ti-TOO-shun
8.	*destitute*	DESS-ti-toot
°9.	*affluence*	AFF-loo-ence
°10.	*affluent*	AFF-loo-ent
°11.	*opulence*	OP-yoo-lence
°12.	*opulent*	OP-yoo-lent
13.	*vicarious*	vye-KAIR-ee-us

14.	*evanescent*	ev-a-NESS-ent
15.	*evanescence*	ev-a-NESS-ence
16.	*evanesce*	ev-a-NESS
*17.	*euphemistic*	yoo-fe-MISS-tic
*18.	*euphony*	YOO-fo-nee
*19.	*euphonic*	yoo-FON-ik
*20.	*euphonious*	yoo-FO-nee-us
21.	*eulogy*	YOO-lo-jee
22.	*eulogistic*	yoo-lo-JISS-tik
23.	*eulogize*	YOO-lo-jyze
*24.	*euphoria*	yoo-FOR-ee-a
*25.	*euphoric*	yoo-FOR-ik
26.	*euthanasia*	yoo-tha-NAY-zha (*zh* like the *s* in *measure*)
*27.	*persiflage*	PUR-si-flahzh
*28.	*cliché*	klee-SHAY
29.	*bromide*	BRO-myde
*30.	*bromidic*	bro-MID-ik
31.	*platitude*	PLAT-i-tood
32.	*platitudinous*	plat-i-TOO-din-us
*33.	*anodyne*	AN-o-dyne

Can you work with the words? (I)

Match words and meanings.

1. penurious	a. poor
2. indigent	b. inoffensive
3. affluent	c. flat, trite
4. evanescent	d. feeling tiptop
5. euphemistic	e. wealthy
6. euphonious	f. pleasant in sound
7. euphoric	g. stingy
8. platitudinous	h. fleeting

KEY: 1–g, 2–a, 3–e, 4–h, 5–b, 6–f, 7–d, 8–c

Can you work with the words? (II)

1. parsimony	a. lavish luxury
2. destitution	b. painless death

3. opulence   c. pleasant sound

4. evanescence   d. trite remark

5. euphony   e. impermanence

6. euphoria   f. feeling of well-being

7. euthanasia   g. niggardliness

8. platitude   h. poverty

KEY: 1—g, 2—h, 3—a, 4—e, 5—c, 6—f, 7—b, 8—d

Can you work with the words? (III)

1. anodyne   a. light, teasing banter

2. bromide   b. tightfistedness

3. persiflage   c. statement intended to allay anxiety

4. eulogy   d. poverty, want

5. penuriousness   e. high, formal praise

6. indigence   f. wealth

7. affluence   g. trite statement

KEY: 1—c, 2—g, 3—a, 4—e, 5—b, 6—d, 7—f

Can you work with the words? (IV)

1. parsimonious   a. begin to vanish

2. destitute   b. stingy, frugal

3. opulent   c. highly praising

4. vicarious   d. hackneyed phrase

5. euphonic   e. ostentatiously wealthy

6. eulogistic   f. stilted in expression

7. evanesce   g. pleasant-sounding

8. eulogize   h. in want

9. bromidic   i. secondhand

10. cliché   j. praise

KEY: 1—b, 2—h, 3—e, 4—i, 5—g, 6—c, 7—a, 8—j, 9—f, 10—d

Do you understand the words? (I)

React quickly to these questions.

1. Does a *penurious* person satisfy his extravagant desires?	YES	NO
2. Is *penuriousness* the characteristic of a miser?	YES	NO
3. If you are *parsimonious* with praise, do you lavish it on others?	YES	NO
4. Are people with low incomes forced to live a life of *parsimony*?	YES	NO
5. Is *indigence* a sign of wealth?	YES	NO
6. Are *indigent* people sometimes reduced to seeking government relief?	YES	NO
7. If you live in a state of *destitution*, do you have all the money you need?	YES	NO
8. Is a completely *destitute* person likely to have to live in extreme want?	YES	NO
9. Does a man of *affluence* generally have petty money worries?	YES	NO
10. Are *opulent* surroundings indicative of great wealth?	YES	NO

KEY: 1—no, 2—yes, 3—no, 4—yes, 5—no, 6—yes, 7—no, 8—yes, 9—no, 10—yes

Do you understand the words? (II)

1. Can you engage in *vicarious* exploits by reading *Horatio Hornblower*?	YES	NO
2. Does an *evanescent* feeling remain for a considerable time?	YES	NO
3. Do parents generally indulge in *euphemisms* in front of young children?	YES	NO
4. Is poetry generally *euphonious*?	YES	NO
5. Does a sincere *eulogy* indicate one's feeling of admiration?	YES	NO
6. Is *euphoria* a feeling of malaise?	YES	NO
7. Is *euthanasia* practiced on animals?	YES	NO
8. Is *persiflage* an indication of seriousness?	YES	NO

9. Does a liberal use of *clichés* show independent
thinking?   YES   NO

10. Is an *anodyne* intended to relieve fears?   YES   NO

KEY: 1—yes, 2—no, 3—yes, 4—yes, 5—yes, 6—no, 7—yes, 8—no,
9—no, 10—yes

Do you understand the words? (III)

1. Is a *platitude* flat and dull?   YES   NO

2. If a person believes *bromides,* is he likely to be
intellectually alert?   YES   NO

3. If you indulge in *persiflage,* are you being
facetious?   YES   NO

4. Are the works of Stravinsky considered
euphonious?   YES   NO

5. Can parents receive a *vicarious* thrill from their
children's triumphs?   YES   NO

KEY: 1—yes, 2—no, 3—yes, 4—no, 5—yes

Can you recall the words?

Now that you have cudgeled your brain over these thirty-
three related words, matching them to their meanings in four
different tests, thinking about them, pronouncing them, and
thereby becoming more and more familiar with them, you are
ready to test your ability to recall them when short definitions
are offered. Let the initial letter guide you. Your aim, of
course, is to make a perfect score from beginning to end—do
you think you can?

1. a statement, usually untrue,
meant to alleviate fear   1. A_____

2. light banter   2. P_____

3. a hackneyed phrase 3. C_____

4. fleeting—lasting a very short time (adj.) 4. E_____

5. laudatory—delivered in tones of formal praise (adj.) 5. E_____

6. process of painlessly putting to death a victim of an incurable disease 6. E_____

7–8. stingy (two adjs.) 7. P_____

 8. P_____

9. in want (adj.) 9. D_____

10. great and increasing wealth 10. A_____

11. lavish expenditure of wealth 11. O_____

12. adverb describing the manner of receiving an emotional impact from another's acts 12. V_____

13–14. stinginess (2 nouns) 13. P_____

 14. P_____

15–16. poverty (2 forms) 15. I_____

 16. D_____

17. impermanence 17. E_____

18. pleasing sound 18. E_____

19. inoffensive substitution of words (adj.) 19. E_____

20. sense of well-being 20. E_____

21. trite remark 21. B_____

22. banal remark 22. P_____

23. begin to vanish 23. E_____

24. poverty-stricken 24. I_____

25–26. wealthy (two adjs.) 25. A_____

 26. O_____

27. feeling tiptop (adj.) 27. E_____

309

28–29. pleasant in sound
    (2 adj. forms)   28. E_____

                                      29. E_____

30. formal praise   30. E_____

31. trite (adj.)   31. B_____

32. flat, dull   32. P_____

33. to praise   33. E_____

KEY: 1—anodyne, 2—persiflage, 3—cliché, 4—evanescent, 5—eulogistic, 6—euthanasia, 7–8—parsimonious, penurious, 9—destitute,
10—affluence, 11—opulence, 12—vicariously, 13–14—parsimony,
penuriousness, 15—indigence, 16—destitution, 17—evanescence,
18—euphony, 19—euphemistic, 20—euphoria, 21—bromide, 22—
platitude, 23—evanesce, 24—indigent, 25—affluent, 26—opulent,
27—euphoric, 28–29—euphonic, euphonious, 30—eulogy, 31—
bromidic, 32—platitudinous, 33—eulogize

ORIGINS AND RELATED WORDS: II

1. people are the craziest animals

Bovine, placid like a cow, stolid, patient, unexcitable, is
built on the Latin word for *ox* or *cow, bovis,* plus the common
ending *ine.* To call someone *bovine* is of course far from
complimentary, for this adjective is considerably stronger than
phlegmatic, and implies a certain mild contempt on the part
of the speaker. A *bovine* person is somewhat like a vegetable:
he eats and grows and lives, but apparently is lacking in any
strong feelings.

Humans are often compared to other animals, as the following adjectives will show:

1. *leonine*—like a lion in appearance or temperament. John L.
Lewis, with his bushy eyebrows and shock of gray hair,
was often described as *leonine,* or as having a *leonine*
countenance.

2. *canine*—like a dog. As a noun the word refers to the species to which dogs belong. Our *canine* teeth are similar to those of a dog.
3. *feline*—catlike. We may speak of *feline* grace; or (insultingly) of *feline* temperament when we mean that a woman is "catty."
4. *porcine*—piglike.
5. *vulpine*—foxlike, in appearance or temperament. When applied to people, this adjective usually refers to a fox's shrewdness.
6. *ursine*—bearlike.

These adjectives are all pronounced with a long final syllable—to rhyme with *mine*.

2. you can't go home again

Nostalgia, which is built on the two Greek roots *nostos, a return to home,* and *algia, pain* (as in *neuralgia*), is a feeling you can't ever understand until you've experienced it—and if you're normal you have experienced it whenever some external stimulus has crowded your mind with scenes from an earlier day.

You know how life always seems much pleasanter in retrospect. Your conscious memory tends to store up the pleasant experiences of the past (the unpleasant experiences get buried in the *unconscious*—but these are the ones that can play havoc with your personality), and when you are lonely or unhappy you may begin to relive these pleasant occurrences. It is then you feel the emotional pain and longing which we call *nostalgia*.

The adjective is *nostalgic,* as in "*Only Yesterday* is a *nostalgic* account of life in America between the Great War and the Great Depression," or "He feels *nostalgic* whenever he passes 138th Street and sees the house in which he grew up."

3. soundings

Cacophony is itself a harsh-sounding word—and is the only one which exactly describes the unmusical, grating, ear-offending noises you are likely to hear in man-made surroundings: the subway, the streets of a big city, a steel mill, an automobile factory, et cetera. The adjective is *cacophonous*, the emphasis remaining on the second syllable—ka-KOFF-o-nus.

Cacophony combines the Greek roots *kakos, bad,* and *phone, sound.*

Phone, sound, is found also in:

1. *telephone*—sound traveling from afar
2. *euphony*—pleasant sound
3. *phonograph*—writer of sound
4. *saxophone*—a musical instrument (hence *sound*) invented by Adolphe Sax
5. *xylophone*—a musical instrument which makes sounds come through wood
6. *phonetics*—the science of the sounds of language

4. the flesh and all

Carnivorous combines *carnis, flesh,* and *vorare, to devour.* A *carnivorous* animal or, as it is also called, a *carnivore,* is one whose main diet is meat.

Vorare, to devour, has given us three other words referring to eating habits:

1. *herbivorous*—subsisting on grains and grasses, as cows, deer, horses, and vegetarians.
2. *omnivorous*—eating everything, meat, grains, grasses, fish, insects, and anything else digestible. Naturally, the only species so indiscriminate in its eating habits is the human species.
   Omnivorous, which adds the Latin word *omni, all,* to *vorare, to devour,* is not restricted to food. An *omnivorous* reader is one who reads everything in great quantities (that is, he devours all kinds of reading matter). An *omnivorous* theatergoer or moviegoer may be described in similar terms.
3. *voracious*—literally *devouring,* means *greedy, gluttonous,* and may refer either to food or to any other habits. One may be a *voracious* eater, *voracious* reader, *voracious* in one's pursuit of money, pleasure, et cetera. The noun is *voracity.*

The *omni (all)* of *omnivorous* builds certain other valuable words:

1. *omnipotent*—all-powerful, an adjective usually applied to God, or, by extension, to any ruler whose governing powers are unlimited.
2. *omniscient*—all-knowing *(scio, to know,* as in *science)*; hence, infinitely wise.
3. *omnipresent*—present in all places at once. Fear was *omnipresent* in Europe during 1939. A synonym of *omnipresent,* with humorous tone, is *ubiquitous,* as in the phrase, the *ubiquitous Good Humor Man,* referring to the fact that he seems to be all over at the same time, ringing his little bells just when you wish Johnnie wouldn't ask for ice cream, now that supper is almost ready.
4. *omnibus*—*for all, including all,* et cetera. In the shortened form *bus* we have a public vehicle for *all* who can pay; in a John Galsworthy *omnibus* we have a book containing all of Galsworthy's works; in an *omnibus* legislative bill we have a bill containing all the miscellaneous provisions and appropriations left out of other bills.

Omnipotent, omniscient, omnipresent, and *ubiquitous* have noun forms as follows: *omnipotence, omniscience, omnipresence,* and *ubiquitousness.*

To return to *carnivorous, meat-eating:* the root *carnis, flesh,* occurs in:

1. *carnelian*—a reddish color, the color, the color of red flesh.
2. *carnival*—originally the season of merrymaking just before Lent, when people took a last fling before saying "Carne Vale," "Oh Flesh, farewell!" Now, of course, it may be a kind of circus or any kind of exuberant or riotous merry-making.
3. *carnal*—most often found in phrases like *carnal* pleasures or *carnal* appetites, the word refers to pleasures or appetites of the flesh rather than of the spirit—hence, sensual, sexy, lecherous, et cetera.

(The noun *carnality* means indulgence of one's sexual appetite.)

4. *carnage*—great destruction of life (that it, human flesh), as in war.

5. *reincarnation*—a return to another body (or *flesh*) after death; hence, a rebirth or reappearance. Believers in *reincarnation* stoutly maintain that one's soul persists after it has fled the flesh, and eventually reappears in the body of a newborn infant. Some of us, according to this interesting and macabre philosophy, were once Napoleon, Alexander the Great, Cleopatra, et cetera.

6. *incarnate*—in the *flesh*. If we refer to someone as the devil *incarnate*, we mean that here is the devil in the flesh. Or we may say that someone is evil *incarnate*, that is, the personification of evil, the quality of evil invested with human or bodily form. Watch your pronunciation of this word—say in-KAHR-nit.

5. dark secrets

Clandestine comes from *clam, secretly* (compare "shut up like a *clam*") and implies secrecy or concealment in the working out of a plan which is evil or illegal. It is a close synonym of *surreptitious*, which means *stealthy, sneaky, furtive,* generally because of fear of detection. The two words cannot always, however, be used interchangeably.

We may speak of either *clandestine* or *surreptitious* meetings or arrangements; but usually only of *clandestine* plans and only of *surreptitious* movements or actions.

Clandestine has no noun form, only an adverb, *clandestinely: surreptitious* has both noun and adverb: *surreptitiousness* and *surreptitiously.*

USING THE WORDS: III

Can you pronounce the words?

  °1. *leonine*   LEE-o-nyne

  °2. *canine*   KAY-nyne

  °3. *feline*   FEE-lyne

  °4. *porcine*   POR-syne

  °5. *vulpine*   VUL-pyne

°6. *ursine*   UR-syne

7. *nostalgic*   noss-TAL-jik

°8. *cacophonous*   ka-KOFF-o-nus

9. *phonetics*   fo-NET-iks

°10. *carnivore*   KAR-ni-vor

°11. *herbivorous*   hur-BIV-er-us

°12. *omnivorous*   om-NIV-er-us

13. *voracious*   vor-AY-shus

14. *voracity*   vor-ASS-i-tee

°15. *omnipotent*   om-NIP-o-tent

°16. *omniscient*   om-NISH-ent

°17. *omnipresent*   OM-nee-prez-ent

°18. *ubiquitous*   yoo-BIK-wi-tus

19. *omnibus*   OM-ni-bus

20. *carnelian*   kar-NEE-lyun

21. *carnal*   KAR-n'l

22. *carnality*   kar-NAL-i-tee

23. *carnage*   KAR-nidge

24. *surreptitious*   sur-rep-TISH-us

25. *reincarnation*   REE-in-kahr-NAY-shun

°26. *incarnate*   in-KAHR-nit

Can you work with the words? (I)

Match words and definitions.

1. leonine	a.	doglike
2. canine	b.	greedy, devouring
3. feline	c.	foxlike
4. porcine	d.	all-powerful
5. vulpine	e.	stealthy, clandestine
6. ursine	f.	lionlike
7. voracious	g.	all-knowing
8. omnipotent	h.	bearlike
9. omniscient	i.	catlike
10. surreptitious	j.	piglike

KEY: 1—f, 2—a, 3—i, 4—j, 5—c, 6—h, 7—b, 8—d, 9—g, 10—e

Can you work with the words? (II)

1.	nostalgic	a.	harsh-sounding
2.	cacophonous	b.	eating everything
3.	herbivorous	c.	lewd, lecherous
4.	omnivorous	d.	found everywhere
5.	ubiquitous	e.	homesick
6.	carnal	f.	grass-eating
7.	incarnate	g.	in the flesh

KEY: 1—e, 2—a, 3—f, 4—b, 5—d, 6—c, 7—g

Can you work with the words? (III)

1.	phonetics	a.	universality
2.	carnivore	b.	a color
3.	voracity	c.	infinite power
4.	omnipotence	d.	furtiveness
5.	omniscience	e.	lechery
6.	omnipresence	f.	infinite wisdom
7.	omnibus	g.	science of sound
8.	carnelian	h.	slaughter
9.	carnality	i.	a collection of all things
10.	carnage	j.	greediness
11.	surreptitiousness	k.	meat eater
12.	reincarnation	l.	return to life in a new body

KEY: 1—g, 2—k, 3—j, 4—c, 5—f, 6—a, 7—i, 8—b, 9—e, 10—h, 11—d, 12—l

Do you understand the words? (I)

Are the following statements *true* or *false?*

1.	A man of *leonine* appearance looks like a tiger.	TRUE	FALSE
2.	*Canine* habits refers to the habits of dogs.	TRUE	FALSE
3.	*Feline* grace means catlike grace.	TRUE	FALSE

316

4. *Porcine* appearance means wolflike
   appearance.   TRUE   FALSE
5. *Vulpine* craftiness means foxlike craftiness.   TRUE   FALSE
6. *Ursine* means bearlike.   TRUE   FALSE
7. *Nostalgic* feelings refer to a longing for
   past experiences.   TRUE   FALSE
8. *Cacophonous* music is pleasant and sweet.   TRUE   FALSE
9. An elephant is a *carnivore*.   TRUE   FALSE
10. Deer are *herbivorous*.   TRUE   FALSE

KEY: 1—false, 2—true, 3—true, 4—false, 5—true, 6—true, 7—true,
    8—false, 9—false, 10—true

Do you understand the words? (II)

1. An *omnivorous* reader does very little
   reading.   TRUE   FALSE
2. A *voracious* eater is gluttonous.   TRUE   FALSE
3. True *omnipotence* is probably
   unattainable by human beings.   TRUE   FALSE
4. No one is *omniscient*.   TRUE   FALSE
5. Fear of economic ruin was practically
   omnipresent in the early nineteen-thirties.   TRUE   FALSE
6. When an airplane lands for refueling, the
   ubiquitous little red gasoline wagon comes
   rolling up.   TRUE   FALSE
7. An author's *omnibus* contains all his
   published writings.   TRUE   FALSE
8. *Carnelian* is a deep blue color.   TRUE   FALSE
9. *Carnality* is much respected in present-day
   society.   TRUE   FALSE
10. There was considerable *carnage* in the
    battle of Okinawa.   TRUE   FALSE
11. A *surreptitious* glance is meant to be
    conspicuous.
12. A man who is evil *incarnate* is doubtless a
    very vicious character.   TRUE   FALSE

KEY: 1—false, 2—true, 3—true, 4—true, 5—true, 6—true, 7—true,
    8—false, 9—false, 10—true, 11—false, 12—true

Can you recall the words?

I—adverbs

1-2. secretly (two forms)	1. C_____
	2. S_____
3. in a harsh and noisy manner	3. C_____
4. in a homesick manner	4. N_____
5. in a greedy, devouring manner	5. V_____

KEY: 1—clandestinely, 2—surreptitiously, 3—cacophonously, 4—nostalgically, 5—voraciously

---

II—nouns

1. greediness	1. V_____
2. unlimited power	2. O_____
3. infinite knowledge	3. O_____
4. a gathering of all things	4. O_____
5. lechery; indulgence in fleshly pleasures	5. C_____
6. slaughter	6. C_____
7. stealthiness; secretiveness	7. S_____
8. harsh sound	8. C_____
9. science of sound	9. P_____
10. return to life	10. R_____

KEY: 1—voracity, 2—omnipotence, 3—omniscience, 4—omnibus, 5—carnality, 6—carnage, 7—surreptitiousness, 8—cacophony, 9—phonetics, 10—reincarnation

III—adjectives

1. lionlike	1. L_____
2. doglike	2. C_____
3. catlike	3. F_____
4. cowlike	4. B_____
5. foxlike	5. V_____
6. bearlike	6. U_____
7. homesick	7. N_____
8. grating in sound	8. C_____
9. meat-eating	9. C_____
10. grass-eating	10. H_____
11. all-eating: indiscriminate	11. O_____
12. devouring; greedy	12. V_____
13. in the flesh	13. I_____

KEY: 1—leonine, 2—canine, 3—feline, 4—bovine, 5—vulpine, 6—ursine, 7—nostalgic, 8—cacophonous, 9—carnivorous, 10—herbivorous, 11—omnivorous, 12—voracious, 13—incarnate

IV—more adjectives

1. all-powerful	1. O_____
2. all-knowing	2. O_____
3. found everywhere (serious)	3. O_____
4. found everywhere (humorous)	4. U_____
5. lewd	5. C_____
6. furtive	6. C_____

KEY: 1—omnipotent, 2—omniscient, 3—omnipresent, 4—ubiquitous, 5—carnal, 6—clandestine

Can you recall root-meanings?

Fill in the meaning of each root.

ROOT		RELATED WORD
1. *ine*	_____	leonine
2. *phone*	_____	euphony
3. *algia*	_____	nostalgia
4. *omni*	_____	omnibus
5. *vor*	_____	omnivorous
6. *carn*	_____	carnage
7. *esce*	_____	putrescent
8. *van*	_____	evanesce
9. *eu*	_____	euphemism

KEY: 1—similar, like, 2—sound, 3—pain, 4—all, 5—devour, 6—flesh,
7—begin to, 8—depart, 9—good

CHAPTER REVIEW

Can you recognize the words?

Check the word which most closely fits each definition.

1. Utter want:
    (a) affluence, (b) opulence, (c) penury
2. Experienced secondhand:
    (a) ephemeral, (b) vicarious, (c) evanescent
3. Inoffensive circumlocution:
    (a) badinage, (b) persiflage, (c) euphemism
4. Homesick:
    (a) nostalgic, (b) bromide, (c) clandestine
5. Meat-eating:
    (a) herbivorous, (b) voracious, (c) carnivorous

6. Stingy:
   (a) indigent, (b) parsimonious, (c) opulent
7. Extreme financial need:
   (a) destitution, (b) affluence, (c) parsimony
8. Great and increasing wealth:
   (a) penuriousness, (b) affluence, (c) opulence
9. Remaining for a short time:
   (a) euphemistic, (b) evanescent, (c) eulogistic
10. Sweet-sounding:
    (a) euphonious, (b) cacophonous, (c) euphoric
11. Highly praise:
    (a) evanesce, (b) eulogize, (c) disparage
12. Sense of physical well-being:
    (a) euthanasia, (b) euphoria, (c) persiflage
13. Hackneyed expression:
    (a) anodyne, (b) badinage, (c) cliché
14. Catlike:
    (a) leonine, (b) feline, (c) canine
15. Bearlike:
    (a) vulpine, (b) ursine, (c) porcine
16. All-knowing:
    (a) omnipotent, (b) omniscient, (c) omnipresent
17. Found everywhere:
    (a) ubiquitous, (b) omnivorous, (c) omnibus
18. Destruction:
    (a) carnage, (b) carnality, (c) reincarnation
19. Stealthy:
    (a) voracious, (b) surreptitious, (c) incarnate

KEY: 1—c, 2—b, 3—c, 4—a, 5—c, 6—b, 7—a, 8—b, 9—b, 10—a, 11—b, 12—b, 13—c, 14—b, 15—b, 16—b, 17—a, 18—a, 19—b

---

GETTING USED TO NEW WORDS

Reference has been made, in previous chapters, to the intimate relationship between reading and vocabulary building. Good books and the better magazines will not only acquaint you with a host of new ideas (and, therefore, new words, since every word is the verbalization of an idea), but also will help you gain a more complete and a richer understanding of the hundreds of words you are learning through your work in this book. If you have been doing a sufficient amount of stimulating reading—and that means, at minimum, several magazines a week and at least three books of nonfiction a month—you have been meeting, constantly, over and over again, the new words you have been learning in these pages. Every such encounter is like seeing an old friend in a new place. You know how much better you understand your friends when you have a chance to see them react to new situations; similarly, you will gain a much deeper understanding of the friends you have been making among words as you see them in different contexts and in different places.

My recommendations in the past have been of nonfiction titles, but novels too are a rich source of additions to your vocabulary—provided you stay alert to the new words you will inevitably meet in reading novels.

The natural temptation, when you encounter a brand new word in a novel, is to ignore it—the lines of the plot are perfectly clear even if many of the author's words are not. (For example, Harold Bell Wright's novels were at one time extremely popular, especially among the less cultivated types of readers. Yet, paradoxically, Wright's vocabulary was often quite erudite, sometimes even abstruse—however, his ideas were so simple and obvious that his readers enjoyed his works despite the vocabulary obstacles.)

I want to counsel strongly that you resist the temptation to ignore the unfamiliar words you may meet in your novel reading: resist it with every ounce of your energy, for only by such resistance can you keep building your vocabulary as you read.

What should you do? Don't rush to a dictionary, don't bother underlining the word, don't keep long lists of words that you will eventually look up *en masse*—these activities are likely to become painful and you will not continue them for any great length of time.

Instead, do something quite simple—and very effective.

When you meet a new word, underline it with a *mental* pencil. That is, pause for a second and attempt to figure out its meaning from its use in the sentence or from its etymological root, if it contains one you have studied. Make a mental note of it, say it aloud once or twice—and then go on reading.

That's all there is to it. What you are doing, of course, is developing the same type of mind-set toward the new word

322

that you have developed toward the words you have studied in this book. And the results, of course, will be the same—you will begin to notice the word occurring again and again in other reading you do, and finally, having seen it in a number of varying contexts, you will begin to get enough of its connotation and flavor to come to a fairly accurate understanding of its meaning. By this means you will be developing alertness not only to the words you have consciously studied in this book, but to all expressive and meaningful words. And your vocabulary will keep growing.

But of course that will happen only if you keep reading. Therefore, to get you started, I should like to suggest a number of novels which I have particularly enjoyed and which you too may find rewarding.

RECOMMENDED NOVELS

1. *Of Human Bondage,* by W. Somerset Maugham (Doubleday).
2. *Lust for Life,* by Irving Stone (Longmans, Green).
3. *Never Love a Stranger,* by Harold Robbins (Knopf).
4. *Night and the City,* by Gerald Kersh (World).
5. *Song of the Flea,* by Gerald Kersh (Doubleday).
6. *Success,* by Lion Feuchtwanger (Viking).
7. *Ethan Frome,* by Edith Wharton (Scribner).
8. *Giants in the Earth,* by O. E. Rolvaag (Harper).
9. *Hunger,* by Knut Hamsun (Knopf).
10. *H. M. Pulham, Esquire,* by John P. Marquand (Little, Brown).
11. *The Lost Weekend,* by Charles Jackson (Farrar & Rinehart).
12. *Hold Autumn in Your Hand,* by George Sessions Perry (Viking).
13. *The Store,* by T. S. Stribling (Garden City Pub. Co.).
14. *Arrival and Departure,* by Arthur Koestler (Macmillan).

BRIEF INTERMISSION ELEVEN:
TAKE THIS SPELLING TEST

Even in the most painstakingly edited of magazines, a silly little misspelling of a perfectly common word will occasionally appear. How the error eluded the collective and watchful eyes of the editor, the associate editor, the assistant editor, the typesetter and the proofreader, no one will ever know—for practically every reader of the magazine spots it at once and writes an indignant letter, beginning: "Didn't you ever go to school . . . ?"

Even if you went to school, you're going to have plenty of trouble spotting the one misspelled word in each group below. And not one of these words will be a demon like *sphygmomanometer* (a device for measuring blood pressure) or *piccalilli* (a highly seasoned relish), which no one in his right mind would ever dare spell without first checking with a dictionary. On the contrary, every word will be of the common or garden variety which you might use every day in your social or business correspondence.

Nevertheless, you're letting yourself in for ten minutes of real trouble, for you will be working with fifty particularly difficult spelling words. So put on your thinking cap before you begin.

A half dozen high-school teachers who took this test were able to make an average score of only five proper choices. Can you do better? Six or seven right is *very good*, eight or nine right is *excellent*, and 100-per cent success marks you as an absolute expert in English spelling.

Directions: Check the only misspelled word in each group.

A: 1—surprise, 2—disappear, 3—innoculate, 4—description, 5—recommend

B: 1—privilege, 2—separate, 3—incidentally, 4—dissipate, 5—occurence

C: 1—analize, 2—argument, 3—assistant, 4—comparative, 5—truly
D: 1—grammar, 2—drunkeness, 3—parallel, 4—sacrilegious, 5—conscience
E: 1—precede, 2—exceed, 3—accede, 4—procede, 5—concede
F: 1—pronunciation, 2—noticable, 3—desirable, 4—holiday, 5—anoint
G: 1—wierd, 2—seize, 3—achieve, 4—receive, 5—leisure
H: 1—superintendent, 2—persistent, 3—resistant, 4—insistent, 5—preseverence
I: 1—accessible, 2—permissible, 3—inimitable, 4—irresistable, 5—irritable
J: 1—pursue, 2—pastime, 3—kidnaped, 4—rhythmical, 5—exhillarate

---

KEY: A—3, B—5, C—1, D—2, E—4, F—2, G—1, H—5, I—4, J—5

15

HOW TO TALK
ABOUT EVERYDAY ATTITUDES

—— TEASER PREVIEW ——————————————

What verb, ending in -*ate*, means:

1. To exhaust	1._____ate
2. To scold severely	2._____ate
3. To deny onself	3._____ate
4. To repeat the main points	4._____ate
5. To be a victim of mental or intellectual stagnation	5._____ate
6. To feign	6._____ate
7. To hint	7._____ate
8. To lighten	8._____ate
9. To show sympathy	9._____ate
10. To waver indecisively	10._____ate

———————————————————————————

WORDS are symbols of ideas—and we have been learning, discussing, and working with words as they revolve around certain basic concepts.

Starting with an idea (personality types, doctors, occupations, science, lying, actions, speech, insults, compliments, et cetera), we have explored the meanings and uses of ten basic

326

words; then, working from each word, we have wandered off toward any idea which that word might have suggested.

By this natural and logical method, we have been able to make meaningful and lasting contact with fifty to a hundred words in each chapter. And I have proved to you, I think, that while five *isolated* words may be difficult to learn in one day, fifty to a hundred *related* words are easy to learn in a single sitting.

Now that we are approaching the end of our work together, I am going to offer a change of pace and conclusive proof that so long as there is some relationship between words, no matter how slight, no matter how tenuous (this expressive word—*tenuous*—will be discussed in Chapter 17), words can be learned in practically wholesale quantities.

In this chapter we shall discuss words which are related only by the ending -*ate*—this being as slight and tenuous a relationship as I can think of.

And yet, since *some* relationship will exist, you will find your learning as effortless and pleasant as it was when a much more basic relationship existed—the relationship of ideas and meaning.

We shall still, of course, learn our new words as expressions of ideas—that is the only sensible, lasting method.

IDEAS, ORIGINS, AND RELATED WORDS

1. complete exhaustion

You have stayed up all night—but literally all night. And what were you doing? Playing poker, a very pleasant way of whiling away time? No. Making love to your favorite girl—or boy—friend, an even pleasanter way? No. Engaging in some creative activity, like writing a short story, planning a military campaign, discussing fascinating questions with stimulating friends? No.

The examples I have offered are exciting, stimulating—and as psychologists have discovered, it is not work or effort that causes fatigue, but boredom, ennui, tedium, dissatisfaction, frustration, and other similar feelings.

You have stayed up all night with a very sick husband, wife, child, or dear friend. And despite all your ministrations, the patient is sinking. You can see how this long vigil contains all the elements of monotony, loneliness, frustration, et cetera, which contribute to mental, physical, and nervous fatigue.

And so you are bushed—but completely bushed. Your exhaustion is mental, it is physiological, it is emotional.

One verb, ending in -*ate*, describes the reaction on you of your night's activity.

to enervate

NOUN: *enervation*

ADJECTIVE: *enervated, enervating*

APPLICATION: He was *enervated* by his tour of duty. He had never felt such *enervation* before. An *enervating* experience.

DERIVATION: Latin, *enervis, weak.* No relation to *energy,* despite the similar sound.

2. tongue-lashing

You may recall Clendennin J. Ryan and the celebrated New York wire-tapping investigation of 1949.

Ryan, heir to the Thomas Fortune Ryan millions, lashed out at the O'Dwyer administration with a fierceness such as had rarely been equaled in the civic affairs of our most exciting city. The rebuke was public, bitter, uninhibited.

Or you recall when Harry Truman, running for re-election in 1948, stumped the country, attacking in no mild or equivocal terms the "do-nothing" Eightieth Congress. Truman, like Ryan, pulled no punches—his censure had a sting which his victims will long remember, as will the Republicans.

One verb, ending in -*ate*, describes the severe, public, tongue-lashing administered by Ryan and Truman.

to castigate

NOUN: CASTIGATION

ADJECTIVE: *castigating*

APPLICATION: Truman's *castigation* of the Eightieth Congress.

Ryan's *castigating* attacks on O'Dwyer.

He *castigated* his opponents.

DERIVATION: Latin, *castigare, to correct.*

3. altruistic

Phyllis is selfless and self-sacrificing to an astonishing and abnormal degree. Her husband's desires are of paramount importance, even when they conflict with her own. Clothes for her two daughters are her first concern—even if she has to wear a seven-year-old coat and outmoded dresses so that Paula and Evelyn can look smart and trim. At the dinner table, she heaps everyone's plate—and herself often goes without; but seeing her family well-fed is better nourishment than meat and potatoes. She will deny herself, will scrimp and save and walk blocks out of her way if she can buy for a few pennies less—all to the end that she may offer her husband and children the luxuries to which she has accustomed them.

What verb, ending in *-ate*, accurately describes Phyllis's attitude?

to self-abnegate

NOUN: *self-abnegation*
ADJECTIVE: *self-abnegating*
APPLICATION: a *self-abnegating* attitude.
  Extreme *self-abnegation*.
DERIVATION: Latin, *negare, to deny*
RELATED WORDS: *negative, negation*

4. repetition

You have delivered a long, complicated, lecture to your class, and now, to make sure that they will remember the important points, you restate the key ideas, the main thoughts. You offer, in short, a kind of brief summary, step by step, omitting all extraneous details.

One verb, ending in *-ate*, best describes what you are doing.

to recapitulate

NOUN: *recapitulation*
ADJECTIVE: *recapitulatory*
APPLICATION: Let me *recapitulate*. . . .
  I think we'll need some *recapitulation*.
DERIVATION: Latin, *re, again*, plus *capitulum, a small chapter heading*, from *caput, head*
RELATED WORDS: *Capital, decapitate, captain*. The *capital* is the seat of the *head* of the government; to *decapitate* is to *behead*; a *captain* is the *head* of a group.

5. no joie de vivre

Perhaps you wake up some gloomy Monday morning (why is it that Monday is always the worst day of the week?) and begin to think of the waste of the last five years. Intellectually, there has been no progress—you've read scarcely half a dozen books, haven't made one new, exciting friend, haven't had a startling or unusual thought. Economically, things are no better—same old debts to meet, same old hundred dollars in the bank, same old job, same old routine of the eight-five to work, the tuna-fish or chicken-salad sandwich for lunch, the five-sixteen back home.

What a life! No change, nothing but routine, sameness, monotony —and for what? (By now you'd better get up—this type of thinking never gets you anywhere, as you've long since learned.)

One verb, ending in -ate, describes how you've lived for the past five years.

to vegetate

NOUN and ADJECTIVE: vegetating
APPLICATION: What a *vegetating* existence! I'm just *vegetating*. What have you done besides *vegetate*?
DERIVATION: Latin *vegetare*, to grow, to live. To *vegetate* is to lead a passive existence, to do little but eat and grow, to be like a vegetable.
RELATED WORDS: *vegetable, vegetation,* et cetera

6. pretense

Your neighbor, Mrs. Brown, comes in to tell you of her latest troubles with (a) her milkman, (b) her maid, (c) her husband, (d) her children, and/or (e) her masseuse.

Since Florence Brown is dull to the point of ennui, and anyway you have a pile of ironing you were planning to light into, you find it difficult to concentrate on what she is saying. However, you do not wish to offend her by sending her packing, or even by appearing to be uninterested, so you pretend rapt attention, nodding vacantly at what you hope are the right places.

One verb, ending in -ate, accurately describes this feigning of interest.

to simulate

ADJECTIVE: *simulated*
NOUN: *simulation*
APPLICATION: *Simulated* (i.e., not real) pearls; he *simulated* interest; he decided on a *simulation* of insanity so that the draft board would reject him.
DERIVATION: Latin, *similis, like, similar*
RELATED WORDS: *similar, dissimilar,* et cetera

7. suggestion, no more

You are an author and are discussing with your publisher the possible avenues of publicity and advertising for your new book. At one point in the conversation the publisher makes several statements which might—or might not—be construed to mean that he is going to allocate some big money for an ambitious advertising campaign. (He may have said, "If we could get some money to put behind this, we might sell a few copies," or "I wonder if it's the type of book which would respond well to a few full pages . . . , might or mightn't. . . ." You see, publishers are a canny, hard-bitten lot, and never make a direct statement, no matter how hard you push them.)

One verb, ending in -*ate*, expressively describes this delicate, indirect act of hinting.

to intimate

NOUN: *intimation*

APPLICATION: He *intimated* that he had discovered your infidelity. We looked for an *intimation* of his feelings.

DERIVATION: Latin, *intimus, inmost*, an *intimation* being an expression of an innermost thought

8. helpful

Aspirin doesn't cure anything—at least not so far as I know. Yet this popular and inexpensive drug (in some stores you can buy a hundred tablets for as little as nine cents) is used to soften and relieve various unpleasant symptoms such as pain, fever, et cetera.

One verb, ending in -*ate*, means to lighten or lessen physical or mental discomfort.

to alleviate

NOUN: *alleviation*

ADJECTIVE: *alleviating*

APPLICATIONS: This medicine will *alleviate* your pain; What measures of *alleviation* shall we take?; What can I say to *alleviate* your anxiety?

DERIVATION: Latin, *levis, light*

RELATED WORDS: *levity*, lightness, lack of seriousness
levitation, lifting bodies off the ground, as in demonstrations of magic

9. when the bell tolls

John Donne's lines (made famous by Ernest Hemingway):

No man is an Iland, intire of it selfe; every man is a peece of the Continent, *a part of the* maine; *if a Clod bee washed away by the* Sea, Europe *is the lesse, as well as if a* Promontorie *were, as well as if a* Mannor *of thy* friends *or of* thine owne *were; any mans* death *diminishes* me, *because I am involved in* Mankinde;

331

*And therefore never send to know for whom the bell tolls; It tolls
for thee.*

are truer than you may think; any mortal who can view another's
suffering with complete composure is denying himself a taste of
genuine emotion.

When someone has suffered a bereavement (as through death);
when he has lost his job and may not be able to find another:
when he has been wounded by life or by friend; then is the time
he most needs to feel that he is not alone, that you share his
misery with him even if you cannot directly alleviate his sadness.
Your sympathy and sharing of emotion are alleviation enough.

One verb ending in *-ate*, signifies this vicarious sharing of the
emotion of sorrow with someone who directly suffers.

to commiserate (with)

NOUN: *commiseration*
ADJECTIVE: *commiserating*
APPLICATIONS: I have come to *commiserate* with you on your
loss.
As a token of my deep *commiseration* . . . ; if you're looking
for *commiseration* . . . ; in *commiserating* tones.
DERIVATION: Latin, *miser, miserable, wretched.* When you *com-
miserate* with someone, you are saying, in effect, "I am as
miserable as you, even though it didn't happen to me."
RELATED WORDS: *Miser, miserable, misery,* et cetera

10. when two men propose

Should you marry John or George? John is handsome, virile,
tender; George is stable, a good provider. George loves you
deeply; John is more exciting. You decide on John, naturally.

But, wait—marrying John would mean continuing to work
after marriage. With George, you could begin to enjoy life. So
you change your mind—it's George, on more mature reflection.

But how happy can you be with a husband who is not exciting?
Maybe John would be best after all . . .

The pendulum swings back and forth all night—you cannot
make up your mind and stick to it. (You fail to realize that your
indecision proves that you're not really ready to marry either
man.) First it's one, then it's back to the other, then back to one
. . . et cetera.

One verb, ending in *-ate*, best describes your indecision.

to vacillate

NOUN: *vacillation*
ADJECTIVE: *vacillating*
APPLICATION: A victim of her own *vacillation;* she *vacillates* between yes and no; a *vacillating* state of mind.
DERIVATION: Latin, *vacillare, move to and fro*

USING THE WORDS

To recapitulate, these are the ten words we have discussed:

1. *enervate*—exhaust completely, deprive of force, vigor, strength
2. *castigate*—censure severely and publicly; tongue-lash
3. *self-abnegate*—suppress one's ego; deny oneself; be excessively self-sacrificing
4. *recapitulate*—repeat the main ideas of; summarize
5. *vegetate*—stagnate intellectually; lead a routine, monotonous existence; do little more than eat and grow
6. *simulate*—make a pretense of; assume the appearance or characteristics by imitation
7. *intimate*—hint at most indirectly
8. *alleviate*—lessen or lighten physical or mental discomfort
9. *commiserate*—express one's sympathy; show one's feeling of sharing another's unhappiness
10. *vacillate*—waver mentally; be unable to come to a definite decision

The lengthy explanations of the ideas behind the words of this chapter plus the recapitulation of their definitions has helped you, I submit, to learn them fully and quickly. The tests to follow will set them firmly in your mind and therefore aid you to retain them in your memory.

Can you pronounce the words?

1.	*enervate*	EN-er-vayt
2.	*castigate*	KASS-ti-gayt
°3.	*self-abnegate*	SELF-AB-ne-gayt
°4.	*recapitulate*	re-ka-PICH-yoo-layt
5.	*vegetate*	VEDGE-e-tayt
°6.	*simulate*	SIMM-yoo-layt
°7.	*intimate*	IN-ti-mayt
8.	*alleviate*	a-LEE-vee-ayt
°9.	*commiserate*	ko-MIZZ-er-ayt
10.	*vacillate*	VASS-i-layt

Can you work with the words?

Match words and definitions.

1. enervation	a. ego denial
2. castigation	b. stagnation
3. self-abnegation	c. suggestion
4. recapitulation	d. sympathy
5. vegetating	e. wavering
6. simulation	f. exhaustion
7. intimation	g. lessening
8. alleviation	h. summary
9. commiseration	i. pretense
10. vacillation	j. censure

KEY: 1—f, 2—j, 3—a, 4—h, 5—b, 6—i, 7—c, 8—g, 9—d, 10—e

Do you understand the words? (I)

React quickly to the following questions.

1. Should you feel *enervated* after a good night's sleep?   YES   NO
2. Do motorists who have been caught speeding sometimes start *castigating* the traffic officer?   YES   NO
3. Is complete *self-abnegation* possibly a symptom of repressed hostility?   YES   NO
4. Is the purpose of a *recapitulation* to teach new material?   YES   NO
5. Do people possessed of *joie de vivre* usually feel that they are *vegetating*?   YES   NO
6. When you *simulate* alertness, do you purposely act somnolent?   YES   NO
7. Is an *intimation* a direct statement?   YES   NO
8. Does aspirin often have an *alleviating* effect?   YES   NO
9. Do people who have suffered a bereavement generally expect *commiseration*?   YES   NO
10. Does *vacillation* show a decisive character?   YES   NO

KEY: 1—no, 2—yes, 3—yes, 4—no, 5—no, 6—no, 7—no, 8—yes, 9—yes, 10—no

Do you understand the words? (II)

Decide whether each pair of words is *similar* or *opposite* in meaning.

1. enervated—exhilarated	SIMILAR	OPPOSITE
2. castigate—condone	SIMILAR	OPPOSITE
3. self-abnegation—egoism	SIMILAR	OPPOSITE
4. recapitulate—summarize	SIMILAR	OPPOSITE
5. vegetate—stagnate	SIMILAR	OPPOSITE
6. simulate—pretend	SIMILAR	OPPOSITE
7. intimate—hint	SIMILAR	OPPOSITE
8. alleviate—aggravate	SIMILAR	OPPOSITE
9. commiserate—sympathize	SIMILAR	OPPOSITE
10. vacillate—decide	SIMILAR	OPPOSITE

KEY: 1–3—opposite; 4–7—similar; 8—opposite; 9—similar; 10—opposite

Can you recall the words?

Write the word that fits each definition.

1. pretend   1. S_____

2. scold   2. C_____

3. sacrifice one's desires   3. S_____

4. waver   4. V_____

5. exhaust   5. E_____

6. sympathize with   6. C_____

7. summarize   7. R_____

8. lighten   8. A_____

9. hint   9. I_____

10. stagnate   10. V_____

KEY: 1—simulate, 2—castigate, 3—self-abnegate, 4—vacillate, 5—enervate, 6—commiserate, 7—recapitulate, 8—alleviate, 9—intimate, 10—vegetate

PICKING YOUR FRIENDS' BRAINS

You can build your vocabulary, I have said, by increasing your familiarity with new ideas and by becoming alert to the new words you will meet in your reading of magazines and books.

There is still another productive method, one that will be particularly applicable in view of all the new words you are learning from your study of these pages.

That method, to put it somewhat inelegantly, is *picking your friends' brains*.

I have noticed that every intelligent person is interested in words, probably (though he may not consciously realize it) because words are symbols of ideas and the man with an alert mind is always interested in ideas.

You may be amazed, if you have never tried it, to find that you can stir up an animated discussion by asking, in a social group that you attend, "What does _____ mean?" (Use any word that particularly fascinates you.) Someone in the group is likely to know, and almost everyone will be willing to make a guess. From that point on, others in the group will ask questions about their own favorite words (most people do have favorites) or about words which they themselves have in some manner recently learned. As the discussion continues along these lines, you will be introduced to new words yourself, and if your friends have fairly good vocabularies you may strike a rich vein of pay dirt (to use an interesting metaphor) and come away with a large number of words to add to your vocabulary.

This method of picking your friends' brains is particularly fruitful because you will be learning not from a page of print (as in this book or as in your other reading) but from real live persons—the same sources that children use to increase their vocabularies at such prodigious rates. No learning is quite as effective as the learning that comes from other people—no information in print can ever be as vivid as information which comes from another human being. And so the words you pick up from your friends will have an amazingly strong appeal, will make a lasting impression on your mind.

Needless to say, your own rich vocabulary, now that you have come this far in the book, will make it possible for you to contribute to your friends' vocabulary as much as, if not more than, you take away—but since giving of oneself is one of the greatest sources of true happiness, you can hardly complain about this extra dividend.

BRIEF INTERMISSION TWELVE:
HOW TO SPELL A WORD

The spelling of English words is archaic, it's confusing, it's needlessly complicated, and, if you have a sense of humor, it's downright comical. In fact, any insulting epithet you might wish to level against our weird methods of putting letters together to form words would probably be justified—but it's our spelling, and we're stuck with it.

How completely stuck we are is illustrated by a somewhat ludicrous event that goes back to 1906, and which cost philanthropist Andrew Carnegie $75,000.

Working under a five-year grant of funds from Carnegie, and headed by the esteemed scholar Brander Matthews, the Simplified Spelling Board published in that year a number of recommendations for bringing some small semblance of order out of the great chaos of English spelling. Their suggestions affected a mere 300 words out of the half million then in the language. Here are a few examples, to give you a general idea:

SPELLING THEN CURRENT	SIMPLIFIED SPELLING
mediaeval	medieval
doubt	dout
debtor	dettor
head	hed
though	tho
through	thru
laugh	laf
tough	tuf
knife	nife
theatre	theater
centre	center
phantom	fantum

These revisions seemed eminently sensible to no less a personage than the President of the United States, Theodore Roosevelt. So delighted was he with the new garb in which these 300 words could be clothed that he immediately ordered that all government documents be printed in simplified spelling. And the result? Such a howl went up from the good citizens of the republic, from the nation's editors and school-teachers and businessmen, that the issue was finally debated in the halls of Congress. Almost to a man, senators and representatives stood opposed to the plan. Teddy Roosevelt, as you have doubtless heard, was a stubborn fellow—but when Congress threatened to hold up the White House stationery appropriation unless the President backed down, Teddy rescinded the order. Roosevelt ran for re-election some time later, and lost. That his attitude toward spelling contributed to his defeat is of course highly doubtful—nevertheless an opposition New York newspaper, the day the returns were in, maliciously commented on the outgoing incumbent in a one-word, simplified-spelling, editorial: "THRU!"

Roosevelt was not the first president to be justifiably outraged by our ridiculous orthography. About one hundred years ago, when Andrew Jackson was twitted on his poor spelling, he is supposed to have made this characteristic reply, "Well, Sir, it is a damned poor mind that cannot think of more than one way to spell a word!" And according to one apocryphal version, it was Jackson's odd spelling which gave birth to the expression "O.K." Jackson thought, so goes the story, that "all correct" was spelled "orl korrect," and he used O.K. as the abbreviation for these words when he approved state papers.

In more recent times, the British playwright George Bernard Shaw offered a dramatic proposal for reducing wartime England's huge taxes. Just eliminate unnecessary letters from our unwieldy spelling, he said, and you'll save enough money in paper and printing to cut everyone's tax rate in half. Maybe it would work, but it's never been put to the test—and the way things look now, it never will be. Current practice more and more holds spelling exactly where it is, bad though it may be. It is a scientific law of language that if enough people make a "mistake," the "mistake" becomes acceptable usage. That law applies to pronunciation, to grammar, to word meanings, but not to spelling. Maybe it's because of

339

our misbegotten faith in and worship of, the printed word—maybe it's because written language tends to be static, while spoken language constantly changes. Whatever the cause, spelling today successfully resists every logical effort at reform, "English spelling," said Thorstein Veblen many years back, "satisfies all the requirements of the canons of reputability under the law of conspicuous waste. It is archaic, cumbrous, and ineffective." Perfectly true. Notwithstanding, it's here to stay.

Your most erudite friend doubtless misspells the name of the Hawaiian guitar. I asked half a dozen members of the English department of a large Eastern college to spell the word—without exception they responded with *ukelele*. Even a pocket-size dictionary lists the word that way. Yet the only accepted form is *ukulele*. Judging from my experience with adult classes at the City College of New York, half the population of the country must think the word is spelled *alright*. Yet *all right* is the only pattern permitted us. Seventy-five per cent of the members of my classes—and they're all educated people—can't spell *embarrassing* or *coolly*. People will go on misspelling these four words, but the authorized spelling will remain impervious to change.

Well, you know the one about Mohammed and the mountain. Though it's true that we have modernized spelling to a microscopic extent in the last thirty-nine years (*traveler, center, theater, medieval, labor,* and *honor,* for example, have pretty much replaced *traveller, centre, theatre, mediaeval, labour,* and *honour*), still the resistance to change has not observably weakened. If spelling won't change, as it probably won't, those of us who consider ourselves poor spellers will have to. We'll just have to get up and go to the mountain.

Is it hard to become a perfect speller? I have demonstrated over and over again in my adult classes at City College that anyone of normal intelligence and average educational background can become a perfect speller in very little time.

What makes the task so easy?

First—investigations have proved that 95 per cent of the spelling errors that educated people make occur in just 100 words. Not only do we all misspell the same words—but we misspell them in about the same way.

Second—correct spelling relies exclusively on memory, and

340

the most effective way to train memory is by means of association or, to use the psychological term, mnemonics.

If you fancy yourself an imperfect or even a terrible speller, the chances are very great that you've developed a complex solely because you misspell some or all of the 100 words with which this chapter deals. When you have conquered this single list, and I shall immediately proceed to demonstate how easy it is, by means of mnemonics, to do so, 95 per cent of your spelling difficulties will in all likelihood vanish.

Let us start with twenty-five words from the list. In the first column you will find the correct spelling of each, and in the second column the simple mnemonic that will forevermore fix that correct spelling in your memory.

CORRECT SPELLING	MNEMONIC
1. all right	Two words, no matter what it means. Keep in mind that it's the opposite of *all wrong*.
2. coolly	Of course you can spell *cool*—simply add the adverbial ending—ly.
3. supersede	This is the only word in the language ending in *-sede* (the only one, mind you—there isn't a single other one so spelled.)
4. succeed	The only three words in the entire
5. proceed	language ending in *-ceed*. When you
6. exceed	think of the three words in the order given here, the initial letters form the beginning of SPElling.
7. cede, precede, recede, et cetera	All other words with a similar-sounding final syllable end in *-cede*.
8. procedure	One of the double *e's of proceed* moves to the end in the noun form, *procedure*.
9. stationery	This is the word that means paper, and notice the *er* in *paper*.
10. stationary	In this spelling, the word means standing, and notice the *a* in *stand*.
11. recommend	*Commend*, which we all spell correctly, plus the prefix *re-*.
12. separate	
13. comparative	Look for *a rat* in both words.
14. ecstasy	to *sy* (sigh) with ecstasy.
15. analyze	The only two nontechnical words in the
16. paralyze	whole language ending in *-yze*.

341

17. repetition	First four letters identical with those in the allied form, *repeat*.
18. irritable	
19. inimitable	Think of allied forms, *irritate* and *imitate*.
20. absence	Think of the allied form, *absent*, and you will not be tempted to misspell it *abscence*.
21. superintendent	The superintend*ent* in an apartment house collects the *rent*—thus you avoid *superintendant*.
22. conscience	*Science* plus prefix *con-*.
23. anoint	Think of *an ointment*, hence no double *n*.
24. ridiculous	Think of the allied form, *ridicule*, which we usually spell correctly, thus avoiding *rediculous*.
25. despair	Again, think of another form—*desperate*—and so avoid *dispair*.

Whether or not you have much faith in your spelling ability, you will need very little time to conquer the preceding twenty-five demons. Spend a few minutes, now, on each of those words in the list that you're doubtful of, and then test your success by means of the exercise below. Perhaps to your astonishment, you will find it easy to make a perfect score.

A test of your learning

Instructions: After studying the preceding list of words, fill in the missing letters correctly.

1. a_____right

2. coo_____y

3. super_____

4. suc_____

5. pro_____

6. ex_____

7. con_____

8. proc_____dure

9. station_____ry (paper)

10. station_____ry (still)

11. sep_____rate

12. compar_____tive

13. esta_____y

14. anal_____e

15. paral_____e

16. rep_____tition

17. irrit_____ble   21. con_____nce

18. inimit_____ble   22. a_____oint

19. ab_____ence   23. r_____diculous

20. superintend_____nt   24. d_____spair

Mere repetitious drill is of no value in learning to spell a word correctly. You've probably heard the one about the youngster who was kept after school because he was in the habit of using the ungrammatical expression, "I have went." Miss X was going to cure her pupil, even if it required drastic measures. So she ordered him to write "I have gone" 1000 times. "Just leave your work on my desk before you go home," she said, "and I'll find it when I come in tomorrow morning." Well, there were twenty pages of neat script on her desk next morning, 1000 lines of "I have gone's," and on the last sheet was a note from the child. "Dear Teacher," it read, "I have done the work and I have went home." If this didn't actually happen, it logically could have, for in any drill, if the mind is not actively engaged, no learning will result. If you drive a car, or sew, or do any familiar and repetitious manual work, you know how your hands can carry on an accustomed task while your mind is far away. And if you hope to learn to spell by filling pages with a word, stop wasting your time. All you'll get for your trouble is writer's cramp.

The only way to learn to spell those words that now plague you is to devise a mnemonic for each one.

If you are never quite sure whether it's *indispensible* or *indispensable,* you can spell it out 100, 1000, or 1,000,000 times—and the next time you have occasion to write it in a sentence, you'll still wonder whether to end it with *ible* or *able.* But if you say to yourself *just once* that *able* men are generally *indispensable,* that thought will come to you whenever you need to spell the word; in a few seconds you've conquered another spelling demon. By engineering your own mnemonic through a study of the architecture of a troublesome word, you will become so quickly and completely involved with the correct spelling of that word that it will be impossible for you ever to be stumped again.

Let us start at once. Below you will find another twenty-five words from the list of 100 demons, each offered to you in both the correct form and in the popular misspelling. Go through the test quickly, checking off what you consider a proper choice in each case. In that way you will discover which of the twenty-five you would be likely to get caught on. Then devise a personal mnemonic for each word you flunked, writing your ingenious result out in the margin of the page. And don't be alarmed if some of your mnemonics turn out kind of silly—the sillier they are, the more likely you are to recall them in an emergency. One of my pupils, who could not remember how many *l*s to put into *tranquillity* (or is it *tranquility*?), shifted his mind into high gear and came up with this: "In the old days life was more *tranquil* than today, and people wrote with *quills* instead of fountain pens. Hence—*tranquillity!*" Another pupil, a girl who always chewed her nails over *irresistible* before she could decide whether to end it with *ible* or *able*, suddenly realized that a certain brand of *lipstick* was called *irresistible*, the point being of course that the only vowel in *lipstick* is *i*—hence, *ible!* Silly, aren't they? But they work. Go ahead to the test now; and see how clever—or silly—you can be.

SPELLING TEST

Check a or b, whichever you think is the correct form:

1. a. supprise	b. surprise
2. a. inoculate	b. innoculate
3. a. definitely	b. definately
4. a. priviledge	b. privilege
5. a. incidently	b. incidentally
6. a. predictible	b. predictable
7. a. dissipate	b. disippate
8. a. descriminate	b. discriminate
9. a. description	b. discription
10. a. baloon	b. balloon
11. a. occurence	b. occurrence
12. a. truely	b. truly
13. a. arguement	b. argument
14. a. assistant	b. asisstant
15. a. grammer	b. grammar

16. a. parallel   b. paralell
17. a. drunkeness   b. drunkenness
18. a. suddeness   b. suddenness
19. a. embarassment   b. embarrassment
20. a. weird   b. wierd
21. a. pronounciation   b. pronunciation
22. a. noticeable   b. noticable
23. a. developement   b. development
24. a. vicious   b. viscious
25. a. insistent   b. insistant

KEY: 1—b, 2—a, 3—a, 4—b, 5—b, 6—b, 7—a, 8—b, 9—a, 10—b, 11—b, 12—b, 13—b, 14—a, 15—b, 16—a, 17—b, 18—b, 19—b, 20—a, 21—b, 22—a, 23—b, 24—a, 25—a

---

By now you're well on the way toward developing a definite superiority complex about your spelling—which isn't a half-bad thing, for I've learned, working with my students, that many people think they're awful spellers, and have completely lost faith in their ability, solely because they get befuddled over no more than two dozen or so common words that they use over and over again and always misspell. Every other word they spell perfectly, but they still think they're prize boobs in spelling until their self-confidence is restored. So if you're beginning to gain more assurance, you're on the right track. The conquest of the 100 common words most frequently misspelled is not going to assure you that you will always come out top man in a spelling bee, but it's certain to clean up your writing and bolster your ego.

So far you have worked with fifty of the 100 spelling demons. Here, now, is the remainder of the list. Test yourself, or have someone who can keep a secret test you, and discover which ones are your Waterloo. Study each one you miss as if it were a problem in engineering. Observe how it's put together and devise whatever association pattern will fix the correct form in your mind.

Happy spelling!

SPELLING DEMONS

These fifty words complete the list of 100 words which most frequently stump the inexpert spellers:

1. embarrassing
2. judgment
   (preferred spelling)
3. indispensable
4. disappear
5. disappoint
6. corroborate
7. sacrilegious
8. tranquillity
   (preferred spelling)
9. exhilaration
10. newsstand
11. license
    (preferred spelling)
12. irresistible
13. persistent
14. dilemma
15. perseverance
16. until (but till)
17. tyrannize
18. vacillate
19. oscillate
20. accommodate
21. dilettante
22. changeable
23. accessible
24. forty
25. desirable
26. panicky
27. seize
28. leisure
29. receive
30. achieve
31. holiday
32. existence
33. pursue
34. pastime
35. possesses
36. professor
37. category
38. rhythmical
39. vacuum
40. benefited
41. committee
42. grievous
43. conscious
44. plebeian
45. tariff
46. sheriff
47. connoisseur
48. necessary
49. sergeant
50. misspelling

16

HOW TO TALK
ABOUT A VARIETY OF CONDITIONS

—— TEASER PREVIEW ——————————————

What word, ending in *—ous*, would aptly describe someone who is:

1. fawning, servilely attentive   1._____ous

2. nagging, dissatisfied   2._____ous

3. snobbish, haughtily contemptuous   3._____ous

4. noisily troublesome; unmanageable   4._____ous

5. habitually short of cash   5._____ous

6. attentive to women   6._____ous

7. harmless   7._____ous

8. fond of liquor   8._____ous

9. gaunt, haggard   9._____ous

10. melancholy, sorrowful   10._____ous

———————————————————————————

THERE are thousands of English words which end in the letters—*ous*—a useful suffix which denotes *full of*.

The central theme about which the words in this chapter revolve is the idea of "fullness"—and as you will shortly see, you can be full of compliance and servility; full of complaints; full of snobbery; full of noise; full of no money; full of horsemanship; full of harmlessness; full of liquor; full of deathly pallor; and full of sorrows.

For each of these ideas English has a word—and the person with a rich vocabulary knows the exact word to describe what he's full of.

IDEAS, ORIGINS, AND RELATED WORDS

1. compliance

The Latin root *sequi* means *to follow*—and those who follow rather than lead are usually in a menial, subordinate, or inferior position. People who engage in certain fields of endeavor—waiters, clerks, and servants, for example—are forced, often contrary to their natural temperaments, to act excessively courteous, pleasant, obliging, even subservient and humble. They must *follow* the lead of their customers or employers, bending their own wills according to the desires of those they serve. They are, etymologically, *full of following after*, or—

obsequious

RELATED WORDS:

1. *obsequies*—In a funeral cortege, the mourners *follow after* the corpse. Hence, *obsequies* are the burial ceremonies, the funeral rites.
2. *subsequent*—A *subsequent* letter, paragraph, time, et cetera, is one which *follows* another.
3. *sequel*—A *sequel* may be a literary work, such as a novel, which *follows* another, continuing the same subject, dealing with the same people or village, et cetera; or it may be an occurrence which grows out of or *follows* another, as in the sentence, "Just wait until you hear the *sequel* to the story!"
4. *sequence*—In order, one item *following* another, as in, "The *sequence* of events of the next few days left him breathless."

Any other word containing letters *sequ* is likely to have some relationship to the idea of *following*.

2. complaints

The Latin root *queri* means *to complain*—and anyone full of complaints, constantly nagging, harping, fretful, petulant, whining, never satisfied, may accordingly be called—

querulous

3. snobbery

The Latin root *cilium* means *eyelid;* *super* means *above;* and above the eyelid, as anyone can plainly see, is the eyebrow. Now there are certain obnoxious people who go around raising their eyebrows in contempt, disdain, and sneering arrogance at ordinary mortals like you and me. Such contemptuous, sneering, overbearingly conceited people are called—

supercilious

4. noise

The Latin root *strepere* means *to make a noise*—anyone who is unruly, boisterous, resistant to authority, unmanageable—all in a noisy, troublesome manner, is—

obstreperous

5. moneyless

The Latin root *pecus* means *cattle*—and at one time in human history a man's wealth was measured not by his stocks and bonds but by his stocks of domestic animals, which was a lot more logical, since you get milk and leather and meat from cattle—true wealth—and all you get from the stock market is a headache.

Someone who had lots of "pecus," then, was rich—someone without "pecus" was indigent, destitute, "broke." And so today we call someone who is habitually without funds, who seems generally to be full of a complete lack of money—

impecunious

(This word is not a synonym of *indigent, destitute,* or *poverty-stricken;* it does not necessarily imply living in reduced circumstances or want, but quite simply being short of cash—habitually.)

RELATED WORD:

1. *pecuniary—pertaining to money*, as in, a *pecuniary* consideration; *pecuniary* affairs, et cetera

6. horses

The French root *cheval* means *horse;* and in medieval times only gentlemen and knights rode on horses—common people walked. Traditionally (but not, I understand, actually) knights were courteous to women, attentive to female desires, and self-

349

sacrificing when their own interests came in conflict with those of the fair sex. Hence, we call a modern man who has a knightly attitude to women—

chivalrous

RELATED WORDS:

(*cheval, horse*, comes from Latin *caballus*, an inferior horse. *Caballus* is found in English words in the spelling *caval*.)

1. *cavalcade*—a procession of persons on horseback, as in a parade
2. *cavalier*—as a noun, *cavalier* means simply a military man of certain rank, or a mounted soldier. As an adjective, *cavalier* describes actions and attitudes that are *haughty, unmindful of other's feelings, too offhand*, such attributes often being associated with people in power (the military being one of the powers-that-be). Thus, "He answered in a *cavalier* manner" would signify that he was arrogant in his answer, as if the questioner was taking a little too much privilege with him. Or, "After the *cavalier* treatment I received, I never wished to return," signifying that I was pretty much made to feel unimportant and inferior. Or, "After her *cavalier* refusal, I'll never invite her to another party," signifying that the refusal was, perhaps, curt, offhand, without any attempt at apology or courtesy.
3. *cavalry*—the mounted, or "horsed" part of an army

Another Latin word for horse is *equus*, found in such English words as:

1. *equestrian*—a horseman
2. *equestrienne*—a horsewoman
3. *equine*—horselike, similar in construction to *bovine, feline, vulpine*, et cetera

7. no harm done

The Latin root *nocere* means *to injure;* someone who need cause you no fear, so harmless is he, so unable to interfere, so unlikely to get you into trouble, is called—

innocuous

RELATED WORDS:

1. *innocent*—not guilty of crime or injury
2. *noxious*—harmful, poisonous; unwholesome

8. alcoholic

The Latin root *bibere* means to *drink;* and one who is generally found with one foot up on the brass rail, who likes to tipple beyond the point of sobriety—who, in short, has an overfondness for drinks with a pronounced alcoholic content, is called, usually humorously—

bibulous

RELATED WORD:

imbibe—to drink in, soak up, absorb. If we use this verb without specifying what is drunk, as in "He likes to *imbibe*," the implication, of course, is always liquor; but *imbibe* may also be used in patterns like *"imbibe* learning" or "in early infancy she *imbibed* a respect for her parents."

9. like death itself

The Latin root *cadere* means *to fall*—one's fall is of course always in death, and so someone who looks like a corpse (figuratively speaking), who is pale, gaunt, thin, haggard, his eyes deep-sunk, his limbs wasted, in other words the extreme opposite of the picture of glowing health, is called—

cadaverous

RELATED WORDS:

1. *cadaver*—a corpse, literally
2. *decadent*—literally, *falling down* (*de* is a prefix meaning *down*, as in *descend*, climb down; *decline*, turn down; et cetera). If something is in a *decadent* state, it is deteriorating, becoming corrupt or demoralized. *Decadence* is a state of *decay*—*decay* itself being the shortened verb form of *decadent*. Generally *decadent* and *decadence* are used figuratively—they refer not to actual physical *decay* (as of a dead body), but to moral or spiritual *decay*. Both *decadent* and *decadence* are preferably accented on the second syllable.

10. pain and misery

The Latin root *dolere* means *to suffer*—one who is mournful and sad, whose melancholy comes from physical pain or mental distress is called—

dolorous

1. *dolor*—a poetic synonym of grief
2. *doleful*—a word applied somewhat humorously to exaggerated dismalness, sadness, or dreariness

USING THE WORDS

I have built this chapter, as you have noticed, directly on the roots found in our basic ten words; roots that are not particularly common but which, once they are recognized and understood, add to the richness and meaningfulness of the words you are studying. Just looking at the roots once again will probably serve to bring the words back to mind. Try it.

ROOT	MEANING	
1. *sequi*	follow	1. _____
2. *queri*	complain	2. _____
3. *cilium*	eyelid	3. _____
4. *strepere*	make noise	4. _____
5. *pecus*	cattle	5. _____
6. *cheval*	horse	6. _____
7. *nocere*	injure	7. _____
8. *bibere*	to drink	8. _____
9. *cadere*	to fall	9. _____
10. *dolere*	to suffer	10. _____

And of course there were the two other roots we turned up in our discussion:

11. *caballus (caval)*	horse	11. _____
12. *equus*	horse	12. _____

Now let's recapitulate by restating the words and their meanings.

1. *obsequious*—servilely attentive, fawningly polite, as to customers or superiors
2. *querulous*—nagging, discontented, complaining
3. *supercilious*—haughtily disdainful, snobbish, sneeringly contemptuous
4. *obstreperous*—noisily unmanageable, troublesome
5. *impecunious*—habitually "broke"
6. *chivalrous*—attentive and courteous to women
7. *innocuous*—harmless
8. *bibulous*—addicted to alcoholic stimulation (humorous)
9. *cadaverous*—gaunt, corpselike, (haggard)
10. *dolorous*—melancholy, sorrowful

A. THE BASIC WORDS

Can you pronounce the words?

°1.	*obsequious*	ob-SEEK-we-us
°2.	*querulous*	KWER-oo-lus
°3.	*supercilious*	soo-per-SILL-ee-us
°4.	*obstreperous*	ob-STREP-er-us
°5.	*impecunious*	im-pe-KYOO-nee-us
°6.	*chivalrous*	SHIV-IL-rus
°7.	*innocuous*	in-NOCK-yoo-us
°8.	*bibulous*	BIB-yoo-lus
°9.	*cadaverous*	ka-DAV-er-us
°10.	*dolorous*	DOLL-er-us

Note: All these adjectives, with the exception of *chivalrous*, become nouns by the simple addition of *NESS. Chivalrous* becomes *chivalry.* Another form of *chivalrous* is *chivalric,* pronounced shi-VAL-rik.

Can you work with the words? (I)

Matching words and meanings.

1. obsequious	a. snobbish
2. querulous	b. harmless

3. supercilious	c. gaunt
4. obstreperous	d. short of funds
5. impecunious	e. fawning
6. chivalrous	f. sorrowful
7. innocuous	g. addicted to drink
8. bibulous	h. courteous to females
9. cadaverous	i. complaining
10. dolorous	j. unmanageable

KEY: 1—e, 2—i, 3—a, 4—j, 5—d, 6—h, 7—b, 8—g, 9—c, 10—f

Can you work with the words? (II)

Match each word in the first column with another from the second column which is *opposite* in meaning.

1. obsequious	a. content
2. querulous	b. affluent
3. supercilious	c. healthy
4. obstreperous	d. rude
5. impecunious	e. sober
6. chivalrous	f. dangerous
7. innocuous	g. humble
8. bibulous	h. misogynous
9. cadaverous	i. gay
10. dolorous	j. quiet

KEY: 1—d, 2—a, 3—g, 4—j, 5—b, 6—h, 7—f, 8—e, 9—c, 10—i

Do you understand the words?

React quickly to each question.

1. Do *obsequious* people usually command our respect?	YES	NO
2. Are *querulous* women satisfied with their lot?	YES	NO
3. Are *supercilious* people usually popular?	YES	NO
4. Is a man of affluence *impecunious?*	YES	NO
5. Do women like *chivalrous* men?	YES	NO

354

6. Are *innocuous* people dangerous?   YES   NO
7. Is a *bibulous* character a teetotaler?   YES   NO
8. Is a *cadaverous*-looking individual the picture of health?   YES   NO
9. Is a *dolorous* attitude characteristic of jovial people?   YES   NO
10. Is an *obstreperous* child difficult to manage?   YES   NO

KEY: 1—no, 2—no, 3—no, 4—no, 5—yes, 6—no, 7—no, 8—no, 9—no, 10—yes

Can you recall the words?

1. sorrowful   1._____
2. servilely attentive   2._____
3. haggard   3._____
4. complaining   4._____
5. addicted to alcohol   5._____
6. arrogant   6._____
7. harmless   7._____
8. noisily unmanageable   8._____
9. attentive to women   9._____
10. short of money   10._____

KEY: 1—dolorous, 2—obsequious, 3—cadaverous, 4—querulous, 5—bibulous, 6—supercilious, 7—innocuous, 8—obstreperous, 9—chivalrous, 10—impecunious

B. RELATED WORDS

Discussion of the roots of our ten basic words has turned up eighteen others. Can you say them correctly?

°1. *obsequies*   OB-se-kweez
  2. *subsequent*   SUB-se-kwent

3. *sequel*   SEE-kwel
4. *sequence*   SEE-kwence
⁕5. *pecuniary*   pe-KYOO-nee-er-ee
6. *noxious*   NOK-shus
7. *imbibe*   im-BYBE
⁕8. *dolor*   DOE-ler
9. *doleful*   DOLE-ful
10. *cavalcade*   KAV-il-kayd
11. *cavalier* (adj.)   KAV-a-leer
12. *cavalry*   KAV-il-ree
13. *equestrian*   ee-KWESS-tree-in
14. *equestrienne*   ee-KWESS-tree-ENN
⁕15. *equine*   EE-kwyne
⁕16. *cadaver*   ka-DAV-er
⁕17. *decadent*   de-KAY-dent
⁕18. *decadence*   de-KAY-dence

Can you work with the words?

Match words and meanings.

1. obsequies	a. proper order
2. subsequent	b. drink, absorb
3. sequel	c. harmful, poisonous
4. sequence	d. pain, sorrow (poetic)
5. pecuniary	e. coming later
6. noxious	f. procession of mounted riders
7. imbibe	g. offhand, haughty
8. dolor	h. a following event or literary work
9. doleful	i. horsewoman
10. cavalcade	j. pertaining to money
11. cavalier (adj)	k. mounted military division
12. cavalry	l. funeral rites
13. equestrian	m. exaggeratedly sorrowful
14. equestrienne	n. horselike
15. equine	o. horseman
16. cadaver	p. spiritual decline
17. decadent	q. morally decaying
18. decadence	r. corpse

KEY: 1—l, 2—e, 3—h, 4—a, 5—j, 6—c, 7—b, 8—d, 9—m, 10—f, 11—g, 12—k, 13—o, 14—i, 15—n, 16—r, 17—q, 18—p

Do you understand the words? (I)

React quickly to each question.

1. Are speeches usually made during *obsequies?*   YES NO
2. Did Margaret Mitchell write a *sequel* to *Gone with the Wind?*   YES NO
3. Are these numbers in *sequence:* 5, 6, 7, 8, 9, 10, 11?   YES NO
4. Do banks often handle the *pecuniary* details of an estate?   YES NO
5. Is arsenic a *noxious* chemical?   YES NO
6. Do children sometimes *imbibe* wisdom from their parents?   YES NO
7. If a song is sung in tones of *dolor*, is it a happy song?   YES NO
8. Is a *doleful* countenance a happy one?   YES NO
9. Does a *cavalcade* contain horses?   YES NO
10. Does a *cavalier* attitude show a spirit of humility?   YES NO

KEY: 1—yes, 2—no, 3—yes, 4—yes, 5—yes, 6—yes, 7—no, 8—no, 9—yes, 10—no

---

Do you understand the words? (II)

1. Is a *cavalry* officer usually a good horseman?   YES NO
2. Would an *equestrian* statue of General Grant show him with or on a horse?   YES NO
3. Is an *equestrienne* a man?   YES NO
4. Do humans possess many *equine* characteristics?   YES NO
5. Is a *cadaver* alive?   YES NO
6. Is an iconoclast likely to consider religion a *decadent* institution?   YES NO
7. Is *decadence* a desirable quality?   YES NO

Do you understand the words? (III)

Is each pair of words the same or opposite in meaning?

1. obsequies—rites   SAME OPPOSITE
2. subsequent—preceding   SAME OPPOSITE

3. pecuniary—financial SAME OPPOSITE
4. sequence—order SAME OPPOSITE
5. noxious—harmful SAME OPPOSITE
6. imbibe—drink SAME OPPOSITE
7. dolor—delight SAME OPPOSITE
8. doleful—merry SAME OPPOSITE
9. cavalier—courteous SAME OPPOSITE
10. cadaver—corpse SAME OPPOSITE
11. decadent—resurgent SAME OPPOSITE

KEY: 1—s, 2—o, 3—s, 4—s, 5—s, 6—s, 7—o, 8—o, 9—o, 10—s, 11—o

Can you recall the words?

Write the word that fits each definition.

1. harmful

1. N_____

2. a literary work or an event that follows another

2. S_____

3. drink in

3. I_____

4. poetic word for sorrow

4. D_____

5. burial ceremonies

5. O_____

6. horseman

6. E_____

7. horsewoman

7. E_____

8. horselike

8. E_____

9. following

9. S_____

10. relating to money

10. P_____

11. exaggeratedly sad

11. D_____

12. items in proper order

12. S_____

13. parade of mounted riders

13. C_____

14. offhand, unmindful of another's feelings

14. C_____

15. mounted military division

15. C_____

16. a corpse

16. C_____

17. morally deteriorating   17. D_____

18. spiritual decay   18. D_____

KEY: 1—noxious, 2—sequel, 3—imbibe, 4—dolor, 5—obsequies, 6—equestrian, 7—equestrienne, 8—equine, 9—subsequent, 10—pecuniary, 11—doleful, 12—sequence, 13—cavalcade, 14—cavalier, 15—cavalry, 16—cadaver, 17—decadent, 18—decadence

---

CHAPTER REVIEW

Can you recognize the words?

Check the word that fits each definition.

1. Excessively polite and fawning:
   (a) querulous, (b) obsequious, (c) supercilious
2. Noisily troublesome:
   (a) querulous, (b) impecunious, (c) obstreperous
3. Courteous and attentive to women:
   (a) querulous, (b) chivalrous, (c) supercilious
4. Complaining, nagging:
   (a) querulous, (b) supercilious, (c) innocuous
5. Haughtily disdainful:
   (a) supercilious, (b) bibulous, (c) dolorous
6. Gaunt, corpselike:
   (a) noxious, (b) cadaverous, (c) doleful
7. High-handed:
   (a) supercilious, (b) cavalier, (c) decadent
8. Moral decay:
   (a) decadence, (b) obsequies, (c) sequence

KEY: 1—b, 2—c, 3—b, 4—a, 5—a, 6—b, 7—b, 8—a

OPENING YOUR MIND TO NEW IDEAS

If you have arrived at this point in the book *honestly*—that is, by actual study, not by merely dipping in at random—I have a simple and interesting exercise for you.

In the spaces below, write down ten new words that you have recently learned either from your work in this book or from any of the suggested methods of vocabulary building.

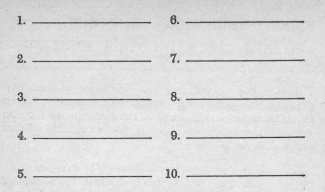

1. ——————— 6. ———————

2. ——————— 7. ———————

3. ——————— 8. ———————

4. ——————— 9. ———————

5. ——————— 10. ———————

That was simplicity itself, wasn't it?

Now ask some other person to try a similar job—writing down ten new words that *he* has learned in the last few weeks.

You know what the result will probably be. The chances are he'll draw a blank, or at best be able to think of only one or two brand new words that he has actually learned recently.

Think what this means.

The average adult effectively (but unnecessarily) puts a brake on his learning after his formal schooling is over (new words, I repeat, are verbal symbols of new learning), practically wraps his mind in an almost impenetrable jacket, virtually (though unconsciously, of course) says: "I know so much and it's enough."

You begin to see, then, how increasing your vocabulary through methodically learning new words and consciously opening your mind to new ideas can change the entire intellectual climate of your life.

I repeat that if you have arrived at this point in the book honestly—by faithfully doing all the work and some of the suggested reading—it cannot be otherwise than that you begin to feel the newness and richness of the changed intellectual climate in which you are now living.

And as we begin to approach the end of our work together and you begin to reap some of the benefits, I wish only to ask: "Was it not effort well-expended?"

BRIEF INTERMISSION THIRTEEN:
ANOTHER CHECK ON YOUR SPELLING

In each line you will find four words—one of them purposely, subtly, and perhaps unexpectedly misspelled. It's up to you to check the single error. If you can come out top man at least fifteen times out of twenty, you're probably a better speller than you realize.

1. (a) alright, (b) coolly, (c) supersede, (d) disappear
2. (a) inoculate, (b) definately, (c) irresistible, (d) recommend
3. (a) incidentally, (b) dissipate, (c) seperate, (d) balloon
4. (a) argument, (b) ecstasy, (c) occurrance, (d) analyze
5. (a) sacrilegious, (b) weird, (c) pronunciation, (d) repitition
6. (a) drunkeness, (b) embarrassment, (c) weird, (d) irritable
7. (a) noticeable, (b) superintendant, (c) absence, (d) development
8. (a) vicious, (b) conscience, (c) panicy, (d) amount
9. (a) accessible, (b) pursue, (c) exhilarate, (d) insistant
10. (a) naïveté, (b) necessary, (c) catagory, (d) professor
11. (a) rhythmical, (b) sergeant, (c) vaccuum, (d) assassin
12. (a) benefitted, (b) allotted, (c) corroborate, (d) despair
13. (a) diphtheria, (b) grandeur, (c) rediculous, (d) license
14. (a) tranquillity, (b) symmetry, (c) occassion, (d) privilege
15. (a) tarrif, (b) tyranny, (c) battalion, (d) archipelago
16. (a) bicycle, (b) geneology, (c) liquefy, (d) bettor
17. (a) defense, (b) batchelor, (c) kidnaped, (d) parallel
18. (a) whisky, (b) likable, (c) bookkeeper, (d) accomodate
19. (a) comparitive, (b) mayonnaise, (c) indispensable, (d) dexterous
20. (a) dictionary, (b) cantaloupe, (c) existance, (d) ukulele

---

KEY: 1—a (all right), 2—b (definitely), 3—c (separate), 4—c (occurrence), 5—d (repetition), 6—a (drunkenness), 7—b (superintendent), 8—c (panicky), 9—d (insistent), 10—c (category), 11—c (vacuum), 12—a (benefited), 13—c (ridiculous), 14—c (occasion), 15—a (tariff), 16—b (genealogy), 17—b (bachelor), 18—d (accommodate), 19—a (comparative), 20—c (existence)

17

HOW TO TALK
ABOUT COMPLICATED IDEAS

────── **TEASER PREVIEW** ──────────────────

What word ending in *-ous* would aptly and vividly describe something which:

1. is a sign of coming danger	1. _____ous
2. deviates from the general rule	2. _____ous
3. is said or done entirely without provocation	3. _____ous
4. is made up of similar parts	4. _____ous
5. is exhibited to the public after the death of its creator	5. _____ous
6. is done in language that is low, vulgar, and coarse	6. _____ous
7. is extremely thin, subtle, abstract	7. _____ous
8. is harmful to the human system	8. _____ous
9. causes humiliation and disgrace	9. _____ous
10. traps you when you are least prepared	10. _____ous

NOT only people, but things, circumstances, actions, speech, and other such intangibles can also be *"full of."* For example, the words in this chapter will explore the ideas of fullness of danger threats; of similarity; of "after-death exhibition"; of coarse indecency; of abstractness; of irregularity; of harm; of disgrace; of wiliness. And to return to previous organization of the material, after our short change of pace in Chapters 15 and 16, we shall first examine the ideas behind ten basic words, then the host of related and derived forms which these words bring to our notice.

IDEAS

1. unexpected difficulties

President Truman was re-elected, in 1948, on a liberal and reform program: housing, civil rights, a pro-labor bill to substitute for the Taft-Hartley law, et cetera. After the Eighty-first Congress met, the Republicans and Southern Democrats formed a coalition which successfully defeated almost every administration measure. Truman then found himself in a most contradictory, irregular, abnormal position; his party, his candidates, his platform had won— but he couldn't get his bills through.

What adjective, ending in -ous, describes Truman's position?

anomalous

2. trouble ahead

In early 1949, there were what seemed unmistakable signs that the much heralded Great Depression was not far off—mounting unemployment, curtailed production, decreased buying, breaks in the price structure, et cetera. Such circumstances were deemed by some economists to be a foreshadowing of disaster.

What adjective, ending in -ous, means a sign of coming trouble?

ominous

3. with their own kind

In many large schools, students of approximately the same intelligence are placed in the same class. The purpose of such grouping is to permit the teacher to work more efficiently by scaling her instruction on the level suitable to all the members of the class. The problem of what may be too fast for some being too slow for others is thus obviated.

What adjective, ending in -ous, describes a grouping or collection of people or things which are essentially similar?

homogeneous

363

4. after death

Sometimes a book is published after the author has died—there being a certain time lag (about six months) between the submission of a manuscript and its appearance between covers. Sometimes a work of art—a statue or painting, say—is exhibited for the first time to the public after the artist has died. And also it may happen (again because of the time lag that exists between conception and appearance) that a child is born after its father has died.

What adjective, ending in *-ous*, describes a book, a work of art, or a baby which appears after the death of its creator or father?

posthumous

5. the lower depths

Often in political campaigns, a point is reached at which the candidates take off their gloves and start slugging with bare fists. This means that all kinds of abusive language is used; coarse implications are made; indecent accusations are aired; and in general the attack is on such a low level that students of American government realize that politics hasn't changed a bit in the last fifty years.

What adjective, ending in *-ous*, describes attacks made in vulgar, low, or indecent language?

scurrilous

6. elusive

Imagine something so thin, so insubstantial, so subtle and abstract (it may be a thought, an argument, the plot of a novel, or similar things) that there seems no part of it that you can grab hold of and really look at.

What adjective, ending in *-ous*, most aptly describes such figurative thinness, such complete intangibility?

tenuous

7. unexpected

You are entertaining some guests in your home. Suddenly one of them makes an insulting remark about your wife's appearance.

364

Not only was the remark insulting—more, it was uncalled for, totally unprovoked, completely unnecessary.

What adjective, ending in *-ous*, describes a remark for which there was no provocation and which seems to serve no purpose?

gratuitous

8. bad for what ails you

The diabetic must generally avoid sugar as much as possible. When an excess of sugar gets into the diabetic's system (and for him an excess is an amount that might not even begin to interest a normal or healthy person) it causes fairly unpleasant results: dizziness, fainting, even coma.

What adjective, ending in *-ous*, describes the harmful effect that substances may have on the human body?

deleterious

9. scandalous

You have been forced to do something which fills you with humiliation, which can be productive of nothing but disgrace. What the particular action was is of no consequence—people have differing standards and what may seem respectable and noble to one may be nothing short of debasing to another. What is important is the shameful feeling which the act gives you—such a feeling growing out of the low opinion of you that you believe your act will produce among your friends or in the public mind.

What adjective, ending in *-ous*, describes an act which can overwhelm the doer with humiliation and disgrace?

ignominious

10. trap, well-concealed

Cancer creeps up on you—you seem perfectly healthy until the first crucial symptoms appear. Then, when you recognize the disease, it is often too late. That is why doctors so solemnly warn of the necessity for periodic cancer examinations.

What adjective, ending in *-ous*, aptly describes something which can, like cancer, weave a trap around you so inconspicuously that you do not realize what is happening until you're caught?

insidious

USING THE WORDS: I

Can you pronounce the words?

°1. *anomalous*   a-NOM-a-lus
°2. *ominous*   OM-in-us
°3. *homogeneous*   hoe-moe-JEE-ne-us
°4. *posthumous*   POSS-choo-mus
°5. *scurrilous*   SKURR-i-lus
 6. *tenuous*   TEN-yoo-us
°7. *gratuitous*   gra-TOO-i-tus
°8. *deleterious*   del-e-TEER-ee-us
°9. *ignominious*   ig-no-MINN-ee-us
10. *insidious*   in-SID-ee-us

Can you work with the words?

Match words and definitions.

1. anomalous	a. after-death
2. ominous	b. threatening
3. homogeneous	c. thin, insubstantial
4. posthumous	d. disgraceful
5. scurrilous	e. unprovoked
6. tenuous	f. deceitful; subtly tricky
7. gratuitous	g. irregular
8. deleterious	h. harmful
9. ignominious	i. indecent
10. insidious	j. similarly constituted

KEY: 1—g, 2—b, 3—j, 4—a, 5—i, 6—c, 7—e, 8—h, 9—d, 10—f

Do you understand the words?

React quickly to each question.

1. Is it *anomalous* for a child to love its parents?   YES   NO
2. Is increasing unemployment an *ominous* sign of bad times?   YES   NO

3. Is America composed of a *homogeneous* population? YES NO

4. Do courteous people indulge in *scurrilous* attacks on their neighbors? YES NO

5. Has a *posthumous* child ever seen its father? YES NO

6. If a book is published *posthumously,* is the author still alive? YES NO

7. Is a *tenuous* argument convincing? YES NO

8. Is a *gratuitous* remark generally unpleasant? YES NO

9. Does poison have a *deleterious* effect? YES NO

10. Is one usually proud of an *ignominious* act? YES NO

11. Is it easy to defend oneself against *insidious* attacks? YES NO

KEY: 1—no, 2—yes, 3—no, 4—no, 5—no, 6—no, 7—no, 8—yes, 9—yes, 10—no, 11—no

---

Can you recall the words?

Write the word that fits each definition.

1. harmful   1. _____

2. foreshadowing disaster   2. _____

3. tending to trap or mislead   3. _____

4. uncalled-for   4. _____

5. published, born, or exhibited after the death of the author, father, or artist   5. _____

6. disgraceful and humiliating   6. _____

7. all of one kind   7. _____

8. deviating from the normal or expected   8. _____

9. thin, insubstantial   9. _____

10. abusive, indecent   10. _____

KEY: 1—deleterious, 2—ominous, 3—insidious, 4—gratuitous, 5—posthumous, 6—ignominious, 7—homogeneous, 8—anomalous, 9—tenuous, 10—scurrilous

---

Can you use the words?

From the ten basic words, choose the one which will best fit each of the following ideas:

1. A mere hint of a theme runs through a musical composition.   1. _____

2. A substance causes illness when taken into the body.   2. _____

3. A line of argument pulls you, against your will, to a conclusion which you do not wish to reach.   3. _____

4. A child is born to a woman who has lost her husband.   4. _____

5. A speech by Hitler indicated that he was going to invade Poland.   5. _____

6. Attacks were made by "America Firsters" on defenseless minorities.   6. _____

7. A defeat of an army shows its cowardice and corruption.   7. _____

8. A class is made up of feebleminded students, all with I.Q.'s between forty-five and fifty.   8. _____

9. An offensive statement is made for which there is no discernible reason.   9. _____

10. A rich man's only interests are the alleviation of the lot of indigent communists.   10. _____

KEY: 1—tenuous, 2—deleterious, 3—insidious, 4—posthumous, 5—ominous, 6—scurrilous, 7—ignominious, 8—homogeneous, 9—gratuitous, 10—anomalous

---

DERIVATIONS AND RELATED WORDS: I

1. an irregularity

Anything *anomalous* is way off the beaten path—it violates our need for order and fitness, it deviates from the rules on which we like to rely, it is a kind of paradox or contradiction.

For example, since most birds fly, we are surprised and puzzled by one that stays on the ground—we call it an *anomaly*.

If we were used to thinking of moneyed men as conservative, we would consider a person like Marshall Field III, the wealthy department-store tycoon, an *anomaly*. Field is a liberal and the one-time financial backer of the newspaper *PM*, which militantly plumped for the right of the common man. Franklin D. Roosevelt was an *anomaly* in the same way—though his background was one of wealth, his interests were with the downtrodden, with the ill-clothed, ill-housed third of our nation.

Anomalous is from two Greek roots: the negative particle *an*, which we have met before in *anachronous* (not in time with its surroundings); and *homalos*, *even* or *regular*. Anything *anomalous* is *irregular*, *contrary to rule*.

2. not so

When you see *an* at the beginning of an English word you cannot be sure that it is the Greek negative particle, for these two letters may have a number of meanings; but in the following words, *an* does serve as a negative force:

1. *anarchy*—no rule or government; lawlessness. The *anarchist* believes that all government is evil; therefore he stands for terroristic resistance to constituted authority. The root *arch*, *rule* or *government*, is also found in *hierarchy*, the top *ruling* caste, as in the church, in any big organization, or in any large government bureau (the archbishops and bishops form, with the Pope, the hierarchy of the Catholic church; Khrushchev and the Politbureau form the *hierarchy* of Russia; the president and cabinet secretaries are the *hierarchy* of the Federal government); *patriarch*, the *ruling* father person; *monarch*, the one, single, *ruler*, et cetera.
2. *analgesia*—no pain, hence insensibility to pain. An *analgesic* is a drug or lotion which soothes or alleviates pain. The root in *analgesia* is of course related to *algia*, which we met in *neuralgia* (nerve pain) and *nostalgia* (pain and longing for the past.)
3. *anesthetic*—no feeling. An *anesthetic*, such as chloroform or ether, removes sensation so that an operation can be

369

performed. There are the general *anesthetics* which remove all feeling by numbing the brain, and the local *anesthetics,* such as novocaine, which numb only certain localities. (A dentist, for example, will inject novocaine into your gums so that he can work on a certain tooth without making you jump out of the chair.) In the rest of your body you are fully alive—in the region of the injection you are without feeling. The doctor who administers the *anesthesia* is an *anesthetist* and is working in the field of *anesthesia.* An *esthetic* person has keen feelings, sharp sensitivity, especially for what is beautiful. If something violates your *esthetic* sense, it offends your ideals of beauty.

4. *anemia*—etymologically, *not blood,* from Greek *haima, blood. Anemia* is the condition in which the red corpuscles of the blood are reduced in number or deficient in *hemoglobin,* an important constituent of the blood. The malady causes paleness, shortness of breath, palpitations of the heart, and other unpleasant symptoms. Therapeutic doses of liver or vitamin B are usually prescribed to alleviate the condition. The adjective *anemic* is applied to anyone who looks thin, pale, or undernourished, and things can be called *anemic* if they lack richness or fullness.

5. *anonymous*—*no name.* You will recall *nym* from our discussion of *patronymic* (name from the father); *synonym* (same name or meaning); *antonym* (opposite name or meaning); and *homonym* (similar name or meaning). Anything *anonymous,* like a letter, a story, et cetera is without a name. If we say that the crime was committed by an *anonymous* person, we mean that the perpetrator of the misdeed doubtless had a name, but we do not know it—hence, to all practical purposes, he is *nameless.* The noun is *anonymity.*

3. signs, portents and prophecies

Ominous, from the Latin root *omen, a sign of coming catastrophe,* may be applied to an event, a speech, a tone of voice, an action which seems to indicate dire misfortune in the future.

The announcer on the "March of Time" newsreels generally speaks in *ominous* tones—in the trade he is known as "the voice of doom." Or we may refer to *"ominous* rumblings of thunder" if we believe such sounds presage a violent storm. The thunder, like the storm, may be actual weather, or may refer to political or economic events.

4. same and different

In *homogeneous* we find two Greek roots: *homos, same,* and *genos, kind* or *type.* Any *homogeneous* group, then, is made up of individuals who in some way are of the same kind. *Homos,* same, is also found in *homosexual,* the adjective that describes the abnormal attraction which some people feel toward members of the *same sex; homeopath,* a physician who believes in treating diseases (*path, suffering*) with minutes doses of drugs which would cause in a healthy patient the *same* symptoms of which the patient complains; and *homonyms,* words of the *same* sound but different spelling and meaning, as *sighs—size, break—brake, bail—bale,* et cetera. *Homicide* (see page 216) has no relation to Greek *homos;* it comes from Latin *homo, mankind.*

The opposite of *homogeneous is heterogeneous,* which uses the Greek root *heteros, other.* A *heterogeneous* population, mixture, class, or other group is made up of individuals of *other* or different kinds, and *heterosexual* love is directed toward members of the *other* or opposite sex. The opposite of *homeopathy,* the technique practiced by the *homeopath,* is *allopathy*—here we use another Greek root for *other, allos. Homeopathy* was a popular technique among physicians several generations back; today almost all doctors are *allopaths*—they believe in curing diseases by administering drugs that cause *other* or opposite symptoms. For example, if a child runs a high temperature, a believer in *allopathic* medicine will prescribe aspirin, which reduces temperature in youngsters.

In *homogeneous* and *heterogeneous* the accent is on the *ge;* in the noun forms, *homogeneity* and *heterogeneity,* the accent shifts to the next syllable: hoe-mo-JEE-ne-us, hoe-moe-je-NEE-i-tee; het-er-o-JEE-ne-us, het-er-o-je-NEE-i-tee.

In *homogenized* milk, the butterfat does not separate from the rest of the milk—the entire content of the bottle then, is of the *same* consistency, hence, say the manufacturers, more digestible, and also, by the way, usually more expensive.

5. after and before

In *posthumous* you can recognize the common Latin prefix *post, after*. Any book, child, or work of art which we call *posthumous* is published, born, or exhibited *after* the author, father, or artist has been buried in the *ground (humus)*. We may also speak of a man's *posthumous* effect—as when his will creates a trust fund, or as when F.D.R., though dead, still has an influence on the Democratic party.

Post, after, is found in many simple words: *postpone, post-date*, P.M. *(post meridiem), postscript*, et cetera. Other, less common words, also contain the prefix:

1. *posterior*—the *"after"* part of the anatomy, hence the back or buttocks. This word is contrasted to *anterior*, the front.
2. *post-mortem*—*after-death*. A *post-mortem* examination on a corpse is an autopsy; in nonmedical parlance, a *post-mortem* is a discussion, usually in tones of complaint, of some difficulty *after* the event. "No post-mortems," one bridge partner will say to another who complains about the way the hand was played; or the husband who likes to engage in *post-mortems* complains to his wife about what she should have done in some circumstance instead of what she actually did. Needless to say, those who are addicted to the habit of making *post-mortems* are not particularly popular.

The Latin prefix *ante* is the opposite of *post*, and means *before*. It is found in such common words as *antique*, belonging to the age way *before; anteroom*, a room *before* another; *antecedent*, something which goes *before;* and also in the interesting word *antediluvian*, literally *before* the flood, that is, the flood in which Noah and his Ark figured so prominently. Call a person or a technique *antediluvian* and you are saying that he or it is about as antiquated and behind the times as one can well imagine—naturally, the adjective is used contemptuously. *Anterior*, the "before" or front part of the anatomy, is contrasted to *posterior*. Do not confuse *ante, before*, with *anti, against*, as in *antiseptic, against* contamination; *antipathy*, a feeling *against; antonyms*, words with "against" or opposite meanings, as *bad—good, high—low*, et cetera.

6. coarse language

Scurra is the Latin for *buffoon* or *jester;* but *scurrilous,* which is built on the Latin root, is much stronger than its source would indicate. A *scurrilous* letter is abusive, vulgar, coarse; a *scurrilous* book, a *scurrilous* attack, a *scurrilous* remark, et cetera contains abusive vituperation and possibly indecent language. The noun is *scurrility.*

USING THE WORDS: II

Let us pause for a moment to review what we have learned. Let us take another look at the words which our study of roots has turned up.

I. an, ana—a Greek negative prefix:
1. *anomaly,* something not according to rule
2. *anarchy,* lack of law, opposition to government
3. *analgesia,* lack of pain
4. *anasthesia,* insensibility to feeling
5. *anemia,* lack of important elements in the blood
6. *anonymity,* lack of a name

II. arch—Greek root meaning *rule:*
1. *anarchist,* one opposed to government
2. *hierarchy,* the higher echelons of church, government, business, et cetera

III. esthet—*feeling*
1. *anasthetic,* no feeling
2. *esthetic,* appealing to the feelings

IV. nym—*name, meaning*
1. *anonymous,* without a name
2. *homonyms,* words of same sound
3. *synonym,* words of same meaning
4. *antonyms,* words of opposite meaning

V. homos—*same*
1. *homogeneity,* same kind
2. *homosexual,* pertaining to the same sex
3. *homeopathy,* treatment to produce *same* symptoms

VI. heteros—*other, different*

1. *heterogeneity*, different kind
2. *heterosexual*, pertaining to the other sex

VII. post—a Latin prefix meaning *after*

1. *posterior*, back, bottom, afterpart
2. *posthumous*, after burial
3. *post-mortem*, after death

VIII. ante—a Latin prefix meaning *before*

1. *antediluvian*, before the flood
2. *antecedent*, coming before
3. *anterior*, forepart, the front

IX. anti—a Greek prefix meaning *against*

1. *antiseptic*, against contamination
2. *antonyms*, words of opposite meanings
3. *antipathy*, hostility, a feeling against

X. scurra—*jester*

1. *scurrilous*, abusive
2. *scurrility*, abusiveness

Can you pronounce the words?

1.	*anomaly*	a-NOM-a-lee
2.	*anarchy*	AN-er-kee
°3.	*hierarchy*	HIE-er-ar-kee
°4.	*analgesia*	an-al-JEE-zee-a
°5.	*analgesic*	an-al-JEE-zik
6.	*anesthetic*	an-es-THET-ik
7.	*anesthetist*	an-ESS-the-tist
°8.	*anesthesia*	an-es-THEE-zha
9.	*esthetic*	ess-THET-ik
10.	*anemia*	a-NEE-mee-a
11.	*anonymous*	a-NON-a-mus
°12.	*anonymity*	a-no-NIMM-i-tee
13.	*homosexual*	hoe-moe-SEK-shoo-al
°14.	*homeopath*	HOE-mee-o-path
15.	*homonym*	HOM-o-nym
°16.	*homeopathy*	hoe-mee-OP-a-thee
°17.	*allopath*	ALL-o-path
°18.	*allopathy*	al-OP-a-thee

°19.	*heterogeneous*	het-er-o-JEE-nee-us
°20.	*heterogeneity*	het-er-o-je-NEE-i-tee
°21.	*homogeneity*	hoe-mo-je-NEE-i-tee
22.	*heterosexual*	het-er-o-SEK-shoo-al
23.	*posterior*	po-STEER-ee-er
24.	*anterior*	an-TEER-ee-er
25.	*post-mortem*	POST-MOR-tem
°26.	*antediluvian*	AN-tee-di-LOO-vee-in
27.	*antiseptic*	an-ti-SEP-tik
°28.	*antipathy*	an-TIP-a-thee
29.	*antonym*	AN-to-nim
°30.	*scurrility*	skur-RILL-i-tee

Can you work with the words? (I)

Match words and definitions.

1. anomaly	a. top ruling caste
2. anarchy	b. numbing of pain
3. hierarchy	c. lawlessness
4. analgesia	d. lack of identification
5. anesthesia	e. alleviation of pain
6. anonymity	f. irregularity

KEY: 1–f, 2–c, 3–a, 4–e, 5–b, 6–d

Can you work with the words? (II)

1. homonym	a. word with same meaning
2. synonym	b. one who administers ether, et cetera
3. antonym	c. doctor who prescribes remedies that produce opposite effects
4. homeopath	d. variety
5. allopath	e. similarity
6. anesthetist	f. abusiveness
7. antipathy	g. word that sounds like another
8. scurrility	h. hostility, aversion
9. homogeneity	i. doctor who prescribes remedies that produce similar effects
10. heterogeneity	j. word with opposite meaning

KEY: 1–g, 2–a, 3–j, 4–i, 5–c, 6–b, 7–h, 8–f, 9–e, 10–d

Can you work with the words? (III)

1. analgesic	a. pain-removing
2. anesthetic	b. wan, pale
3. esthetic	c. pertaining to one's own sex
4. anemic	d. nameless
5. anonymous	e. pain-soothing
6. homosexual	f. pertaining to the other sex
7. heterosexual	g. appealing to sense of beauty

KEY: 1—e, 2—a, 3—g, 4—b, 5—d, 6—c, 7—f

Can you work with the words? (IV)

1. posterior	a. very antiquated
2. anterior	b. front
3. post-mortem	c. clean; free of germs
4. antediluvian	d. irregular
5. antiseptic	e. threatening; foreboding evil
6. scurrilous	f. after death; after the event
7. anomalous	g. after death of author, et cetera
8. ominous	h. back
9. posthumous	i. abusive

KEY: 1—h, 2—b, 3—f, 4—a, 5—c, 6—i, 7—d, 8—e, 9—g

Do you understand the words? (I)

React quickly to the following questions.

1. If a man of great wealth was an ardent supporter of communism, would he be considered an *anomaly*?   YES   NO
2. Is *anarchy* a political philosophy in good standing?   YES   NO
3. Do the shipping clerks belong to the *hierarchy* of a business?   YES   NO

4. If you have a sprained muscle, is it advisable to apply an *analgesic* ointment? YES NO

5. Is some form of *anesthesia* usually administered during childbirth? YES NO

6. Does an artist normally have a keenly developed *esthetic* sense? YES NO

7. Is *anemia* a blood condition? YES NO

8. If you wish to preserve your *anonymity*, do you make your name known far and wide? YES NO

9. Is *homosexual* love normal? YES NO

10. Is *heterosexual* love normal? YES NO

11. Do most doctors today practice *homeopathic* medicine? YES NO

12. Do most doctors today practice *allopathic* medicine? YES NO

KEY: 1—yes, 2—no, 3—no, 4—yes, 5—yes, 6—yes, 7—yes, 8—no, 9—no, 10—yes, 11—no, 12—yes

Do you understand the words? (II)

1. Are *veil* and *vale* homonyms? YES NO

2. Is the *posterior* region in front? YES NO

3. Is the *anterior* region in back? YES NO

4. Is a *post-mortem* conducted on a cadaver? YES NO

5. Are *antediluvian* attitudes modern? YES NO

6. Does an *antiseptic* help ward off infection? YES NO

7. Do you feel great *antipathy* to people you love? YES NO

8. Are *good* and *bad* antonyms? YES NO

9. Is *scurrility* respectful? YES NO

10. Does New York City have a fairly *heterogeneous* population? YES NO

11. Is *homogeneity* a desirable factor for successful teaching? YES NO

KEY: 1—yes, 2—no, 3—no, 4—yes, 5—no, 6—yes, 7—no, 8—yes, 9—no, 10—yes, 11—yes

Can you recall the words?

Write the word that fits each definition.

1. against contamination   1. A_____

2. abusive attack   2. S_____

3. aversion, dislike   3. A_____

4. a word opposite in meaning to
   another word   4. A_____

5. before the flood   5. A_____

6. an irregularity   6. A_____

7. after death   7. P_____

8. political lawlessness   8. A_____

9. ventral   9. A_____

10. pain-relieving   10. A_____

11. dorsal   11. P_____

12. sense-deadening   12. A_____

13. pertaining to love for
    opposite sex   13. H_____

14. appealing to sense of beauty   14. E_____

15. similarity in kind   15. H_____

16. blood deficiency   16. A_____

17. made up of many different
    kinds   17. H_____

18. nameless   18. A_____

19. pertaining to love for the
    same sex   19. H_____

20. a word identical in sound, but
    different in spelling and meaning,
    to another word.   20. H_____

_____

KEY: 1—antiseptic, 2—scurrility, 3—antipathy, 4—antonym, 5—
antediluvian, 6—anomaly, 7—post-mortem, 8—anarchy, 9—an-

378

terior, 10—analgesic, 11—posterior, 12—anesthetic, 13—heterosexual, 14—esthetic, 15—homogeneity, 16—anemia, 17—heterogeneous, 18—anonymous, 19—homosexual, 20—homonym

---

Can you recall roots?

Write the root that has each of the following meanings:

1. not	1. _____
2. rule	2. _____
3. feeling	3. _____
4. pain	4. _____
5. name	5. _____
6. same	6. _____
7. other	7. _____
8. before	8. _____
9. after	9. _____
10. against	10. _____

KEY: 1—*an*, 2—*arch*, 3—*esthet*, 4—*alg*, 5—*nym*, 6—*homo*, 7—*hetero*
or *allo*, 8—*ante*, 9—*post*, 10—*anti*

ORIGINS AND RELATED WORDS: II

1. thinner and thinner

Though *tenuous* comes from the Latin word *tenuis, thin,*
the thinness is usually not actual, literal, or physical, but
generally figurative and abstract. We do not, of course, refer
to "a *tenuous* woman" or "a *tenuous* slice of roast beef."
Rather the word is used in such combinations as "*tenuous*
logic," "*tenuous* feeling," or "a *tenuous* thread of melancholy
throughout the book." This is one of those words which
practically defy explanation or definition, and which you
can best learn by watching for it in your reading. Synonyms

of *tenuous* are *flimsy, insubstantial, insignificant, subtle;* and Webster's Dictionary of Synonyms says that something is *tenuous* if it "is so finespun or so fine-drawn as to be exceedingly subtle, abstruse, visionary, or the like" and offers as examples of its use:

"a *tenuous* idealism . . ."

—Bunyan

"poetry so *tenuous* in thought and feeling . . ."

—Grandgent

"golden, *tenuous* imaginings . . ."

—Galsworthy

The noun is *tenuousness.*

The root of *tenuous (tenuis*—thin) is found in two other valuable words:

1. *attenuate*—to thin (figuratively) by robbing of richness, impact, or vitality; to weaken or lessen the force. Thus, rent control was *attenuated* by Congress in March, 1949, according to critics of the measure. The provisions that landlords could sue for "fair return" and that communities, with the consent of the state governor, might decontrol themselves, *thinned* the bill down to practically nothing, again according to its critics.

2. *extenuating*—moderating, justifying. If there are "*extenuating* circumstances" behind an offense or crime, these serve to explain or justify the offense or crime, or, etymologically, to *thin* out its seriousness. Thus, if you have killed someone, the fact that he first attacked you and you simply hit back in self-defense is an *extenuating* circumstance. At your trial, you will offer in *extenuation* of your offense the fact that there was practically nothing else to do. "*Extenuating* evidence" is that evidence which helps to explain the reasons for an act and therefore to lessen its seriousness. There can be "*extenuating* factors" to account for and soften the gravity of a misdeed. It is true, let us suppose, that the assistant manager of the bank disappeared, and with him $690,000—but there were *extenuating* factors: the money was always lying around to tempt him; there was a cute blonde who kept demanding mink coats and gold bracelets; et cetera

2. an etymological anomaly

Gratuitous comes from Latin *gratus, agreeable, thankful;* yet a *gratuitous* remark, insult, or act is far from pleasing— we have here one of those etymological flip-flops that occasionally happen in English.

Understand two things about a gratuitous act: it is perpetrated without reason, cause, or justification; and it is always unpleasant, in that it offends or harms someone. For example, you and your wife have been having a most pleasant conversation, in the course of which you both agree that Mr. P, your neighbor, often beats his wife, but with good cause (i.e., there are *extenuating* factors). Suddenly your wife says: "I bet you've often wanted to beat me but haven't dared."

Of course your mouth drops open. Everything has been honey and light up to this point—and now this *gratuitous,* unexpected insult. Do you see the flavor of the word?

3. please and thank you

Gratus, pleasing, is found more sensibly in a number of other words in which it ties up logically with the meaning:

1. *gratis*—free, without charge, merely to *please* rather than for money. As in, "The material costs $4.25; my labor is *gratis.*"

2. *gratuity*—a tip, offered because the service has been, or is expected to be, *pleasing.*

3. *gratitude—thankfulness,* because of a feeling of being pleased. (The idea of *thanks* is most graphically seen in "*gracias,*" which comes from the same Latin root, and which is the Spanish word for "*thank you.*"

4. *ingrate*—someone who feels or shows no gratitude or *thankfulness,* though any normal person would. Obviously a term of censure or contempt.

5. *Ingratiate*—to be especially and not quite sincerely *pleasing,* for the sake of winning someone's favor; to get into someone's good graces. An *ingratiating* person goes out of his way to please, not because he is devoted, but because he either has a psychological need to avoid conflict or because he has some ulterior motive. Psychoanalysts recognize that some excessively sweet or *ingratiating* per-

sonalities actually feel a great deal of hostility to the world —but this feeling is largely unconscious and rather than express it they go to the other extreme and may become practically self-abnegating. In a sense, they are trying to punish themselves—they are always sweet and kind and polite, yet look how they're stepped on, imposed on, and mistreated! On the other hand, *ingratiation* may be a calculated technique for winning favor, and as such is not of course a symptom of neurotic behavior.

There are other common words with the same root. If you *congratulate* someone, you are saying, in effect, "I am *pleased* at your success—my pleasure goes *together (con)* with yours." A *grateful* person is full of thanks, he is so well-*pleased*. If you feel *gratified*, you feel *pleased* with what has happened.

4. rub it out, O'Toole!

Deleterious, harmful to health, injurious, is from a Greek root from which the verb *delete* also stems. *Delete* means simply *to erase, take out,* as in "Let's *delete* that word." The noun is *deletion*. The connection in meaning is that normally one *deletes* what is harmful; but the verb *delete* has lost such connotation and is used quite neutrally.

5. about names

An *ignominious* act is infamous, shameful, scandalous, dishonorable, the sort that will bring public disgrace down upon you. You will see in the word the letters *nomin*, since *ignominious* comes from the Latin *nomen, nominis, name*. What has one's name to do with disgrace? *Ig* is a Latin prefix with negative force—if you do something *ignominious*, you have gotten a *bad* name. The noun form is *ignominy*.

Nominate, nomenclature, nom de plume, cognomen, and *nominal* come from the same root, *nomen, nominis, name*.

1. *nominate*—place someone's *name* up for election. A person so *nominated* may be called a *nominee*.
2. *cognomen*—your last *name*. The cog (sometimes spelled *con,* as in *congratulate,* or *col,* as in *collaborate*) means *together*—your *cognomen* is the name you share together with the rest of your family.

382

3. *nominal*—in *name* only. If you call someone the *nominal* ruler of a country, you mean that he has the name of ruler, but someone else is really in power. If the price is *nominal,* or the salary is *nominal,* it is so low that, though we call it by the name of *price* or *salary,* it doesn't compare with other prices or salaries. "There will be a *nominal* fee" means that just to be able to say we've collected a fee we'll charge something, but it will be very little, and will not of course reflect the true value of the services. Or, we may say that Mr. Brown is *nominally* in charge of the school—that he has the *name* of principal, perhaps. Really we imply, someone else, perhaps the assistant principal, runs the institution.

4. *nomenclature*—a system of *names.* When you study biology, for example, you must become familiar with the names given to various classifications, for example *phylum, species, primates, coelenterata, arthropoda,* et cetera.

5. *nom de plume*—literally, *pen name.* This word has come to us through French, though the basic root is still the Latin *nomen.* Authors use a *nom de plume,* or a fictitious name which appears on their work, for various reasons: to forestall creditors, so their neighbors will not realize they don't have an honest job, et cetera. Sinclair Lewis wrote books for boys under the *nom de plume* of Tom Graham, adult fiction under his true name. Another term for *nom de plume* is *pseudonym,* literally a *false name.* You recognize the *nym* as our old Greek friend from *homonym, synonym, anonymous,* et cetera. *Pseudo* is from a Greek verb meaning *to deceive,* and can be used as a word in its own right with the significance of *false or pretended* (as in "Phrenology is a *pseudo* science") or as a prefix, as in "pseudointellectual," "pseudoscientific," et cetera. Movie stars often travel under *pseudonyms* to deceive the autograph hounds and avoid the sycophants.

Pseudonym and *nom de plume* should not be confused with *alias.* For private reasons of their own, honest people prefer to use a fictitious name—in writing, a *nom de plume,* on other occasions a *pseudonym.* But only a criminal uses an *alias,* and then solely for criminal purposes or to throw the police off his scent.

6. patiently sitting

Insidious is from the Latin *insidiae*, an ambush. Picture soldiers waiting in a well-concealed ambush, then suddenly pouncing on the surprised enemy, and you have a good idea of the connotation of *insidious*. Anything *insidious* sneaks up on you and catches you unaware—usually when it's too late for you to protect yourself. In a word, you're trapped—and *insidious* vices, *insidious* diseases, *insidious* persuasions are so subtle, so camouflaged, that before you realize what has happened, or how, you're ensnared.

Insidious is related to many other words containing the letters *sid, sed,* or *sess.* (The Latin noun *insidiae*, an *ambush,* is derived from the Latin verb *sedeo, to sit,* which has the forms *sedeo, sedere, sessi, sessum*—the soldiers *sit* patiently *in* an ambush waiting for their prey.) A *sedentary* occupation, such as that of a writer, a bookkeeper, a clerk, et cetera, is one in which the person spends his days sitting quietly instead of doing what nature intended him to do—get out in the open and exercise his large muscles. Laborers lead a much more natural life than *sedentary* workers, hence they sleep better, rarely suffer from insomnia, eat well, and do not look cadaverous. Perhaps that is why they are paid so little—there are many other compensations in their work.

Sediment is the matter that settles to the bottom of a liquid —it *sits* down at the bottom.

To *reside* is to *sit* in your home, etymologically speaking.

If one law *supersedes* another, it *sits above (super)* it—that is, it takes its place. Realizing that *supersede* derives from *sedeo,* to sit, you will never be tempted to misspell it *super-cede.* This, incidentally is the only word in the entire language that ends in the letters sede.

When you *preside* over a meeting, you *sit before (pre)* the members or audience. *President* comes from the same root.

When Congress is in *session,* it is *sitting* to discuss laws, appropriations, and, sometimes, how to annoy the President.

USING THE WORDS: III

Can you pronounce the words?

1.	*attenuate*	a-TEN-yoo-ayt
2.	*extenuate*	eks-TEN-yoo-ayt
*3.	*gratis*	GRAY-tis
4.	*gratuity*	gra-TOO-i-tee
5.	*ingrate*	IN-grayt
6.	*ingratiating*	in-GRAY-shee-ay-ting
7.	*delete*	de-LEET
8.	*deletion*	de-LEE-shun
*9.	*ignominy*	IG-no-mi-nee
10.	*nominee*	nom-i-NEE
*11.	*nomenclature*	NO-men-klay-choor
12.	*nom de plume*	nome de PLOOM
13.	*nominal*	NOM-in-'l
*14.	*pseudonym*	SOO-do-nim
*15.	*sedentary*	SED-en-ta-ree
16.	*supersede*	soo-per-SEED
*17.	*alias*	AY-lee-is
*18.	*cognomen*	kog-NO-men

Can you work with the words? (I)

Match words and definitions.

1. attenuating	a.	justifying
2. extenuating	b.	taking precedence over
3. ingratiating	c.	excessively pleasant
4. sedentary	d.	without charge
5. superseding	e.	robbing of force
6. gratis	f.	not physically active
7. nominal	g.	in name only

KEY: 1—e, 2—a, 3—c, 4—f, 5—b, 6—d, 7—g

Can you work with the words? (II)

1. gratuity	a.	classification by name
2. ingrate	b.	pen name

3. deletion	c. removal from the record
4. nominee	d. fictitious name for criminal purposes
5. nom de plume	e. fictitious name
6. pseudonym	f. one whose name has been offered
7. ignominy	g. unappreciative person
8. nomenclature	h. tip
9. alias	i. shame, disgrace

KEY: 1—h, 2—g, 3—c, 4—f, 5—b, 6—e, 7—i, 8—a, 9—d

Can you work with the words? (III)

1. tenuous	a. last name
2. gratuitous	b. wily, ensnaring
3. deleterious	c. slight, subtle
4. ignominious	d. disgraceful
5. insidious	e. uncalled-for and offensive
6. cognomen	f. harmful

KEY: 1—c, 2—e, 3—f, 4—d, 5—b, 6—a

Do you understand the words?

React quickly to each question.

1. Do proponents of a legislative bill attempt to *attenuate* its provisions?	YES	NO
2. Do *extenuating* circumstances normally lessen the severity of a crime?	YES	NO
3. If something is done *gratis,* is there a charge?	YES	NO
4. Do waiters expect *gratuities?*	YES	NO
5. Does an *ingrate* feel thankful?	YES	NO
6. Is an *ingratiating* tone hostile?	YES	NO
7. Does an eraser help you *delete* an error?	YES	NO
8. Do people normally enjoy *ignominy?*	YES	NO
9. Is *nomenclature* a system of labeling?	YES	NO
10. Is a *nom de plume* sometimes used by writers?	YES	NO

386

11. Is a *nominal* fee usually small?	YES	NO
12. Is a *pseudonym* one's real name?	YES	NO
13. Is a bookkeeper a *sedentary* worker?	YES	NO
14. Is a *superseded* law still in effect?	YES	NO
15. Is it considered respectable to have an *alias*?	YES	NO
16. Do you and your brother have the same *cognomen*?	YES	NO

KEY: 1—no, 2—yes, 3—no, 4—yes, 5—no, 6—no, 7—yes, 8—no, 9—yes, 10—yes, 11—yes, 12—no, 13—yes, 14—no, 15—no, 16—yes

Can you recall the words? (I)

Here I intend to test your ability to think of any of the words we have studied in this chapter. Review first, if you think such action necessary.

1. threatening	1. O_____
2. exhibited after death	2. P_____
3. abusive	3. S_____
4. contrary to rule	4. A_____
5. of one kind	5. H_____
6. of different kinds	6. H_____
7. tending to alleviate pain	7. A_____
8. appealing to one's sense of the beautiful	8. E_____
9. of unknown name or authorship	9. A_____
10. pale, wan, lacking in important blood elements	10. A_____
11. word of opposite meaning	11. A_____

KEY: 1—ominous, 2—posthumous, 3—scurrilous, 4—anomalous, 5—homogeneous, 6—heterogeneous, 7—analgesic, anesthetic, 8—esthetic, 9—anonymous, 10—anemic, 11—antonym

Can you recall the words? (II)

| 1. pertaining to the opposite sex | 1. H_____ |
| 2. back | 2. P_____ |

3. front 3. A_____

4. antiquated; literally, before the flood 4. A_____

5. slight, almost imperceptible 5. T_____

6. justification 6. E_____

7. unprovoked 7. G_____

8. tip 8. G_____

9. erase 9. D_____

10. humiliation 10. I_____

11. free of germs 11. A_____

12. last name 12. C_____

KEY: 1—heterosexual, 2—posterior, 3—anterior, 4—antediluvian, 5—tenuous, 6—extenuation, 7—gratuitous, 8—gratuity, 9—delete, 10—ignominy, 11—antiseptic, 12—cognomen

---

Can you recall the words? (III)

1. pen name 1. N_____

2. fictitious name 2. P_____

3. fictitious name of a criminal 3. A_____

4. subtly trapping 4. I_____

5. take the place of 5. S_____

6. physically inactive 6. S_____

7. system of names 7. N_____

8. in name only 8. N_____

9. system of treating diseases with similar remedies 9. H_____

10. a word that sounds like another 10. H_____

11. hostility   11. A_____

12. excessively sweet   12. I_____

KEY: 1—nom de plume, 2—pseudonym, 3—alias, 4—insidious, 5—
supersede, 6—sedentary, 7—nomenclature, 8—nominal, 9—homeopathy, 10—homonym, 11—antipathy, 12—ingratiating

---

Can you recognize roots?

Fill in the meaning of each root.

ROOT	EXAMPLE	MEANING
1. *anti*	antipathy	_____
2. *ante*	antediluvian	_____
3. *post*	posterior	_____
4. *homos*	homogeneous	_____
5. *heteros*	heterosexual	_____
6. *arch*	anarchy	_____
7. *esthet*	esthetic	_____
8. *an*	anesthetic	_____
9. *sed, sid, sess*	sedentary session preside	_____
10. *nomen, nomin*	cogomen nominal	_____
11. *gratus*	congratulate	_____
12. *tenuis*	tenuous	_____
13. *con, cog, col*	concur cognomen collaborate	_____

KEY: 1—against, 2—before, 3—after, 4—same, 5—other, 6—rule,
7—feeling, 8—not, 9—sit, 10—name, 11—pleasing, 12—thin, 13—
together

CHAPTER REVIEW

Can you recognize the words?

Check the word which most closely fits each definition.

1. Deviating from the rule:
   (a) anomalous, (b) ominous, (c) heterogeneous
2. Of one kind:
   (a) heterogeneous, (b) homogeneous, (c) tenuous
3. Thin, insubstantial:
   (a) tenuous, (b) scurrilous, (c) insidious
4. Uncalled-for:
   (a) deleterious, (b) scurrilous, (c) gratuitous
5. Pain-soothing:
   (a) analgesic, (b) anesthetic, (c) esthetic
6. Of different kinds:
   (a) homeopathic, (b) heterogeneous, (c) homogeneous
7. Before the flood:
   (a) antediluvian, (b) anterior, (c) antiseptic
8. Insinuating oneself in another's good graces:
   (a) extenuating, (b) ingratiating, (c) superseding
9. Erasure:
   (a) deletion, (b) nomenclature, (c) ingrate
10. False name for the purpose of criminal deception:
    (a) pseudonym, (b) nom de plume, (c) alias
11. Disgrace:
    (a) ignominy, (b) nominee, (c) nominal
12. Family name:
    (a) pseudonym, (b) cognomen, (c) nom de plume

KEY: 1—a, 2—b, 3—a, 4—c, 5—a, 6—b, 7—a, 8—b, 9—a, 10—c, 11—a, 12—b

---

In this final week of your work you have covered approximately 165 new words and over forty Greek and Latin roots. Are you clear on everything you've learned? The Achievement Test for the third week, which follows immediately, will show you how well you have done.

18

HOW TO CHECK
YOUR THIRD WEEK'S PROGRESS

I—ROOTS

Direction: In the table below you will find a number of roots we have discussed, with examples of their use. It is your job to fill in the meaning of each one.

ROOT		EXAMPLE
1. *phon*	_____	cacophonous
2. *eu*	_____	euphemism
3. *carn*	_____	carnivorous
4. *omni*	_____	omnivorous
5. *sequ*	_____	obsequious
6. *pecus*	_____	pecuniary
7. *noc*	_____	innocent
8. *caval*	_____	cavalcade
9. *equus*	_____	equestrian
10. *cad*	_____	cadaver
11. *homos*	_____	homogeneous
12. *gratus*	_____	ingrate
13. *nomen*	_____	ignominious
14. *sed, sid*	_____	insidious
15. *an, ana*	_____	anomaly
16. *arch*	_____	hierarchy
17. *esthet*	_____	esthetic

18. *nym* ———————————— synonym

19. *heteros* ———————————— heterogeneous

20. *post* ———————————— posterior

21. *ante* ———————————— antediluvian

22. *pseudo* ———————————— pseudonym

II—SAME OR OPPOSITE?

Directions: If each pair of words is similar in meaning, check S; if more nearly opposite, check O.

1. penury—affluence   S   O
2. vicarious—secondhand   S   O
3. ephemeral—evanescent   S   O
4. badinage—persiflage   S   O
5. cacophony—euphony   S   O
6. clandestine—surreptitious   S   O
7. parsimonious—extravagant   S   O
8. indigent—opulent   S   O
9. destitute—impecunious   S   O
10. euphemistic—indirect   S   O

III—SAME OR OPPOSITE?

Directions: If each pair of words is similar in meaning, check S; if more nearly opposite, check O.

1. cliché—bromide   S   O
2. platitudinous—original   S   O
3. voracious—gluttonous   S   O
4. omniscient—ignorant   S   O
5. omnipresent—ubiquitous   S   O
6. carnal—libidinous   S   O
7. carnage—slaughter   S   O
8. enervated—exhilarated   S   O
9. castigate—condone   S   O
10. simulate—pretend   S   O

IV—RECALL A WORD

Directions: Write the word we have studied that best fits each definition. The initial letter is offered to guide your thinking.

1. lionlike	1. L_____
2. doglike	2. C_____
3. catlike	3. F_____
4. piglike	4. P_____
5. foxlike	5. V_____
6. bearlike	6. U_____
7. horselike	7. E_____
8. all-powerful	8. O_____
9. in the flesh	9. I_____
10. stagnate	10. V_____

V—MATCHING

Match words and definitions.

WORDS	DEFINITIONS
1. alleviating	a. excessively polite
2. cavalier (adj.)	b. gaunt, corpselike
3. vacillating	c. noisy
4. obsequious	d. poisonous
5. querulous	e. high-handed
6. obstreperous	f. sad
7. innocuous	g. nagging
8. cadaverous	h. harmless
9. dolorous	i. soothing
10. noxious	j. constantly changing

VI—MORE MATCHING

Again match words and definitions.

WORDS	DEFINITIONS
1. deleterious	a. of several kinds
2. anomalous	b. threatening
3. ominous	c. uncalled-for
4. homogeneous	d. irregular
5. heterogeneous	e. pain-soothing
6. tenuous	f. wily
7. gratuitous	g. harmful
8. insidious	h. pleasing to the sense of beauty
9. analgesic	i. slight
10. esthetic	j. of one kind

VII—CHOOSE THE RIGHT WORD

Check the word that most closely fits each definition.

1. Words that sound alike:
   (a) antonyms, (b) synonyms, (c) homonyms
2. Very old-fashioned:
   (a) antediluvian, (b) posthumous, (c) antiseptic
3. Hostility:
   (a) scurrility, (b) antipathy, (c) homeopathy
4. Without charge:
   (a) gratuitous, (b) gratis, (c) nominal
5. Pen name:
   (a) alias, (b) pseudonym, (c) nom de plume
6. Unemotional:
   (a) bovine, (b) carnivorous, (c) omnivorous
7. Done in secret:
   (a) ephemeral, (b) evanescent, (c) clandestine
8. A feeling of well-being:
   (a) euphoria, (b) eulogy, (c) euthanasia
9. A statement intended to soothe:
   (a) bromide, (b) euphemism, (c) anodyne
10. To be self-sacrificing:
    (a) vegetate, (b) recapitulate, (c) self-abnegate

VIII—PRONOUNCE A WORD

Directions: Check the correct pronunciation.

1. *cacophony:* a. ka-KOFF-o-nee, b. KAK-a-foe-nee.
2. *parsimony:* a. par-SIM-o-nee, b. PAR-si-moe-nee.
3. *feline:* a. FEE-lyne, b. FELL-in.
4. *omnivorous:* a. om-ni-VOR-ous, b. om-NIV-er-us.
5. *incarnate* (adj.): a. IN-kar-nayt, b. in-KAR-nit.
6. *dolorous:* a. DOLL-er-us, b. do-LORE-us.
7. *decadent:* a. DECK-a-dent, b. de-KAY-dent.
8. *ignominy:* a. ig-NOM-in-ee, b. IG-no-mi-nee.
9. *homogeneity:* a. ho-mo-je-NEE-i-tee, b. ho-mo-JEE-nee-i-tee.
10. *homeopathy:* a. HOE-me-o-path-ee, b. hoe-me-OP-a-thee.
11. *gratis:* a. GRAY-tis, b. GRAT-is.
12. *sedentary:* a. SED-en-ter-ree, b. se-DEN-te-ree.
13. *alias:* a. AY-lee-is, b. a-LYE-is.

IX—CHANGE A WORD

Directions: Write the required part of speech.

1. Change *penury* to an adjective.   1. P_____
2. Change *cacophonous* to a noun.   2. C_____
3. Change *evanescent* to a verb.   3. E_____
4. Change *euphoria* to an adjective   4. E_____
5. Change *dolorous* to a noun.   5. D_____
6. Change *heterogeneous* to a noun.   6. H_____
7. Change *anonymous* to a noun.   7. A_____
8. Change *ignominy* to an adjective.   8. I_____

KEY: I: 1—sound, 2—good, 3—flesh, meat, 4—all, 5—follow, 6—
cattle, 7—injure, 8—horse, 9—horse, 10—fall, 11—same,
12—thanks, pleasing, 13—name, 14—sit, 15—not, 16—rule,
17—feel, 18—name, 19—other, 20—after, 21—before, 22—
false

II: 1—o, 2—s, 3—s, 4—s, 5—o, 6—s, 7—o, 8—o, 9—s, 10—s

III: 1—s, 2—o, 3—s, 4—o, 5—s, 6—s, 7—s, 8—o, 9—o, 10—s

IV: 1—leonine, 2—canine, 3—feline, 4—porcine, 5—vulpine, 6—ursine, 7—equine, 8—omnipotent, 9—incarnate, 10—vegetate

V: 1—i, 2—e, 3—j, 4—a, 5—g, 6—c, 7—h, 8—b, 9—f, 10—d

VI: 1—g, 2—d, 3—b, 4—j, 5—a, 6—i, 7—c, 8—f, 9—e, 10—h

VII: 1—c, 2—a, 3—b, 4—b, 5—c, 6—a, 7—c, 8—a, 9—c, 10—c

VIII: 1—a, 2—b, 3—a, 4—b, 5—b, 6—a, 7—b, 8—b, 9—a, 10—b, 11—a, 12—a, 13—a

IX: 1—penurious, 2—cacophony, 3—evanesce, 4—euphoric, 5—dolor, 6—heterogeneity, 7—anonymity, 8—ignominious

---

SCORING

You have been asked for 103 responses. Allowing once again for normal human frailty, you may consider your learning successful if you came through with a score of 85 or better (each answer credits one point).

Record your score in the appropriate space below and, referring to pages 148 and 290, copy your scores in the preceding achievement tests. You will then have a total comparison chart of all three weeks of your work.

SCORES

First week's Achievement Test

_____ out of *110*

Second week's Achievement Test

_____ out of *110*

Third week's Achievement Test

_____ out of *103*

BRIEF INTERMISSION FOURTEEN:
FINAL CHECK ON YOUR PRONUNCIATION, GRAMMAR, AND SPELLING

TEST I—YOUR PRONUNCIATION

Instructions: Check the preferable pronunciation of each of the following words.

		A	*B*
1.	*after*	AHF-ter	AFF-ter
2.	*human*	HYOO-man	YOO-man
3.	*editor*	ED-i-ter	ED-i-toar
4.	*status*	STAT-us	STAY-tus
5.	*chauffeur*	sho-FURR	SHO-fer
6.	*comparable*	COM-per-able	com-PAR-able
7.	*docile*	DO-syle	DOSS-ill
8.	*coupon*	KOO-pon	KYOO-pon
9.	*chiropodist*	tchi-ROP-o-dist	ki-ROP-o-dist
10.	*grimace*	GRIM-iss	gri-MACE
11.	*genuine*	JEN-yoo-win	JEN-yoo-wyne
12.	*robust*	ROE-bust	ro-BUST
13.	*progress*	PROE-gress	PROG-ress
14.	*again*	a-GAYNE	a-GEN
15.	*orgy*	OR-jee	OR-gee (g as in girl)
16.	*permit* (noun)	PER-mit	per-MIT
17.	*aviator*	AVV-ee-ay-ter	AY-vee-ay-ter
18.	*prestige*	pres-TEEZH	pres-TEEDJ
19.	*often*	OFF-ten	OFF-en
20.	*secretive*	se-CREE-tive	SEEK-re-tive
21.	*flaccid*	FLAK-sid	FLASS-id
22.	*quay*	kway	key
23.	*bouquet*	boo-KAY	bo-KAY
24.	*nausea*	NAW-zee-a	NAW-sha

TEST II—YOUR GRAMMAR

Instructions: Check the word in parentheses which, in your considered opinion, makes each sentence grammatically defensible.

1. Everyone seems to be happy except (a-I, b-me).

2. (a-Lay, b-Lie) your books on the table.

3. The child (a-lay, b-laid) asleep all morning.

4. Our plans have (a-laid, b-lain) idle for many years.

5. Neither of us (a-is, b-are) very happy about your decision.

6. He is one man (a-who, b-whom) I believe can help you.

7. She may not look it, but she's a full inch taller than (a-I, b-me).

8. Just between you and (a-I, b-me), he's pulling your leg.

9. If memory serves me, that package was addressed to my wife and (a-I, b-me).

10. I (a-can, b-can't) hardly believe that he would do such a thing!

11. We (a-stood, b-stayed) home as long as we could.

12. (a-Leave, b-Let) me help you.

13. Mary's brother and father (a-is, b-are) waiting to be discharged from the Navy.

14. Either Frances or Rhoda (a-is, b-are) sure to be at home today.

15. The destroyer as well as the corvette (a-was, b-were) buffeted by the high seas.

16. You should (a-have, b-of) known better.

17. They (a-hung, b-hanged) the murderer at dawn.

18. Was it (a-he, b-him) you were thinking about?

19. It is I who (a-am, b-is) your only true friend.

20. He is one of those men who (a-is, b-are) eternally finding fault.

21. Do you understand the (a-principle, b-principal) of the atomic bomb?

22. The atomic bomb has had a tremendous (a-affect, b-effect) on the world.

TEST III—YOUR SPELLING

Instructions: Of the following twenty-five words, only twelve are spelled correctly. Check the dozen that contain the proper combination of letters and rewrite those which you believe contain errors.

1. all right _____
2. coolly _____
3. drunkeness _____
4. procede _____
5. incidentally _____
6. dissapear _____
7. recommend _____
8. analize _____
9. wierd _____
10. inimitible _____
11. embarrassment _____
12. irresistable _____
13. rediculous _____
14. despair _____
15. disippate _____
16. superintendent _____
17. occurence _____
18. desirable _____
19. sieze _____
20. arguement _____
21. existence _____
22. ukelele _____

23. accommodate _____ 25. ecstasy _____

24. inoculate _____

HOW TO CHECK YOUR
TOTAL ACHIEVEMENT

NOW that you have come to the end of your work, you will be interested, I imagine, to discover how well you've done.

To give you this information, I have made a random selection of ten words from each of the thirteen vocabulary chapters in the book and will use these 130 words to put your learning to the acid test.

You have made creditable scores, let us assume, in the three big achievement tests you've taken. These tests for the most part explored your *understanding* of the words you had learned in each section—and of course understanding is basic to remembering and using the words.

The question is, at this final point, whether the words you have learned have become so *active* a part of your everyday thinking, speaking, and writing vocabulary that you can *recall* any I may ask for if I provide you with a brief definition of each one.

That's the final, acid test of complete and successful learning.

Once again (and for the last time), I will leave it to you whether to review before you go into the test.

FINAL TEST

Directions: Write the word we have studied that best fits each definition. The initial letter is offered to guide your thinking.

I.

1. one who puts another's welfare above his own   1. A_____

2. one whose mind is turned inward   2. I_____

3. one who hates mankind — 3. M_____

4. one who hates females — 4. M_____

5. one who hates marriage — 5. M_____

6. an argument — 6. A_____

7. one's other self — 7. A_____

8. able to use either hand with equal skill — 8. A_____

9. custom of plural marriages — 9. P_____

10. awkward, clumsy, tactless — 10. G_____

II.

1. doctor who treats female disorders — 1. G_____

2. doctor who specializes in child delivery — 2. O_____

3. baby doctor — 3. P_____

4. eye doctor — 4. O_____

5. heart doctor — 5. C_____

6. one who foments political discontent — 6. D_____

7. contemptuous name for a teacher — 7. P_____

8. study of skin disorders — 8. D_____

9. insane — 9. P_____

10. emotional conflict — 10. N_____

III.

1. tooth straightening — 1. O_____

2. foot doctor — 2. C_____

3. handwriting analyst — 3. G_____

4. Freudian practitioner   4. P_____

5. describing the relationship
   between mind and body   5. P_____

6. of psychological origin   6. P_____

7. speaker's stand   7. P_____

8. practitioner who specializes
   in fitting glasses   8. O_____

9. dealer in optical goods   9. O_____

10. handwriting   10. C_____

IV.

1. student of human development   1. A_____

2. student of heavenly phenomena   2. A_____

3. student of formation of the earth   3. G_____

4 student of insect life   4. E_____

5. student of psychological
   effects of word meanings   5. S_____

6. make love triflingly   6. P_____

7. self-governing   7. A_____

8. a cutting in two   8. D_____

9. small part representing the whole   9. E_____

10. examination of live tissue which
    has been cut from the body   10. B_____

V.

1. complete, finished, perfect   1. C_____

2. beyond reform   2. I_____

3. from birth   3. C_____

4. outstandingly bad   4. E_____

5. study of heredity   5. G_____

6. out of time   6. A_____

7. out of place   7. I_____

8. diseased   8. P_____

9. dislike, aversion   9. A_____

10. fond of friends; liking to be
with people   10. G_____

VI.

1. belittle   1. D_____

2. tickle   2. T_____

3. forbid   3. P_____

4. make unnecessary   4. O_____

5. fight against   5. M_____

6. expression with two
meanings, one sexy   6. D_____

7. general feeling of physical
and mental discomfort   7. M_____

8. feeling ill-disposed toward   8. M_____

9. a blessing   9. B_____

10. beyond pleasing   10. I_____

VII.

1. disinclined to conversation   1. T_____

2. practicing an economy of words   2. L_____

3. idly chattering   3. G_____

4. talkative   4. L_____

5. trite and hackneyed in speech   5. B_____

6. unspoken   6. T_____

7. wordiness   7. V_____

8. speak to oneself   8. S_____

9. sleep-inducing   9. S_____

10. sleepwalker   10. S_____

VIII.

1. strict disciplinarian   1. M_____

2. bootlicker   2. S_____

3. obstreperous woman   3. V_____

4. sneerer at tradition   4. I_____

5. dabbler   5. D_____

6. accomplished musician   6. V_____

7. excessively fond of one's wife   7. U_____

8. irresistible urge to set fires   8. P_____

9. irresistible urge to drink   9. D_____

10. irresistible urge to steal   10. K_____

IX.

1. tireless   1. I_____

2. simple, direct, frank   2. I_____

3. noble, forgiving, generous   3. M_____

4. able to do many things well   4. V_____

5. fearless   5. I_____

6. polite, polished, cultured

6. U_____

7. "stomach-minded"

7. V_____

8. boredom, tedium

8. E_____

9. one who is a connoisseur
of good food

9. G_____

10. rough, countrified

10. R_____

X.

1. describing emotions that are
shared or secondhand

1. V_____

2. homesickness

2. N_____

3. harsh sound

3. C_____

4. secret, hidden

4. C_____

5. luxurious, wealthy

5. O_____

6. fleeting

6. E_____

7. speech of praise

7. E_____

8. feeling of well-being

8. E_____

9. hackneyed, stale expression

9. C_____

10. in the flesh

10. I_____

XI.

1. exhausted

1. E_____

2. tongue-lashing

2. C_____

3. self-sacrificing

3. S_____

4. repeat by giving the gist

4. R_____

5. stagnate intellectually

5. V_____

6. pretend

6. S_____

406

7. hint subtly   7. I_____

8. lighten the severity of   8. A_____

9. sympathize with, over misfortune   9. C_____

10. fluctuate, be indecisive   10. V_____

XII.

1. servilely attentive   1. O_____

2. complaining   2. Q_____

3. haughtily disdainful   3. S_____

4. habitually short of funds   4. I_____

5. addicted to drink   5. B_____

6. corpselike   6. C_____

7. melancholy   7. D_____

8. high-handed   8. C_____

9. morally dying   9. D_____

10. something which follows   10. S_____

XIII.

1. deviating from the usual   1. A_____

2. of one kind   2. H_____

3. occurring after the death
   of the creator   3. P_____

4. thin, insubstantial   4. T_____

5. indecently and violently attacking   5. S_____

6. nameless   6. A_____

7. of various kinds   7. H_____

8. explanatory, justifying   8. E_____

9. unprovoked   9. G_____

10. erase, take out   10. D_____

KEY

I: 1—altruist, 2—introvert, 3—misanthrope, 4—misogynist, 5—misogamist, 6—altercation, 7—alter ego, 8—ambidextrous, 9—polygamy, 10—gauche

II: 1—gynecologist, 2—obstetrician, 3—pediatrician, 4—oculist or ophthalmologist, 5—cardiologist, 6—demagogue, 7—pedagogue, 8—dermatology, 9—psychotic, 10—neurosis

III: 1—orthodontia, 2—chiropodist, 3—graphologist, 4—psychoanalyst, 5—psychosomatic, 6—psychogenic, 7—podium, 8—optometrist, 9—optician, 10—chirography

IV: 1—anthropologist, 2—astronomer, 3—geologist, 4—entomologist, 5—semanticist, 6—philander, 7—autonomous, 8—dichotomy, 9—epitome, 10—biopsy

V: 1—consummate, 2—incorrigible, 3—congenital, 4—egregious, 5—genetics, 6—anachronous, 7—incongruous, 8—pathological, 9—antipathy, 10—gregarious

VI: 1—disparage, 2—titillate, 3—proscribe, 4—obviate, 5—militate, 6—*double-entendre*, 7—malaise, 8—malevolent, malignant, maleficent, malign, 9—benediction, 10—implacable

VII: 1—taciturn, 2—laconic, 3—garrulous, 4—loquacious, 5—banal, 6—tacit, 7—verbosity, 8—soliloquize, 9—soporific or somniferous, 10—somnambulist

VIII: 1—martinet, 2—sycophant, 3—virago, 4—iconoclast, 5—dilettante, 6—virtuoso, 7—uxorious, 8—pyromania, 9—dipsomania, 10—kleptomania

IX: 1—indefatigable, 2—ingenuous, 3—magnanimous, 4—versatile, 5—intrepid, 6—urbane, 7—visceratonic, 8—ennui, 9—gourmet, 10—rustic

X: 1—vicarious, 2—nostalgia, 3—cacophony, 4—clandestine, 5—opulent, 6—ephemeral or evanescent, 7—eulogy, 8—euphoria, 9—cliché, 10—incarnate

XI: 1—enervated, 2—castigation, 3—self-abnegating, 4—recapitulate, 5—vegetate, 6—simulate, 7—intimate, 8—alleviate, 9—commiserate, 10—vacillate

XII: 1—obsequious, 2—querulous, 3—supercilious, 4—impecunious, 5—bibulous, 6—cadaverous, 7—dolorous or doleful, 8—cavalier, 9—decadent, 10—sequel

XIII: 1—anomalous, 2—homogeneous, 3—posthumous, 4—tenuous, 5—scurrilous, 6—anonymous, 7—heterogeneous, 8—extenuating, 9—gratuitous, 10—delete.

SCORING

In a difficult test of this nature, and one which covers an entire course of weeks of learning any score which shows 80 per cent success or better is more than satisfactory. So, counting one point for each correct response, consider your learning successful if you came through with a score of 100 or more out of 130.

20

HOW TO KEEP
BUILDING YOUR VOCABULARY

YOUNGSTERS at graduation exercises in elementary and high schools go through a certain unpleasant shock right after they receive their diplomas.

To them, this is the last day—they're finished, they're done, they wish to hear no more about school or studying or books or teachers.

And then the important (and generally self-important) speaker of the evening tells them in no uncertain terms that this is not the end—not by a long shot. It is only the beginning; that's why it is called "commencement" exercises, et cetera, et cetera, the poor kids feeling more and more miserable as he goes on and on.

Of course the speaker is right—no educative process is ever the end; it is always the beginning of more education, more learning, more living.

And that is the case here. What has happened to you as a result of your reaction to the material and suggestions in this book is only the beginning of your development. To stop increasing your vocabulary is to stop your intellectual growth. You will wish, I am sure, to continue growing intellectually so long as you remain alive. And with the great momentum that your three weeks of hard work have given you, continuing will not be at all difficult.

May I offer, as a sort of summary of all I have said throughout the book, a recapitulation of the steps you will want to keep taking so that your vocabulary (and, synonymously, your mental horizons) can continue growing and growing?

STEP ONE. *You must become actively receptive to new words.*

Words won't come chasing after you—you must train yourself to be on a constant lookout, in your reading and listening, for any words that other people know and you don't.

STEP TWO. *You must read more.*

As an adult, you will find most of the sources of your supply of new words in books and magazines. Is your reading today largely restricted to a quick perusal of the daily newspaper? Then you will have to change your habits. If your aim is to have a better vocabulary than the next person, you will have to make the time to read at least one book and several magazines *every week*. Not just this week and next week—but every week for the rest of your life. I have never met a single person who possessed a rich vocabulary who was not also an omnivorous reader.

STEP THREE. *You must learn to add to your own vocabulary the new words you meet in your reading.*

When you see an unfamiliar word in a book or magazine, do not skip over it impatiently. Instead, pause for a moment and say it over to yourself—get used to its sound and appearance. Then puzzle out its possible meaning in the context of the sentence. Whether you come to the right conclusion or not, whether indeed you are able to come to any intelligent conclusion at all, is of no importance. What is important is that you are, by this process, becoming superconscious of the word. As a result, you will suddenly notice that this very word pops up unexpectedly again and again in all your reading— for you now have a mind-set for it. And of course after you've seen it a few times, you will know fairly accurately not only what it means but the many ways in which it can be used.

STEP FOUR. *You must open your mind to new ideas.*

Every word you know is the translation of an idea. And when your vocabulary stops growing, your mind also stops growing—then your ideas, to put it bluntly, are in danger of becoming dull, static, and uninteresting. Think for a few minutes of the areas of human knowledge which may possibly be unknown to you—psychology, psychoanalysis, semantics, science, art, music, or whatever. Then attack one of these areas methodically—by reading books in the field. In every field, from the simplest to the most abstruse, there are several books written for the average, untrained lay reader which will give you both a good grasp of the subject and at the same time add immeasurably to your vocabulary. College students

411

have tremendous vocabularies because they are required to expose themselves constantly to new areas of learning. You must do the same.

STEP FIVE. *You must set a goal.*

If you do nothing about your vocabulary, you will learn, just by the natural process of staying alive, about fifty new words in the next twelve months. *By conscious effort you can learn several thousand.* Set yourself a goal of discovering, and absorbing, five to ten new words *every day.* This may sound ambitious—but you will discover as soon as you start actively looking for new words in your reading, and actively doing reading of a more challenging type, that new words are all around you—that is, if you're ready for them. And understand this: vocabulary building *snowballs.* The results of each new day's search will be greater and greater—once you provide the necessary initial push, the first important momentum.

How to raise a brighter child

These new methods, based on the theories of famous physicians, educators and behavioral scientists, are simple and fun—and they can increase your child's I. Q. by 20 points or more! Start using them as early as possible—even right after birth!

Imagine a 21-month-old with a reading vocabulary of 160 words...a boy of four who enjoys teaching himself major number principles...a girl not yet four who reads at the third grade level! None of these children was born a genius. Yet, through the early learning concepts described in this remarkable new book—HOW TO RAISE A BRIGHTER CHILD—all are being helped to develop above-average intelligence and a joyous love of learning.

Now you can give your little pre-schooler the same happy advantages...and they may well last throughout your child's life. For according to recent research, a child's I. Q. level is not permanently fixed at birth. It can be raised—or lowered by 20 points or even more in the precious years before six, by the way you rear your child at home.

Take the book now for a 30-day FREE trial

Send now for your copy of HOW TO RAISE A BRIGHTER CHILD. When it arrives, turn to the section that applies to your child *right now*, at this particular stage in his life. Apply some of the early learning techniques it shows you how to use. Then if not convinced this one book can make a world of difference in your child's mental development, return it within 30 days and owe nothing. If you decide to keep the book, it is yours for only $5.95 plus a small mailing charge. Take advantage of this opportunity! See your bookseller or mail the coupon today.

Joan Beck is known by millions of readers who follow her syndicated column, "You And Your Child." A graduate of Northwestern University, holding Bachelor's and Master's degrees, she has received several academic and professional awards and honors. She is married to Ernest W. Beck, a medical illustrator. They have two children, aged 15 and 12.

Protect yourself and your family!

Don't be one of the "taken"!

BUYER, BEWARE. Each time you walk into a store, call a serviceman, or sign a contract, you run the risk of being "taken." And not just by fly-by-night operators either. Some of the best-known and respected companies in the country lend their names to unscrupulous practices.

Now, Sidney Margolius, leading consumer authority and an expert in financial management, shows you how to avoid being "tricked" by shady operators and operations. In his book, *The Innocent Consumer vs. The Exploiters,* you'll discover:

- How you can save up to 90 per cent on your drug bills without changing stores. (See page 195)

- The simple "instant" process that lets you calculate the real interest on a loan. (See page 37)

- Why your department store is so anxious to open a revolving charge account for you. (See page 55)

- That you are buying "balloon bread" without realizing it, fruit drinks that are 90 to 97 per cent water, and pre-sweetened cereals that are 45 per cent sugar (at $1.07 a pound.) (See page 115)

- More than an exposé, *The Innocent Consumer vs. The Exploiters* will give you the protection you need every time you open the door to a salesman. Once you've read this book, you won't be tricked—as so many have—into paying more than $400 for a TV set worth $150 which has false guarantees. And you certainly won't be one of the thousands who have their salaries garnisheed every year without even being notified.

10-Day Free Trial

With all these pitfalls, one sure way to get your money's worth when you buy anything would be to bring along a lawyer, an engineer and a man from the Food and Drug Administration. Much simpler, however, is to go to your bookstore *or* fill out the coupon at right to get your copy of Sidney Margolius' revealing and helpful *The Innocent Consumer vs. The Exploiters.* If you do not believe that this book will save you many times its cost, you may return it within ten days for a full refund.

Today they're playing word games.
Before he's five, he can be reading 150 words a minute.

HOW TO GIVE YOUR CHILD A SUPERIOR MIND

A remarkable new book tells how you, yourself—at home—with no special training can actually add as much as thirty points to your child's effective I.Q....how you can help him move ahead quickly in school and enable him to be more successful in an education-conscious world.

Best of all, your child can achieve this early success without being pushed and without interference with a happy, normal, well-adjusted childhood.

GIVE YOUR CHILD A SUPERIOR MIND provides a planned program of home instruction that any parent can start using immediately. *You will learn:*

1. How to awaken your child's inborn desire to learn.
2. How to teach your child to read.
3. How to help your child streak ahead in math.
4. How to give your child the power of abstract reasoning.
5. How to increase your child's effective I.Q.

At all bookstores, or mail coupon today.

75295